Miniature Arts of China and Japan

Miniatures de Chine et du Japon

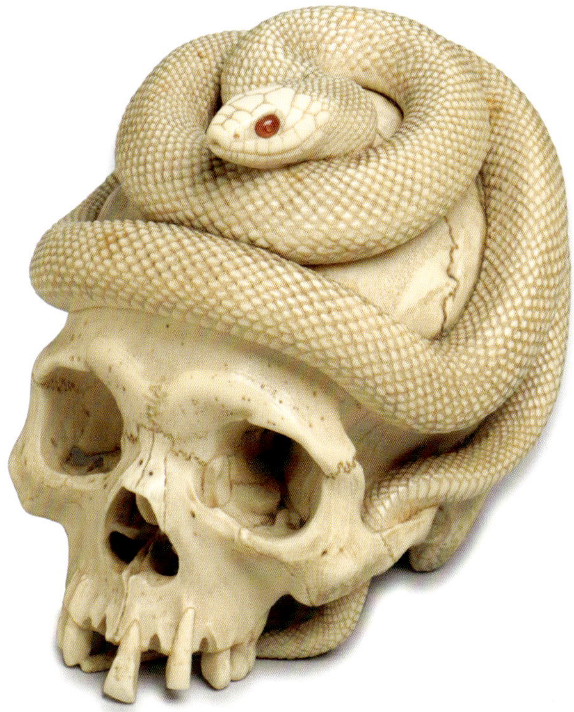

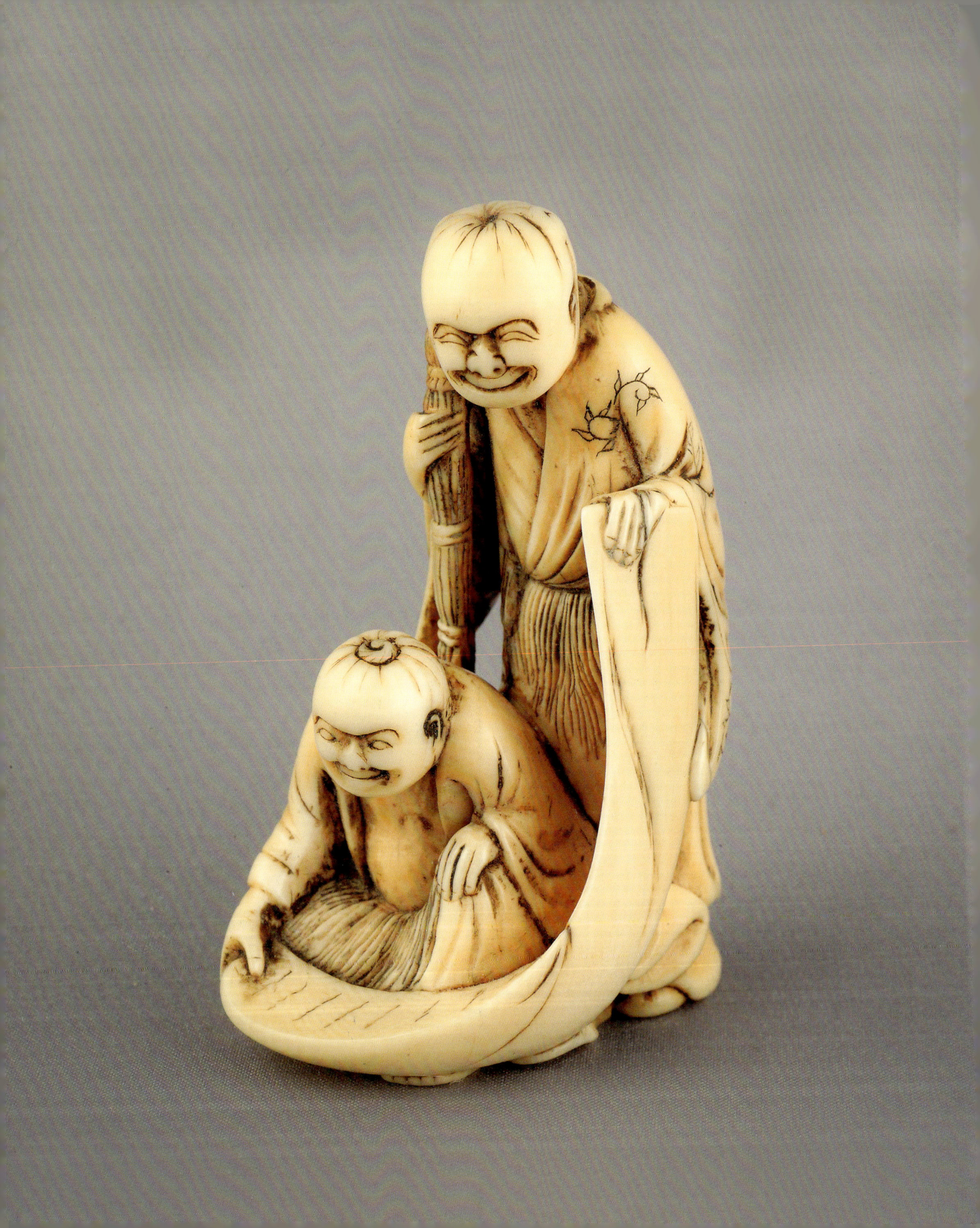

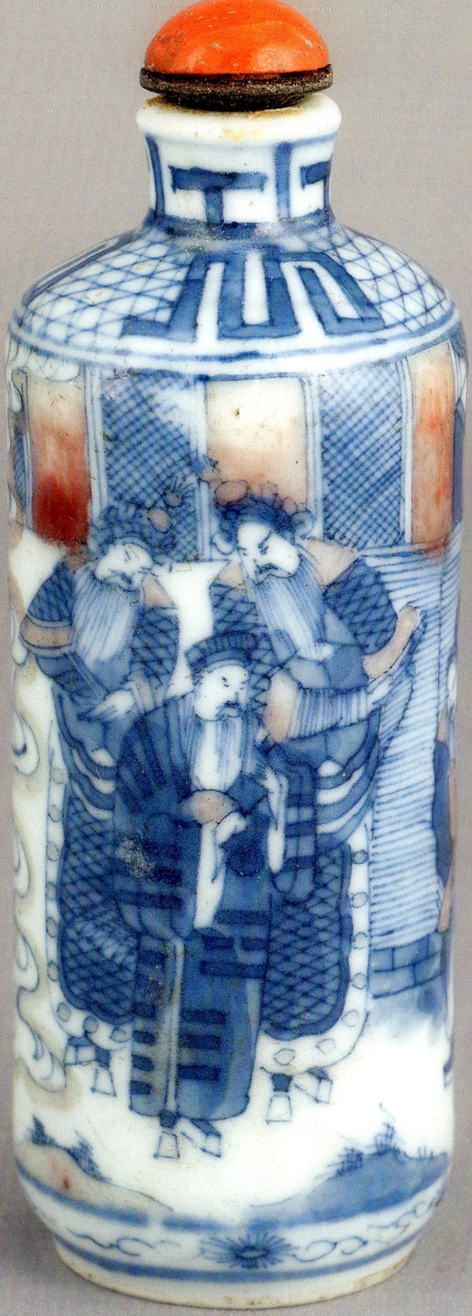

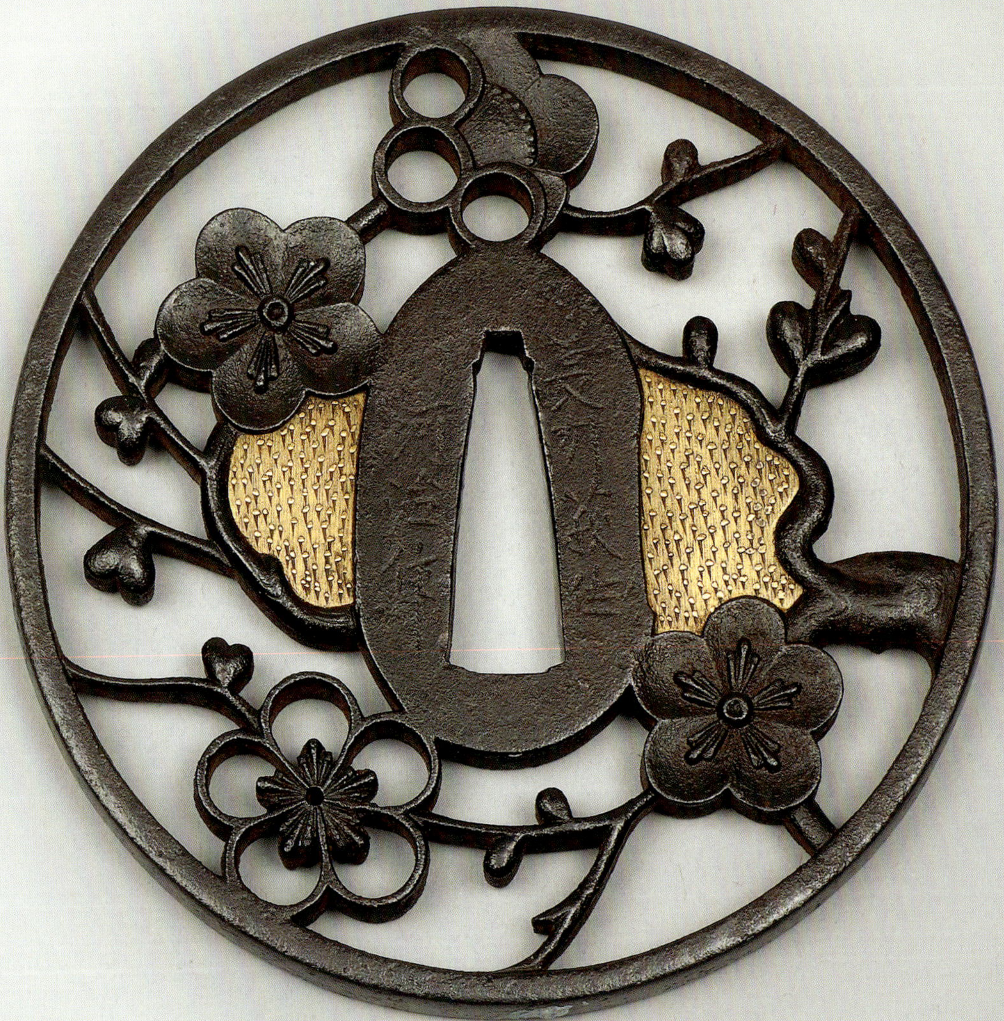

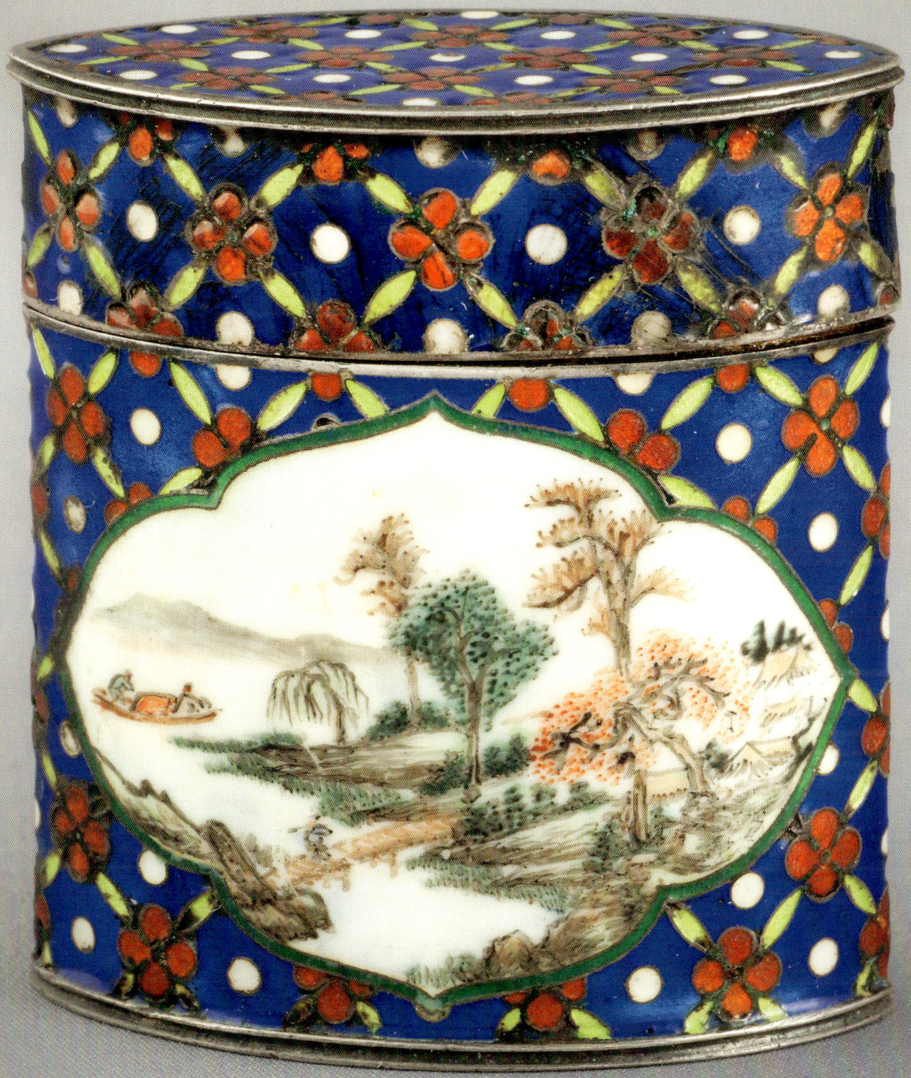

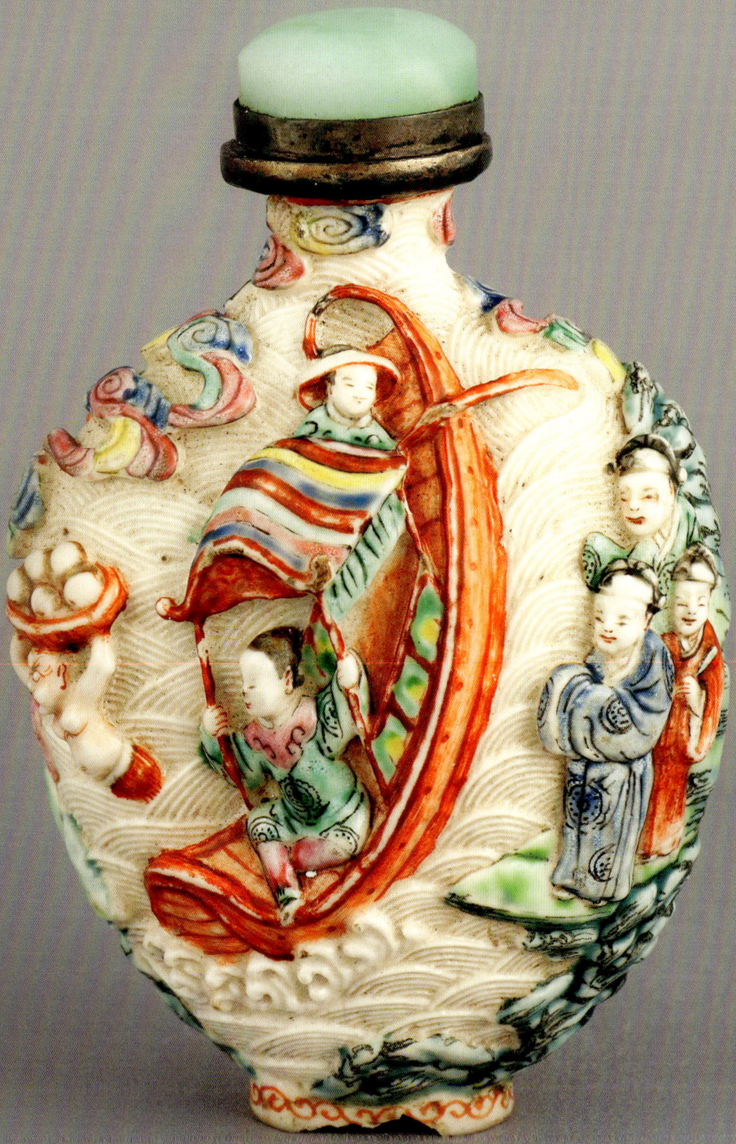

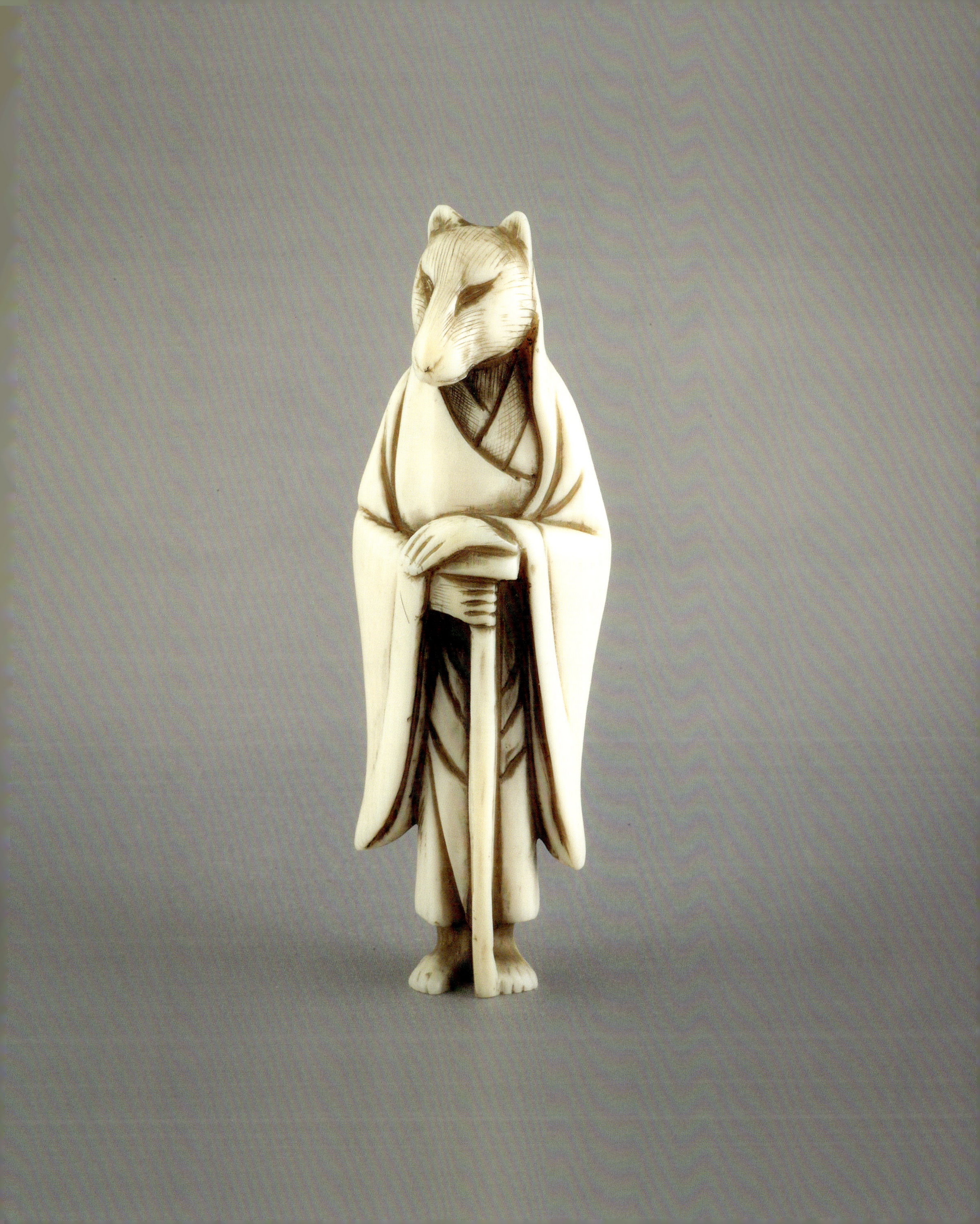

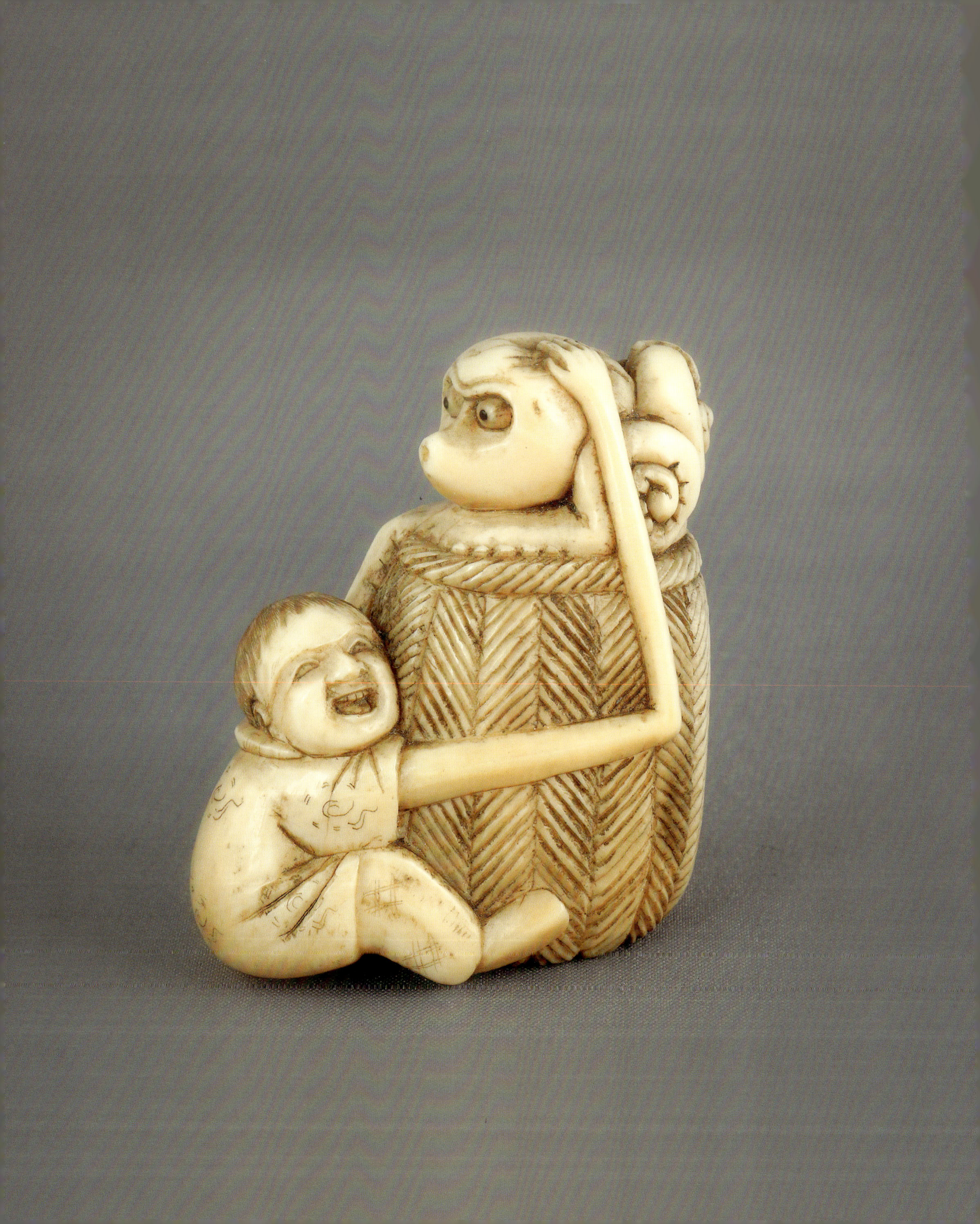

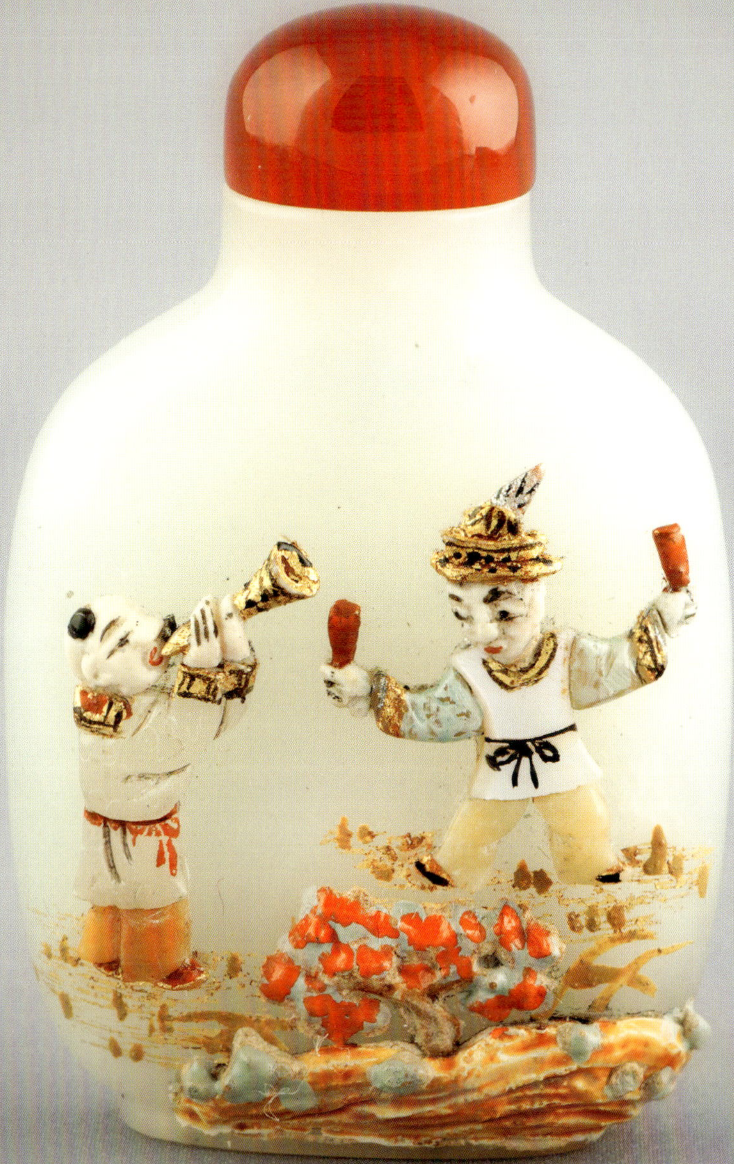

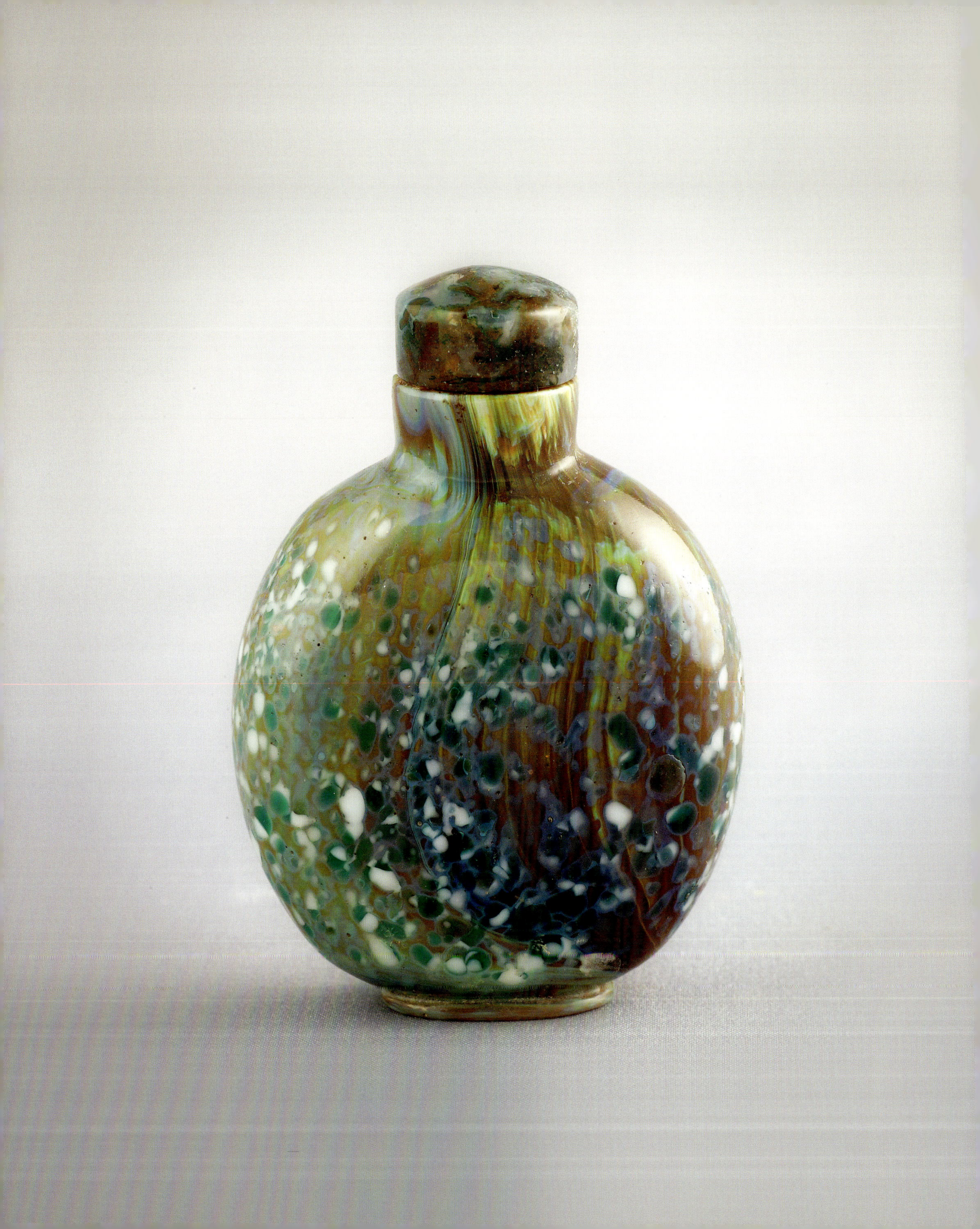

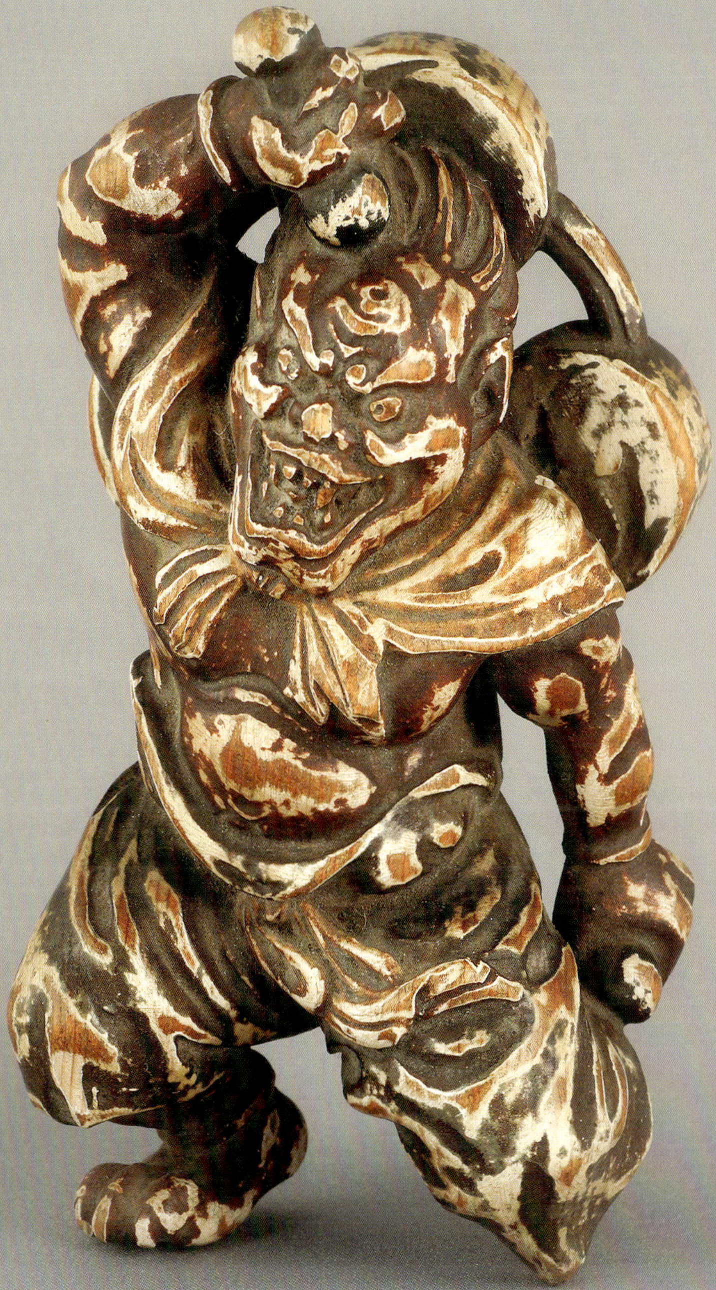

Miniature Art

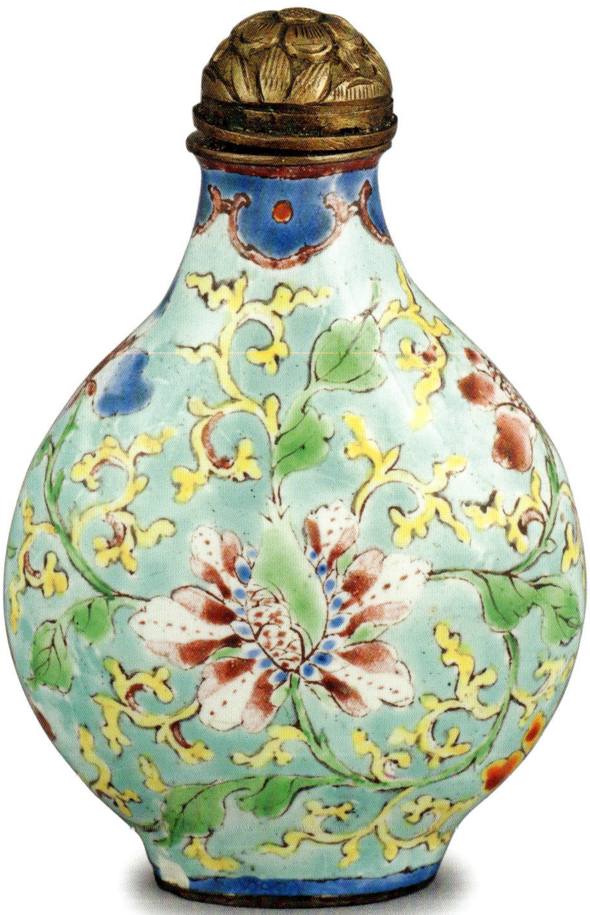

# of China and Japan

Miniatures de Chine et du Japon

Barry Till

Art Gallery of Greater Victoria

2010

Library and Archives Canada Cataloguing in Publication

Till, Barry
Miniature arts of China and Japan = Miniatures de Chine et du Japon / Barry Till.

Includes bibliographical references.
Catalogue of an exhibition held at the Art Gallery of Greater Victoria, September 3, 2010 to January 16, 2011.
Text in English and French.

ISBN 978-0-88885-362-2

1. Miniature art–China–Exhibitions.
2. Miniature art–Japan–Exhibitions.
3. Miniature art–British Columbia–Victoria–Exhibitions.
I. Art Gallery of Greater Victoria II. Title.
III. Title: Miniatures de Chine et du Japon.

N7437.T54 2010 709.51'07471128 C2010-906175-6E

Catalogage avant publication de Bibliothèque et Archives Canada

Till, Barry
Miniature arts of China and Japan = Miniatures de Chine et du Japon / Barry Till.

Comprend des réf. bibliogr.
Catalogue d'un exposition tenue à Art Gallery of Greater Victoria, 3 sept. 2010 – 16 janv. 2011.
Texte en anglais et en français.

ISBN 978-0-88885-362-2

1. Art miniature–Chine–Expositions.
2. Art miniature–Japon–Expositions.
3. Art miniature–Colombie-Britannique–Victoria–Expositions.
I. Art Gallery of Greater Victoria II. Titre.
III. Titre: Miniatures de Chine et du Japon.

N7437.T54 2010 709.51'07471128 C2010-906175-6F

Printed in Canada

Labels for *Miniature Arts of China and Japan* (when in groups, title and credits read from left to right) • Légendes pour les œuvres d'art miniatures de Chine et du Japon (Dans le cas d'œuvres groupées, le titre et les auteurs se lisent de gauche à droite.)

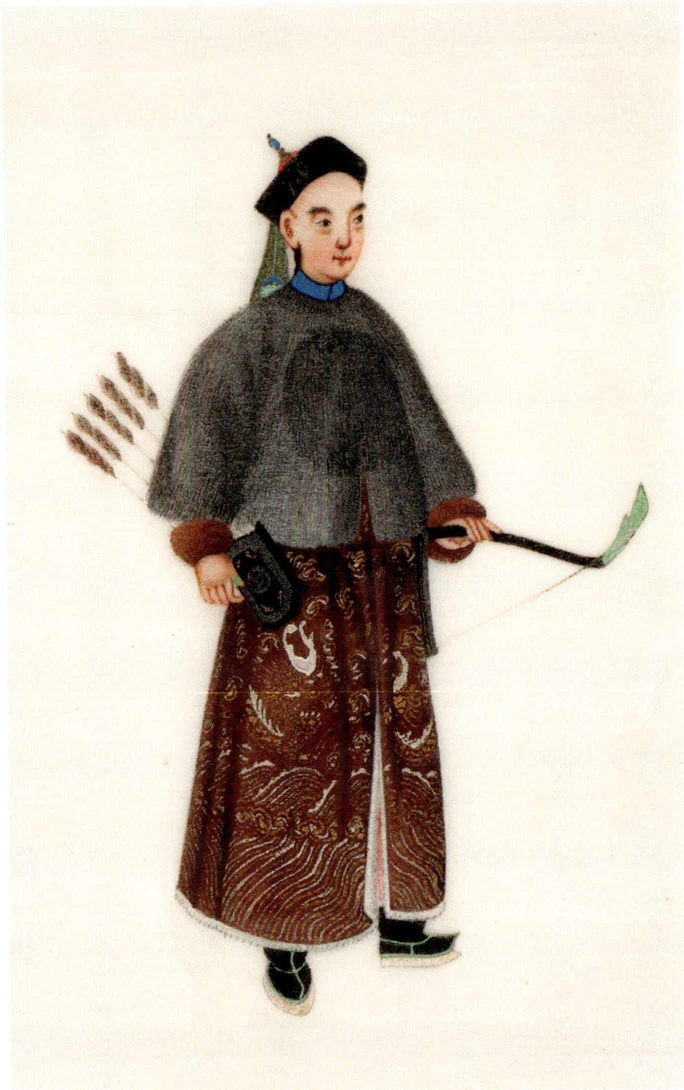

FIRST PAGE • ***okimono*** in the form of a human cranium with snake • ***okimono*** en forme de crâne humain avec un serpent • Edo period, mid 19th century • ivory, carnelian • Gift of David Young, AGGV 1998.047.001

PHOTO ESSAY

PAGE 2 • ***netsuke*** of monks Kanzan and Jittoku holding a broom and reading a scroll • ***netsuke***, moines Kanzan et Jittoku tenant un balai et lisant un rouleau • late 18th/ early19th century • ivory • Gift of the Lewis and Ruth Sherman Foundation, AGGV 2007.016.066

PAGE 3 • **Snuff Bottle** with design of generals meeting • **Tabatière** avec motif représentant une réunion de généraux • Qing dynasty, 19th century • porcelain, underglaze blue and red • Private Collection, Intended Gift

PAGE 4 • Japanese ***tsuba*** sword guard with openwork prunus sprays, signed Koji • La gard du sabre japonaise, le ***tsuba*** avec motif ajouté de grappes de cerisier, signée Koji • iron, gold *numone* • Edo period (1603-1868) • Fred and Isabel Pollard Collection, AGGV 1962.151.001

PAGE 5 • **Opium Box** with floret pattern around two panels of landscape scene • **Flacon à opium** orné de fleurons autour de deux panneaux d'une scène de paysage • Qing dynasty, late 19th century • metal, enamel • Gift of Hy Eiley, AGGV 2002.028.001

PAGE 6 • **Snuff Bottle** with reticulated scene of figures on a boat with others on shore • **Tabatière** avec scène réticulée représentant des personnages dans une embarcation et d'autres sur la rive • Qing dynasty, 19th century • carved porcelain with overglaze enamels • Gift of Helen Sawyer, AGGV 1995.012.012

PAGE 7 • ***netsuke*** of fox priest with a staff, signed Kogyoku, 19th century • ***netsuke***, prêtre loup avec un bâton, signé Kogyoku, 19e siècle • ivory • Gift of James and Joanna Davidson, AGGV 2006.002.036

PAGE 8 • ***netsuke*** of long-armed Tenaga holding an octopus in a basket • ***netsuke***, Tenaga avec un long bras tenant une pieuvre dans un panier • 19th century • ivory • Gift of James and Joanna Davidson. AGGV 2006.002.024

PAGE 9 • **Snuff Bottle** with overlay design of musicians and dancer • **Tabatière** avec scène incrustée représentant des musiciens et un personnage qui danse • early 20th century • glass embellished with mother-of-pearl, enamels • Fred and Isabel Pollard collection, AGGV 1974.229.001

PAGE 10 • **Snuff Bottle • Tabatière** • Qing dynasty, 19th century • mottled glass • Private Collection, Intended Gift

PAGE 11 • ***netsuke*** of Raijin the Thundergod • ***netsuke***, Raijin, le dieu du tonnerre • 19th century • wood, lacquer • Given in Memory of John P. Nind by his Wife and Daughter, AGGV 1974.149.001

TITLE PAGE • **Snuff Bottle** with design of stems and flowers • **Tabatière** ornée de tiges et de fleurs • Qing dynasty, 19th century • enamel on metal • Gift of the Joy DeWeese-Wehen Estate, AGGV 2003.004.027

OPPOSITE PAGE • **Chinese Pith Painting • Peintures chinoises sur papier de moelle** • Series of Chinese and Manchu men and women, (illustrated – archer) • Série de femmes et d'hommes chinois et mandchous, (illustré : archer) • artist unknown, 19th century • ink and colours on pith paper • Gift of Jan and Ardo Muhlack, AGGV 1999.034.001-.006

CONTENTS PAGE • **Snuff Bottles** with design of fish and flowers/of a dragon amidst clouds/of cranes under a pine • **Tabatières** ornées d'un poisson et de fleurs/dragon dans les nuages/grues sous un pin • Qing dynasty, late 19th/early 20th century • lapis lazuli • Gift of the Joy DeWeese-Wehen Estate, AGGV 2003.004.020 • Gift of Helen Sawyer, AGGV 1995.012.021, Private Collection, Intended Gift

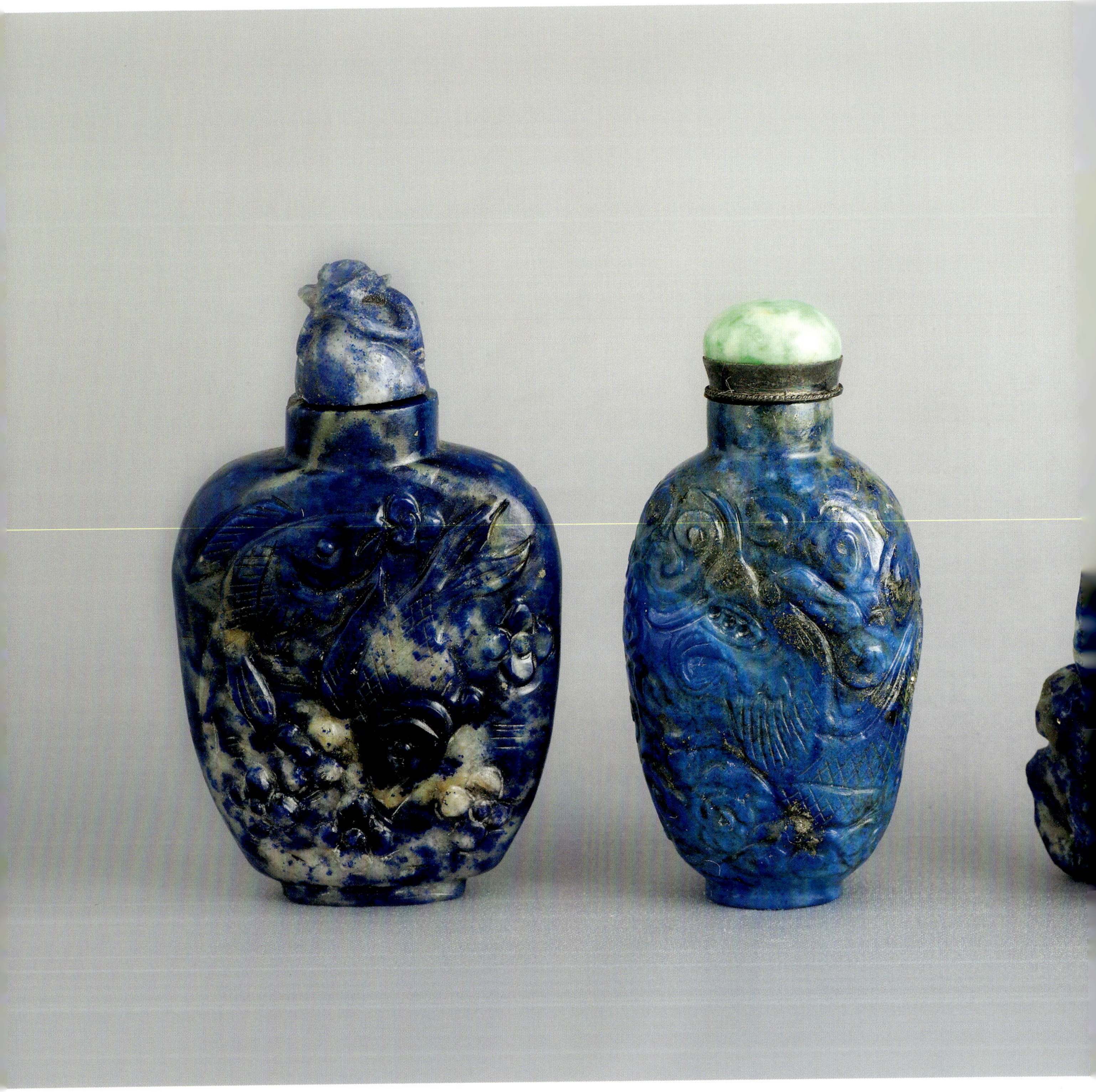

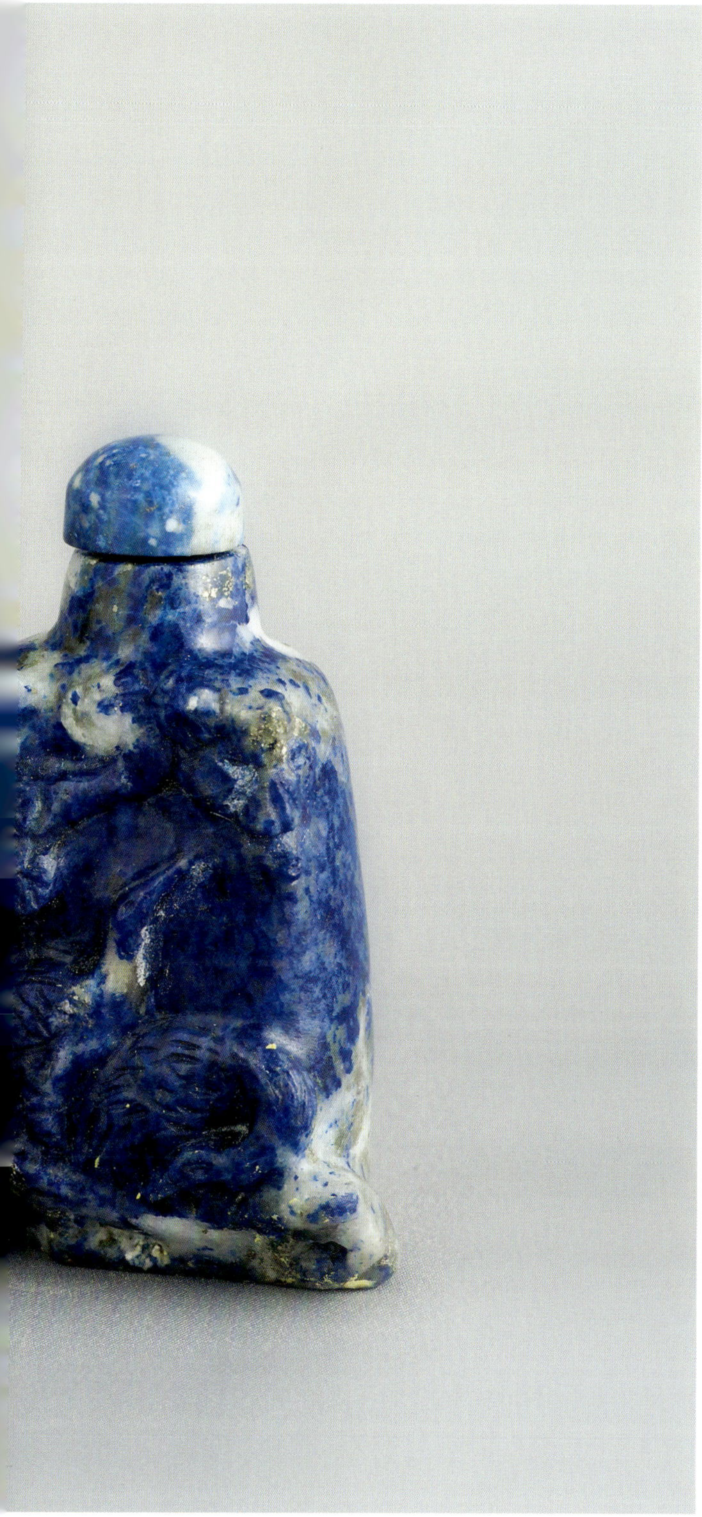

Contents

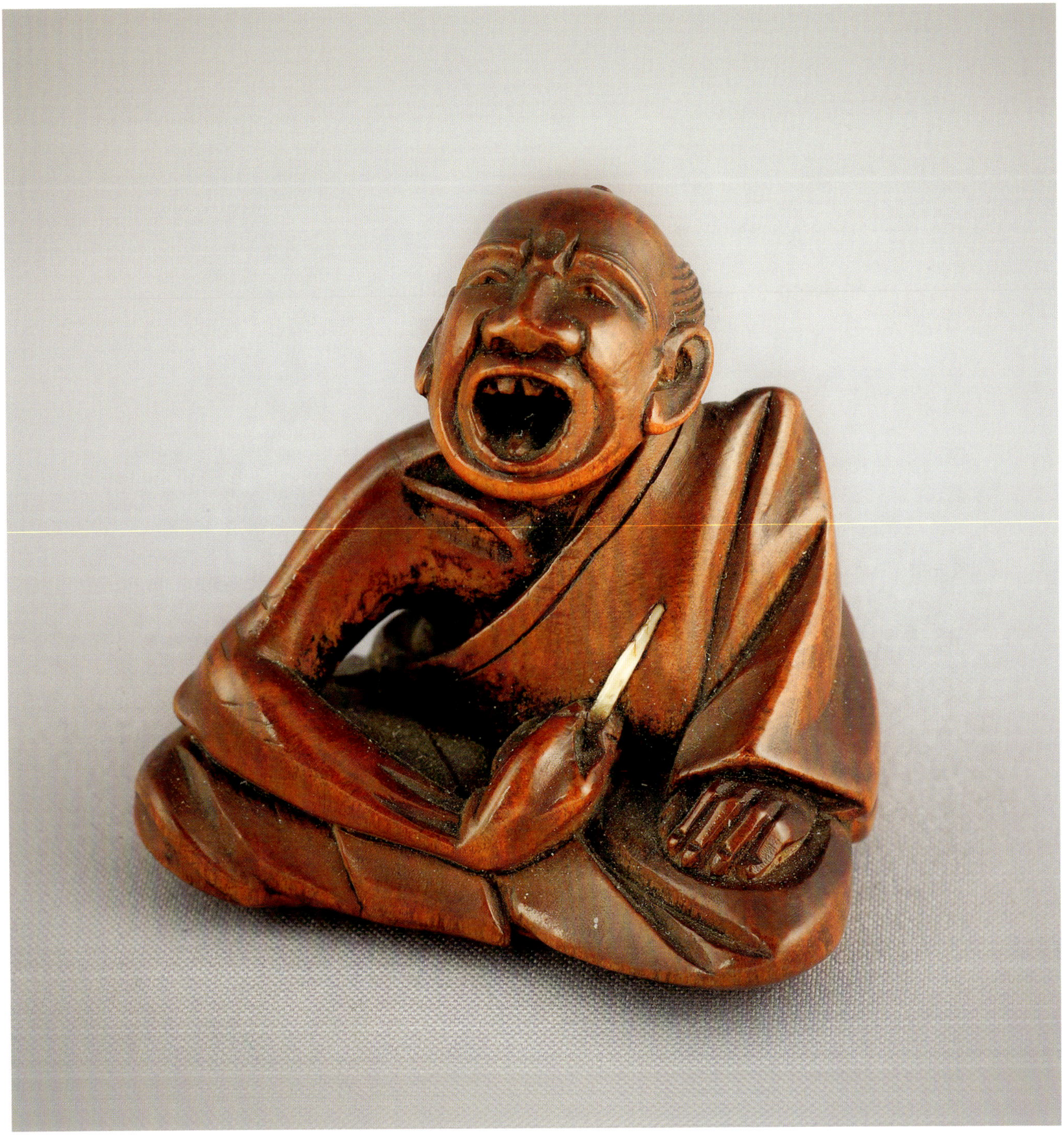

Foreword

The Art Gallery of Greater Victoria is pleased to present *Miniature Arts of China and Japan*. This publication and the exhibition it refers to examines the Chinese and Japanese love of miniature art and the vast variety of treasures they have created.

This exhibition would not have been possible without the support of the Department of Canadian Heritage through its Museum Assistance Program. Thanks must also go to David Lemon of the Health Arts Society for helping to make this project more accessible to a wider audience. The Associates of the Art Gallery of Greater Victoria, the British Columbia Arts Council and the Capital Regional District have all contributed financial assistance, which has enabled the AGGV to undertake this special project.

We would like to thank Barry Till, our esteemed Curator of Asian Art, for his work in developing, organizing and producing this project as well as all the AGGV staff members who assisted him.

Jon Tupper
Director
July 2010

netsuke of a sneezer, signed Hokei 19th century • ***netsuke***, tempête, Signé Hokei, 19e siècle • wood, mother-of-pearl • Edith Low-Beer Collection, AGGV1990.038.003

Avant-propos

L'Art Gallery of Greater Victoria a le plaisir de présenter *Miniatures de Chine et du Japon*. La présente publication et l'exposition à laquelle elle se rapporte se penchent sur l'intérêt que portent les Chinois et les Japonais à l'art miniature et traitent de la très grande variété de trésors qu'ils ont créés.

Cette exposition n'a été rendue possible que grâce à l'appui du ministère canadien du Patrimoine par l'entremise du Programme d'aide aux musées. Il faut également remercier M. David Lemon de la Health Arts Society qui a contribué à rendre ce projet accessible à un plus grand public. Les membres de l'Art Gallery of Greater Victoria, le British Columbia Arts Council et le District régional de la capitale ont tous apporté une contribution financière, ce qui a permis à l'AGGV d'entreprendre ce projet spécial.

Nous aimerions remercier M. Barry Till, notre estimé conservateur du domaine des arts d'Asie, pour son travail consacré à l'élaboration, l'organisation et la production de ce projet, ainsi qu'à tout le personnel de l'AGGV qui l'a aidé.

Le directeur,
Jon Tupper
Juillet 2010

inro with design of Daruma, founder of Zen; ceremonial fly whisk in verso, signed Shibata Zeshin (1807-1891) • ***inro***, motif de Daruma, fondateur du Zen; chasse-mouche de cérémonie au verso, signé Shibata Zeshin (1807 à 1891) wood, lacquer • ***ojime***, glass • ***ojime***, verre • inlaid lapis lazuli • ***netsuke*** in form of enshrouded Daruma and his successor, Eino, signed Gyokuei • ***netsuke*** en forme de Daruma enveloppé et de son successeur, Eino, signé Gyokuei • ivory • late Edo period, mid 19th century • Fred and Isabel Pollard Collection, AGGV 1968.267.001

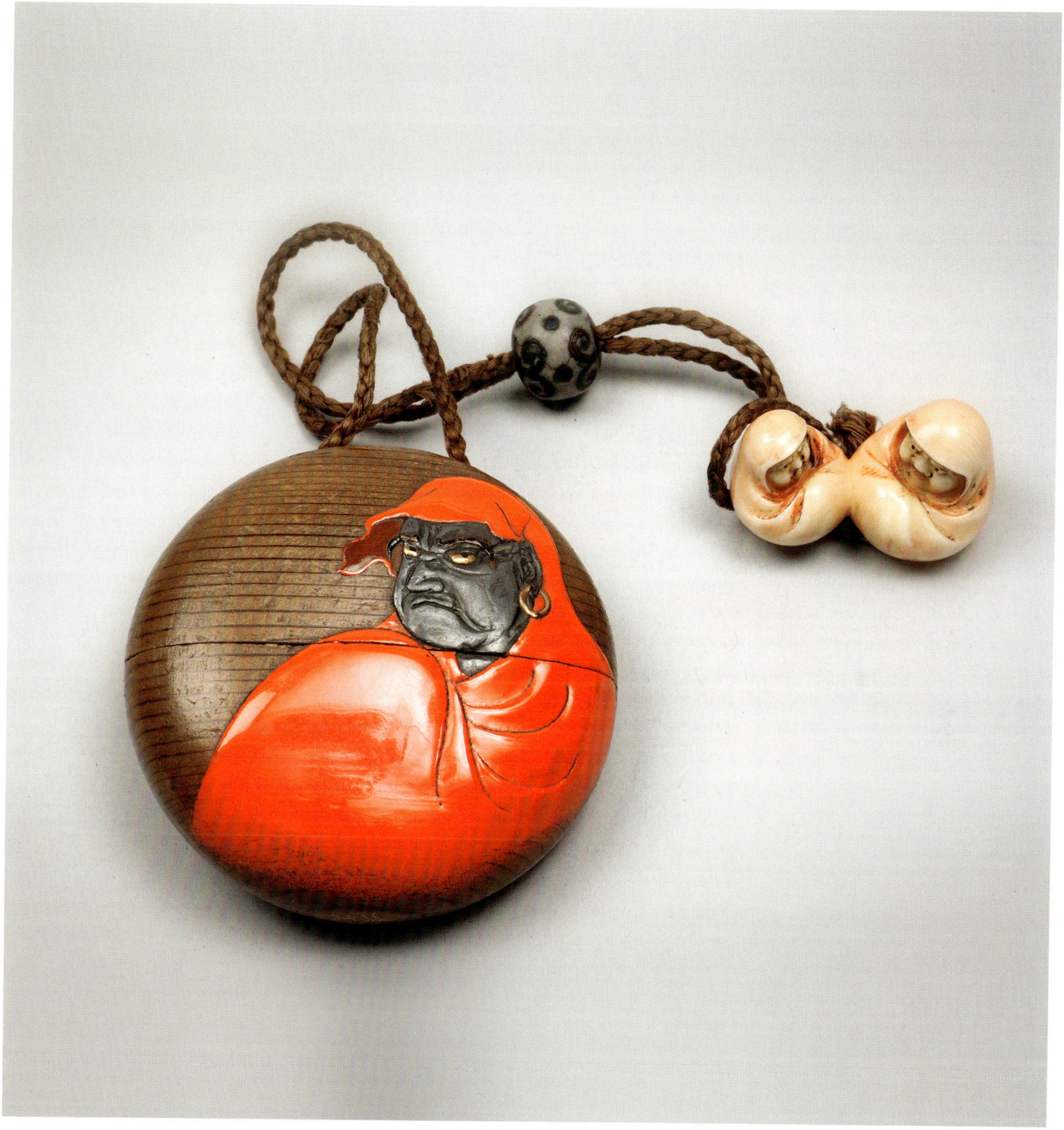

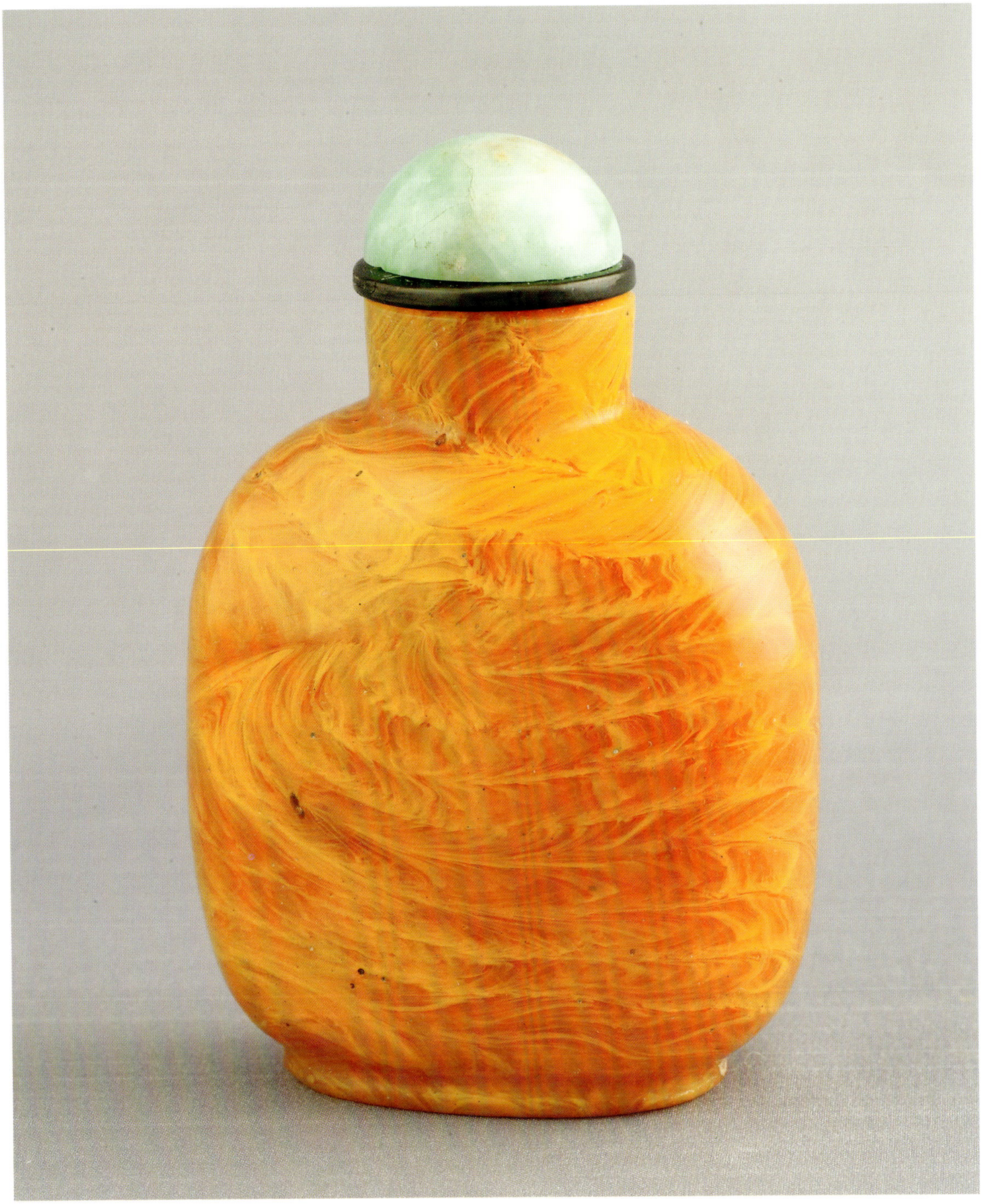

Acknowledgements

The Art Gallery of Greater Victoria is grateful to the Department of Canadian Heritage through its Museum Assistance Program for their financial support, which has made this exhibition and catalogue a reality. This exhibition would not have been possible without the generous donations throughout the years by a number of collectors in both Canada and the United States. A few of the large-scale donors include: Mrs. Helen Sawyer of Victoria, Ms. Joy DeWeese-Wehen of San Francisco and Mr. and Mrs. Francis and Kay Reif of Vancouver, who have donated sizeable collections of Chinese snuff bottles; Mr. and Mrs. James and Joanna Davidson of Victoria, Mr. and Mrs. Lewis and Ruth Sherman of Hamilton, and Mrs. Isabel Pollard of San Francisco, who have donated large Japanese netsuke collections; Mr. Hy Eiley of Toronto, who has donated numerous Chinese opium boxes, and Mr. Colin Graham of Bowen Island, who has donated a nice selection of Chinese pith paintings.

The assistance of the following staff members has been vital to the success of the exhibition: Gillian Booth, Marlaina Buch, Jennifer Cook, Mike Elkink, Lori Graves, Chris Russell, David Seager, Nicole Stanbridge, Stephen Topfer and volunteer, Fran Cornish. Paula Swart should be thanked for proofreading the text and making suggestions, and Joan Padgett for skilfully editing the text. Special thanks go to Bob Matheson for the difficult task of photographing these objects, and Frank Reimer for the carefully considered design of the catalogue. Thanks must also go to Michiko Warkentyne for her help with Romanizing the always difficult Japanese names on the tsuba, netsuke, inro and okimono. A final thank you goes to Marie-Hélène Duval for the French translation.

Snuff Bottle • Tabatière • Qing dynasty, 19th century • mottled pale yellow glass • Private Collection, Intended Gift

In cataloguing the miniature artefacts for this publication, I have relied heavily on the work already completed by the original owners, previous cataloguers, translators, appraisers and art dealers; hence, with so many small works and different people involved, there will undoubtedly be some problems with identification, materials and dating.

Barry Till
Curator of Asian Art
July 2010

Remerciements

L'Art Gallery of Greater Victoria remercie le ministère du Patrimoine canadien pour son appui financier par l'entremise de son Programme d'aide aux musées qui a permis de réaliser l'exposition et le présent catalogue. Cette exposition n'a été rendue possible que grâce aux généreux dons de collectionneurs du Canada et des États-Unis échelonnés au fil des ans. Parmi les plus importants donateurs figurent les noms de Mme Helen Sawyer de Victoria de Mme Joy DeWeese-Wehen de San Francisco et M. et Mme Francis et Kay Reif de Vancouver qui ont donné des collections appréciables de tabatières chinoises; M. et Mme James et Joanna Davidson de Victoria, M. et Mme Lewis et Ruth Sherman de Hamilton, et Mme Isabel Pollard de San Francisco, qui ont de donné de grandes collections de *netsuke* japonais; M. Hy Eiley de Toronto, qui a donné de nombreux flacons à opium chinois, et M. Colin Graham de Bowen Island, qui a donné un beau choix de Peintures chinoises sur papier de moelle.

L'aide des membres du personnel suivants a été de toute première importance pour le succès de cette exposition : M. Gillian Booth, Mme Marlaina Buch, Mme Jennifer Cook, M. Mike Elkink, Mme Lori Graves, M. Chris Russell, M. David Seager, Mme Nicole Stanbridge, M. Stephen Topfer et une bénévole, Mme Fran Cornish. Je tiens également à remercier Mme Paula Swart qui a relu le texte et apporté des suggestions, ainsi que Mme Joan Padgett qui a si habilement révisé le texte. Un merci tout spécial à M. Bob Matheson pour la difficile tâche de photographier ces objets, et à M. Frank Reimer pour le soin consacré à la conception du présent catalogue. Je m'en voudrais d'oublier Mme Michiko Warkentyne pour son aide à la transcription toujours difficile des titres japonais en écriture romaine des *tsuba, netsuke, inro* et *okimono*. Merci enfin à Mme Marie-Hélène Duval qui en a assuré la traduction en français.

En vue de cataloguer les miniatures de la présente publication, je me suis beaucoup inspiré du travail déjà accompli par leurs propriétaires précédents ainsi que par des catalogueurs, traducteurs, évaluateurs et marchands d'œuvres d'art. Par conséquent, compte tenu d'un si grand nombre de petites œuvres, et de personnes ayant apporté leur contribution, il ne fait aucun doute que de petites erreurs puissent s'être glissées dans l'identification, les matières employées et la datation.

Barry Till
Conservateur, art d'Asie
Juillet 2010

NEXT PAGE • **Snuff Bottles** with rectangle form with design of lion masks holding rings on shoulders / one undecorated • **Tabatières** de forme rectangulaire ornées de masques de lion tenant des anneaux sur les épaules/dont une non décorée • Qing dynasty, 18th/19th century • root amber • Francis and Kay Reif Collection, AGGV 1999.023.057, Gift of Helen Sawyer, AGGV 1995.012.002

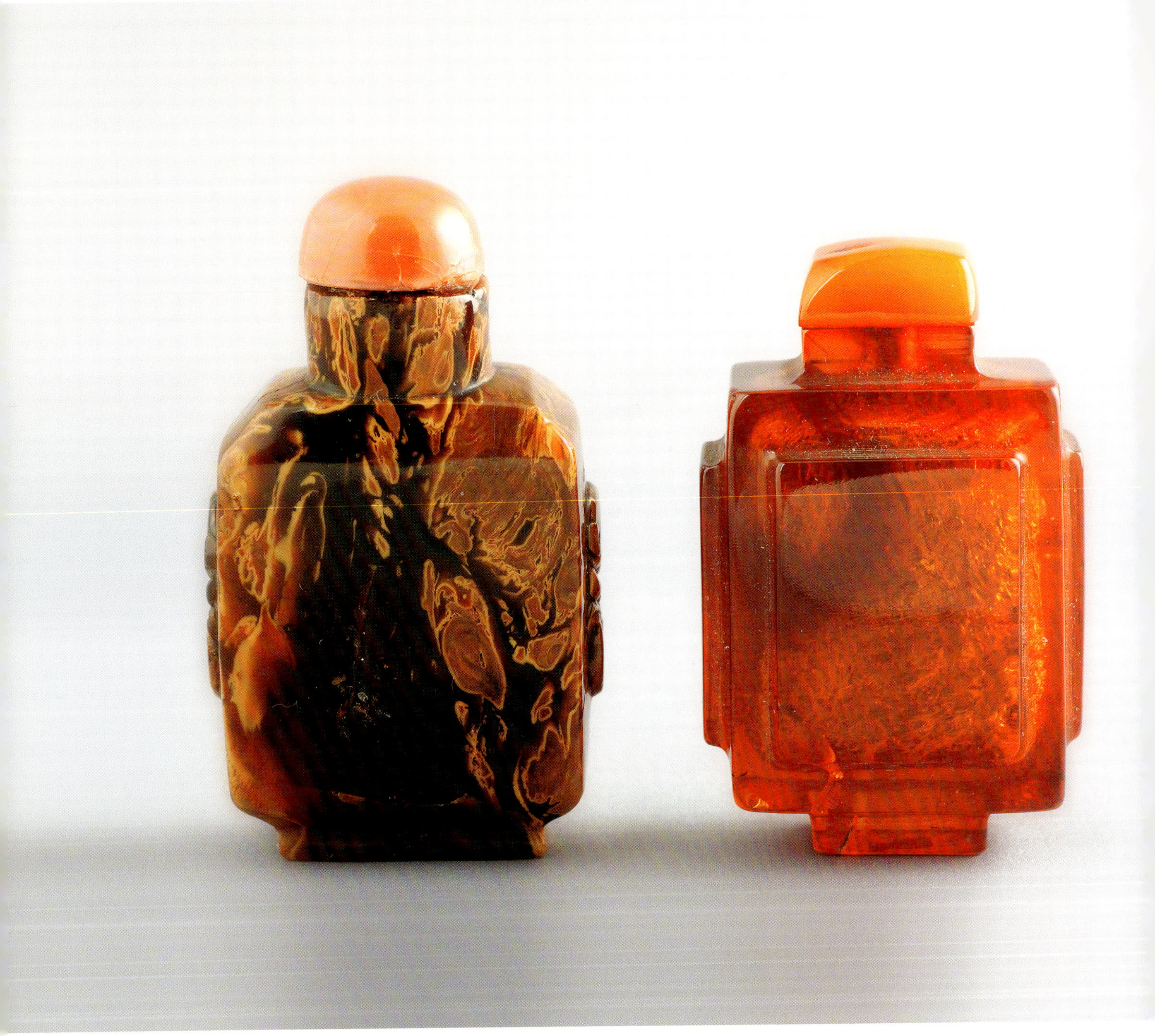

Miniature Arts of China and Japan

THE MINIATURE ART FORMS in this publication express the delight of the Chinese and the Japanese in small things and their aptitude for exquisite workmanship on a miniature scale. Both China and Japan boast a great range of artistic achievements in miniature. Since early times, Chinese and Japanese miniature art has been characterized by exceptional delicacy, preciseness and exquisiteness.

Even though the art forms in this publication are often referred to as the minor arts, they still represent the highest standards of art in China and Japan. Miniature works are more suitable to personal close-up inspection than larger works of art and are meant to be held individually in the palm of one's hand. As a rule, they have a wonderful tactile quality and are very pleasing to the touch. They are popular with collectors because of their size and because they have the power to make a substantial impact on people.

Despite the limitations of the material and the restricted compact space and shape for the designs, the makers of these miniature art pieces have shown extraordinary patience, unique sensitivity, exquisite workmanship, elegance of form and ingenuity in the variety of materials used. They have succeeded in beautifying mundane functional or utilitarian items into objects of great beauty and sophistication. In their miniature treasures, the Chinese and Japanese show their love of nature, of symbolism and of tradition. As a whole, miniature arts in China and Japan stand the test of magnification with much success.

Without exception, all the miniature art types discussed in this publication were collected by foreigners who helped popularize, stimulate and prolong the various miniature arts and crafts of China and Japan. A result of their recognition of the excellence and collectibility of these small treasures was the eventual promotion, preservation, and appreciation of this art form in China and Japan, both of which had for a time abandoned it as irrelevant. Large collections of these miniature arts have been built up in museum and private collections around the world and not just in their native countries.

Chinese Snuff Bottles

Snuff Bottle undecorated • **Tabatière** non décorée • Qing dynasty, late 19th/early 20th century • tiger's eye stone • Gift of the Joy DeWeese-Wehen Estate, AGGV 2003.004.023

Tobacco and then snuff were first brought to China during the Ming dynasty (1368–1644) by Europeans in the late 16th and early 17th centuries. During the early part of the Qing dynasty there was an attempt to ban smoking tobacco, but not snuff, due to the latter's therapeutic significance. Snuff consisted of dried tobacco leaves ground into a fine powder and blended with herbs, spices and various aromatic substances. Chinese snuff had mint, camphor, jasmine and an essence of rose. It was considered a medicine and thought to improve one's feeling of well being, curing a wide variety of diseases. It was used to treat nasal/sinus congestion, dissipate colds, provide relief from migraines, ease tooth pain, relieve pain in the eyes and throat trouble, cause sweats, help relieve asthma, aid digestion and help with intestinal ailments like constipation. Snuff came to play an important social role in the lives of the upper class in China.

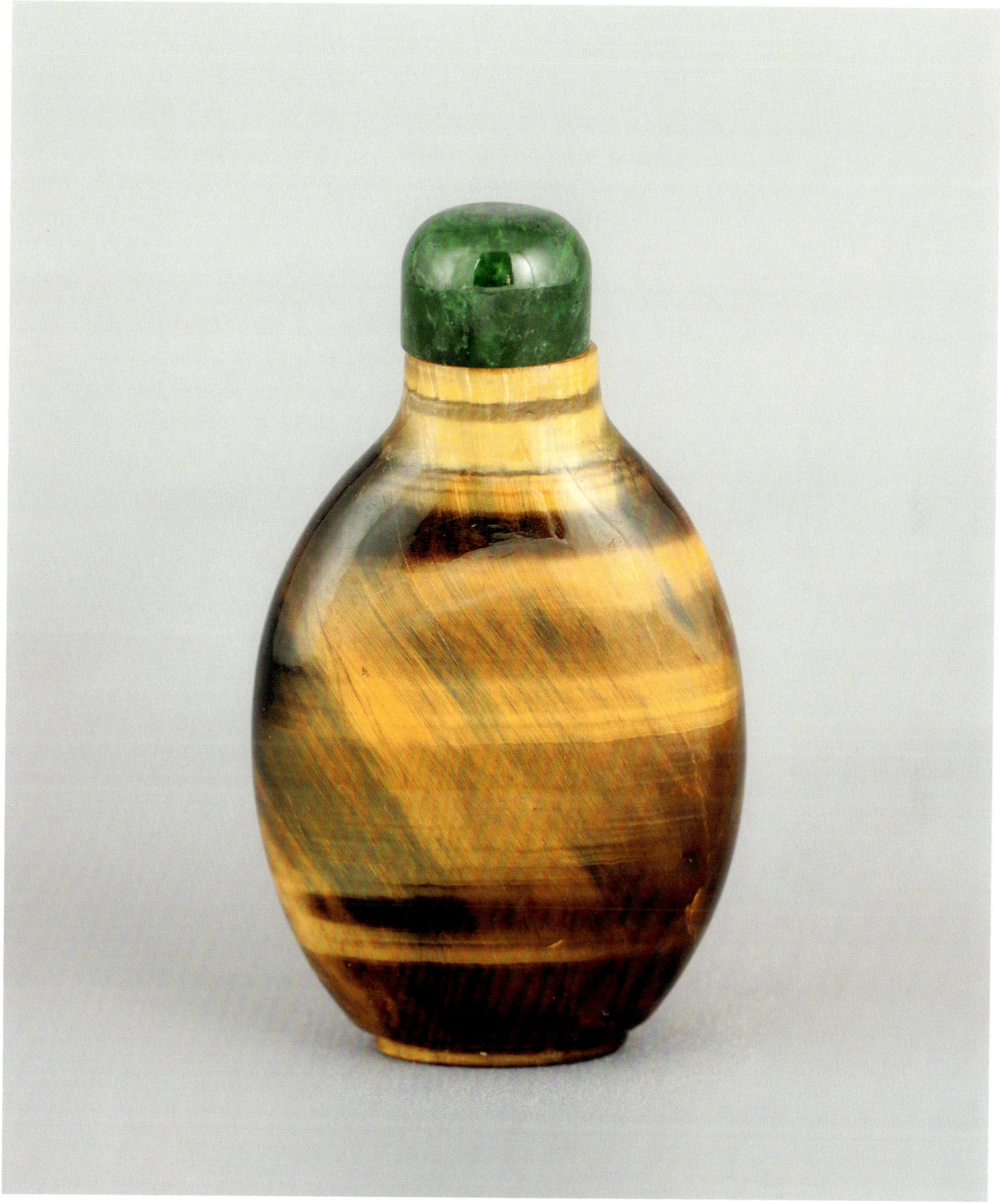

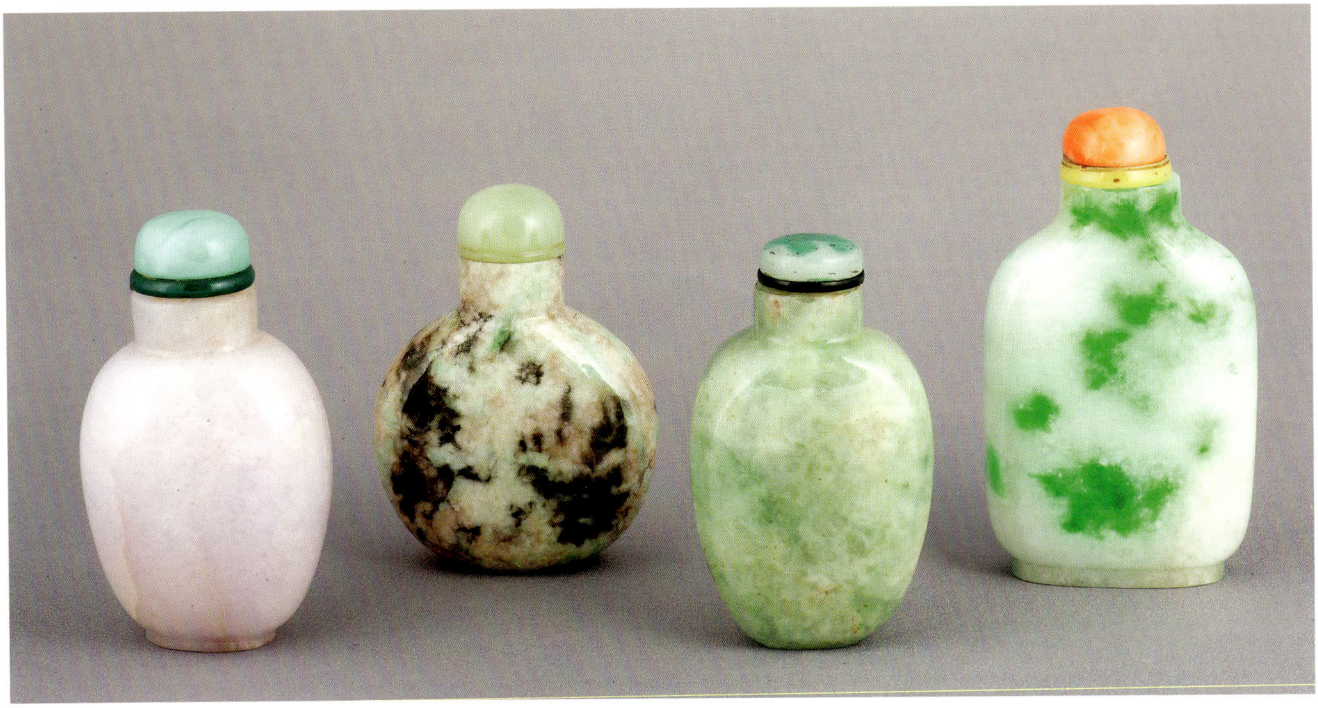

During the reigns of Kangxi (1662–1722), Yongzheng (1723–1735) and Qianlong (1736–1795), European envoys presented snuff and snuff boxes to the Manchu court as a way of promoting cordial relations with China. However, their boxes proved impractical due to China's humid climate, so the Chinese first used small glass medicine bottles for snuff. A tiny spoon, usually of ivory or silver and occasionally tortoise shell, was attached to the inside of the stopper cap and was used to scoop out the snuff from the bottle. The small opening of the bottle kept moisture out, preserved the freshness of the snuff and prevented spillage. These bottles became miniature works of art and highly collectible items. The Manchu emperors made use of snuff bottles as gifts to express imperial favour to civil officials and military men of great merit as well as to foreign envoys and dignitaries. They even set up imperial workshops or ateliers on the palace grounds to produce snuff bottles. Snuff bottles were produced elsewhere in China and sometimes were given as bribes by individuals for political favours. He Shen, a greedy corrupt chief advisor of Emperor Qianlong, had a collection of 2,390 snuff bottles, which would eventually be exploited as evidence of his venality and his crimes.

The use of snuff was originally confined to the wealthy upper classes, but eventually became a staple for all social classes. In order to distinguish their use of snuff, the upper classes began to use beautiful, elegant, unique and expensive materials for the creation of their snuff bottles. Thus, the decorative snuff bottles of China reveal much about the social power and class as well as the economic conditions of the times in which they were produced. Palace workshops were set up in Beijing, Jingdezhen, Suzhou and Yangzhou to create these miniature treasures for the court. Other bottles were made in Guangzhou, Boshan (Shandong province) and Liaoning province, and metal snuff bottles were made in Mongolia and Tibet.

Many Chinese snuff bottles are completely devoid of decoration, letting the material speak for itself, while others are incredibly ornate with decorations or designs that were painted, carved, incised, inlayed or appliquéd. The Chinese snuff bottle can be called the epitome of Chinese arts in microcosm as they combine the skills of painting, calligraphy, carving and inlaying with the handicrafts required to work the various materials. The landscapes, the flora and fauna, and the genre scenes depicted on the blue and white porcelain snuff bottles in particular show the competent hand of skilled monochrome painters.

Snuff Bottles • Tabatières • Qing dynasty, 19th century • jadeite, mottled green and lavender colours • Gift of Helen Sawyer, AGGV 1995.012.008. 1995.012.065, 1995.012.009, (right) Gift of the Joy DeWeese-Wehen Estate, AGGV 2003.004.017

Chinese bottles are made from a seemingly endless range of different materials and can be divided into roughly five main groups: stone, metal, organic, ceramic and glass (including inside painted glass bottles). The caps of the bottles are also made from various materials, contrasting or complementing the aesthetics of the bottle. The different types of stone and their subcategories used to make snuff bottles are vast: jade (nephrite and jadeite), chalcedony, agate, quartz, amethyst, crystal, tourmaline, aquamarine, beryl, lapis lazuli, turquoise, malachite, jasper, topaz, soapstone, inkstone, puddingstone, limestone and jet. Skilled lapidary craftsmen often carved in such a way as to make ingenious use of the inherent natural beauty and different colours naturally occurring in the stone or on the outside surface to create beautiful designs in relief of contrasting colours, as well as to capitalize on the distinctive darker colour inclusions in chalcedony to create "shadow" images. Organic materials used for snuff bottles include coral, amber, wood, bamboo, gourd, walnut, coconut shell, ivory, horn, hornbill, tortoise shell, fish skin, mother-of-pearl and lacquer, especially cinnabar lacquer. Metals employed to make snuff bottles include silver, copper and paktong/ baitong (a copper-nickel alloy), and a metal base was often used for cloisonné and enamel surfaces. Ceramic snuff bottles were made out of high-fired porcelain and brown stonewares from the Yixing kilns in Jiangsu province.

During the Qing dynasty, Chinese potters produced some of the world's greatest ceramic masterpieces, especially at the Imperial kilns at Jingdezhen, located in Jiangxi province. They created magnificent vessels, including snuff bottles, using a great variety of monochromatic glazes, painted underglaze cobalt blue, and overglaze enamelled decoration, and they were even able to make glazes in imitation of ivory, mother-of-pearl, metal, lacquer, wood, bamboo, jade, agate, marble and puddingstone. The plasticity of porcelain also allowed for the moulding and carving of designs. Excluding the magnificent porcelain snuff bottles for the Imperial Court and aristocracy, porcelain snuff bottles were relatively easy to produce in great numbers and were thus more affordable to a wider public. The potters, who made the famous Yixing brown stoneware teapots, also made some snuff bottles that appealed to the sensibilities of the literati.

The earliest and most popular material used in China to make snuff bottles was glass. European glass-making techniques were brought to the Imperial Palace in Beijing by Jesuit missionaries in the reign of Kangxi (1662–1722). This led to the creation of many outstanding glass snuff bottles. By mixing metal oxides, many different colours were created, some with spots, dapples and swirls; this period also saw the inclusion

Snuff Bottles with designs of an elongated dragon/fish and waves/of fruit and blossoms/ of lotus, crabs and fish/of a fisherman and a boat with pavilion on verso • **Tabatières** avec motifs de dragon allongé/poisson et vagues/fruit et fleurs/lotus, crabes et poisson/ pêcheur et une embarcation; un pavillon au verso • Qing dynasty, 19th century • white glass with red overlay • Given in memory of John P. Nind (R.M.L.I. ret.) by his wife Mildred and their daughter Ann Neilson, AGGV 1974.139.001, Given in memory of John P. Nind (R.M.L.I. ret.) by his wife Mildred and their daughter Ann Neilson, AGGV 1974.141.001, Gift of the Joy DeWeese-Wehen Estate, AGGV 2003.004.006, Gift of Helen Sawyer, AGGV 1995.012.003, 1995.012.022

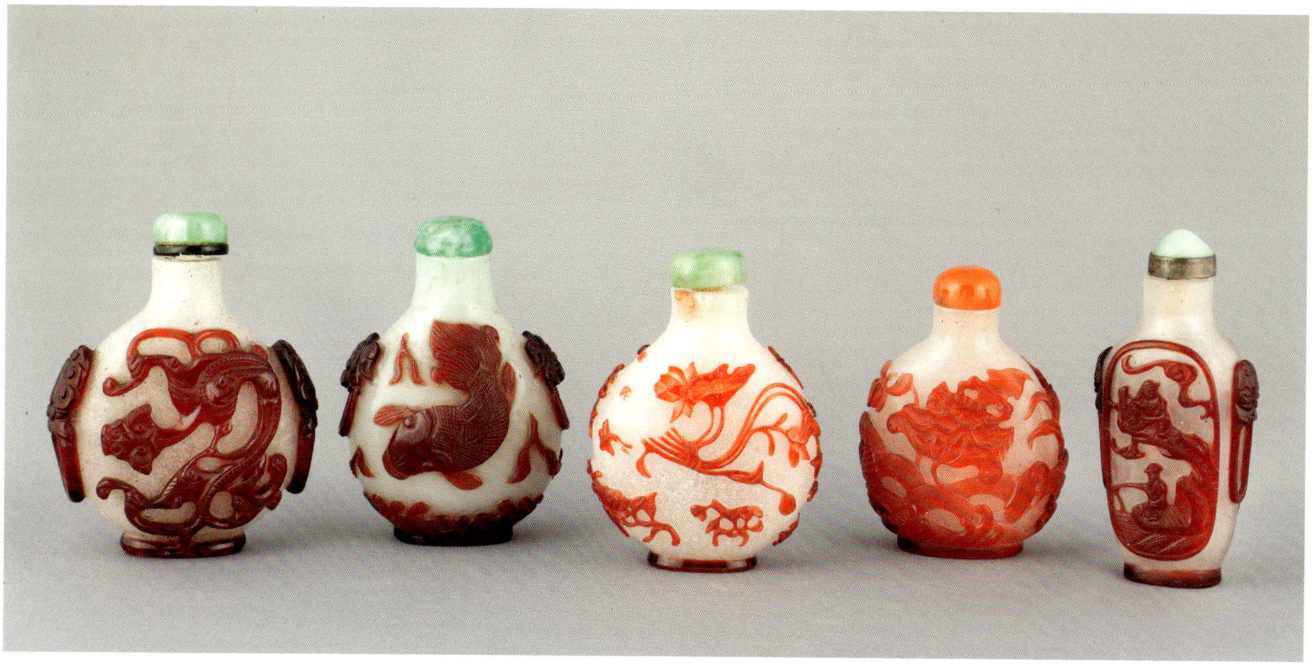

of goldstone. Chinese glass craftsmen mastered all aspects of the technical manufacture of glass like blowing, pressing, casting in moulds, undercutting and chiselling. Like potters, they also were able to imitate other materials in glass such as porcelain, jade, agate, realgar (an arsenic sulphide mineral) and other stones. One popular form of glass snuff bottle decoration was overlay. This technique, also known as Peking glass, was accomplished by dipping a glass bottle in molten glass of a contrasting colour or colours, and then carving through the outside layer to the original base colour, which was usually clear, opaque white or had a "snowflake" appearance. Painted enamels on glass were also a popular form of decoration.

Glass was also used to make inside painted snuff bottles. First, craftsmen would place iron, sand and emery in a glass bottle, shake it, rub it smooth, and then paint the interior with iron oxydal mixed with water to create a milky white surface suitable for taking paint and allowing for intricate detail. A hooked brush inserted into the mouth of the bottle was used to painstakingly create, in reverse, beautiful landscapes, portraits, calligraphy, and flora and fauna scenes. These highly accomplished miniature paintings inside the glass bottles were immensely fascinating and popular with art connoisseurs, and they are still being produced to this day with many artists gaining international renown. Some of the best known artists of inside painted snuff bottles are Ma Shouxuan, Zhou Leyuan, Ding Erzhong, Ye Zhongsan, Yan Yutian, Guan Yutian and Tang Cichuan, to name a few.

The designs, motifs and symbols on snuff bottles are immense and diverse. Symbols are derived from a multitude of sources such as legends, history, religion, philosophy and folklore. Auspicious symbols on Chinese snuff bottles are often in the form of visual puns called rebuses. Since a good number of Chinese words have the same pronunciation, there are plenty of opportunities for punning, but usually only those with a more sophisticated understanding of the Chinese language would understand the nuance. Over many centuries, rebuses came to have established meanings, sometimes hidden ones. The ideas frequently expressed were coded wishes for good health, prosperity, marital bliss, many sons, good luck, happiness, advancement in one's career, longevity and even immortality to the owner or giver of the artefact.

Many foreign traders coming to the Chinese markets in the 18th and 19th centuries wanted to return home with a memento of this strange land. The small and portable snuff bottle was the perfect curio to bring back. Right into the 20th century, foreigners acquired huge numbers of Chinese snuff bottles that can now be found in countless private and museum collections in Europe and America.

A fair number of snuff bottles were produced in Japan during the Meiji period (1868–1912) in response to the Western demand for all things Oriental and also for the Chinese market. The snuff bottles produced in Japan in the late 19th century may have been made by netsuke carvers and can exhibit original designs in Japanese style or simply be direct copies of Chinese snuff bottles. Many Japanese copies have an incised mark of Chinese Emperor Qianlong on the base.

Selected Bibliography

Hall, Robert and Ian Hardy. "Chinese Snuff Bottles, the Japanese Connection." *Arts of Asia*, Vol. 35, No. 5, 2005.

Kleiner, Robert. *Chinese Snuff Bottles from the Collection of Mary and George Bloch.* Hong Kong, 1987.

____________. "The Tuyet Nguyet Collection of Snuff Bottles and Saucers." *Arts of Asia*, Volume 28, No. 6, 1998.

Moss, Hugh M. *Snuff Bottles of China.* London, 1971.

Moss, Hugh M., Victor E. Graham and Kabo Tsang. *The Art of the Chinese Snuff Bottle.* New York and Tokyo, 1993.

Scott, Rosemary. *The Miniature World, An Exhibition of Snuff Bottles from the J and J Collection.* Taipei, 2002.

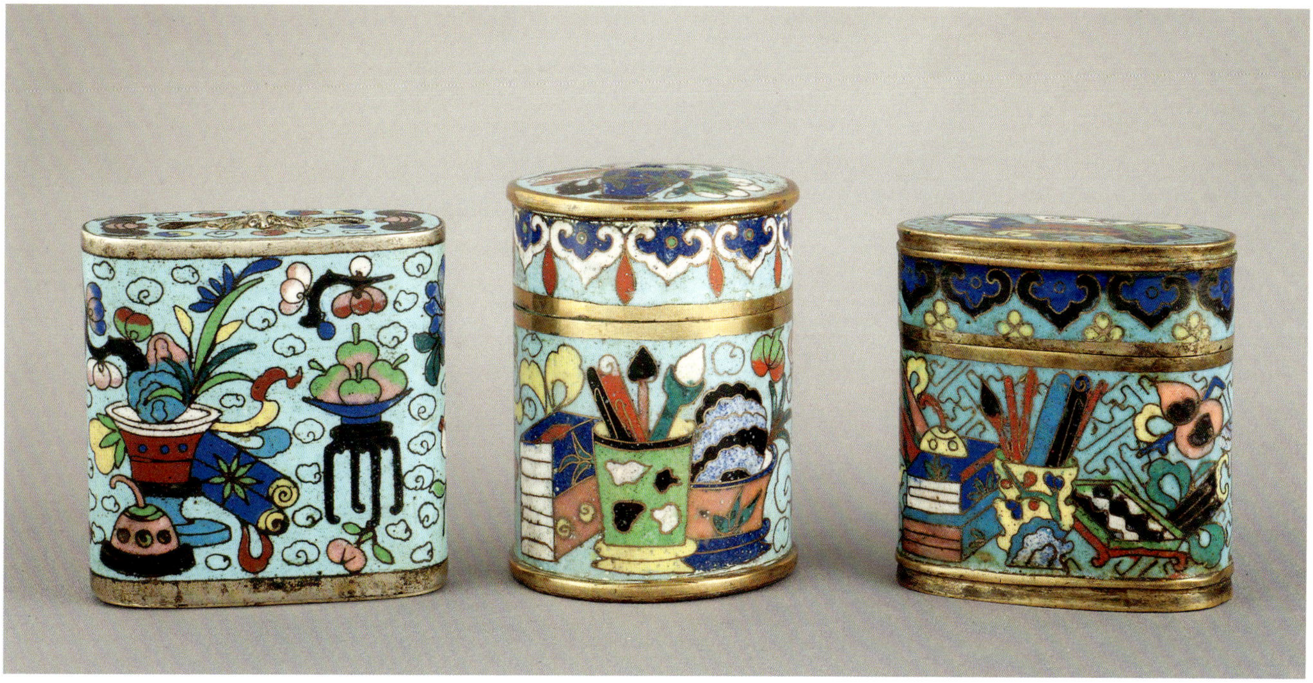

Chinese Opium Boxes

Unlike snuff bottles, miniature opium boxes have not been the subject of widespread collecting. In fact, there are only a small number of collections in private hands and public museums. Nonetheless, these boxes are often quite exquisite, highly decorated and ultimately very collectible. Opium boxes were the personal small portable containers used to store the smoker's supply of opium for use in daily life as well as for special occasions.

Opium, which came to be known euphemistically as "long-life mud," probably made its first appearance in China in the 8th century as a cure-all medicine and aphrodisiac. Sometimes served with either honey, prunes or orange peel, it was believed to relieve diarrhea, asthma, rheumatism, and pain in the heart and stomach. Early European traders introduced the smoking of opium, allowing the drug to reach the bloodstream quicker than eating it. By the late 18th century, opium smoking had spread across China as a recreational drug, and by the 19th century was taken by members of all levels of Chinese society to

Opium Boxes with design of objects for the scholar's desk (Hundred Antiques pattern) • **Flacons à opium** ornés d'objets d'un pupitre de lettré (motif *Hundred Antiques*) • Qing dynasty, 19th/early 20th century • cloisonné • Gift of Hy Eiley, AGGV 2003.012.005, Gift of Margaret N.Cutt, AGGV 2000.024.003, Gift of Mrs. H. J. Mackinnon, AGGV 2000.025.001

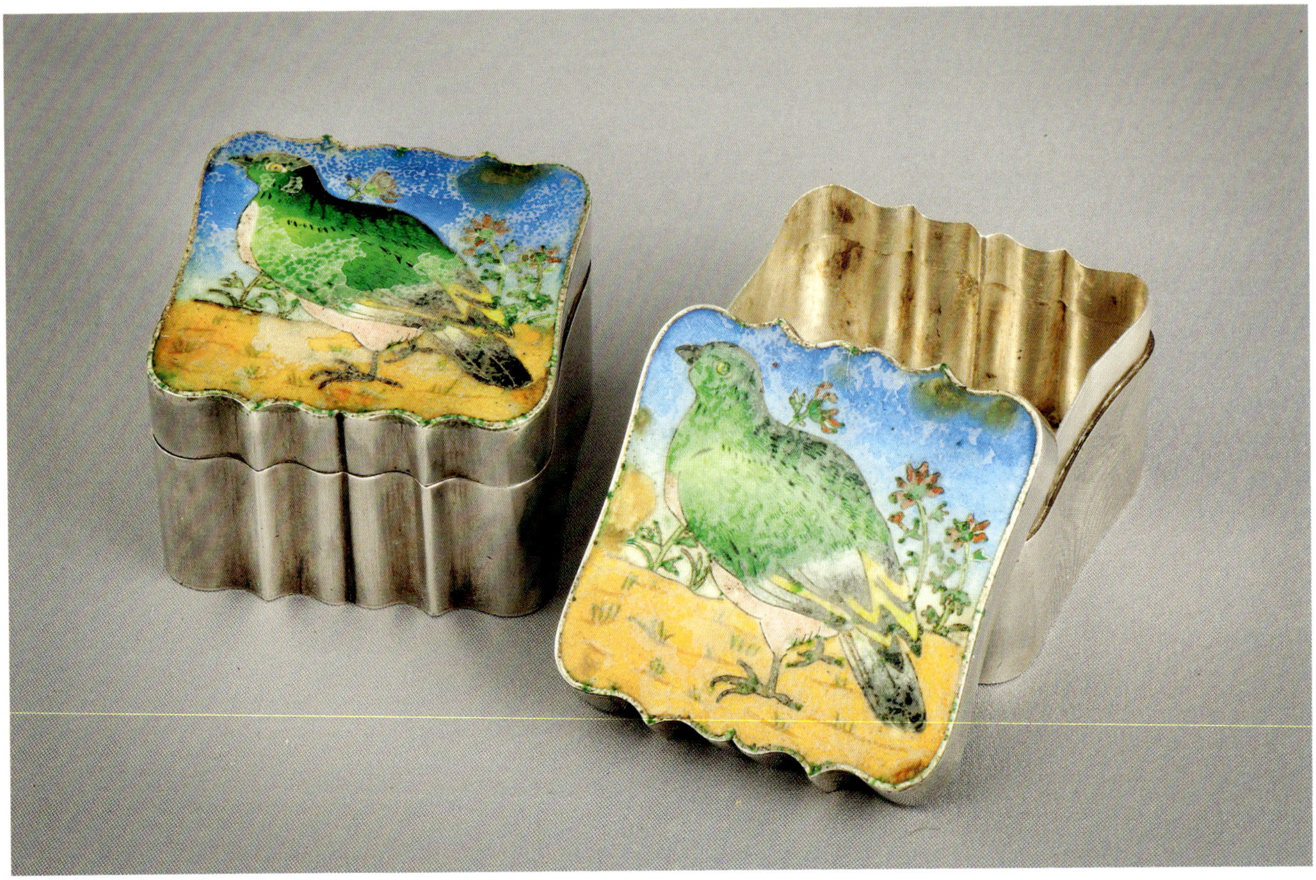

Pair of **Opium Boxes** with design of a quail • Deux **flacons à opium** ornés de cailles • Qing dynasty, late 19th century • silver, enamel • Gift of Hy Eiley, AGGV 2002.028.005 and .006

offer relief from the daily struggles of life. It was believed opium aided masculinity and provided sexual vigour. This idea can occasionally be seen in erotic designs found in hidden parts of the box. Opium smoking often conjures up dark disreputable opium dens, but it was also practised in the homes of the elite and the poor alike. Empress Dowager Cixi (1835-1908) was also reputed to have enjoyed a smoke or two late in the day.

Opium proved to be the perfect commodity for countries like Britain to correct the trade imbalance with China, caused by the huge demand for tea in Europe. In the 19th century Britain defied Chinese drug laws, promoted the lucrative export of Indian opium and would successfully fight two wars (known as the Opium Wars of 1839–1842 and 1857–1860) to keep China's drug market open. It was a legacy that left a myriad of tales of addiction and suffering in China, which would last until the middle of the 20th century, when opium use was stamped out by the newly established People's Republic of China.

Opium had certain paraphernalia attached to its use, like a distinctively shaped pipe, a small lamp, a spoon, a broad needle, a portable scale to weigh an exact dosage, a specially shaped pillow for resting the head and miniature containers or boxes. The opium boxes, which were small enough to fit in the palm of a hand, came in a variety of shapes—cylindrical, oblong and square—and were made from a variety of materials, both organic and inorganic, such as brass, silver, paktong (a mixture of copper, zinc and nickel), cloisonné, enamel, jade, mandarin orange peel, horn and ivory; some were even decorated with exotic materials like porcupine quills. Most boxes were made of metal that was decorated by incising, enamelling or hammering patterns in relief known as repoussé. Some silver boxes were decorated with a technique known as niello, where a mixture of silver, copper, lead, sulphur and borax designs were applied to the engraved silver or metal base and then fired.

Decorative subjects on the boxes include various flora and fauna themes, mythological and folklore subjects, calligraphy, symbols, religious emblems, Daoist immortals and landscapes. Some of the inscriptions on the boxes allude to the pleasures of opium smoking. Elaborately decorated opium boxes were often a display of wealth. For the most part the opium boxes date from the late 18th to early 20th centuries. While they contained a very destructive substance, which caused much political turmoil in China, they are nonetheless interesting examples of miniature works of art. The boxes, which were often given as gifts, had pull-off covers and large openings for the extraction of the gummy and sticky pea-sized blob of opium. Perhaps the reason why opium boxes never really caught on as collectible items was because of their negative connotation, as they served as a reminder of a time when foreign imperialism was rampant in China.

Selected Bibliography

Armero, Carlos, and Ben Rapaport. *The Arts of an Addiction. Qing Dynasty Opium Pipes and Accessories.*(privately printed) 2005.

Hodgson, Barbara. *Opium, A Portrait of the Heavenly Demon.* San Francisco, 1999.

Pagani, Catherine. *Chinese Opium Boxes, H. J. Eiley Collection.* Toronto, 1992.

___________. "Late Ch'ing Dynasty Opium Boxes", Arts of Asia, 1991, Vol. 21, No. 3

___________. "Opium, the Long Life Mud." *Rotunda, the Magazine of the Royal Ontario Museum.* Vol. 24, No. 2, 1991.

Chinese Pith Paintings

Pith paintings appear to have made their first appearance in China sometime in the early 19th century and were made almost exclusively for the export market, being sold as inexpensive souvenirs—like picture postcards of the day—to foreign merchants, sailors and missionaries, and eventually shipped in bulk to satisfy the Western appetite for stereotypical images of Chinese culture. Their heyday appears to have been in the 1830s and 1840s. They were often made in sets and presented in small paper-windowed albums or glass-fronted boxes and could vary greatly in quality. Pith paintings ranged in size from as small as about 10 x 8 cm to a maximum of about 30 x 20 cm. Of the eight known studios of pith painting, six were located in Canton, one in Beijing and one site remains unidentified. The only way of knowing the studio of origin of a painting is when the paintings come in an album, which has a studio plate stamp. As a rule, pith painters did not sign their works, except for the artist Sunqua. Other known pith artists listed in Carl Crossman's book *The China Trade* include Tingqua and Youqua from Canton, Chou Pai Chuen in Beijing and Chow Kwa in Shanghai, the latter two both working in the late 19th century. Tingqua and Chow Kwa are known to have set up studios in Hong Kong after the waterfront factories, or *hongs* of Canton, were burned down in the First Opium War (1839–1841) and in 1856.

Chinese Pith Painting – Trading ships in Canton: steamships, clippers and junks • **Peintures chinoises sur papier de moelle** – Navires commerçants à Canton : paquebots, clippers et jonques • artist unknown, 19th century • ink and colours on pith paper • Gift of Colin C. Graham, AGGV 2004.004.005

Pith paintings were small by necessity. Pith was a cheap, unprocessed, spongy paper-like material cored from the stem of a shrub called *tetrapanax papyrifera*, native to swampy areas in southern China and Taiwan. Pith is soaked before cutting, then short, thin sheet lengths are cut with a razor-sharp blade by a very skilful craftsman while turning the cylindrical stem. After drying in the sun for several days, they were trimmed and used without any further processing. The resulting pith surface is shiny, soft or velvety and translucent, and because the applied paint did not spread, it allows for incredibly detailed images. The bright

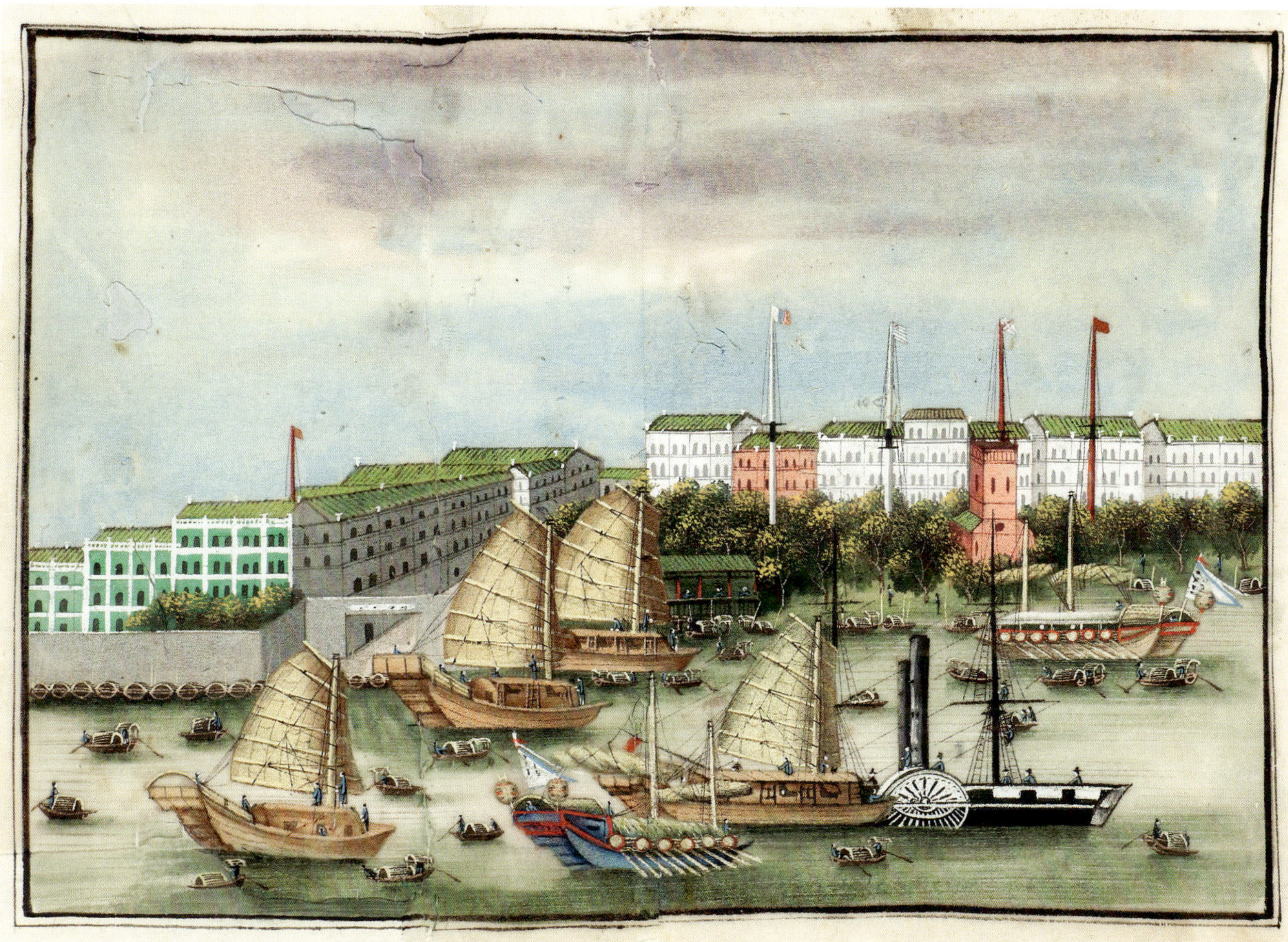

watercolour or tempera applied to the pith surface immediately causes it to swell, as a reaction to the moisture, giving an impression of three-dimensionality or depth perception. The jewel-like brilliance of the vibrant colours creates a look of embroidery or even the appearance of a mosaic. Because the paint does not spread, a brush as thin as a single hair can be used to paint on the surface. Unfortunately the nature of the pith paper makes the paintings very fragile as the pith becomes very brittle and cracks easily, and is almost always in need of conservation.

Little is known of the pith painters, as only a very few ever signed their works. Most paintings were probably produced by teams in studios, perhaps working on a type of assembly line, each doing a different aspect or element of the painting—face, clothing or background—over and over again. Sometimes the faces in a series look overly standardized and simplified. An experienced painter might create the original image, and his stable of assistants would churn out countless copies by stencilling or tracing the general outline and filling in the colours. The themes for the paintings, which played a very important role in revealing Chinese culture to the West, included landscapes, harbour scenes (especially the waterfront factories or the "hongs" in Canton and the ships transporting the products), customs, gambling, festivals, weddings, funerals, torture/punishment scenes, occupations, market scenes, genre scenes of traditional games and pastimes, as well as production sequences like the culturing of tea, the carving of jade, the production of ceramics and the making of silk. Other popular themes were portraits of the locals, from beggars on the street to wealthy Chinese and Manchu aristocrats with their stunning costumes. The flora and fauna were often depicted with great detail, especially the local plants, flowers, birds, insects and fish.

Selected Bibliography

Clunas, Craig. *Chinese Export Watercolours.* 1984.

Crossman, Carl L. *The China Trade: Export Paintings, Furniture, Silver and Other Objects*, Princeton. 1972.

Williams, Ifan. "Beauty in Pursuit of Pleasure." *Apollo.* November, 2006.

____________. "Views from the West, Chinese Pith Paper Paintings." *Arts of Asia*, Volume 31, No. 5, 2001.

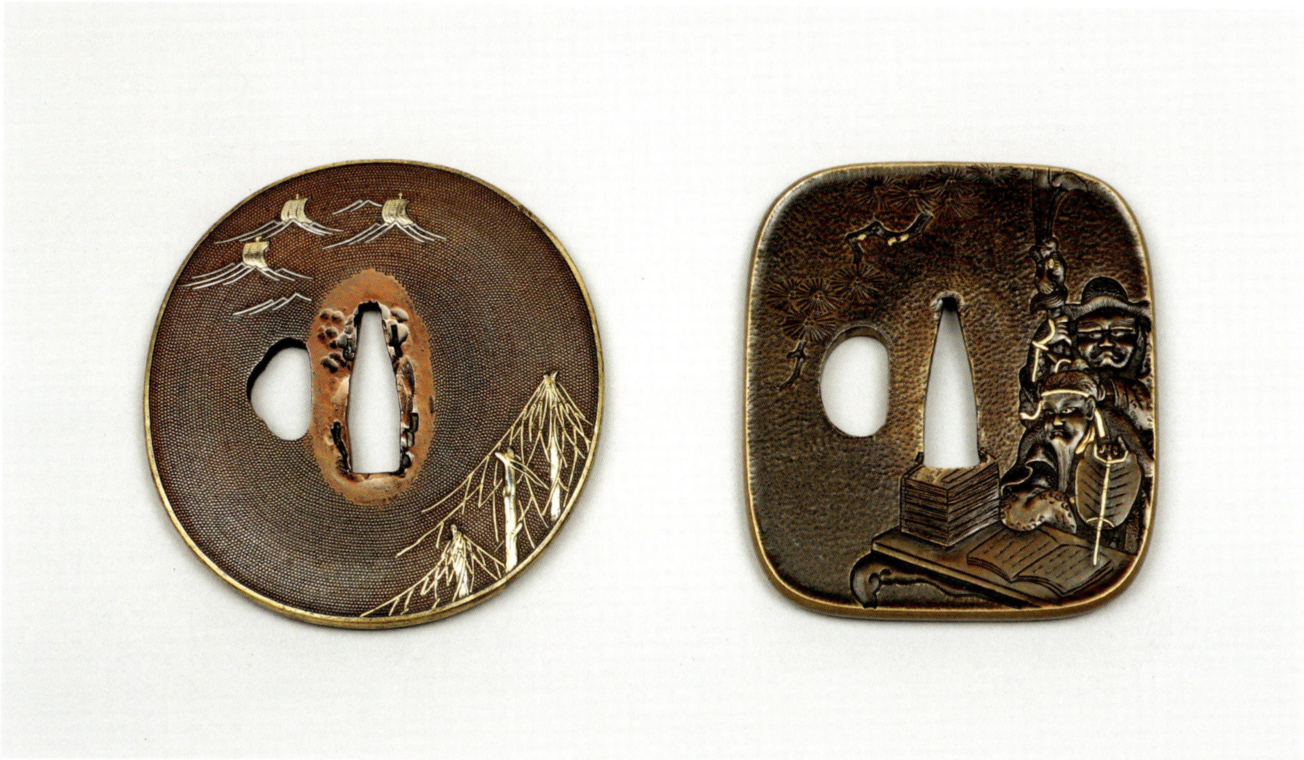

Japanese Sword Guards - Tsuba

The sword was the most highly revered object in the possession of the samurai and is considered "the soul of the samurai," as it was the embodiment of their behavioural code known as *bushido* with its self-discipline, unquestioning devotion and ultimate skill in martial arts. Only the samurai class had the privilege of carrying two swords, a long sword (*katana*) for attack and defence, and a short sword (*wakizashi*) for self-destruction, if necessary. Ancient Japanese swords, made between the 16th and mid-19th centuries, were examples of Japan's highest craftsmanship and were the most nearly perfect fighting weapons of their time, as well as being the finest edged weapons ever crafted. The associated fittings with the blade have been regarded as important works of art and, like the blades, have become highly collectible. The most ornate part of the sword is the sword guard known as the *tsuba,* a flat disc that separates the blade from the handle grip. The tsuba, which needed to be strong and light, contributed to the control and overall balance of

Two of ***tsuba*** sword guards, Edo period (1603-1868) • Duex ***tsuba*** de sabre, période Edo (1603 à 1868) • (left) ***tsuba*** with design of sailboats and fishnets, clams on verso • (à gauche) ***tsuba*** avec motif représentant des voiliers et des filets de pêche, palourdes au versobrass • gold, silver • (right) ***tsuba*** with a design of the God of War and God of Literature Kan-wu (Guan Yu in Chinese) with his assistant reading Confucian texts; pine tree on verso • (à droite) ***tsuba*** avec motif représentant le dieu de la guerre et le dieu de la littérature Kan-wu (Guan Yu en chinois) avec ses aides lisant des textes de Confucius; pin au verso • brass, gold inlay • Intended Gift, Private Collection

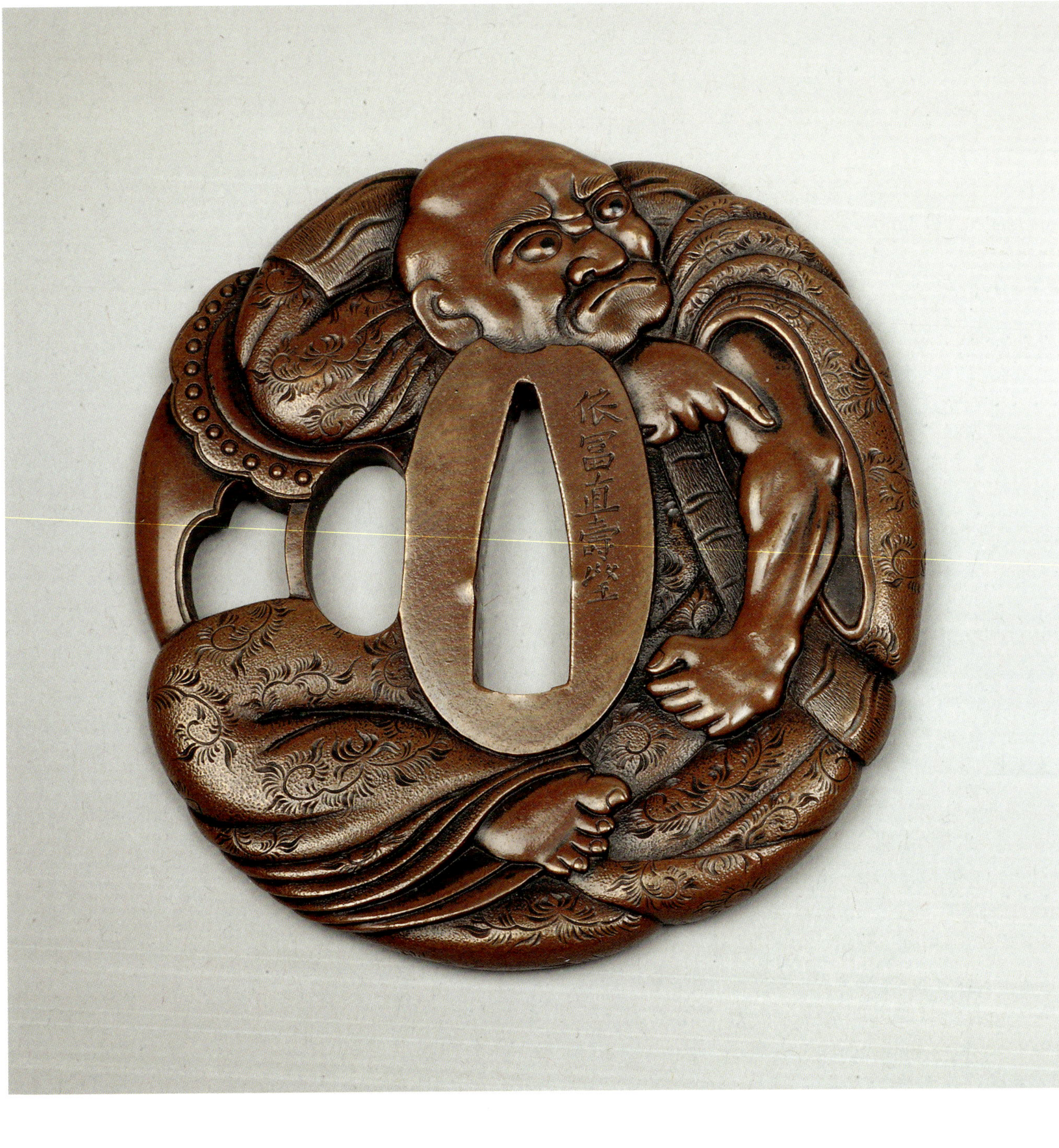
依冨直壽望

the sword by providing an accurate centre of gravity. Its main function was to prevent the hand from sliding onto the blade and being slashed and was also an important accoutrement of defence, used to block an incoming opponent's strike from sliding down the blade to cut the defender's hand.

The development of the tsuba sword guard was closely linked to the evolution of the sword in Japan and was probably originally made by swordsmiths to be fitted on their own swords. Early tsuba from the Muromachi period (1333–1573) and the Momoyama period (1573–1603) were strong and functional, and often traditionally made of iron with minimal openwork or surface decoration. However, during the Edo period (1603–1868), a time of relatively long peace, tsuba reached a zenith in quality and were noted for their soft metal artistry, becoming extremely decorative and less practical, and serving more as a status symbol. These were never intended for battle. The samurai, who formed a large and influential class, patronized the tsuba makers, who flourished in schools of artists with distinctive styles and who passed on the trade secrets to their lineage. Tsuba often have the name of their maker incised on either side of the hole for the blade handle. During the Muromachi period into the Edo period, groups of specialist sword guard makers came into being with a wide and varied decorative repertoire. The samurai owners of the tsuba usually passed them down to family members as heirlooms, wrapped in soft old brocade and stored in exquisite lacquered boxes. Sometimes they were decorated with family crests (*mon*), insignias or seals. Despite reaching new heights of ornamentation during the Edo period, it was not long after the restoration of power to the Emperor during the Meiji period (1868–1912) that the wearing of swords became prohibited by an imperial decree in 1876. With the sword made redundant, the tsuba makers lost their samurai patrons and had to switch to mainly making metal knick knacks for the tourist trade. By the 20th century, brass tsuba were being turned out in great numbers by factories for use by the army. During the

Japanese ***tsuba*** sword guard in the shape of a Rakan (disciple of Buddha), signed Ryu Nusai • La gard du sabre japonaise, le ***tsuba*** en forme de Rakan (disciple de Boudha), Signée Ryu Nusai • copper, *shakudo* eyes and inner sleeve • Fred and Isabel Pollard Collection, AGGV 1962.150.001

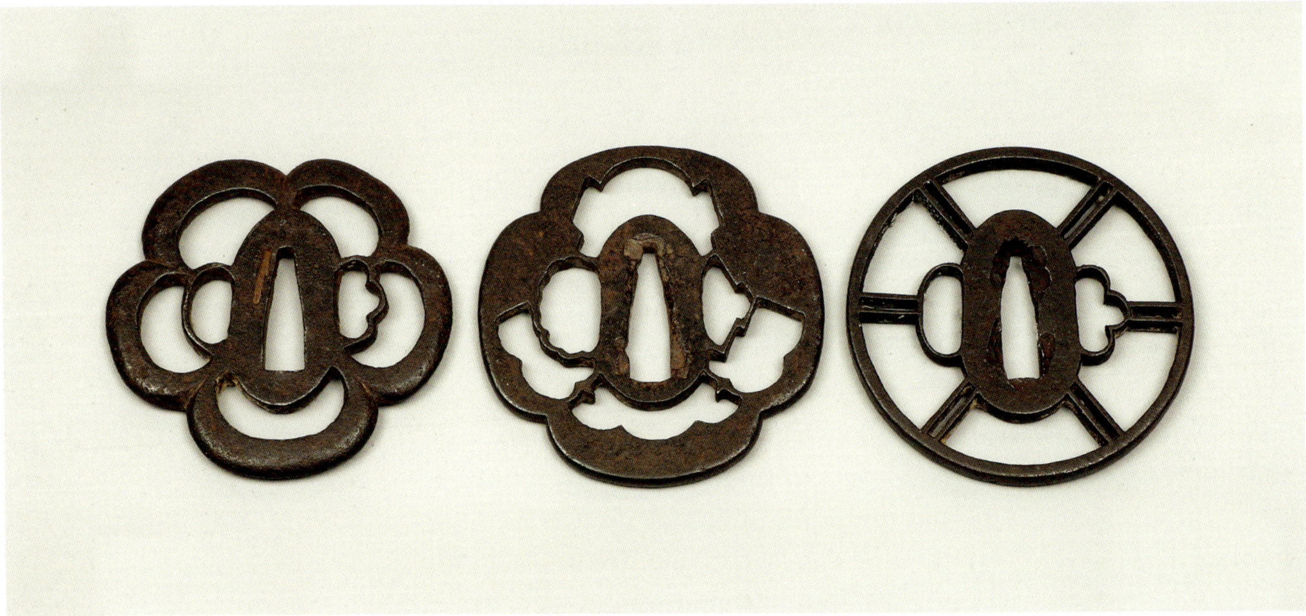

Three **tsuba** sword guards with openwork designs • Trois gardes **tsuba** de sabre japonais avec motifs ajourés • unsigned, Edo period (1603-1868) • iron • Collection of Frank Low-Beer, AGGV 2005.029.011- .016

Meiji period, foreigners saw the beauty in tsuba and began collecting them on a large scale.

The tsuba were made in all kinds of shapes for bladed Japanese weapons, including the *tachi* or *katana* (long sword) and *wakizashi* (short sword) as well as sometimes for the *tanto* (dagger) and *naginata* (spear halberd). The four main shapes for the tsuba are *maru gata*, which is the most common, a roundish shape, often elliptical or oval; *kaku gata*, a squarish shape with rounded corners, occasionally hexagonal or octagonal, or, rarely, trapezoidal; *mokko gata*, a shape with four lobes; and *shitogi*, in the shape of a rice cake, usually reserved for ceremonial swords. On rare occasions, the tsuba were made in the shape of an insect, a snake, a frog or a bird. The tsuba itself usually has three holes: the centre hole is for the tang or handle of the blade to be fitted through; the simple arc or oval hole on the left is for the *kozuka*, which is a handle that holds a small blade called a *kogatana* carried in the scabbard of the main sword; and the hole on the right side, usually with three arcs, is for the *kogai*, a skewer-like implement. Both the *kozuka* and *kogai* project beyond the top of the scabbard; hence, the necessity for the holes in the tsuba. Sometimes the maker of the tsuba is listed on one or both sides of the central tang hole.

Despite their limited surface size, there have been a multitude of themes depicted on tsuba covering all aspects of Japanese culture, ranging from religion, history and mythology to landscapes and nature. There were a number of human figures illustrated on tsuba, which include famous warriors, generals and Chinese legendary figures like the god of war Guanyu or Guandi (Kan'u in Japanese), the demon queller Zhong Kui (Shoki in Japanese), Bodhidarma (Daruma in Japanese), the playful monks Hanshan and Shide (Kanzan and Jittoku in Japanese), to name a few. The landscape designs on tsuba were often based on Chinese paintings. The scenes could include high mountains in the background with trees, a river, a temple, a gateway, travellers or boats in the foreground. Among the most popular creatures represented from nature are the tiger, the monkey, the horse, the snake, the hare, the crane and the carp. Many of the illustrated mythological beasts were inspired by Chinese folklore, such as the dragon, the phoenix and the *qilin (kirin* in Japanese). The dragon was associated with the emperor and the phoenix (*ho* bird) with the empress. The *kirin* symbolized imperial authority.

The techniques and decorative devices for the tsuba were also quite varied. The surface was created by forging and hammering, and in the case of iron, tempering. The traditional material used for sword guards was iron—which could acquire a number of patinas including red, black and brown—as well as soft metals like copper and, later, brass. During the long peace of the Edo period, when the arts were allowed to bloom, the use of copper-based alloys like *shakudo* (containing gold), *shibuichi* (containing silver) and *sentoku* (containing brass) were used to make exquisite tsuba. These were embellished with gold or gilt metal. Usually the tsuba are decorated on both sides with the most visible "handle" side being the most decorative. Tsuba were often decorated with punched and incised designs and perforations, which allowed for inlay techniques. It was not uncommon for samurai to have several interchangeable tsuba for a single cherished blade. The choice of the tsuba might depend on the season or the occasion at which the sword was to be worn.

Selected Bibliography

Caldwell, R.B. "Tsuba, Handguards of the Japanese Sword." *Arts of Asia*. Vol. 23, No. 1, 1993.

Earle, Joe. "Japanese Sword-fittings in the Victoria and Albert Museum." *Orientations*. Vol. 17, No. 12, 1986.

Lorber, D. and H.B. Martin. "Japanese Sword Fittings." *Arts of Asia*, Vol. 7, No. 3, 1977.

Swart, Paula, Robert E. Haynes and John Berta. *The Soul of the Samurai, A Selection of Sword Guards from the Vancouver Museum*. Vancouver, 1993.

inro with design of capped monkey head • ***inro***, motif de langur à capuchon • wood, lacquer, glass • ***ojime*** with rooster • ***ojime***, coq • wood, lacquer, silver • ***netsuke*** in the form of a badger's head; floral spray and conch shell on verso • ***netsuke*** en forme de tête de blaireau; grappe de fleurs et conque au verso • carved wood • late Edo period, mid 19th century • Fred and Isabel Pollard Collection, AGGV 1974.223.001

Japanese Netsuke Toggles, Ojime Beads and Inro Cases

Miniature toggles called netsuke (literally means "root for fastening") were created in Japan at least as early as the late 16th century for both functional and aesthetic decorative purposes. The traditional form of Japanese dress known as *kimono* and *kosode* had no pockets to carry small items. Women could tuck personal items into their sleeves, while men suspended on cords their objects of everyday use, called *sagemono* (hanging objects)—which included tobacco pouches, pipes, brush cases, purses or compartment cases called *inro* —from their *obi* (kimono sash). To secure the cord from slipping through the wearer's sash, a small fashionable netsuke toggle or counterweight with two openings for the cord to pass through, acted as an anchor, and an *ojime* (sliding bead) was strung on the cord between the netsuke and the *sagemono* to tighten or loosen the opening of the *sagemono*. The owners of the three elements sought to bring about the perfect combination of them in colour, material and design. Most often, the three elements were not made by the same group of artists.

To work properly, netsuke toggles had to meet certain basic requirements: they had to be compact, not too heavy, but bulky enough to stop a cord from slipping; durable, to be able to withstand a lot of wear; smooth and comfortable, with no sharp or protruding edges that could cause damage to the wearer's garment or skin; and finally, fashionable, something the wearer could be proud of displaying.

During the Edo or Tokugawa period (1603–1868), people of all classes, from officials and samurai, to wealthy merchants and craftsmen, sought out fine netsuke. Even peasants owned simple netsuke, often made of natural materials like gourds, shells and stones. netsuke became a means to exhibit personal taste through adornment, like one might with jewellery. netsuke production soon evolved from a strictly utilitarian

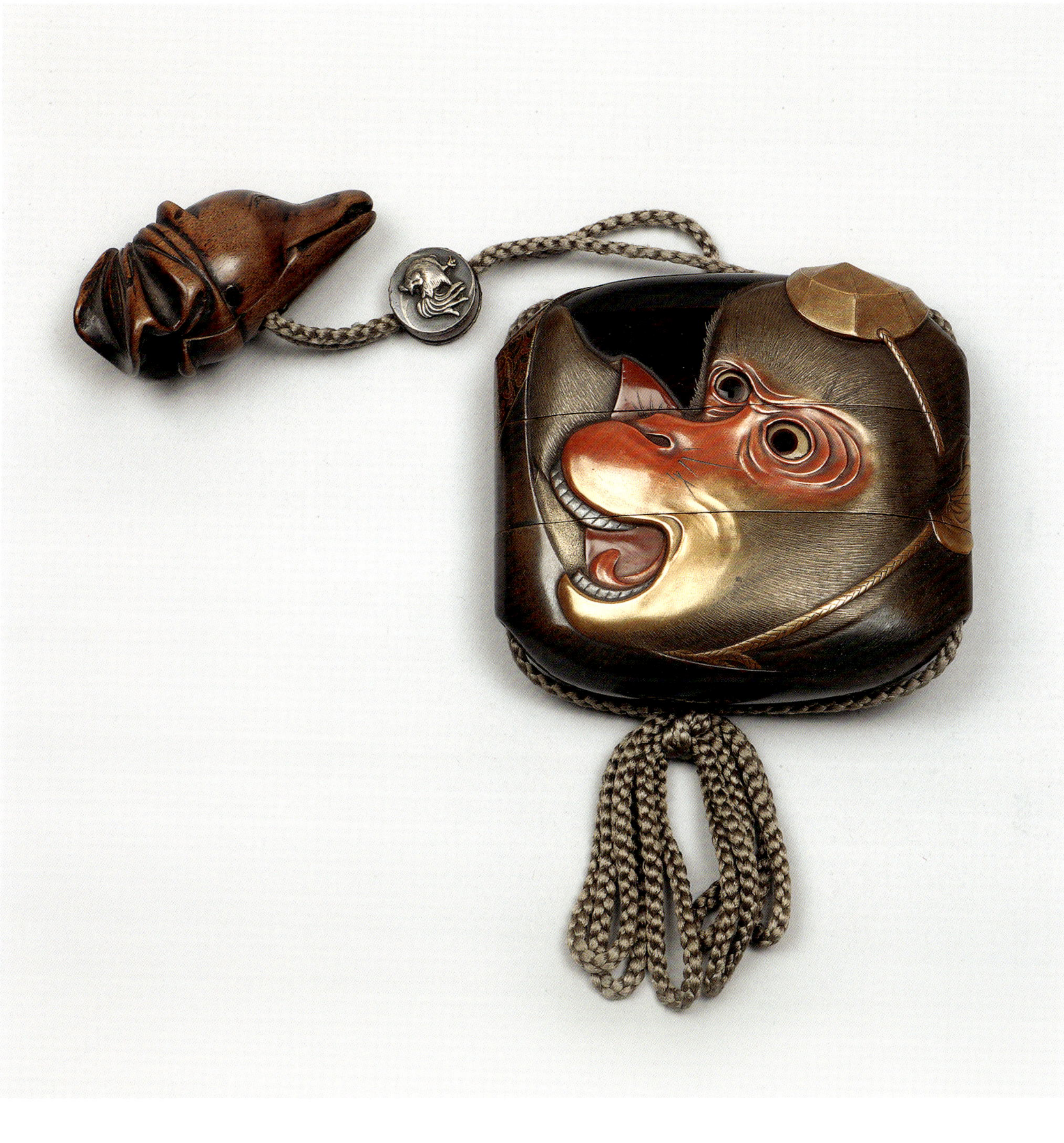

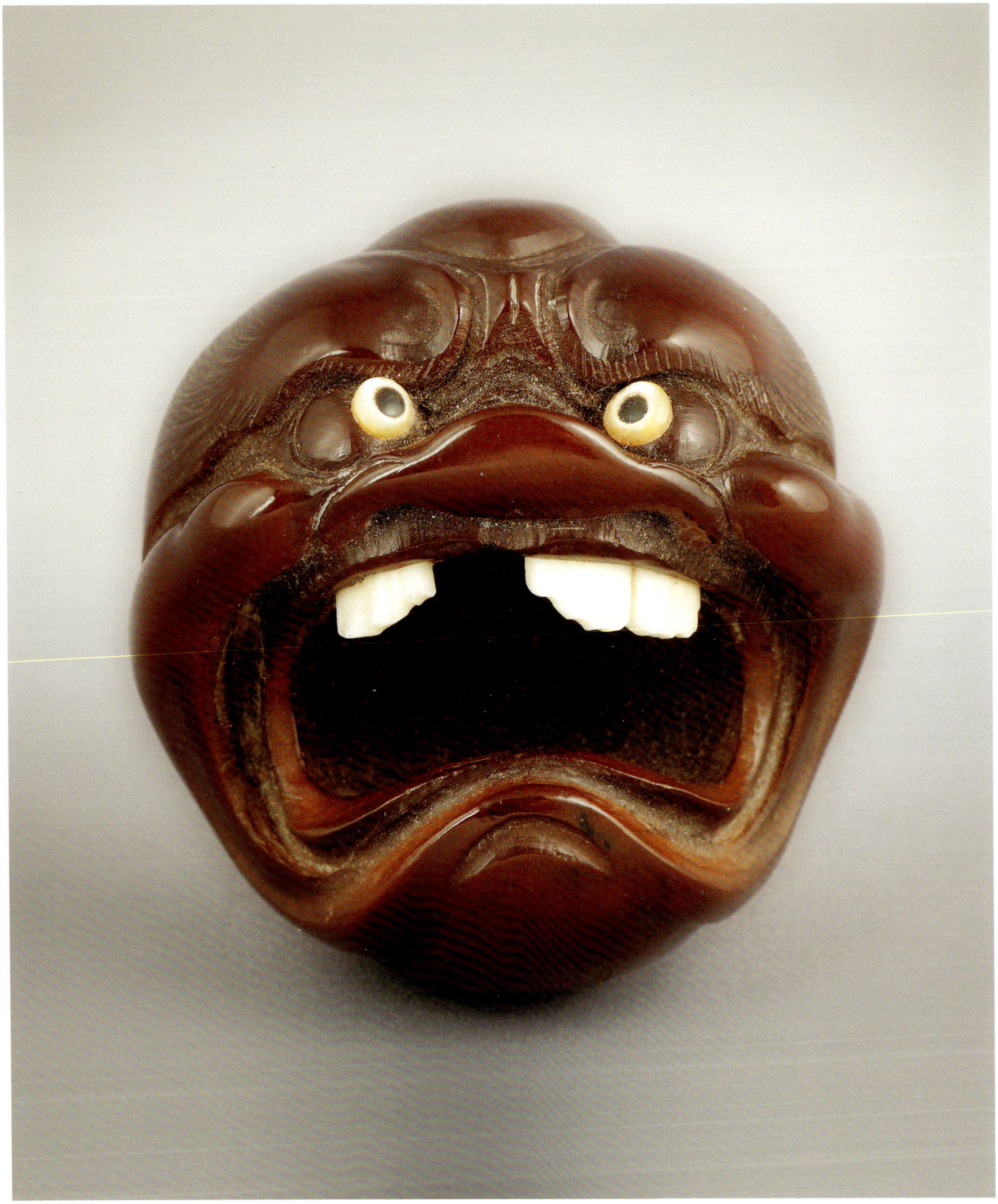

object to a coveted collector's item of great artistic merit and elegant sophistication. netsuke also became a status symbol for their owners, who competed with each other to acquire a collection more elegant than that of their peers. It was because of their individuality, originality and uniqueness that netsuke quickly became highly collectible and a coveted art form. netsuke, like jewellery, also became a sign of social status, as the craftsmanship and the quality of materials used varied among the classes.

By the mid-18th century, netsuke carvers no longer considered their occupation an insignificant pastime or hobby, but as a relevant art form, By the mid-18th century, netsuke carvers no longer considered their occupation an insignificant pastime or hobby, but as a relevant art form. They began to sign their works, became professional carvers and teachers, and eventually formed different regional schools with distinctive styles. They needed proper tools, carving skills, excellent eyesight and a vivid imagination to cater to the great demand, as by this time almost all males in Japan had need of wearing a netsuke. Their designs became increasingly complicated and sophisticated as they developed new carving techniques, experimented with all sorts of materials and dreamed up as many conceivable subjects as possible.

netsuke in the form of grotesque head • ***netsuke*** en forme de tête grotesque • signed Mitsuyuki, 19th century • wood, ivory • Edith Low-Beer Collection, AGGV 1990.038.001

Carvers' reputations were established by the style, skill and cleverness of their work. They seemed to have had more freedom in terms of using parody, satire and parables than artists of other mediums during the Edo period. They seem to have been unfettered by tradition or censorship of subject matter, like painters and print artists. A good number of netsuke bear the master carver's signature, especially during the late Edo period. However, because schools (and the pupils) of a master carver often used the master's signature indiscriminately, the netsuke might not necessarily have been made by the master himself. Even if there is a genuine maker's name inscribed, very little seems to be known about their lives. Although fine old netsuke were only a miniature art form, their painstaking creation was labour intensive, taking a considerable length (left) ***netsuke*** of man with a staff • (à gauche) ***netsuke***, homme avec un bâton • late 19th/early 20th century • bone • Gift of Philip and Georgina Steel, AGGV SC897 • (right) ***netsuke*** of monk • (à droite) ***netsuke***, moine • ca. 1900 • bone • Harold and Vera Mortimer-Lamb Purchase Fund, AGGV 1977.243.001

of time to produce a single piece, perhaps as long as a month or two. As a result, the earnings of a netsuke carver were extremely modest. Since netsuke are three-dimensional sculptures, they were meant to be seen and appreciated from all angles, and thus required being finely finished from every view point. The netsuke also had to have tactile appeal when handled, revealing its depths and textures. Over time, many netsuke develop a fine patina from age and handling.

Netsuke can be made out of a wide variety of different materials, sometimes in combinations or as inlays, with ivory and wood being the most popular materials. Besides elephant ivory, the teeth (loosely defined as ivory) of other creatures were used to make netsuke, including mammoth tusk from Siberia, sperm whale teeth, narwhal horn, walrus tusk, wild boar tusk as well as the ivory of the helmeted hornbill, and occasionally hippopotamus teeth. Wood netsuke were not confined to just one specific tree type. The trees used included cypress, boxwood, camphor, cherry, mulberry, persimmon, plum, camellia as well as bamboo, and imported ebony and teakwood. Other materials used to make netsuke include metal, lacquer, bone, nuts, horn (for example, ox, rhinoceros, deer), tortoise shell, amber, coral, glass, soapstone, semi-precious stones, ceramic, natural and carved gourds, shell, and rattan. These were not just produced by netsuke carvers, but also by other craftsmen—such as lacquer artists, metal casters, silversmiths, sword makers, and potters—as adjuncts to their main crafts.

Netsuke can be categorized into a few main different types: *katabori*, the most common form of netsuke, a compact three-dimensional sculpture depicting human beings, deities, real and mythical animals, and fruits and vegetables; *men*, mask netsuke that were often miniature imitations of full size *noh* and *kyogen* masks, ceremonial Buddhist *gigaku* and *bugaku* masks as well as folk masks used in festivals; *sashi*, a long and thin netsuke; *kagamibuta*, a netsuke that has a metal disc serving as a lid to a shallow bowl, usually of ivory, bone or horn; and *manju*, a flat netsuke,

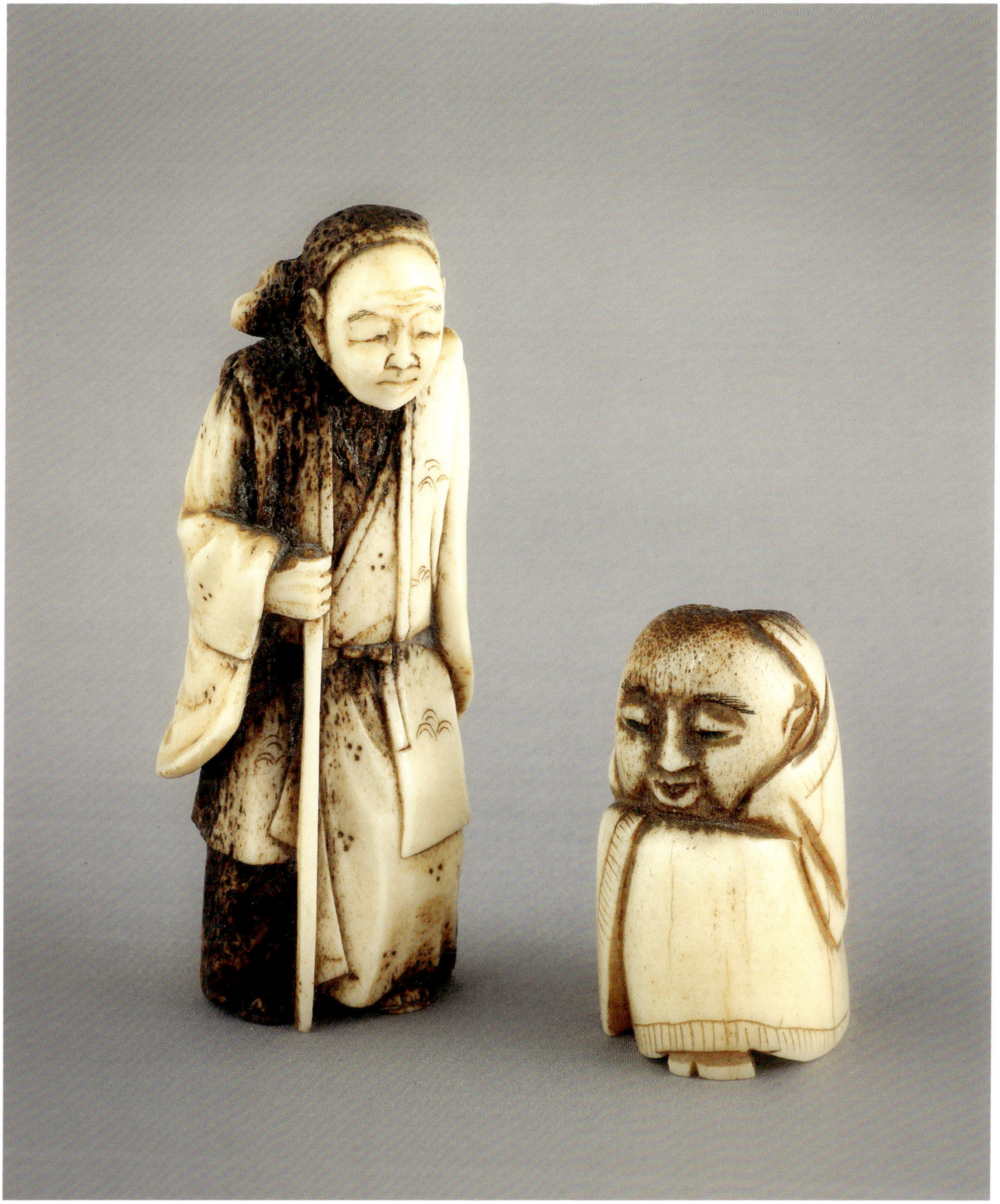

usually round, but sometimes square or oval, that resembles the shape of a rice cake called *manju* and is often made of two ivory halves. Less common types include: *ryusa*, a variety of *manju*, often with designs of flowers and birds made popular by the artist Ryusa; *ichiraku*, often a gourd shaped netsuke made of braided or woven material like bamboo, cane or wire; and *kurawa*, known as ashtray netsuke after their actual use by smokers.

Because of its specific small size, there were limitations to how elaborately netsuke could be carved. netsuke are generally about four centimetres in size, but may vary between two to nine centimetres, and occasionally are larger. As far as netsuke subjects, everyday activities of Edo Japan's various social classes were portrayed, often in a whimsical manner including scenes of monks meditating, pipe smoking, drinking tea, playing games, or performing daily tasks, as well as foreign traders in Western costume. All types of people, real or imaginary, famous or common, old to young, gods and demons, historical to contemporary, foreign or domestic, were ingeniously depicted. Occasionally, sexual themes were also portrayed. Many of the human figures were based on Chinese and Japanese folklore or religious legends, including the *sennin*, legendary hermits, Zhong Kui (Shoki) the demon queller, Bodhidarma (Daruma), the Indian Buddhist saint who founded Chan (Zen), and the Seven Gods of Good Fortune. Among the most popular animal subjects were the twelve zodiac animals, sea creatures, birds, magical animals like the fox and badger, mythical beasts like the dragon, *kirin* (an auspicious beast usually with one horn, sometimes referred to as a unicorn), *baku* (eaters of nightmares), *oni* (demons), *kappa* (impish creatures with webbed hands and feet), *tengu* (goblins of the forest) and *shishi* (lion-dogs), as well as reptiles and bugs. Plants such as chestnuts, mushrooms, flowers and various fruits and vegetables were common themes. Non-living subjects included coins, tools, toys, household objects, musical instruments, and roof tiles. There was also a liking for anything quaint, odd, grotesque or macabre, like human skulls.

netsuke of Pegasus, signed Tanetoshi, contemporary Japanese • ***netsuke***, Pégase, signé Tanetoshi, japonais contemporain • ivory, silver and gold paint, wood, amber, jade, horn • Gift of the Lewis and Ruth Sherman Foundation, AGGV 2007.016.086

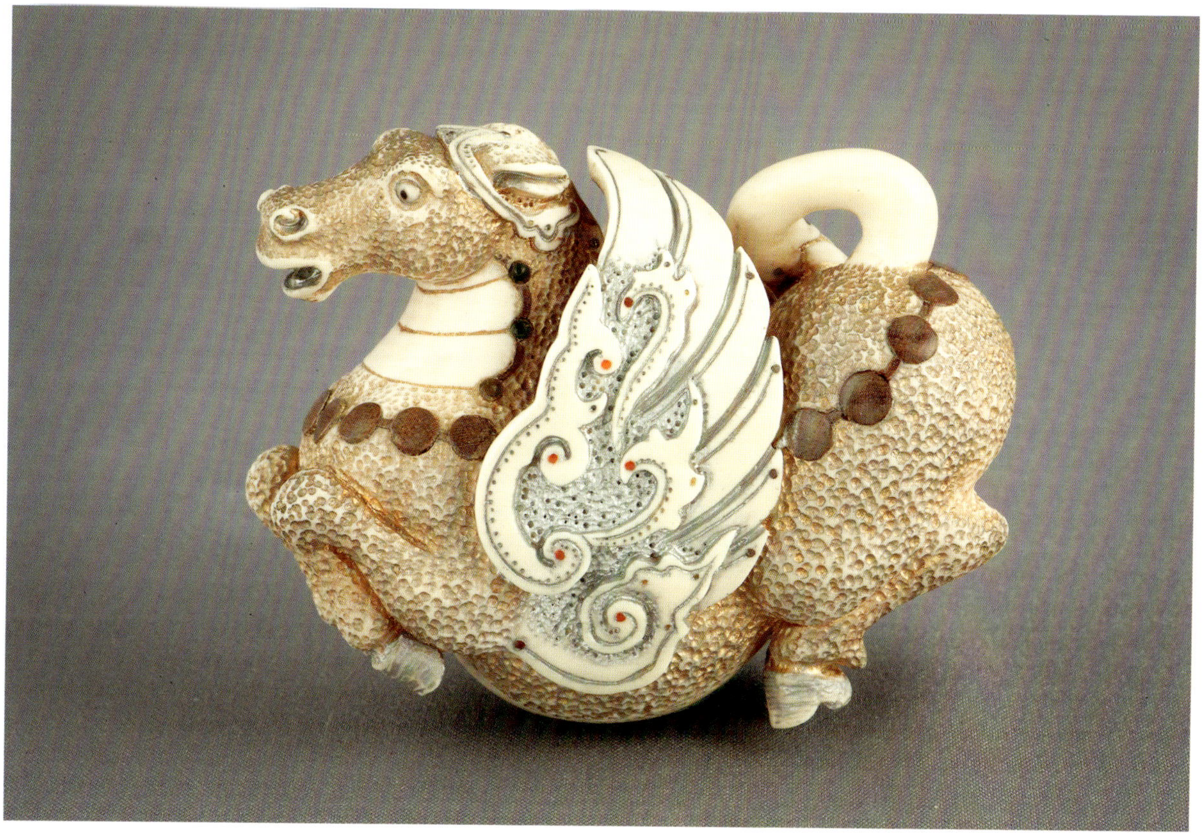

With the end of the feudal Edo period and the beginning of the Meiji period (1868–1912), Western dress with plenty of pockets came to be adopted by the Japanese in place of the traditional kimono, and as a result, netsuke lost their relevance, causing them to disappear as fashion accessories for daily use. Whole heirloom treasure chests of netsuke were set aside by Japanese families as outdated relics. European and American traders immediately recognized netsuke as marvellous examples of art in miniature and began to collect them by the boxfuls. Despite the decline in use of kimono and netsuke, the foreign demand for the prized netsuke kept the industry flourishing. The export boom allowed the livelihood of the netsuke artists to prosper and survive for several more decades. As a result, huge private and museum collections were built up in Holland, England, France and the United States. In fact, because of the Japanese indifference towards netsuke, many of the finest ancient netsuke collections are outside of Japan. Most of the netsuke made from the early Meiji period onwards were never used and were simply

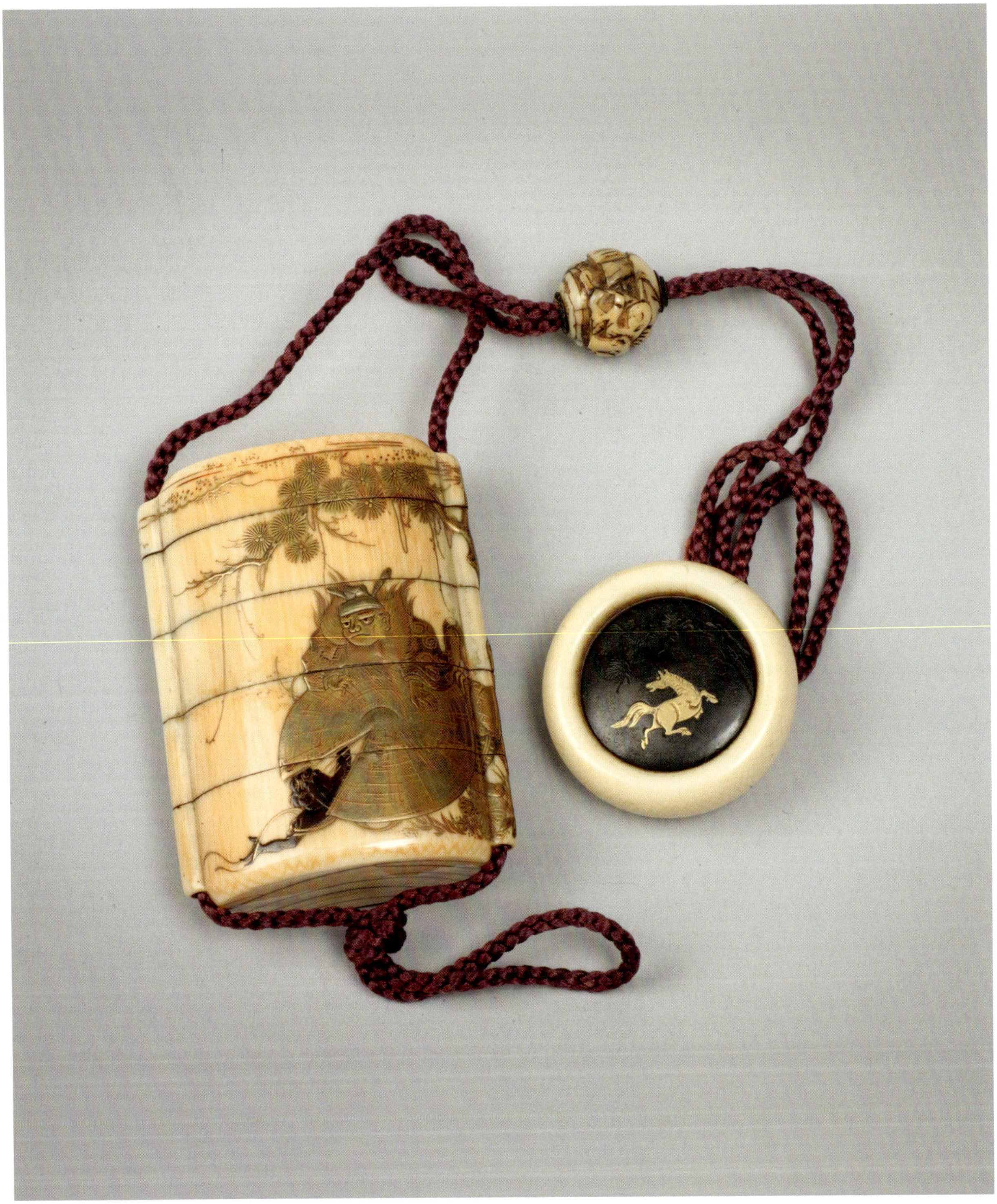

made as export items. They were carved by skilled artisans and were of fine quality, but the large demand for export to the West also led to the production of many minor quality netsuke.

Thus, foreigners (*gaijin*) played an integral role in preserving and sustaining netsuke art, causing the carvers to adapt and cater to the new clientele with new ideas and materials. Erotica even became a fairly common genre in netsuke for export to foreign markets.

Today the value of netsuke can range from a hundred to one hundred thousand dollars, based on the quality of the works and if they were created by well known craftsmen. It is buyer beware, as there are now mass-produced knock-offs being created around the world, especially in China. The artistic tradition of carving netsuke has survived to this day with about a hundred professional artists worldwide (both Japanese and non-Japanese) who continue to produce netsuke of high standard. In fact, an innovative netsuke created by a well known contemporary netsuke artist can sell for a four-digit dollar price.

The contemporary netsuke carvers who have revived the art of netsuke carving often exhibit the same great artistry, craftsmanship and originality of the great old masters. Contemporary Japanese netsuke artists include Kangyoku, Bishu, Hideyuki, Akihide and Keiun. Foreign netsuke carvers who have devoted themselves to this incredible painstaking craft include British carvers Guy Shaw, Nick Lamb and Michael Webb; American carver David Carlin; and Jewish carver George Weil, to name a few. There are also a large number of Chinese craftsmen who have been carving for decades.

As mentioned earlier, the netsuke toggle, the *ojime* bead and the inro case are part of a set for carrying items. The ojime is a bead or small slide that is slid down two strands of cord against the top of the inro to loosen or tighten it. It was usually designed to harmonize with the netsuke and the

inro with design of Shoki and *oni* demon • ***inro***, motif représentant Shoki et un démon *oni* • ivory, gold, lacquer • ***ojime*** in the form of Shoki's face, ivory • ***ojime*** en forme du visage de Shoki, ivoire • ***netsuke*** with design of gold horse with monkey and pine tree, signed Re In or Li Guang • ***netsuke***, orné d'un cheval doré avec un singe et un pin, signé Re In ou Li Guang • ivory, shakudo alloy • late Edo period, mid 19th century • Fred and Isabel Pollard Collection, AGGV 1964.010.001

inro. Like netsuke, it could be fashioned of many materials, with various metals, gold, stone, ivory and wood being among the most popular; and it also incorporated designs of myth, tradition and nature, but because of its limited size and shape, it was destined to have much less detail and appeal.

Inro (meaning personal seal case) are small interlocking, tightly fitted cases. It is said that the samurai class were the first to wear inro, and they were a popular item with them. Eventually, however, prosperous members of other classes also began wearing them. The multi-compartments (usually two to five in number, precisely slot into one another) were used to carry small ink seals, medicinal powders and pills, and aromatic conserves. The inro were flat, rectangular or round in shape, consisting of four or five horizontal compartments, held together by cords that ran through the ends of each compartment. Like the netsuke and ojime, the tiered inro cases could be made of a variety of different materials, but by far the most popular was cypress wood covered with lacquer. Lacquer, a sap from a lacquer tree, was applied in layers (some say as many as sixty layers) to the cypress core, allowed to dry and then polished to bring out the gloss. To create different colours and textures on fine pieces, lacquer artists used a decoration technique called *maki-e*, which involved sprinkling a variety of metal powders including gold, silver, copper, brass, lead, aluminum, platinum, pewter, as well as their alloys, onto the lacquer surface before it dried. A decorator might lavishly apply an outer decoration with different coloured lacquer or make use of appliqué of different materials like mother-of-pearl, ivory, tortoiseshell and coral. Some inro were masterpieces of the lacquer craft, which could be afforded only by the wealthier samurai and later, wealthy merchants. Whereas netsuke were usually three-dimensional sculptures, inro were more like two-dimensional designs sometimes borrowed from classical literature, paintings or woodblock prints. Some of the exquisite decorations on inro are spectacular examples of Japan's finest lacquer workmanship. Like netsuke, they are also highly collectible.

Selected Bibliography

Barker, Richard and Lawrence Smith. *netsuke, The Miniature Sculptures of Japan*. London, 1976.

Bushell, Raymond. *Collectors' netsuke*. Tokyo, 1971.

Davey, Neil K. *netsuke*. London, 1973.

Kotler, Philip. "Judging Quality in netsuke." *Arts of Asia*. Vol. 6, No. 2, 1976.

Okada, Barbra Teri. *netsuke, Masterpieces from the Metropolitan Museum of Art*. New York, 1982.

O'Brien, Mary Louise. *netsuke, Guide for Collectors*. Ruthland and Tokyo, 1973.

Olson, Eleanor. "A Panorama in Miniature: Japanese netsuke". *The Museum*. Vol. 9, No. 4, 1957.

Roth, Stig. *netsuke in the Collections of the Röhss Museum of Arts and Crafts*. Göteborg, 1970.

Ryerson, Egerton. *The netsuke of Japan, Legends, History, Folklore and Customs*. London, 1958.

Stern, Harold P. *The Magnificent Three: Lacquer, netsuke, and Tsuba, Selections from the Collection of Charles A. Greenfield*. London, 1972.

Ueda, Reikichi. *The netsuke Handbook of Ueda Reikichi*, adapted from Japanese by Raymond Bushell. Tokyo, 1961.

Webb, Glenn T. *Masterworks in Miniature: Japanese netsuke*. Vancouver, 1967.

Yoshiko, Kakudo. *netsuke: Myth and Nature in Miniature*. San Francisco, 1981.

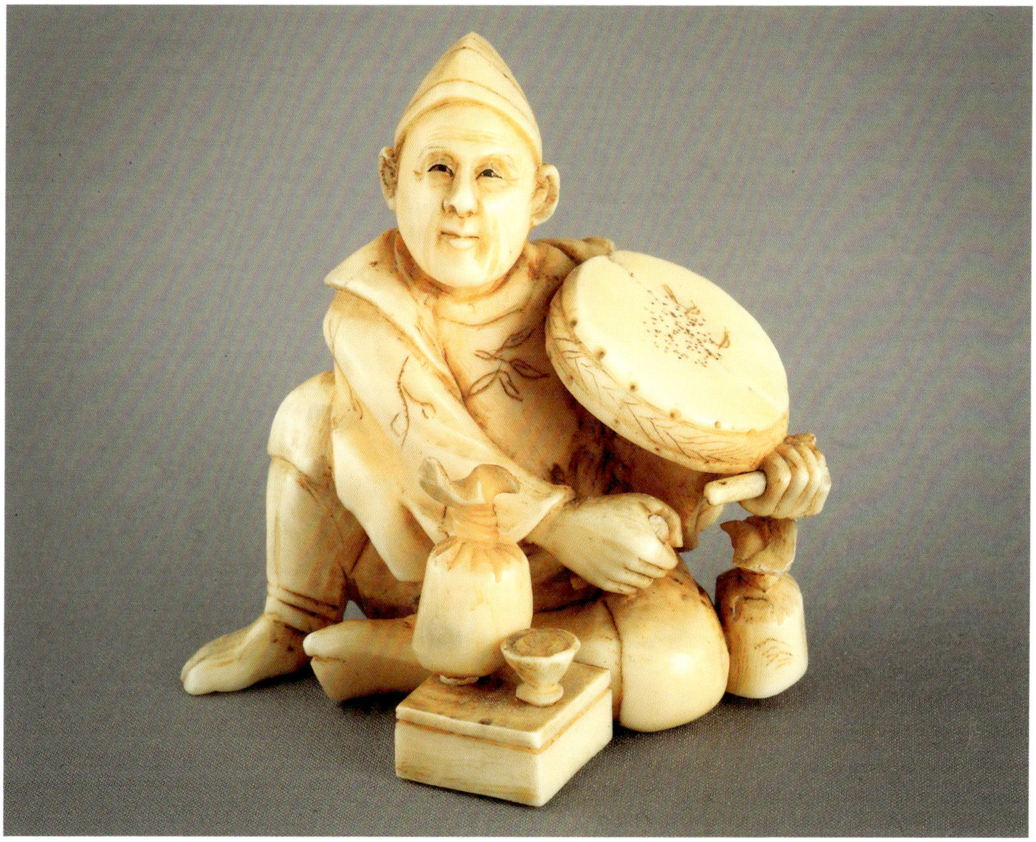

Japanese Okimono Sculptures

okimono of drummer, signed Ariyuki or Kaneyuki or Teruyuki or Mitsuyuki • ***okimono*** d'un joueur de tambour, signée Ariyuki ou Kuneyuki ou Teruyuki ou Mitsuyuki • Meiji period (1868-1912) • ivory • From the Collection of Bruce and Dorothy Brown, Given by their son Tony Brown, AGGV 2005.034.005

Related to the miniature netsuke carvings are larger, non-functional, purely decorative sculpture known as *okimono* (which literally translates as "object for placement") usually displayed in the tokomono or alcove. When the Japanese began wearing Western fashion with pockets during the Meiji period (1868–1912), they no longer needed the netsuke toggles and *sagemono* containers. As a result, many netsuke carvers also began carving larger sculptures to cater to the interests of the prosperous merchants who emerged as the new connoisseur class and patrons of the arts, and to meet the huge demand for Japanese curios or souvenirs in the Western world, especially in the late 19th century. The West craved exquisitely crafted and unique artefacts from Japan. The Japanese government at this time also helped the okimono trade through their participation in international expositions, starting with the Exposition Universelle or Grand Exhibition in Paris in 1867, where foreigners had the opportunity to see products from exotic Japan.

Along with spectacular ceramic, cloisonné, metalwork, lacquer and textile products, okimono sculptures were exhibited in the late 19th century during the Meiji period at domestic industrial expositions as well as at international expositions, where Japan was singled out for its grace and elegance of design and perfection of workmanship.

However, the okimono craftsmen did not alter their distinctly Japanese flavour, but did cater to the foreigners' taste by overloading some sculptures with excessive amounts of finely carved details as well as exhibiting a bias towards Western naturalism. Sculptures of figures and groups, portraying aspects of Japanese traditional occupations, were particularly popular, with mythical and supernatural animals and beings having less appeal. The okimono varied from beautifully sculpted individual pieces to mass-produced objects of mediocre quality. Okimono show a seemingly endless number of subjects and follow many of the same themes as used by netsuke. Most okimono were made of wood and ivory, but lacquer, ceramic, amber, cloisonné and metal materials were also used.

Selected Bibliography

Bordignon, Laura. *The Golden Age of Japanese Okimono, Dr. A. M. Kanter's Collection*. London, 2010.

Earle, James. *Splendors of Imperial Japan: Arts of the Meiji Period from the Khalili Collection*. London, 2002.

Lester, Gerd. "Okimono: Decorative Wood and Ivory Carvings for the Tokonoma." *Arts of Asia*, Vol. 19, No. 6, 1989.

Chinese Snuff Bottles

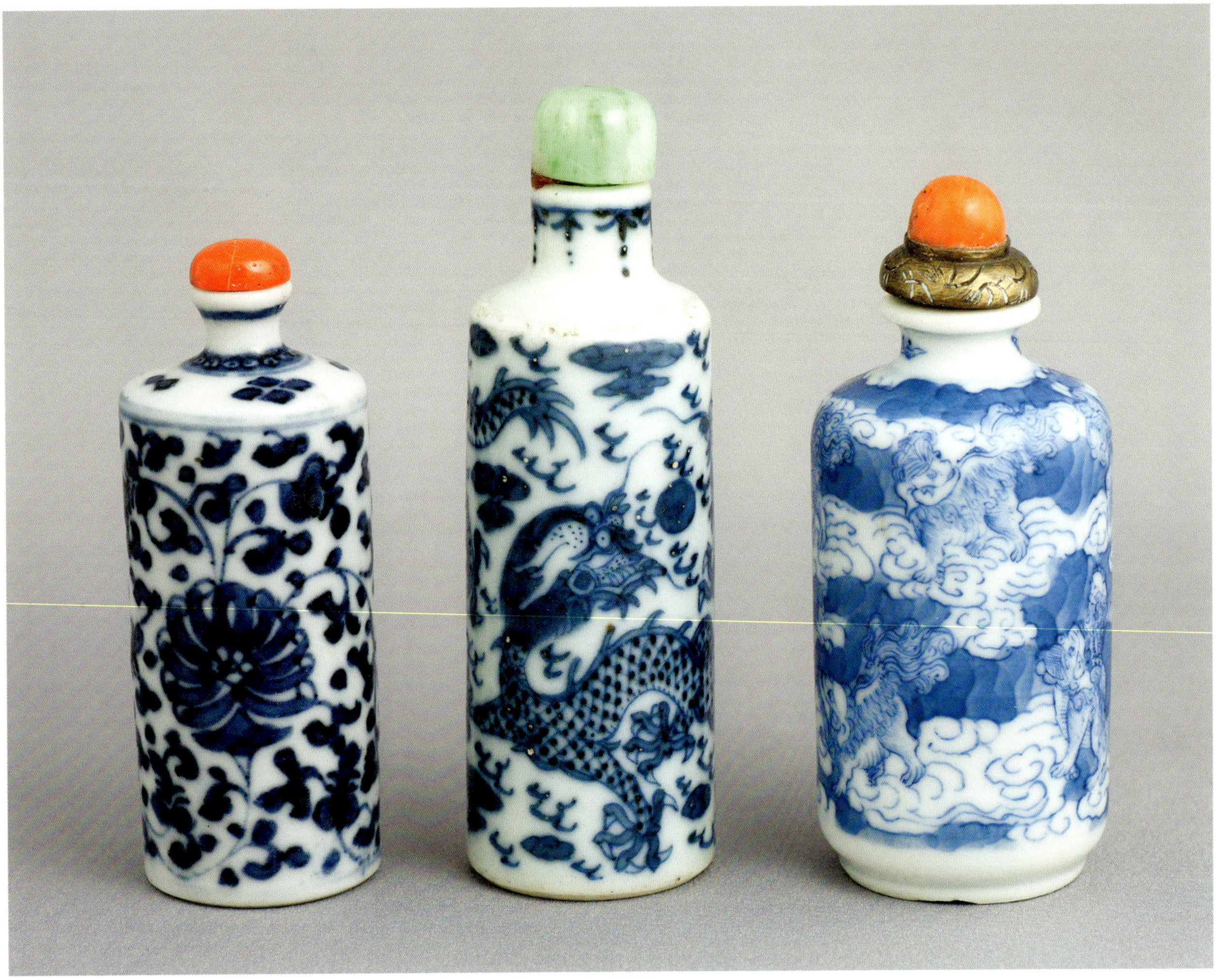

Snuff Bottles with cylindrical shape and design of chrysanthemum scrolls/of a dragon/of *fo* lion dogs amidst clouds • **Tabatières** de forme cylindrique avec enjolivement de chrysanthèmes/dragon/chiens lions (chiens *de fo*) dans les nuages • Qing dynasty, 19th century • porcelain, underglaze blue • Gifts of Helen Sawyer, AGGV 1995.012.069, 1995.012.068, 1995.012.070

Snuff Bottles with cylindrical shape and design of figures in a boat and on shore/of a figure leaving a boat • **Tabatières** de forme cylindrique avec motif représentant des personnages dans une embarcation et sur la rive/personnage qui sort d'une embarcation • Qing dynasty, 19th century • porcelain, underglaze blue • Gift of Helen Sawyer, AGGV 1995.012.037, 1995.012.032

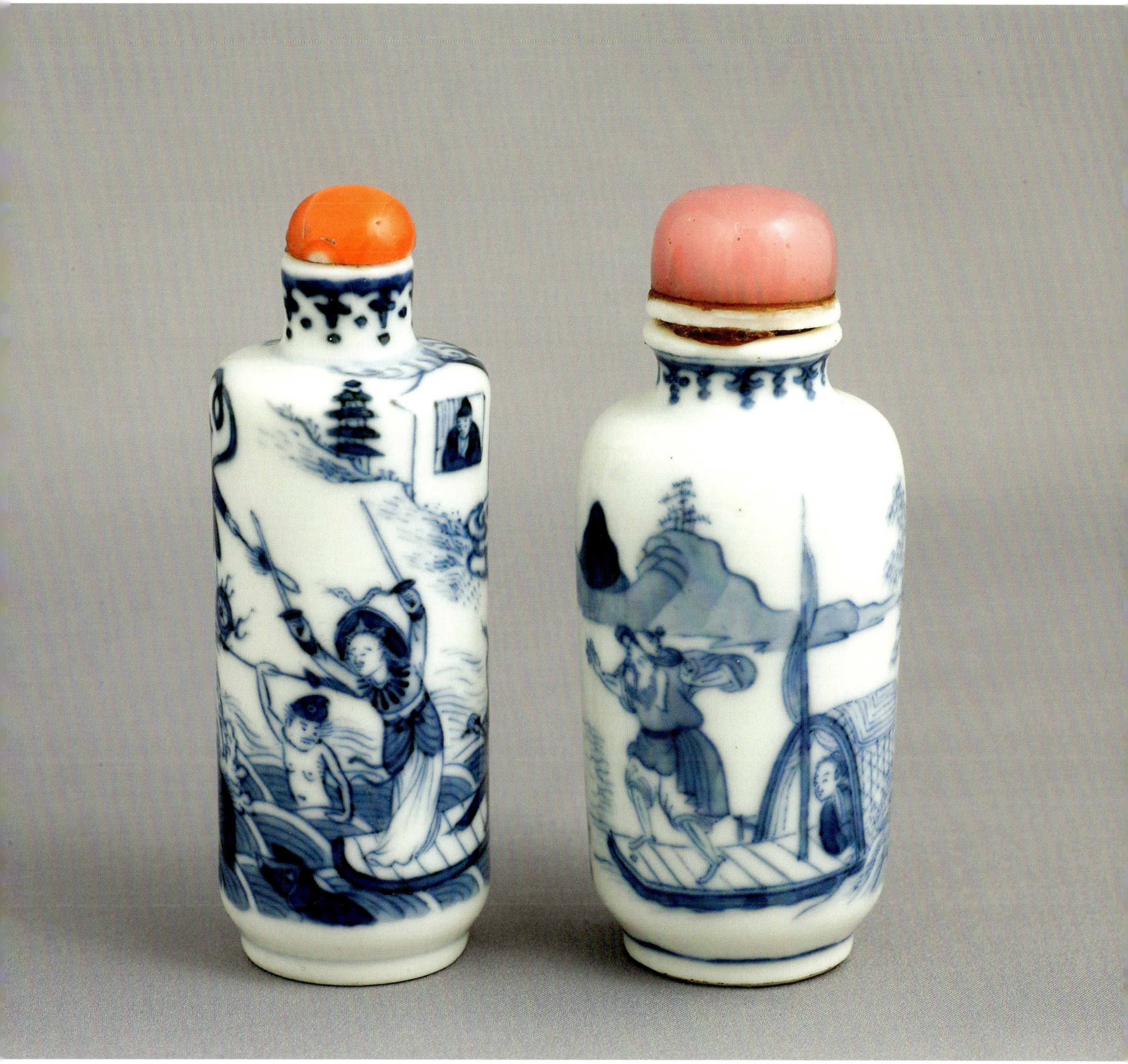

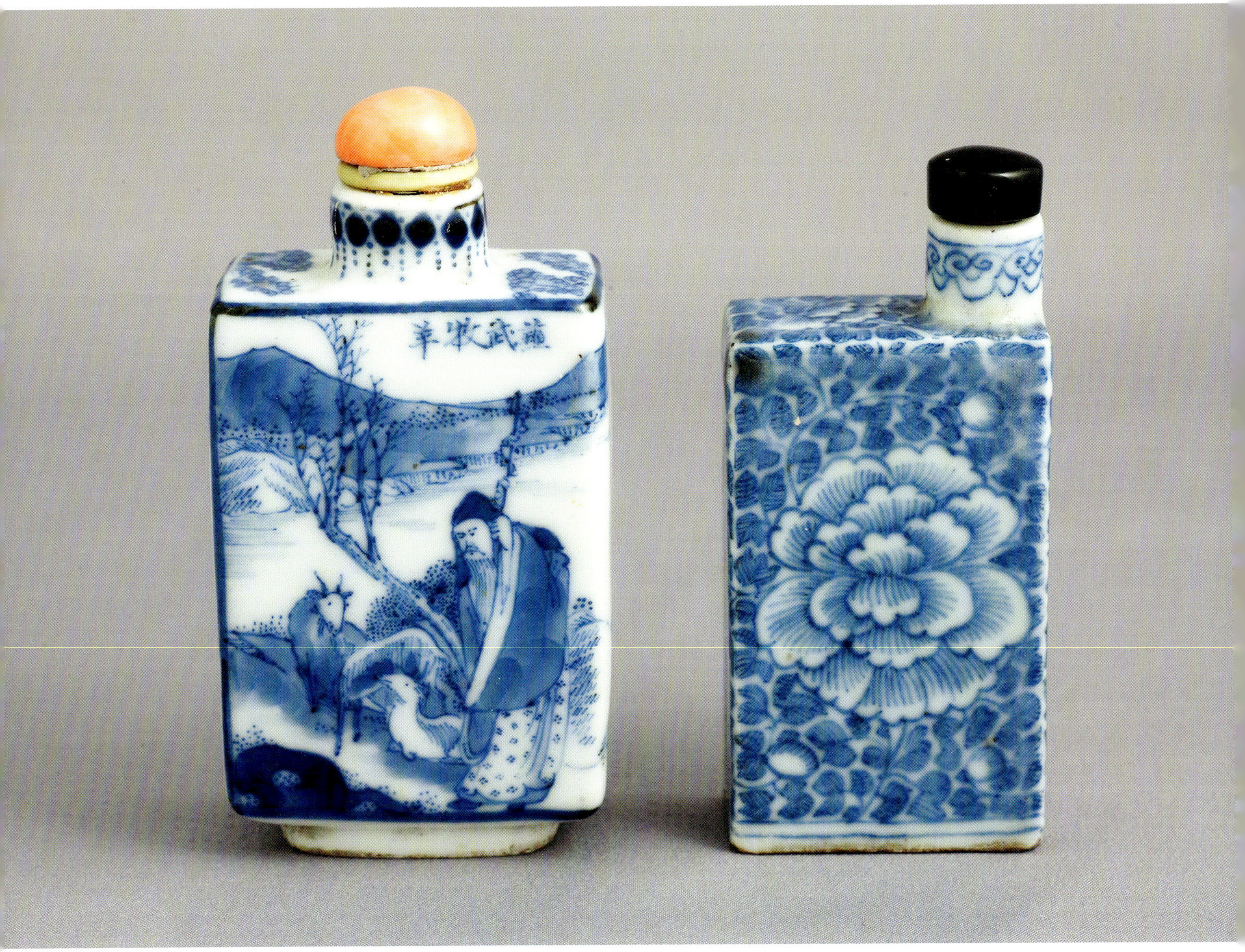

(left) **Snuff Bottle** with design of immortal and goats with Liu Hai and three-legged toad on verso • (à gauche) **Tabatière** avec motif représentant un immortel et des chèvres; avec Liu Hai; et crapaud à trois pattes au verso • Qing dynasty, 19th century • porcelain, underglaze blue • Gift of Helen Sawyer, AGGV 1995.012.033 • (right) **Snuff Bottle** with design of peony scrolls • (à droite) **Tabatière** avec enjolivement de pivoines • late 19th/early 20th century • porcelain, underglaze blue • Given in memory of Woody (E.O.J.) Woodward by his wife Frances Woodward, AGGV 2006.003.004

Snuff Bottles with scene of an official directing a man carrying a pole with baskets and nearby children • **Tabatières** avec la même scène d'un fonctionnaire qui dirige un homme transportant des paniers au bout d'une perche, contenant un produit et des enfants • Qing dynasty, late 18th/early 19th century • soft paste and porcelain, underglaze blue • (left) Gift of Terry J. Waller in memory of Myra L. Waller, AGGV 2009.010.001, (right) Gift of John Boehme, AGGV 2003.014.001

Snuff Bottle with design of group of mounted figures approaching a gate/of boys playing with firecrackers and "Hob-in-the-well" scene • **Tabatière** avec motif illustrant un groupe de cavaliers qui s'approchent d'une porte/garçons qui jouent avec des pétards et scène populaire appelée *Hob in the well* • Qing dynasty, 19th century • porcelain, underglaze blue • Gifts of Helen Sawyer, AGGV 1995.012.031, 1995.012.038

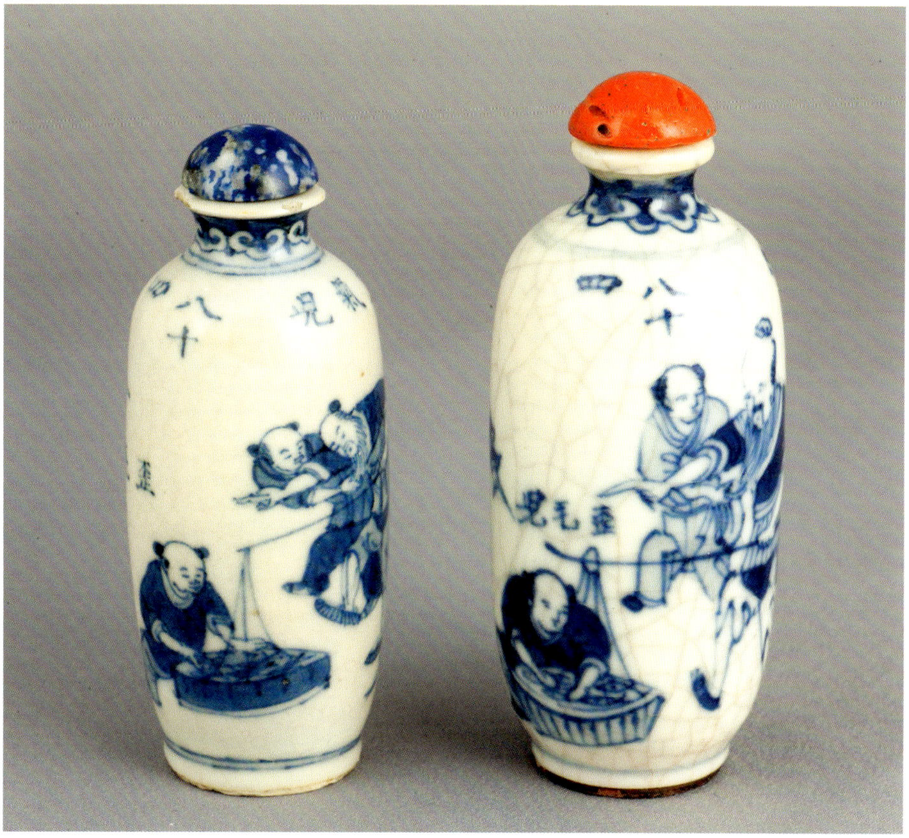

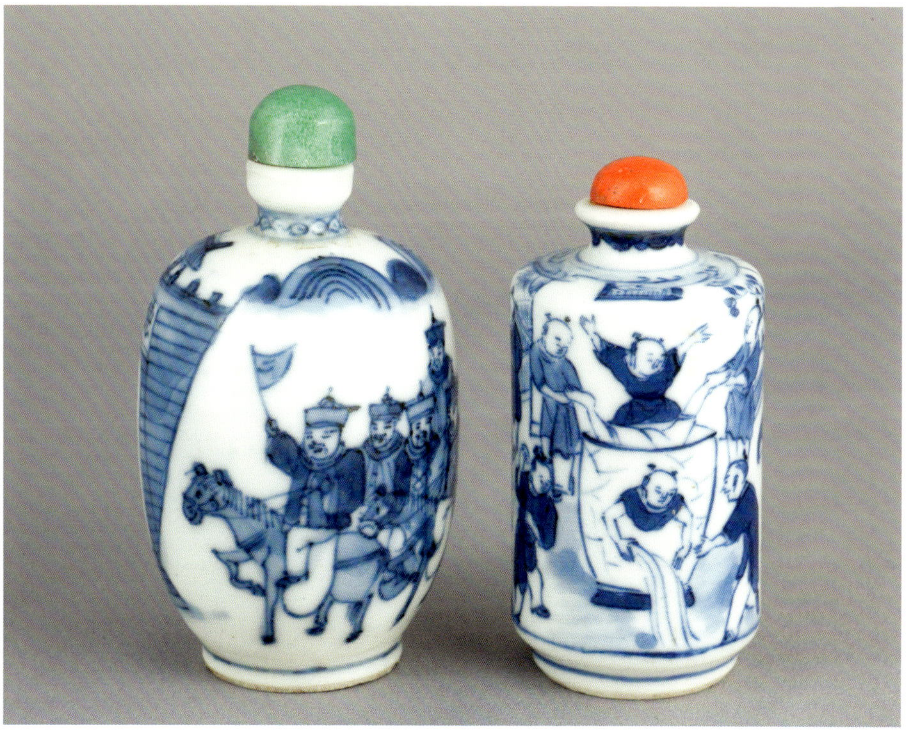

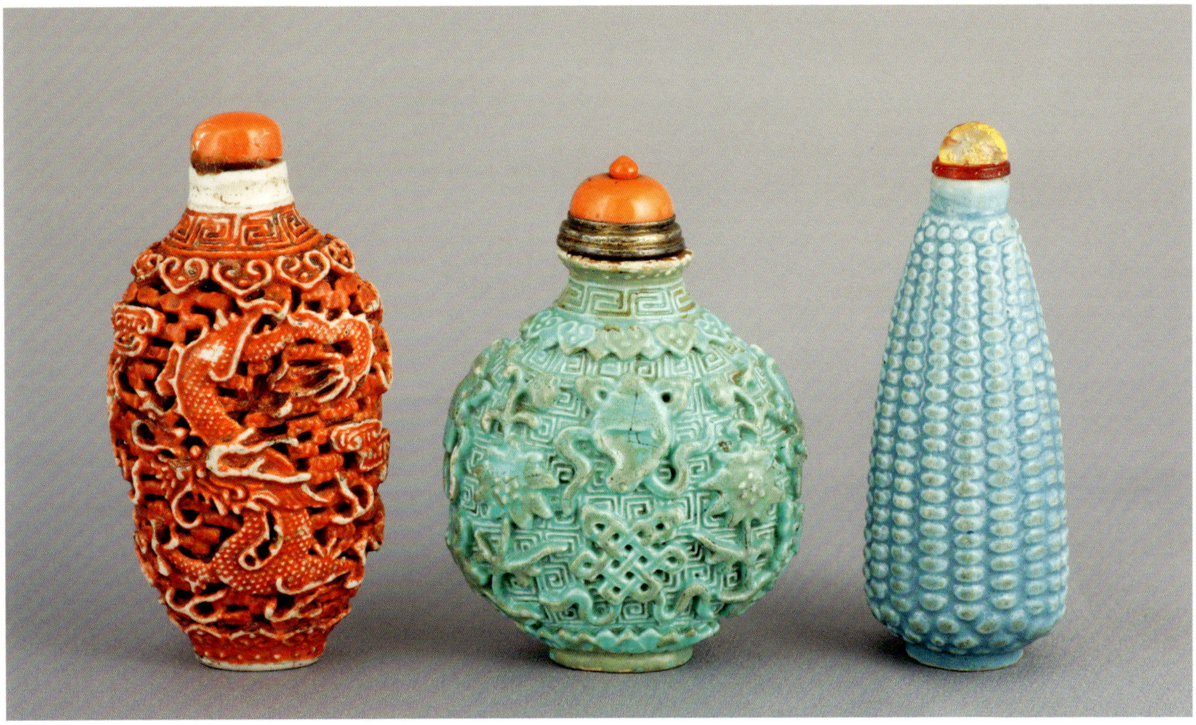

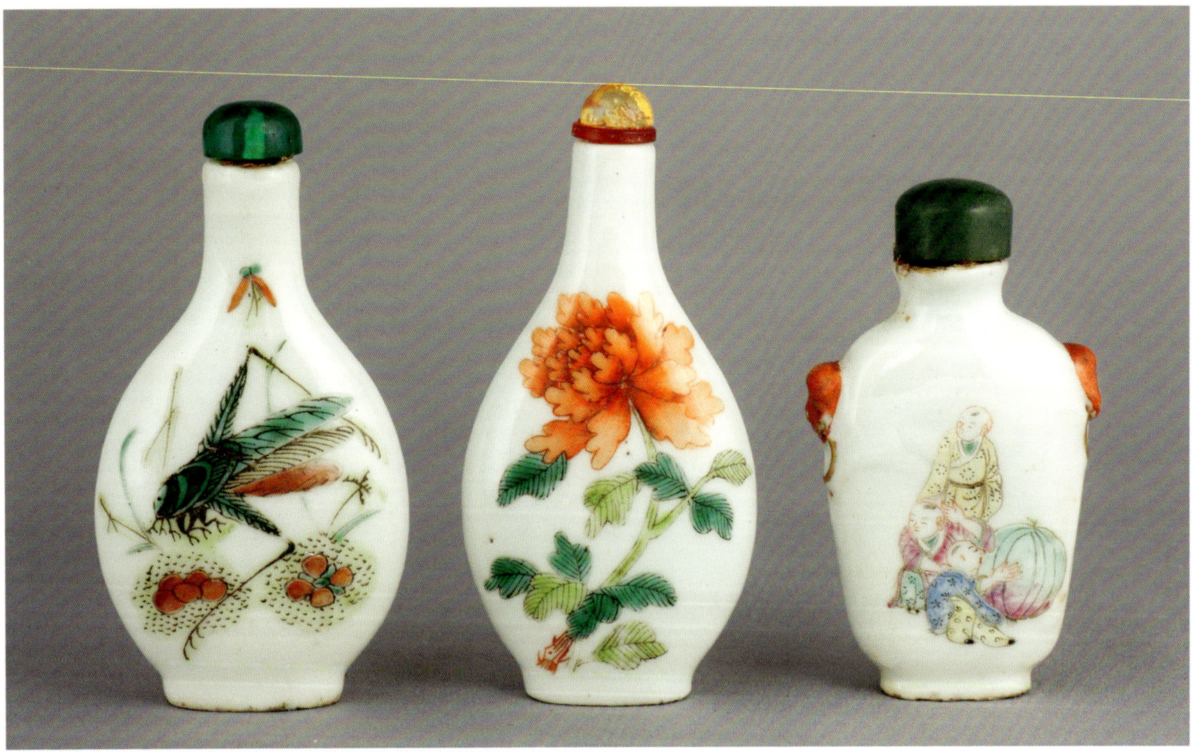

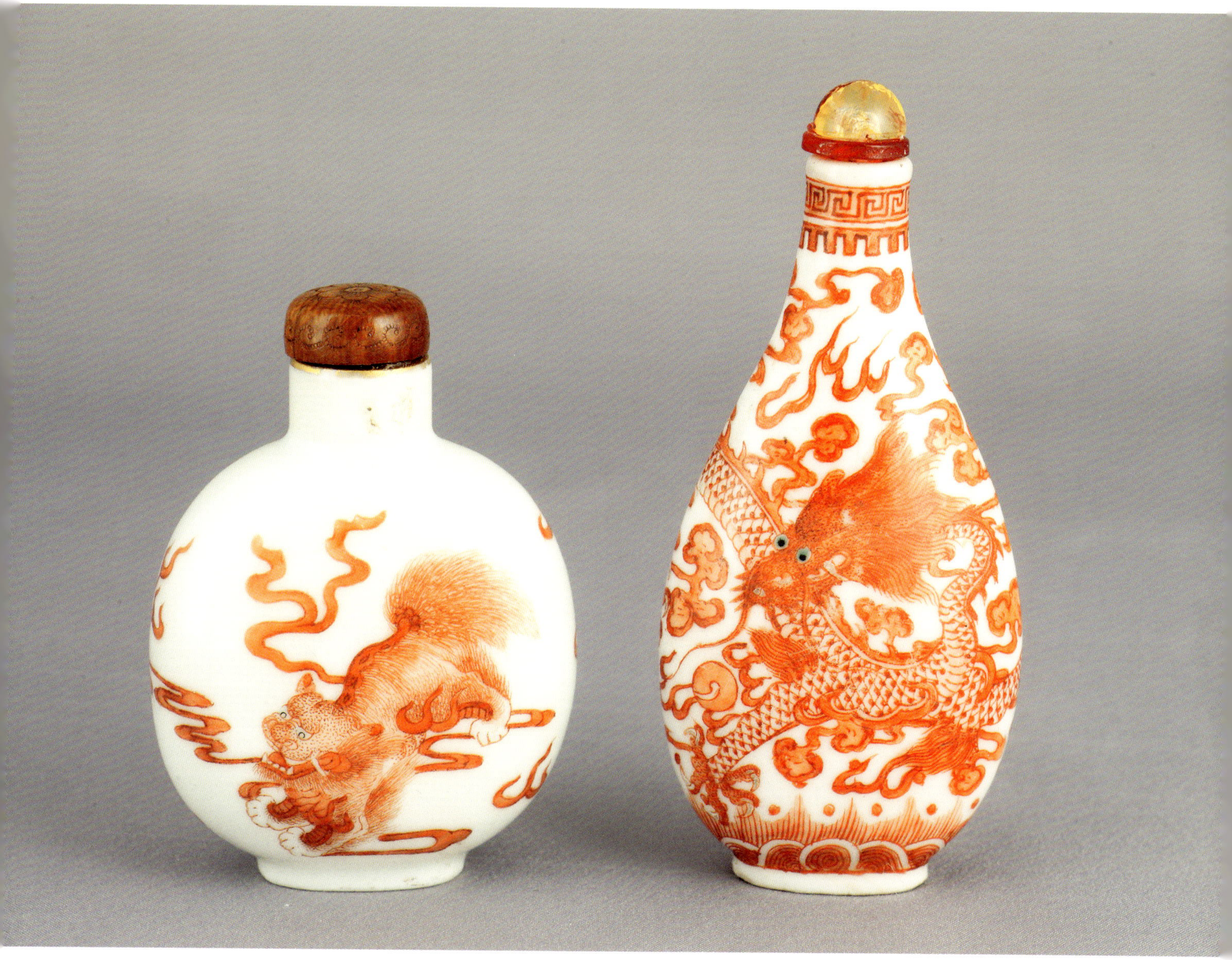

Snuff Bottles with reticulated designs of a dragon and a phoenix amidst clouds/the Eight Buddhist Emblems/of an ear of corn • **Tabatières** avec motifs réticulés représentant les dragon et phœnix dans les nuages/huit emblèmes bouddhistes/épi de maïs • Qing dynasty, 19th century • carved porcelain with turquoise, red and blue glaze • Gift of the Joy DeWeese-Wehen Estate. AGGV 2003.004.013, Gift of Helen Sawyer, AGGV 1995.012.018, Gift of Arthur Menzies, AGGV 2003.029.087

Snuff Bottles with design of cricket and lotus/of flowers/of boys playing with a melon • **Tabatières** ornées de crickets et lotus/fleurs/garçons jouant avec un melon • Qing dynasty, 19th century • porcelain with overglaze enamels • Gift of Helen Sawyer, AGGV 1995.012.052, Anonymous Gift, Gift of Col. Thomas M. Knox, AGGV 1963.087.001, Gift of Helen Sawyer, AGGV 1995.012.056

Snuff Bottles with design of *fo* lion dogs amidst flames/of a coiling dragon amidst flames • **Tabatières** avec motif de chiens lions *(chiens de fo)* dans les flammes/dragon se tortillant dans les flammes • Qing dynasty, 19th century • porcelain, underglaze red • Gift of Helen Sawyer, AGGV 2004.007.010, Given in Memory of John P. Nind (R.M.L.I. ret.) by his wife Mildred and their daughter Ann Neilson, AGGV 1974.143.001

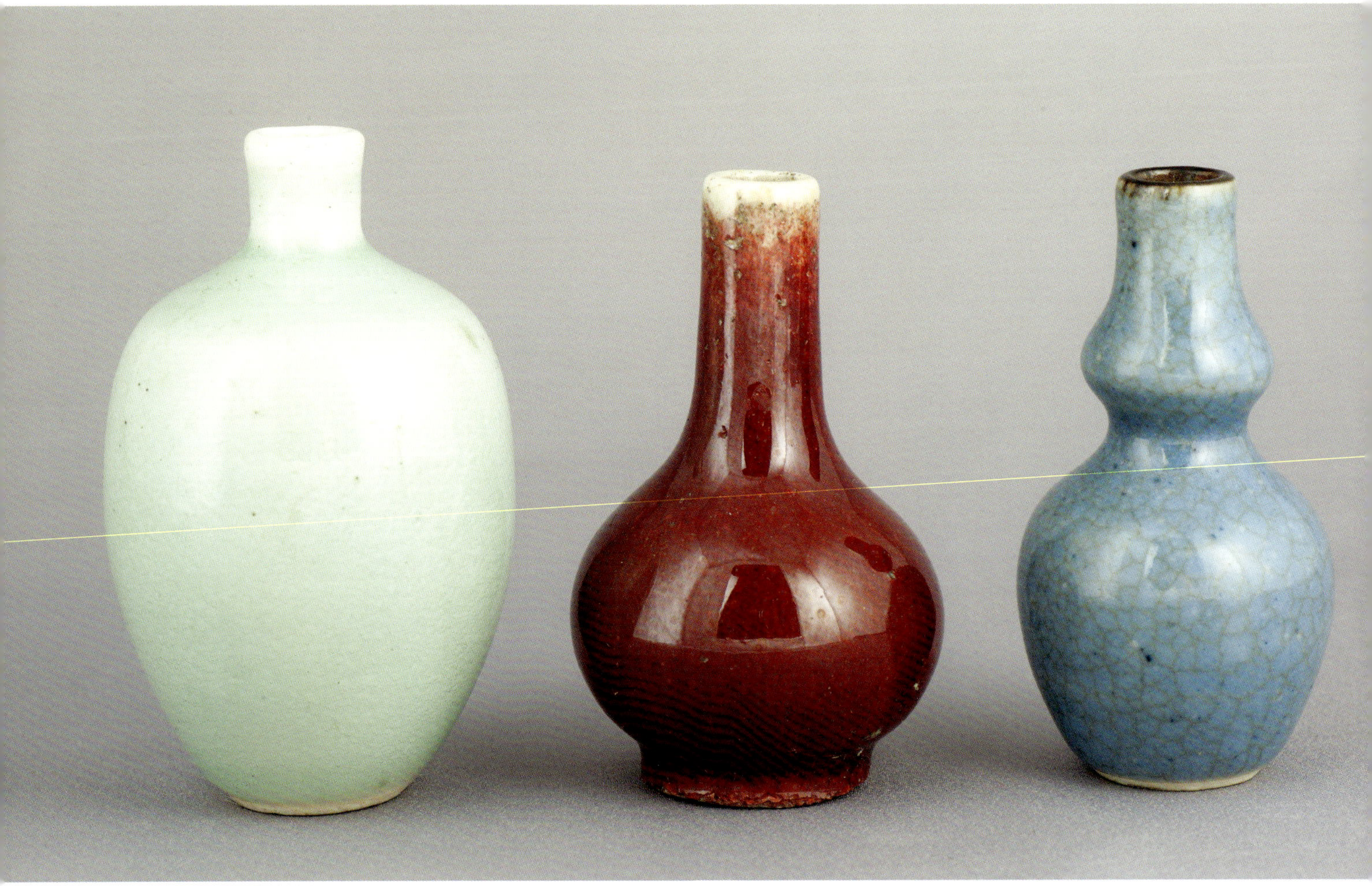

Snuff Bottles • Tabatières • Qing dynasty, 19th century • blue, celadon and oxblood monochrome glazed porcelain • Anonymous Gift, AGGV 1963.180.001, 1963.179.001, 1963.181.001

Snuff Bottle commemorating Chairman Mao and President Nixon meeting in 1972 with design of their faces and flags on verso • **Tabatière** commémorant la rencontre du président Mao et du président Nixon en 1972; avec leur visage et leur drapeau au verso • porcelain, enamels • Private Collection

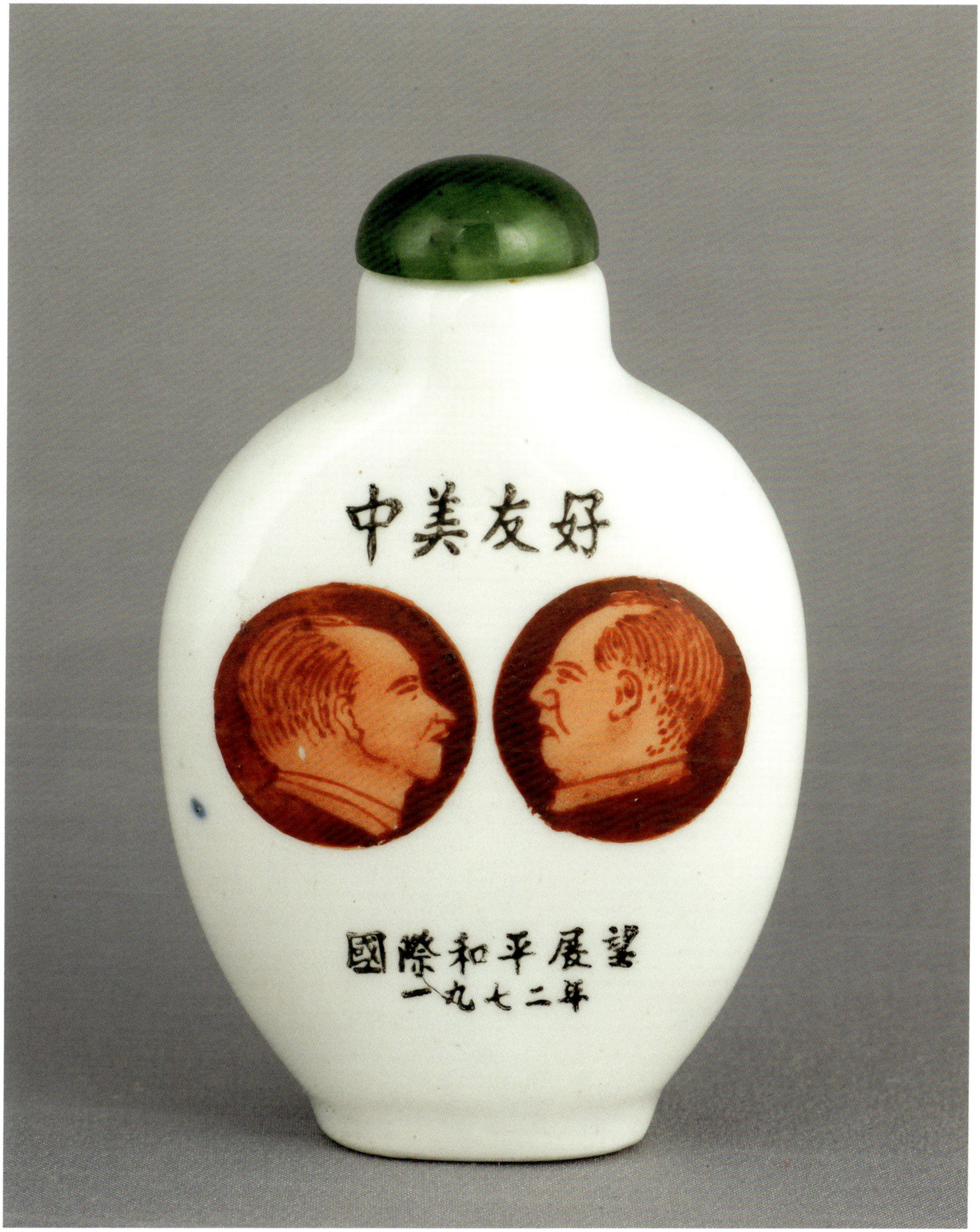
中美友好
國際和平展望
一九七二年

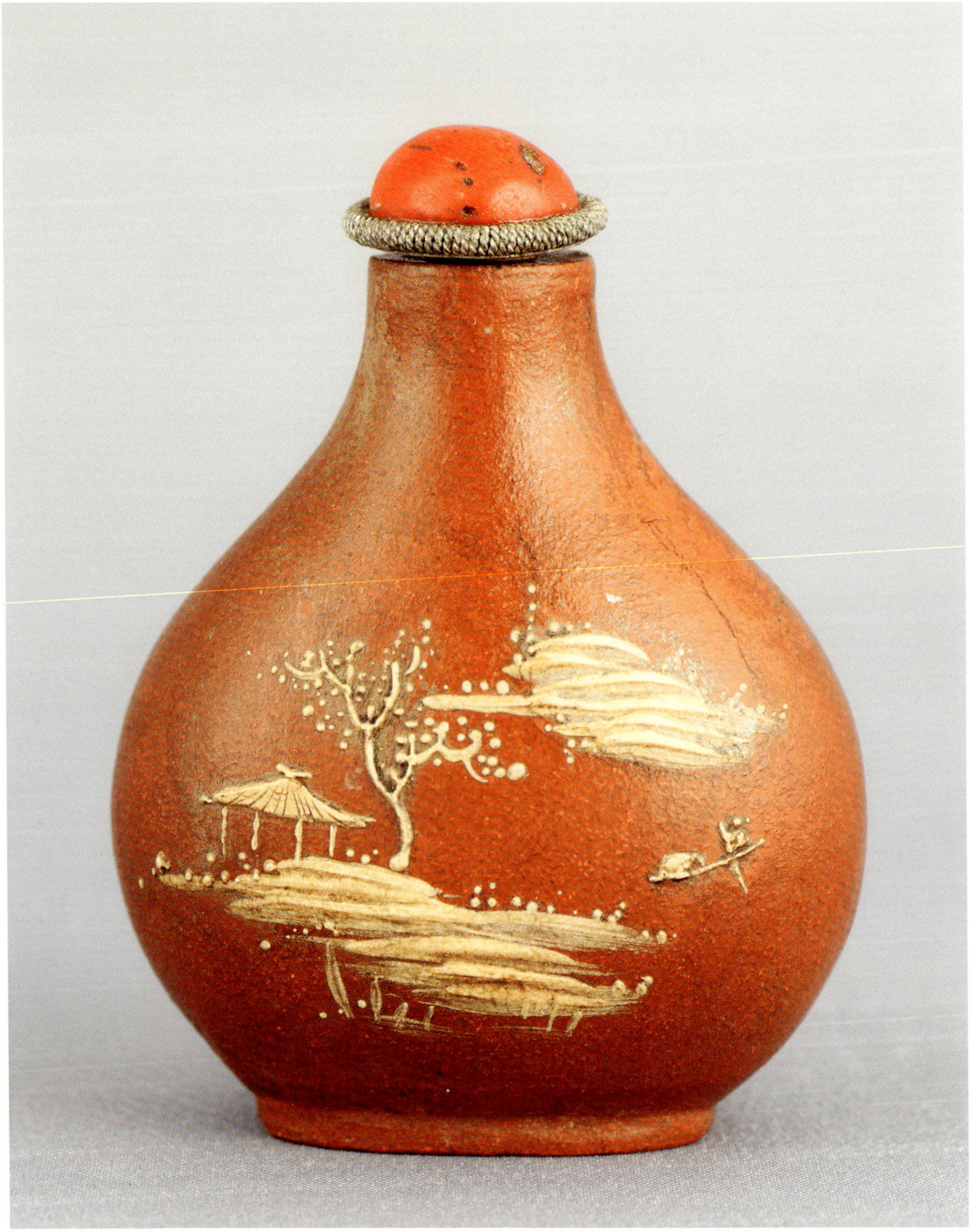

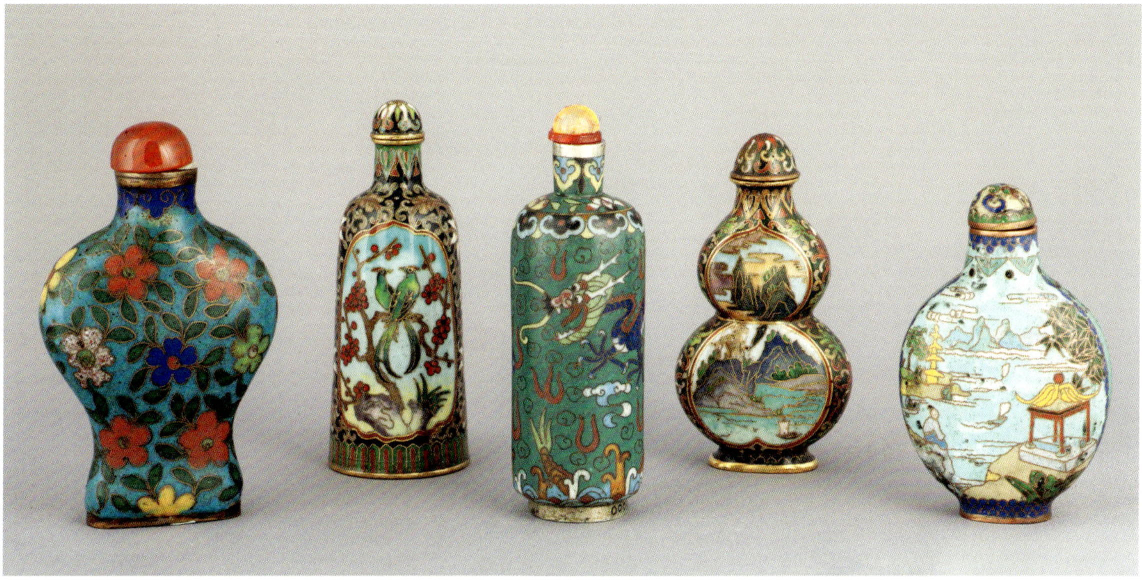

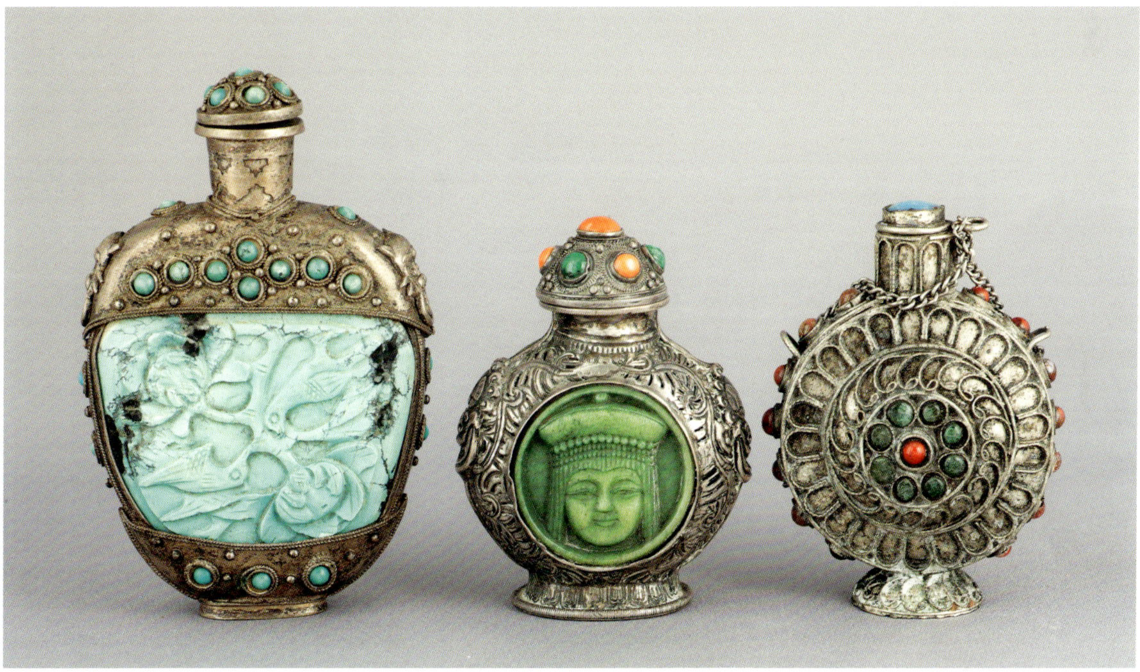

Snuff Bottle with design of landscape on either side • **Tabatière** ornée d'un paysage des deux côtés • Qing dynasty, late 19th century • Yixing stoneware, enamels • Gift of Carol Potter Peckham, AGGV 2010.017.005

Snuff Bottles with design of flowers and leaves/ of two panels of birds and flowers/of a dragon/ of two panels of landscapes/of two landscapes • **Tabatières** ornées de fleurs et feuilles/deux panneaux d'oiseaux et de fleurs/dragon/deux panneaux de paysages/deux paysages • late 19th century/early 20th century • cloisonné • Gift of Helen Sawyer, AGGV 1995.012.020 , Gift of the Joy DeWeese-Wehen Estate, 2003.004.025, Gift of Margaret N.Cutt, AGGV 2000.024.004, (two on right) Private Collection, Intended Gift

Snuff Bottles with turquoise panel of birds on blossoming branches/with portrait in green/with glass beads • **Tabatières** ornées d'un panneau turquoise d'oiseaux sur des branches en fleurs/d'un portrait dans du verre vert/perles de verre • glass and with coral, malachite pieces • silver base • Gift of Myfanwy Pavelic, AGGV 1970.064.00 , Given by Mrs. Mary Irwin from Estate of Miss Janet Gibson, AGGV 1976.090.007, Private Collection, Intended Gift

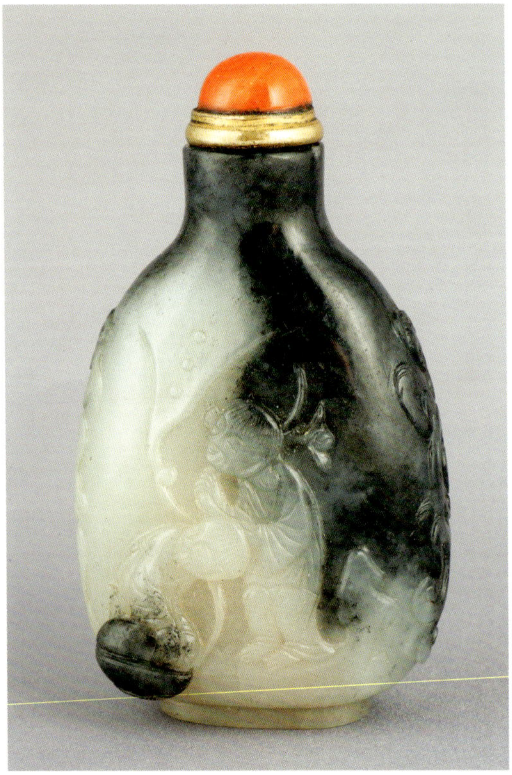

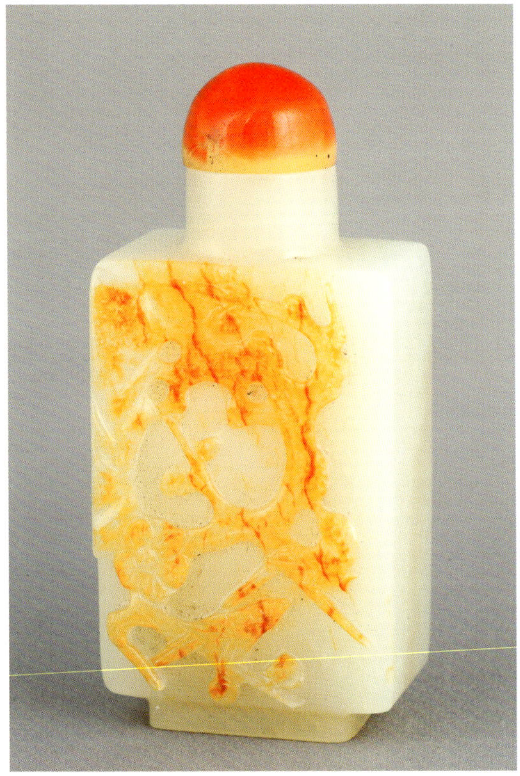

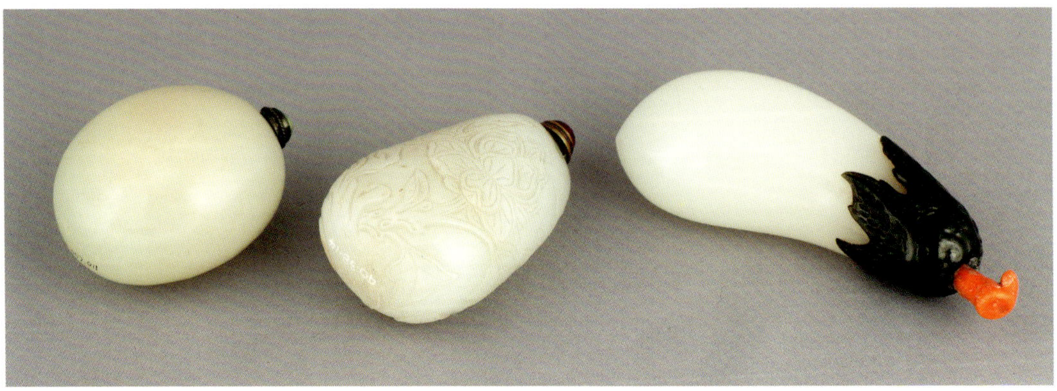

Snuff Bottle with design of two boys with a dragon amidst clouds on verso • Tabatière avec motif représentant deux garçons jouant avec un dragon dans les nuages au verso • Qing dynasty, 19th century • nephrite • Gift of Helen Sawyer, AGGV 2004.007.001

Snuff Bottle with russet relief design of prunus branch with six seal marks on verso • Tabatière avec relief brun roux d'une branche de cerisier; et six marques de seau au verso • Qing dynasty, 19th century • nephrite • Gift of the Joy DeWeese-Wehen Estate, AGGV 2003.004.005

(left, middle) **Snuff bottles** in the form of a pebble; one undecorated and one with design of flower and butterfly with figure in a mountain landscape on verso nephrite • (à gauche, au milieu) **Tabatières** en forme de caillou; une sans décoration et l'autre avec motif de fleur et papillon; personnage dans un paysage montagneux au verso • Qing dynasty, 19th century • Gift of Helen Sawyer, AGGV 2004.007.011 • Edith Low-Beer Collection, AGGV 1990.038.014 • (right) **Snuff Bottle** in the form of an eggplant • (à droite) **Tabatière** en forme d'aubergine • Qing dynasty, 19th century • nephrite • Private Collection, Intended Gift

Snuff Bottle in form of a flattened melon with leaves and vines • **Tabatière** en forme de melon aplati ornée de feuilles et vignes • Qing dynasty, 19th century • nephrite • Gift of Helen Sawyer, AGGV 1995.012.015

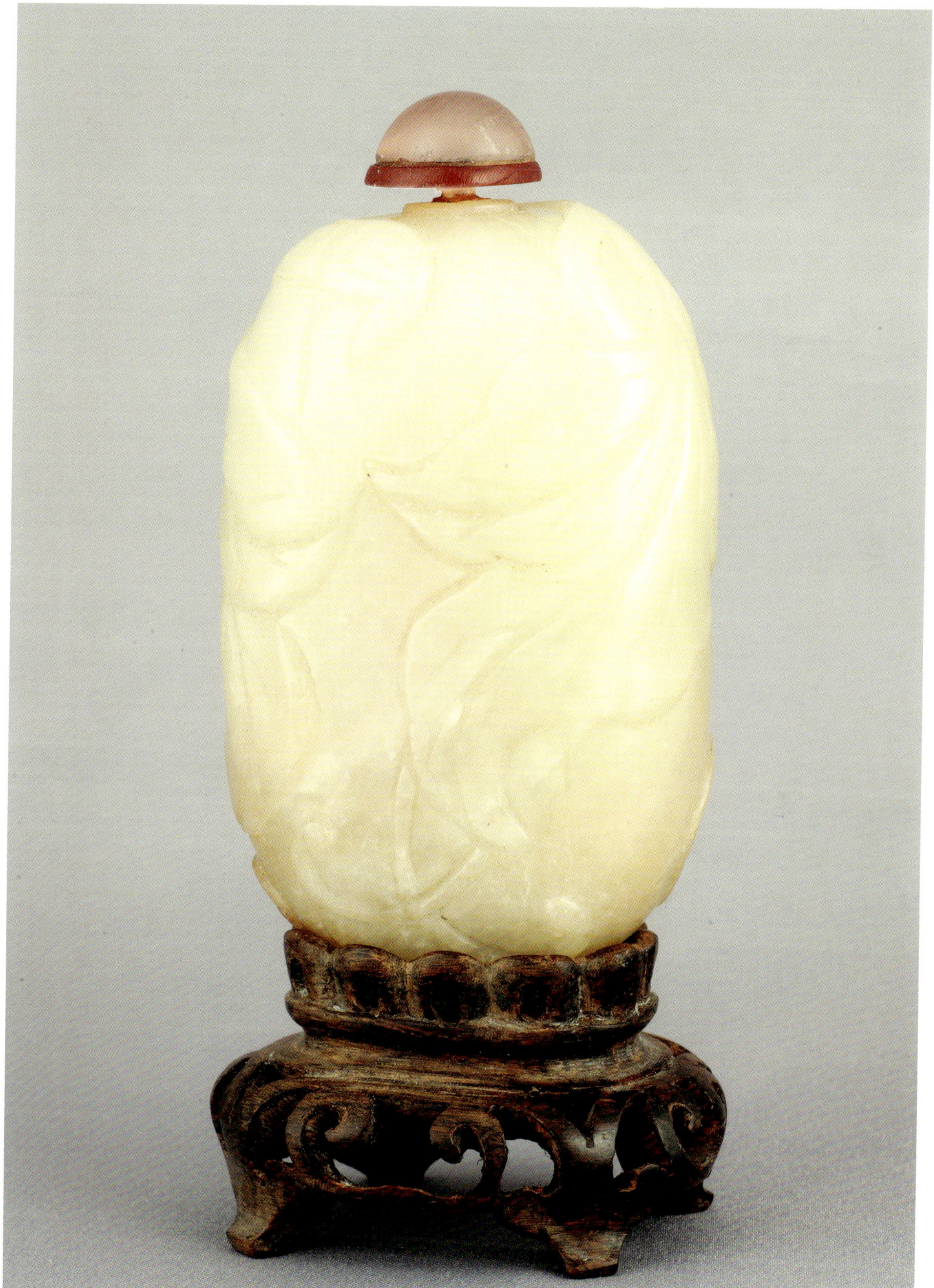

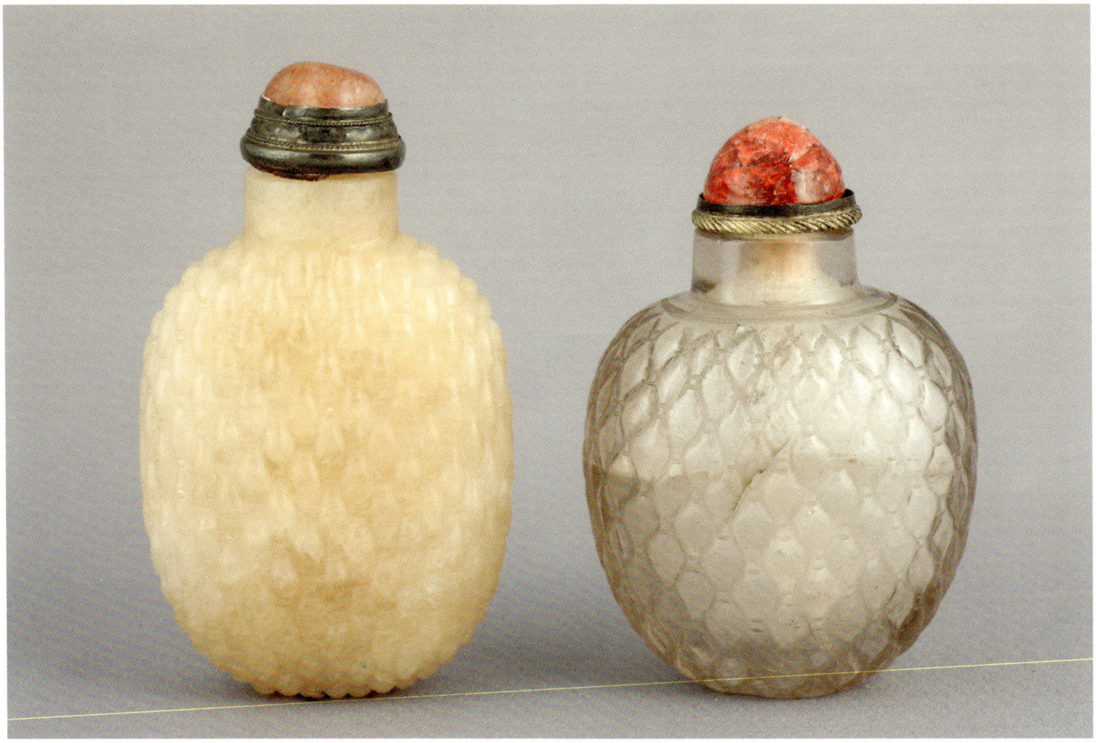

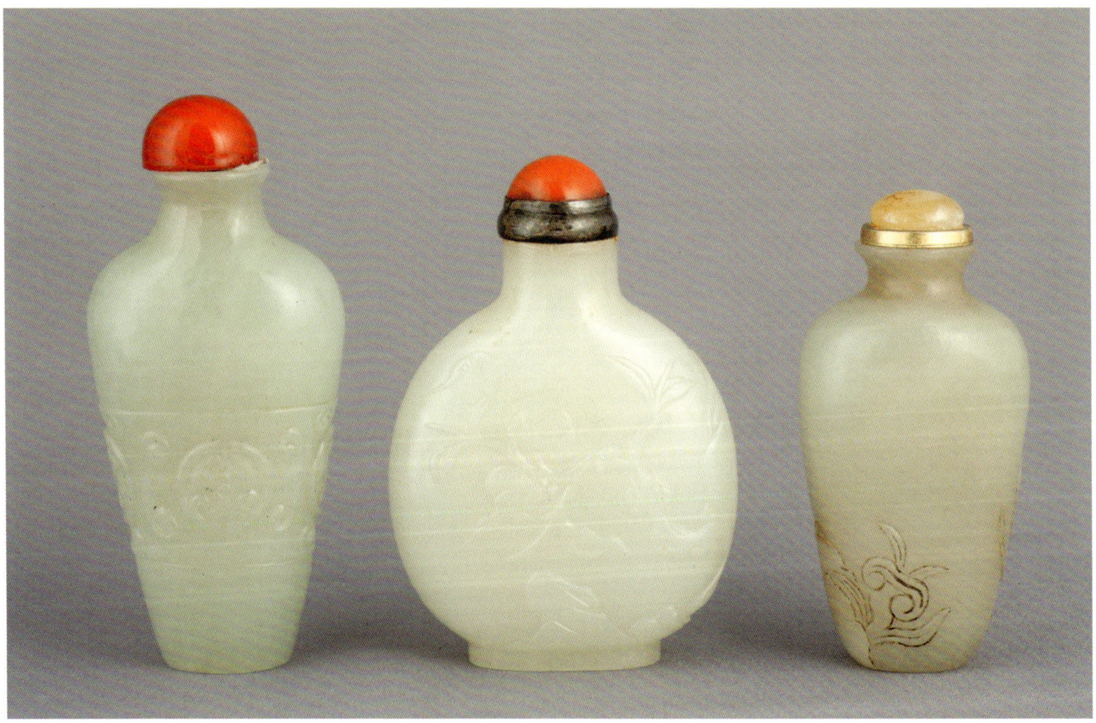

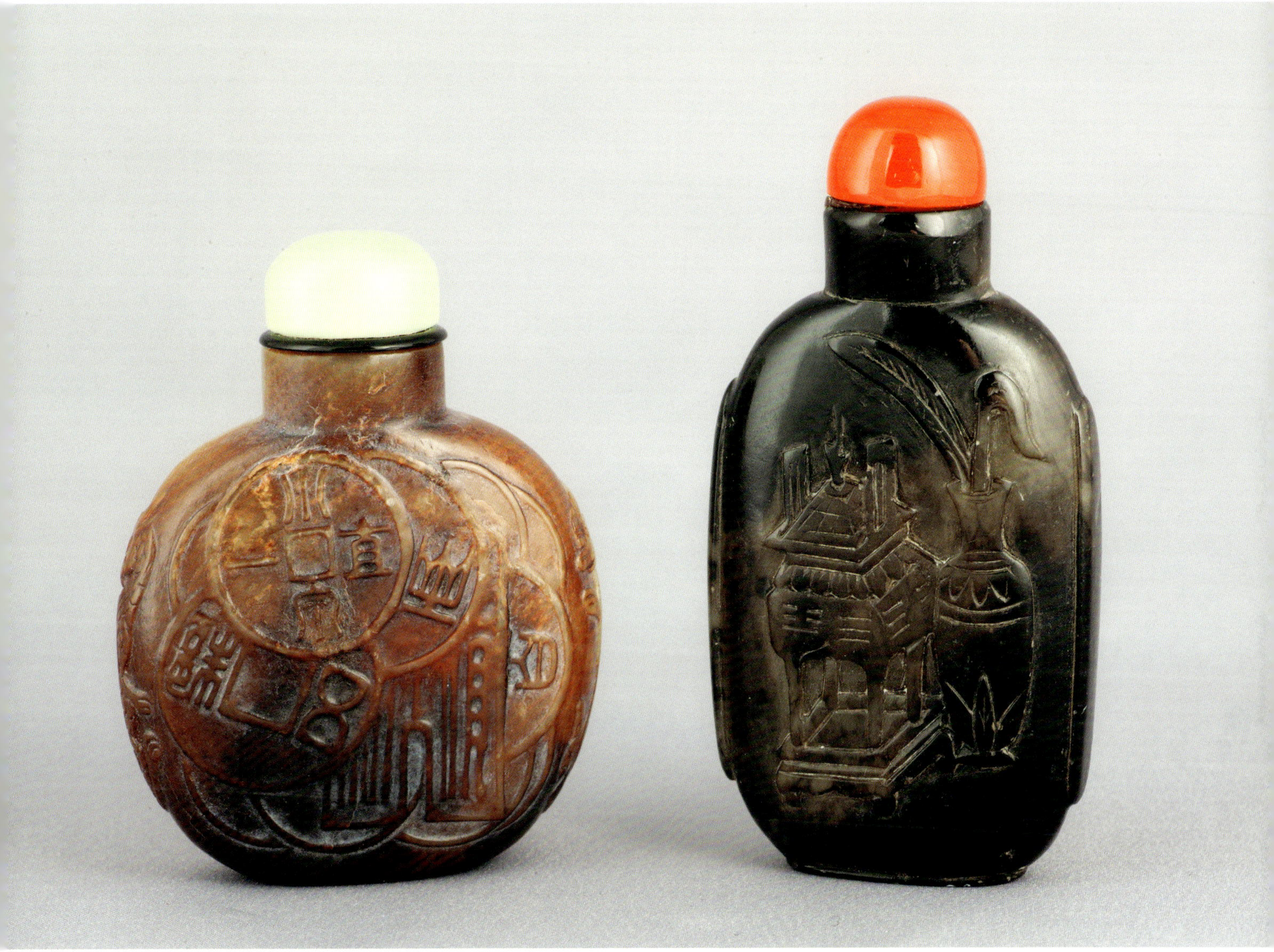

Snuff Bottles with basket weave pattern • **Tabatières** avec motif de panier tressé • Qing dynasty, 19th century • nephrite and quartz/crystal • Gifts of Helen Sawyer, AGGV 1995.012.064, 1995.012.054

Snuff Bottles with design of a band with roundels/of a fruit tree/of plants and fungus • **Tabatières** ornées d'une bande et de cocardes/arbre fruitier/plantes et champignons • Qing dynasty, 19th century • nephrite • Gift of John Boehme, AGGV 2003.014.002, Gift of the Joy DeWeese-Wehen Estate, AGGV 2003.004.001 , Gift of Arthur Menzies, AGGV 2003.029.052

(left) **Snuff Bottle** with russet skin and design of ancient Chinese coins • (à gauche) **Tabatière** avec revêtement brun roux et motif d'ancienne monnaie chinoise • Qing dynasty, 19th century • nephrite • Private Collection, Intended Gift • (right) **Snuff Bottle** with design of vases of flowers, incense burner • Qing dynasty, 19th century • nephrite • Gift of Helen Sawyer, AGGV 1995.012.039

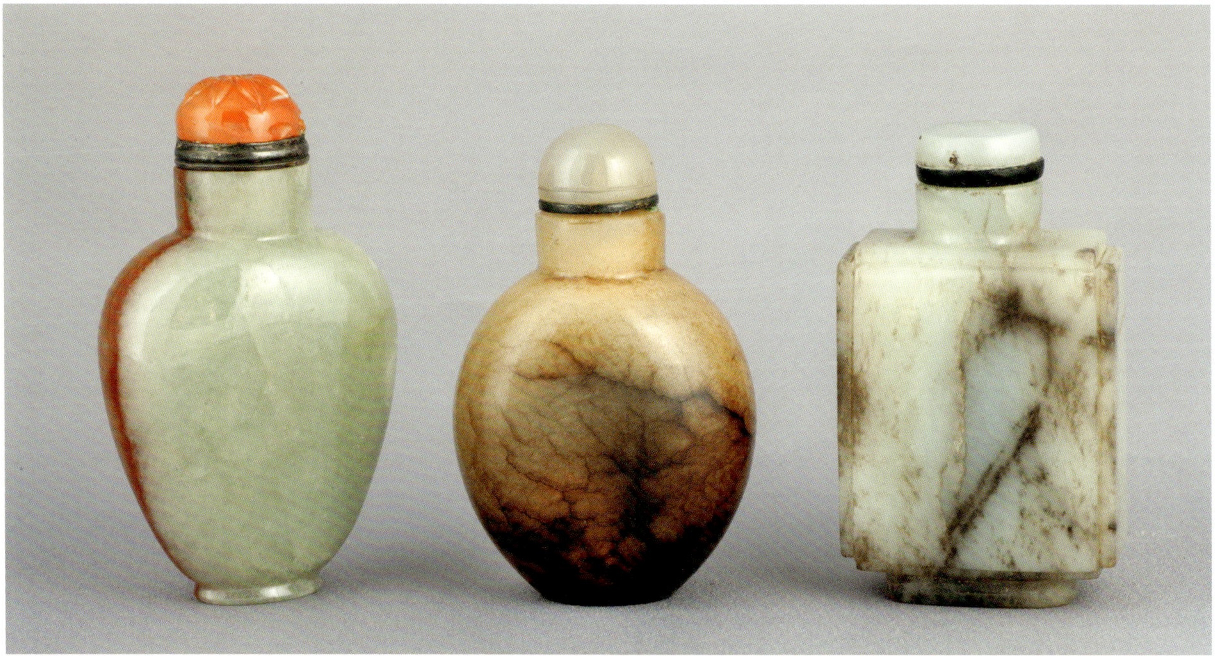

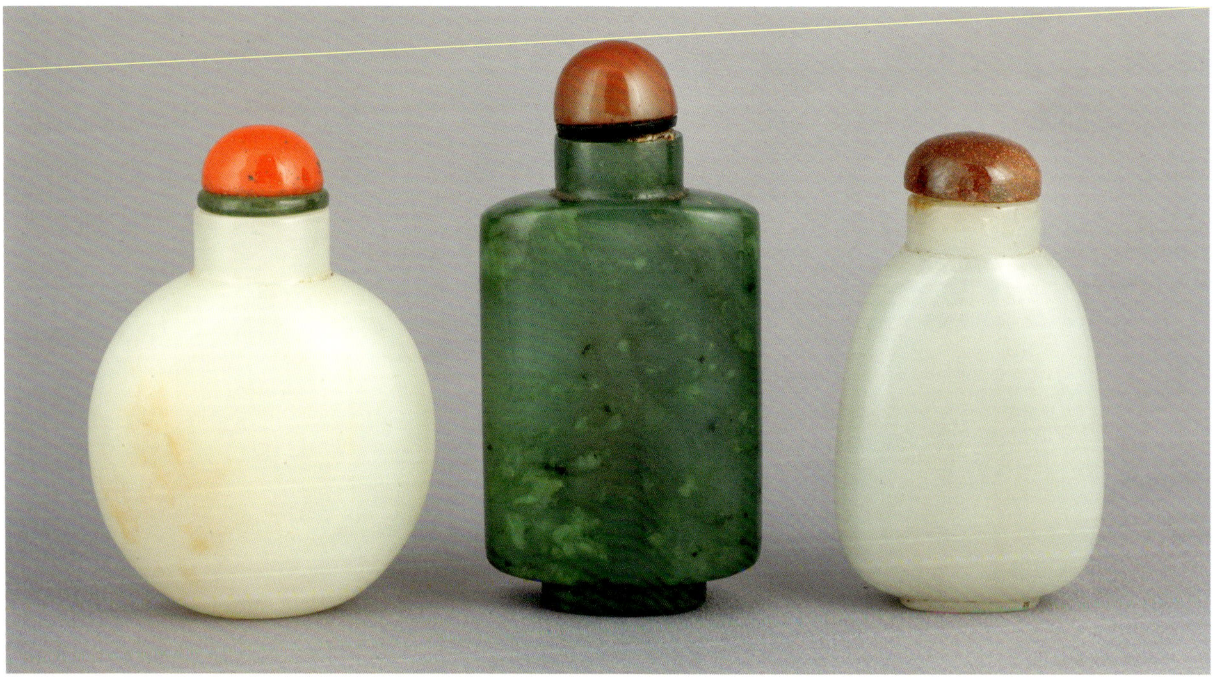

(left) **Snuff Bottle • Tabatière** • Qing dynasty, 19th century • nephrite, pale green with one side russet brown (dyed?) • Gift of the Joy DeWeese-Wehen Estate, AGGV 2003.004.021 • (middle, right) **Snuff Bottles • Tabatières** • Qing dynasty, 19th century • nephrite • Gift of Helen Sawyer, AGGV 1995.012.050, 1995.012.066

Snuff Bottles • Tabatières • Qing dynasty, 19th century • nephrite • Gift of David Young, AGGV 1999.039.003, Gift of Helen Sawyer, AGGV 1995.012.063 , Gift of Mrs. Shih Hua Chao and Mr. Shih Tsun Lee, AGGV 2007.009.008

Snuff Bottle with relief design of a woman, man, birds, trees and shrubs • **Tabatière** avec motif en relief d'une femme, d'un homme, d'oiseaux, d'arbres et d'arbustes • late 19th/early 20th century • chalcedony • From the Collection of Bruce and Dorothy Brown, given by their son Tony Brown, AGGV 2005.034.004

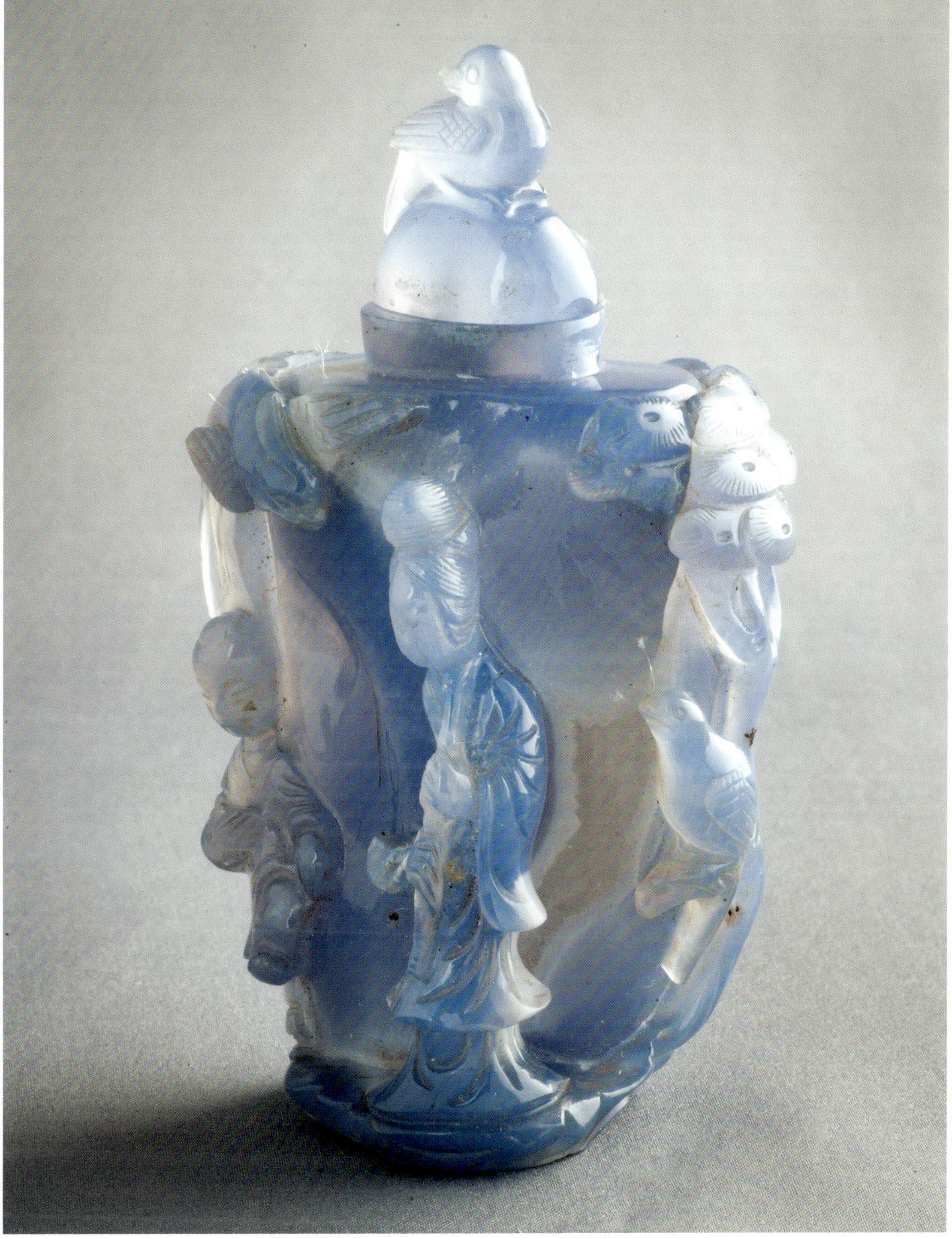

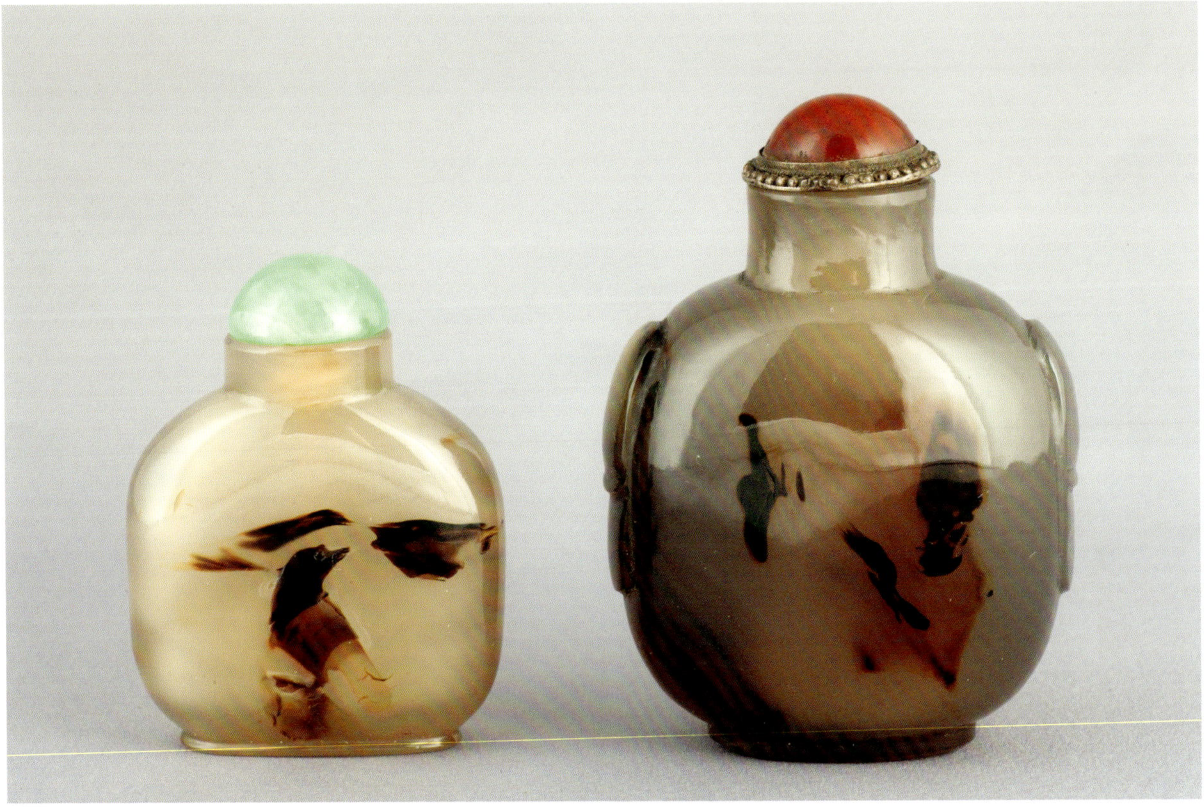

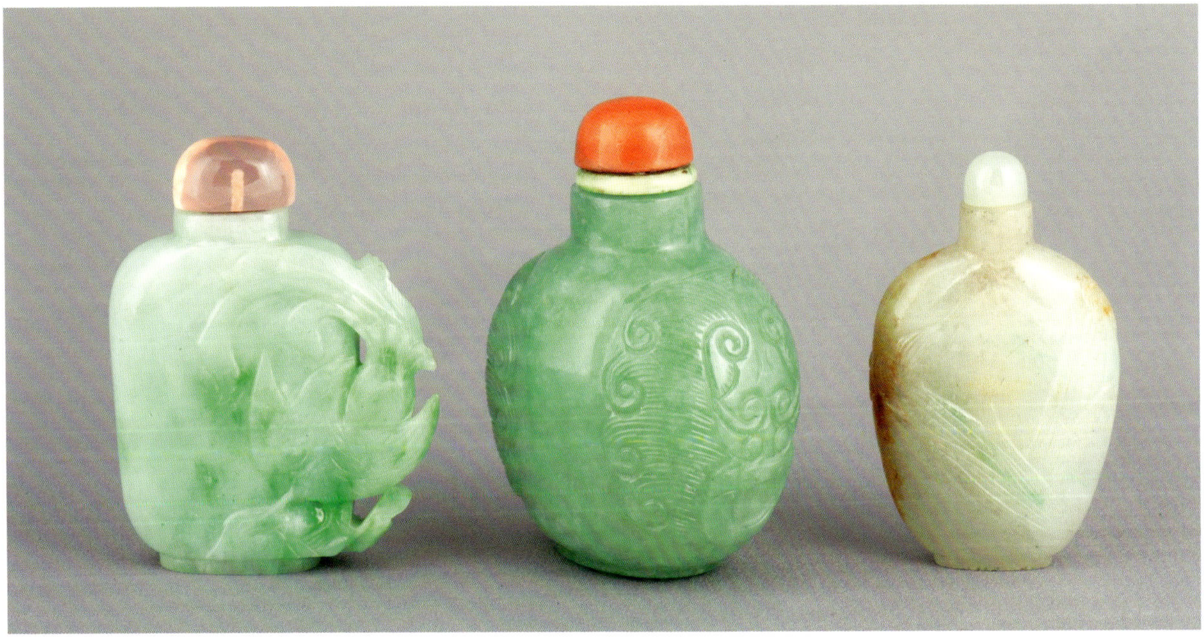

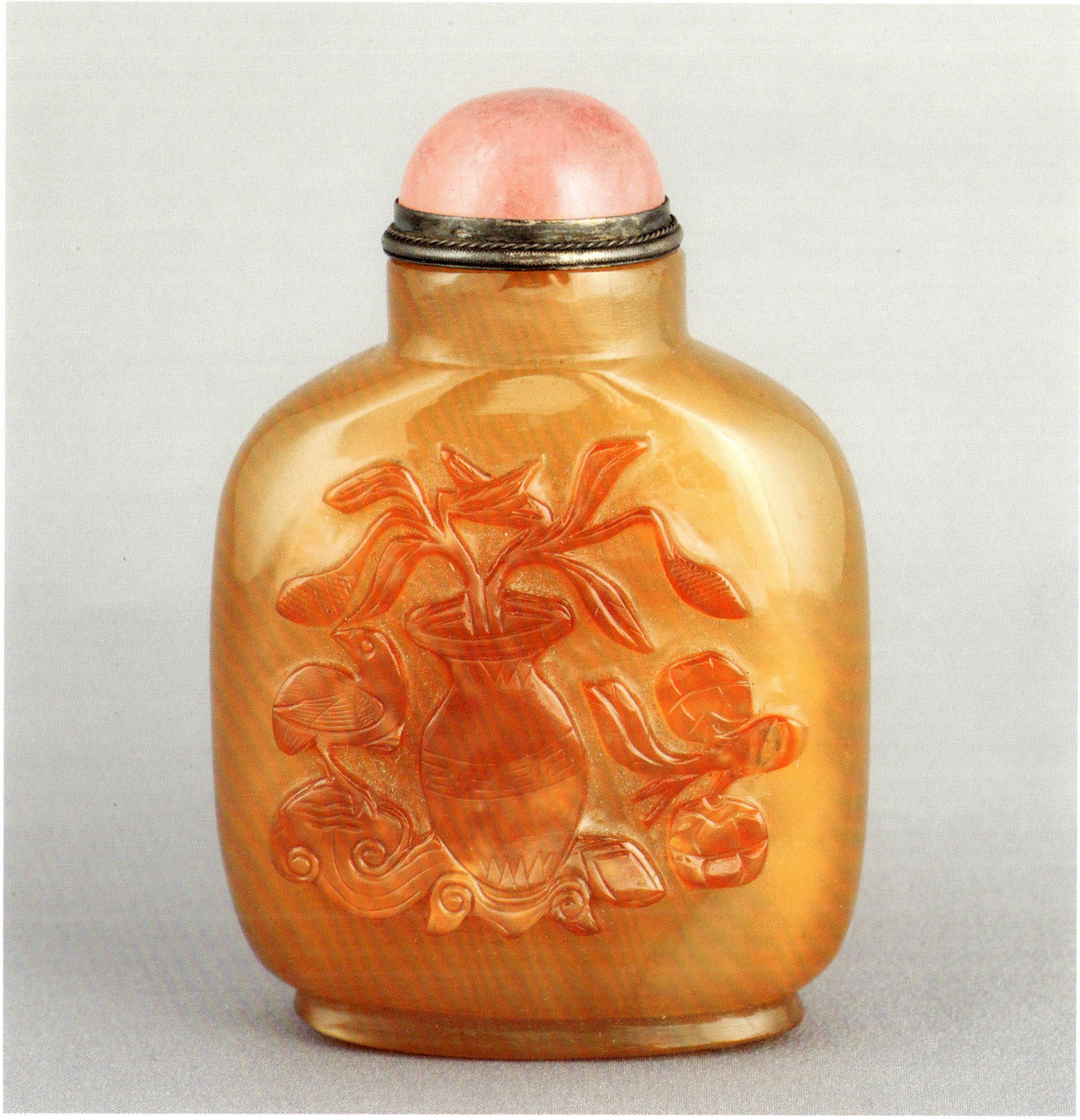

(left) **Snuff Bottle** with shadow design of bird • (à gauche) **Tabatière** ornée de l'ombre d'un oiseau • Qing dynasty, 19th century • chalcedony/agate • Gift of the Joy DeWeese-Wehen Estate, AGGV 2003.004.014 • (right) **Snuff Bottle** with shadow marks • (à droite) **Tabatière** avec ombres • Qing dynasty, 19th century • chalcedony/agate • Gift of the Estate of Elizabeth Stewart, AGGV 2009.029.001

(left) **Snuff Bottle** with phoenix clinging to one side • (à gauche) **Tabatière** avec phœnix se cramponnant d'un côté • Qing dynasty, 19th century • jadeite • Gift of Helen Sawyer, AGGV 2004.007.005 • (middle) **Snuff Bottle** with design of two lion masks holding rings • (au milieu) **Tabatière** ornée de deux masques de lion tenant des anneaux • Qing dynasty, 19th century • jadeite • Gift of Helen Sawyer, AGGV 2004.007.002 • (right) **Snuff Bottle** with design of corn cobs with flowering plant on verso • (à droite) **Tabatière** ornée d'épis de maïs; et plante en fleurs au verso • early 20th century • jadeite • Gift of Mrs. Shih Hua Chao and Mr. Shih Tsun Lee, AGGV 2007.009.004

Snuff Bottle with design of a flower vase • **Tabatière** ornée d'un vase de fleurs • Qing dynasty, 19th century • chalcedony/agate • Gift of the Joy DeWeese-Wehen Estate, AGGV 2003.004.011

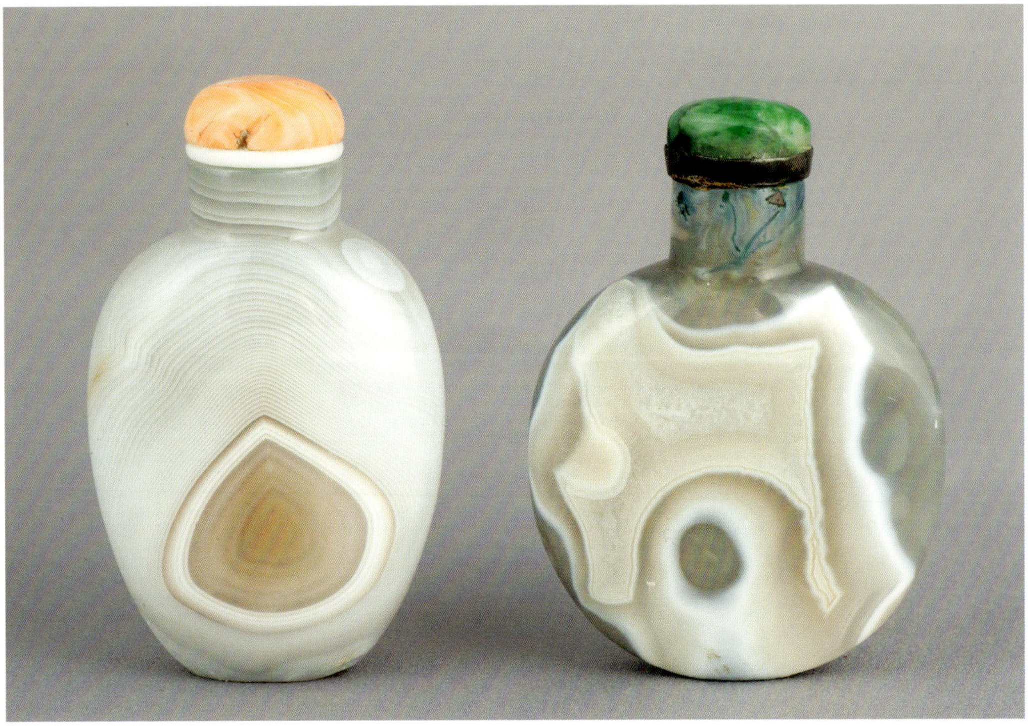

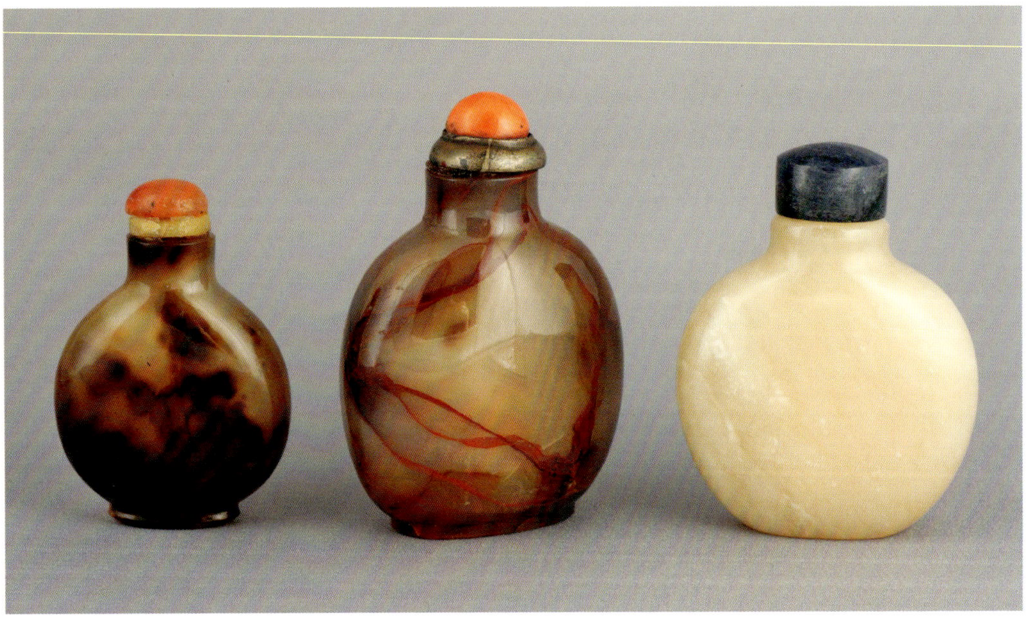

Snuff Bottles • Tabatières • Qing dynasty, 19th century • agate • Gift of Helen Sawyer, AGGV 2004.007.004, 1995.012.014

Snuff Bottles • Tabatières • Qing dynasty, 19th century • chalcedony/agate • Gift of Helen Sawyer, AGGV 1995.012.041, 1995.012.011, 1995.012.044

Snuff Bottles • Tabatières • Qing dynasty, 19th century • amber-coloured agate • Gift of Helen Sawyer, AGGV 2004.007.006, 2004.007.012

Snuff Bottle in the form of Buddha's hand fruit • **Tabatière** en forme de main de Bouddha • Qing dynasty, 19th century • agate • Gift of Helen Sawyer, AGGV 1995.012.062

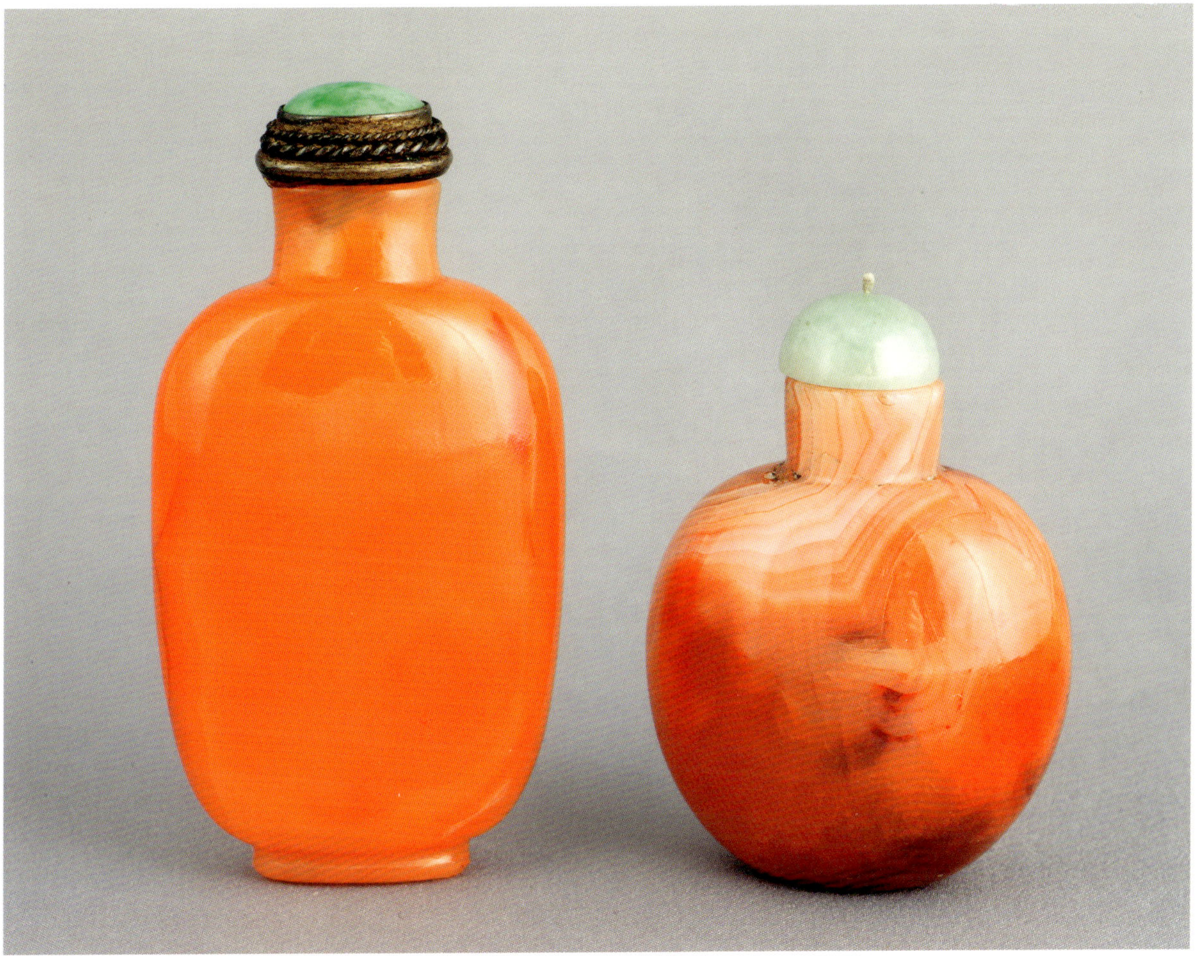

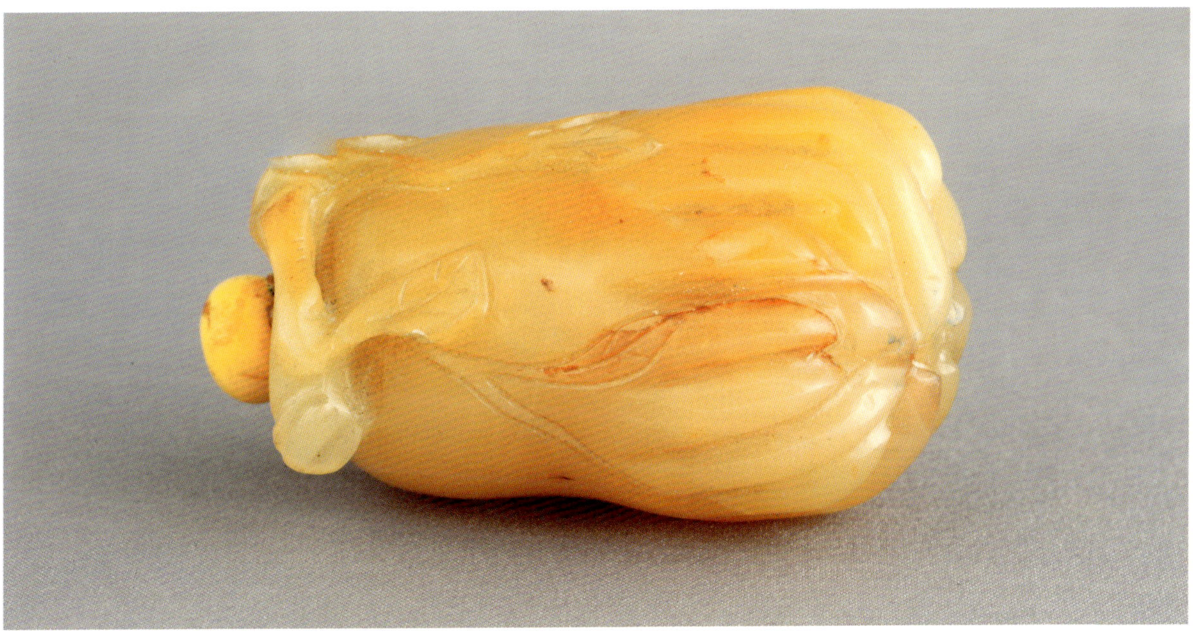

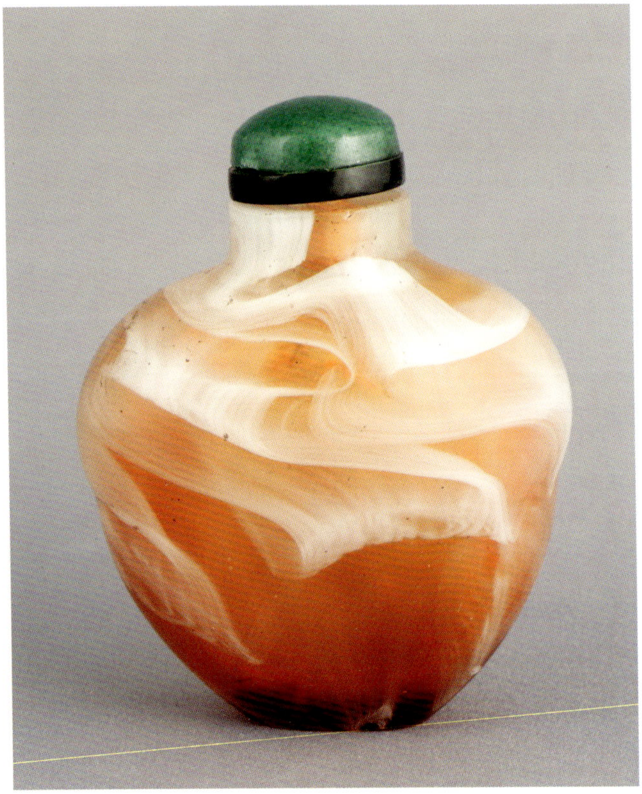

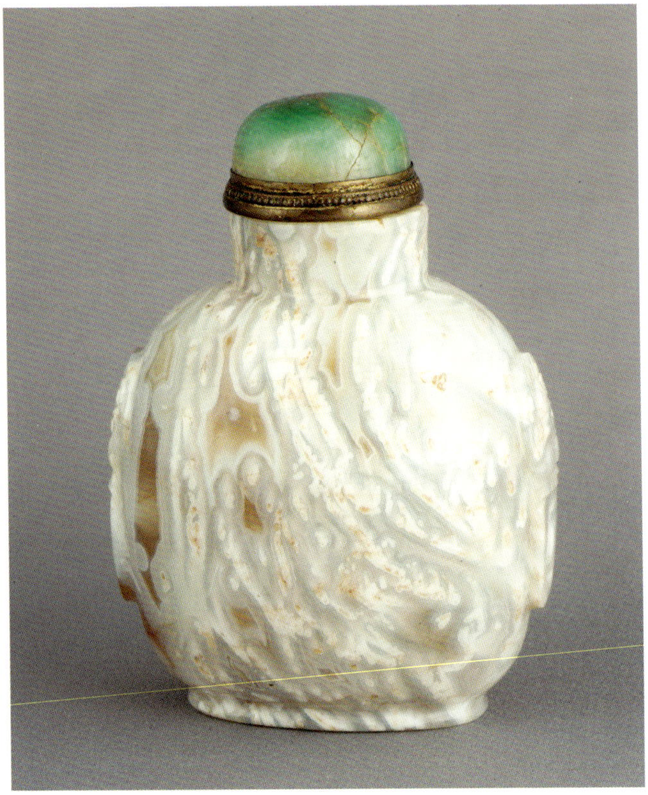

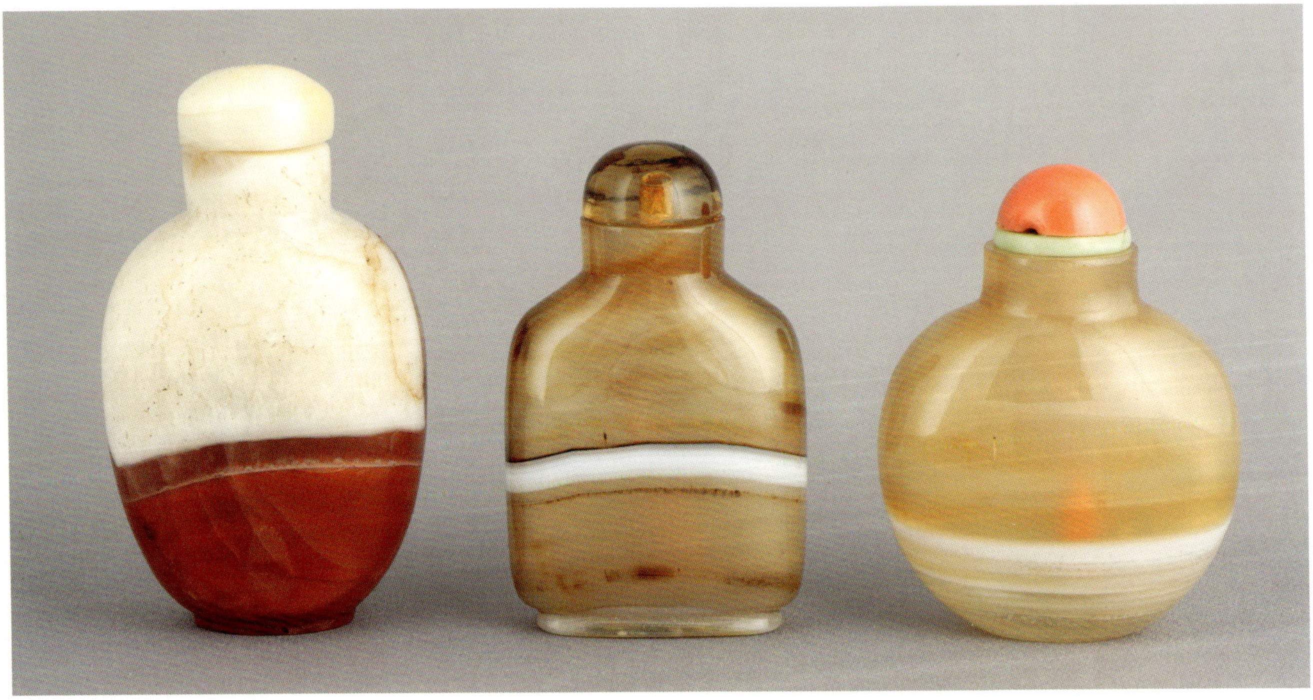

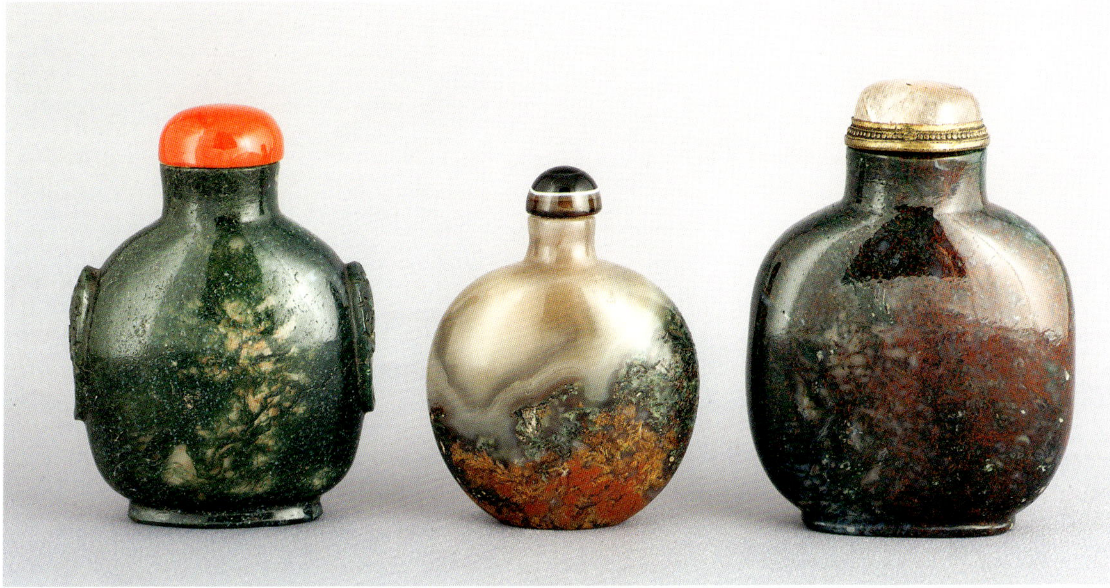

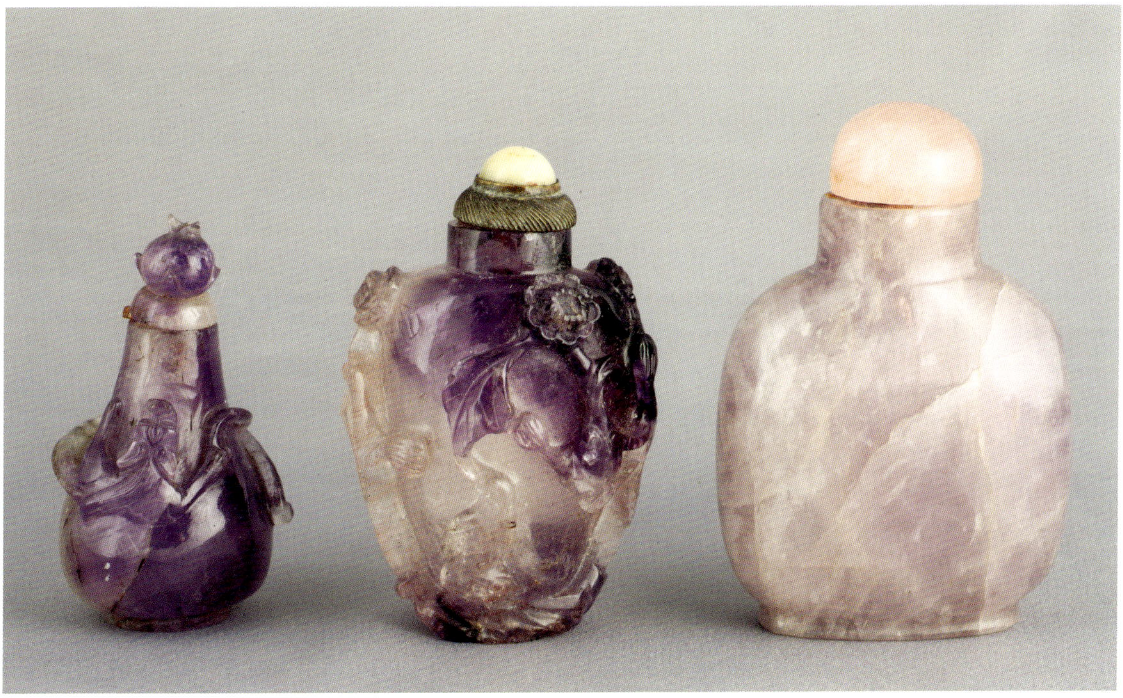

Snuff Bottle • Tabatière • Qing dynasty, 19th century • glass imitating agate • Given in memory of Woody (E.O.J.) Woodward by his wife Frances Woodward, AGGV 2006.003.001

Snuff Bottle • Tabatière • Qing dynasty, 19th century • macaroni agate • Gift of Helen Sawyer, AGGV 1995.012.047

Snuff Bottles • Tabatières • Qing dynasty, 19th century • banded agate • Gift of Helen Sawyer, 1995.012.045, 1995.012.048, (right) Gift of the Joy DeWeese-Wehen Estate, AGGV 2003.004.019

Snuff Bottles • Tabatières • Qing dynasty, 19th century • moss agate • Gift of Helen Sawyer, AGGV 1995.012.043, 1995.012.049, (right) Gift of the Joy DeWeese-Wehen Estate, AGGV 2003.004.022

Snuff Bottles with relief design of an elongated dragon/of plum blossoms and birds/one undecorated **• Tabatières** avec motif en relief d'un dragon allongé/fleurs de prunier et oiseaux/sans motif • late 19th early 20th century • amethyst • Gifts of Helen Sawyer, AGGV 1995.012.055, 1995.012.004 and 1995.012.042

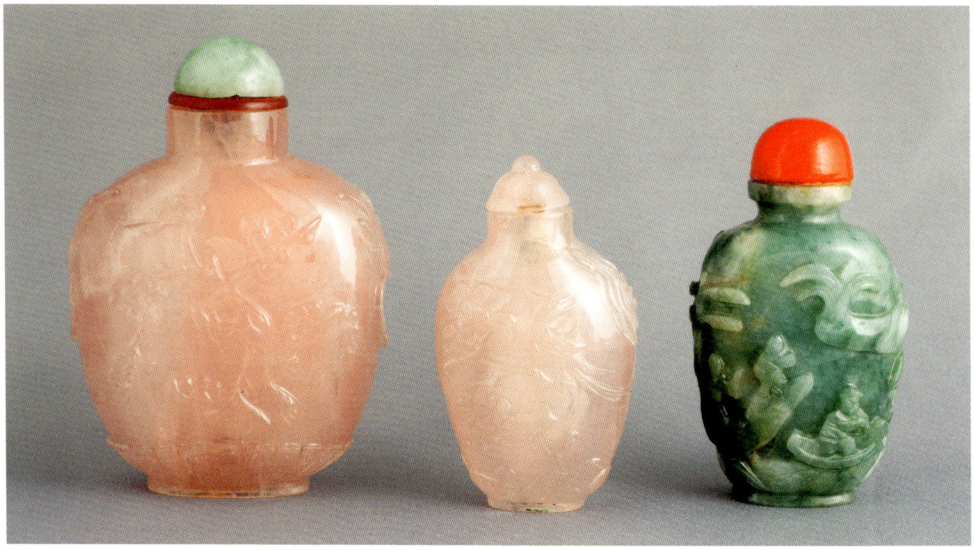

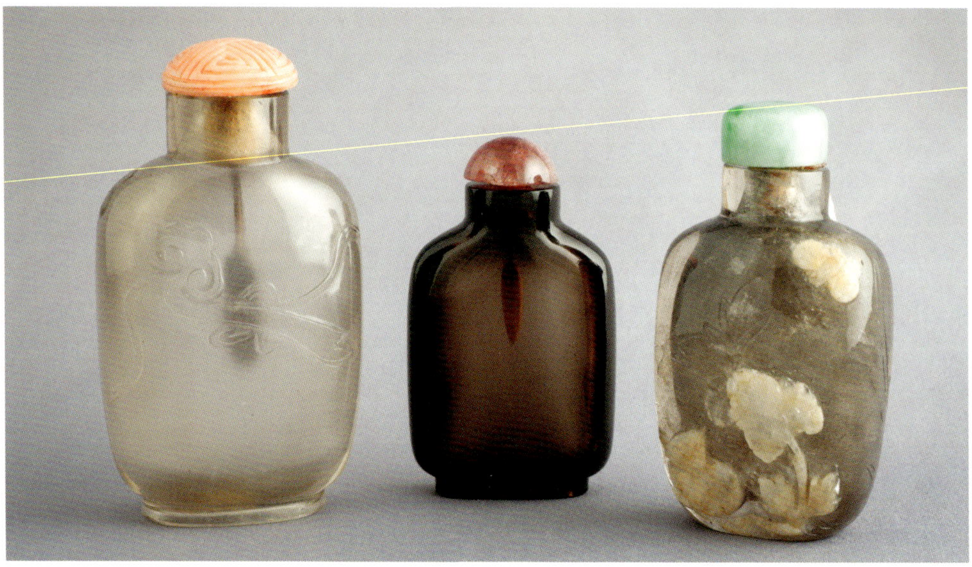

(left, middle) **Snuff Bottles** with design of plum and bamboo with flowers and butterfly on verso/of lotus and phoenix • (à gauche, au milieu) **Tabatières** avec motif de prunier; et bambou avec fleurs et papillon au verso/lotus et phœnix • late 19th/early 20th century • rose quartz • Gift of Helen Sawyer, AGGV 1995.012.013, 1995.012.006 • (right) **Snuff Bottle** with design of figures in boats with man on bridge in verso • (à droite) **Tabatière** ornée de personnages dans des embarcations; un homme sur un pont au verso • Qing dynasty, 19th century • green quartz • From the Estate of Miss Janet Gibson, Given by Mrs. Mary Irwin, AGGV 1976.090.003

(left) **Snuff Bottle** with relief design of iris, cat and butterfly • (à gauche) **Tabatière** avec relief d'iris, chat et papillon • Qing dynasty, 19th century • smoky quartz • Gift of Helen Sawyer, AGGV 1995.012.051 • (middle) **Snuff Bottle** • (au milieu) **Tabatière** • Qing dynasty, 19th century • smoky quartz • Gift of the Joy DeWeese-Wehen Estate, AGGV 2003.004.003 • (right) **Snuff Bottle** with design of *ruyi* sceptre with two butterflies on verso • (à droite) **Tabatière** avec motif de sceptre *ruyi*; et deux papillons au verso • Qing dynasty, 19th century • quartz/crystal • Gift of Helen Sawyer, AGGV 1995.012.007

Snuff Bottles with design of elongated dragon/with shape of a vase and relief design of a cat and flowers • **Tabatières** ornées d'un dragon allongé/en forme de vase avec un chat et des fleurs en relief • early 20th century • malachite • Gift of Helen Sawyer, AGGV 1995.012.035 , Gift of the Joy DeWeese-Wehen Estate, AGGV 2003.004.018

Snuff Bottles with design of birds and flowers/ in shape of a Buddha's hand fruit/one with pebbled surface • **Tabatières** ornées d'oiseaux et de fleurs/en forme de main de Boudha/dont une avec une surface granuleuse • late 19th/20th century • turquoise • Gift of Helen Sawyer, AGGV 1995.012.034 • Gift of Mrs. Shih Hua Chao and Mr. Shih Tsun Lee, AGGV 2007.009.003, Private Collection, Intended Gift

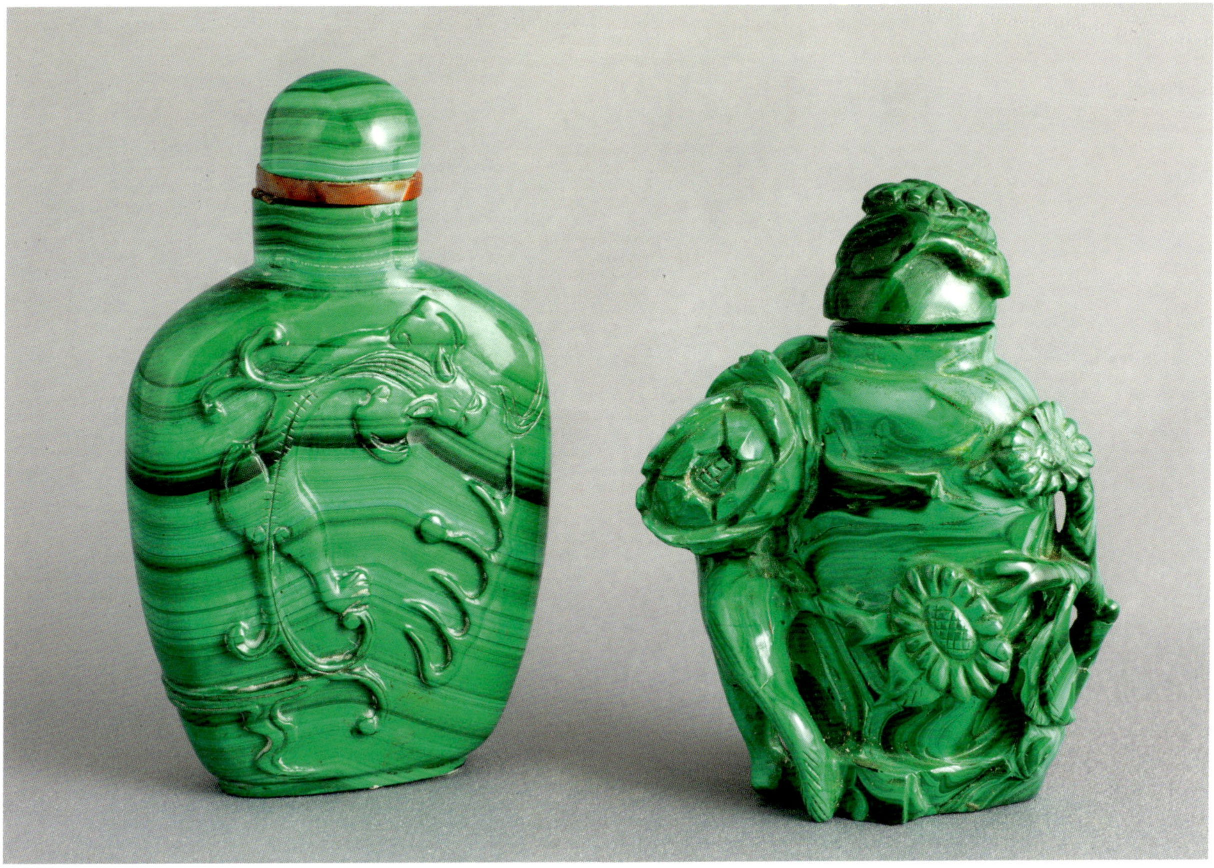

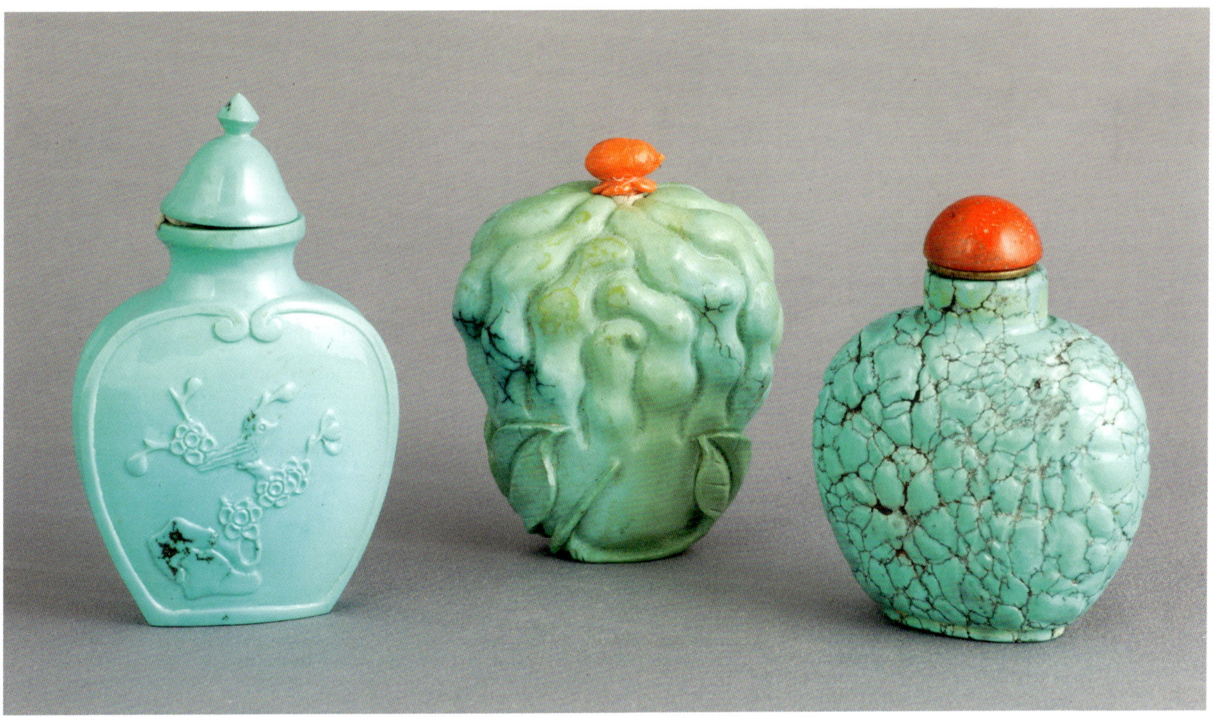

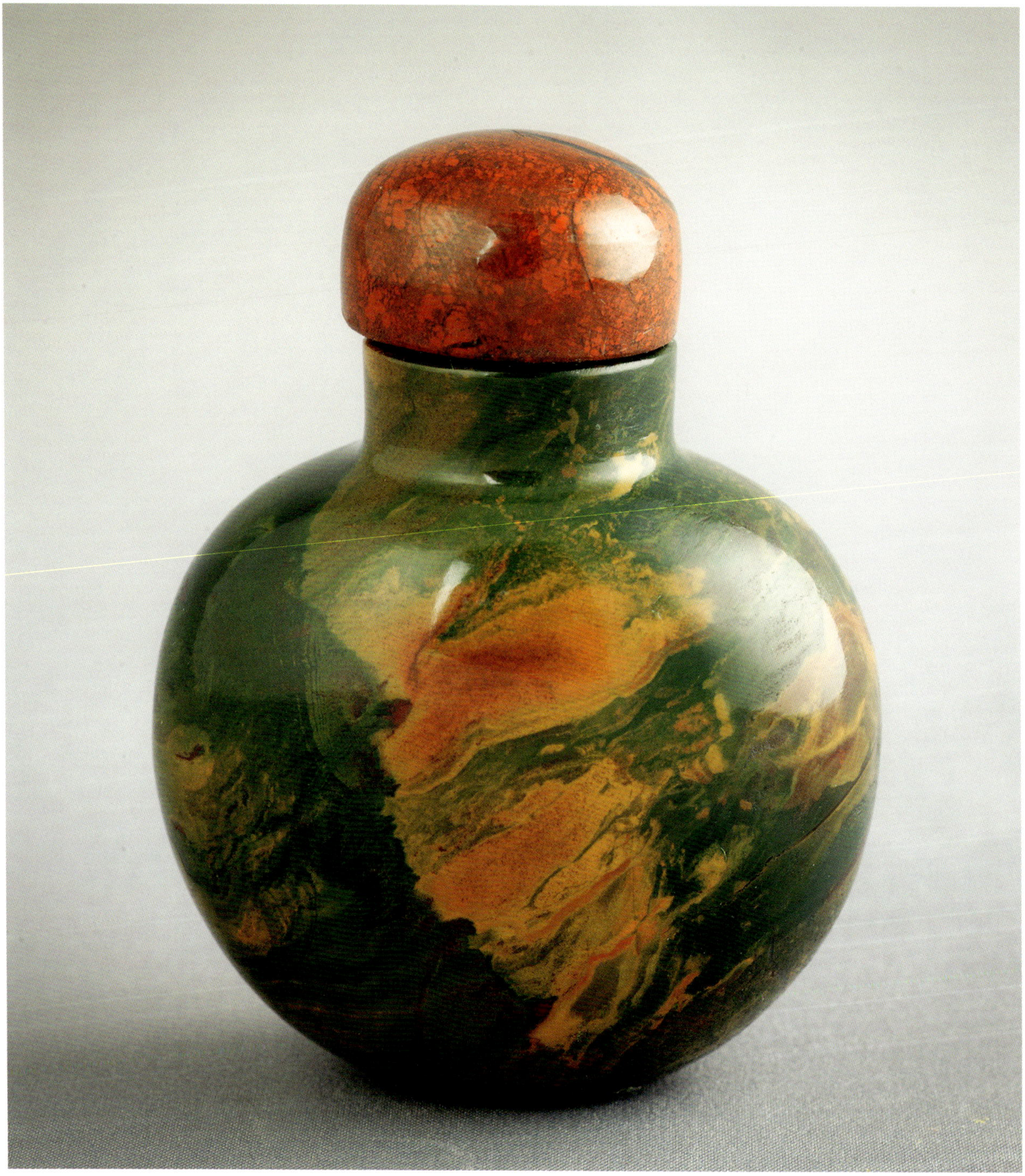

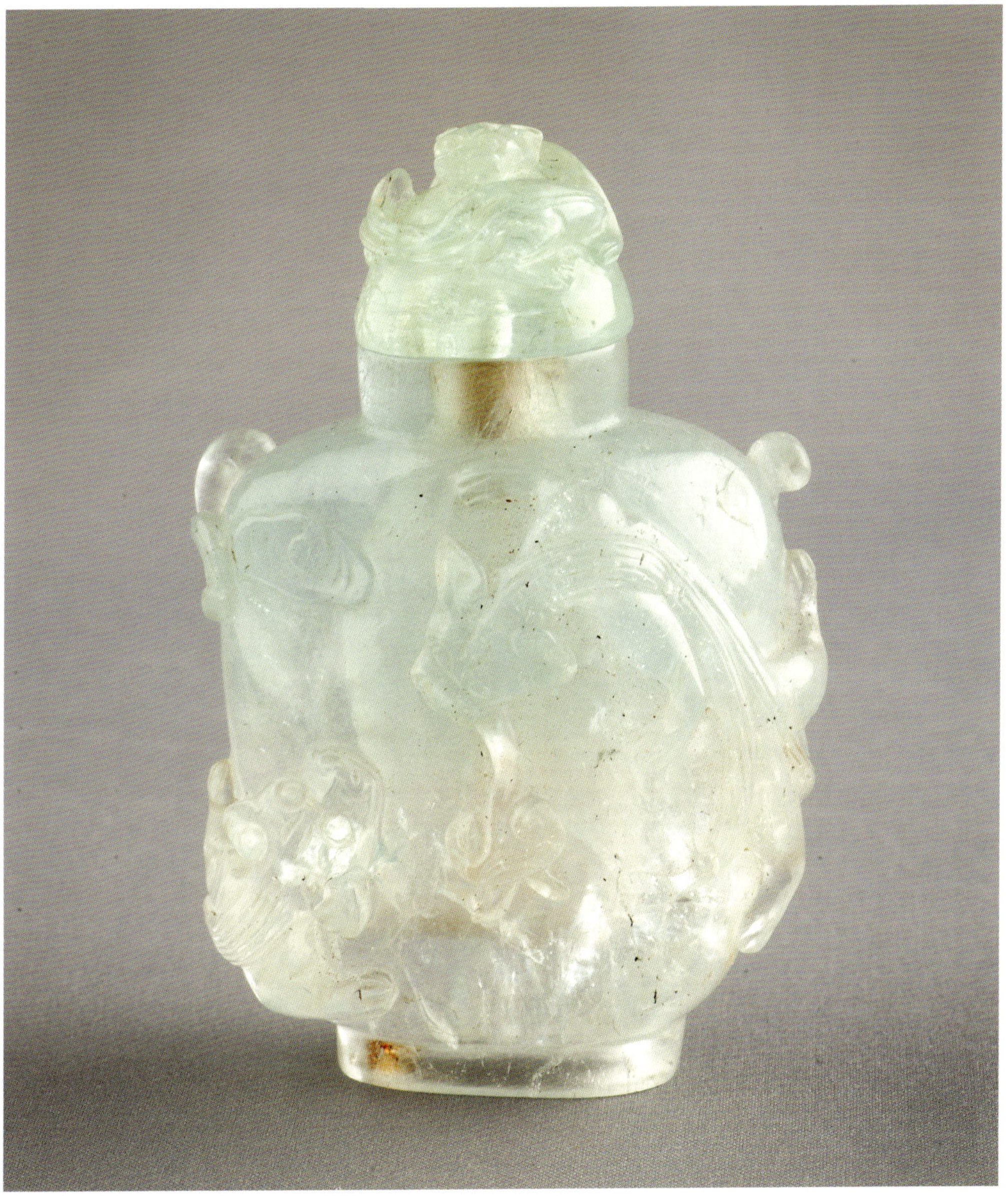

85

Snuff Bottle • Tabatière • Qing dynasty, 19th century • jasper • Gift of Helen Sawyer, AGGV 1995.012.046

Snuff Bottle with relief design of coiling dragons • **Tabatière** avec motif en relief de dragons se tortillant • late 19th/early 20th century • aquamarine • Gift of the Joy DeWeese-Wehen Estate, AGGV 2003.004.008

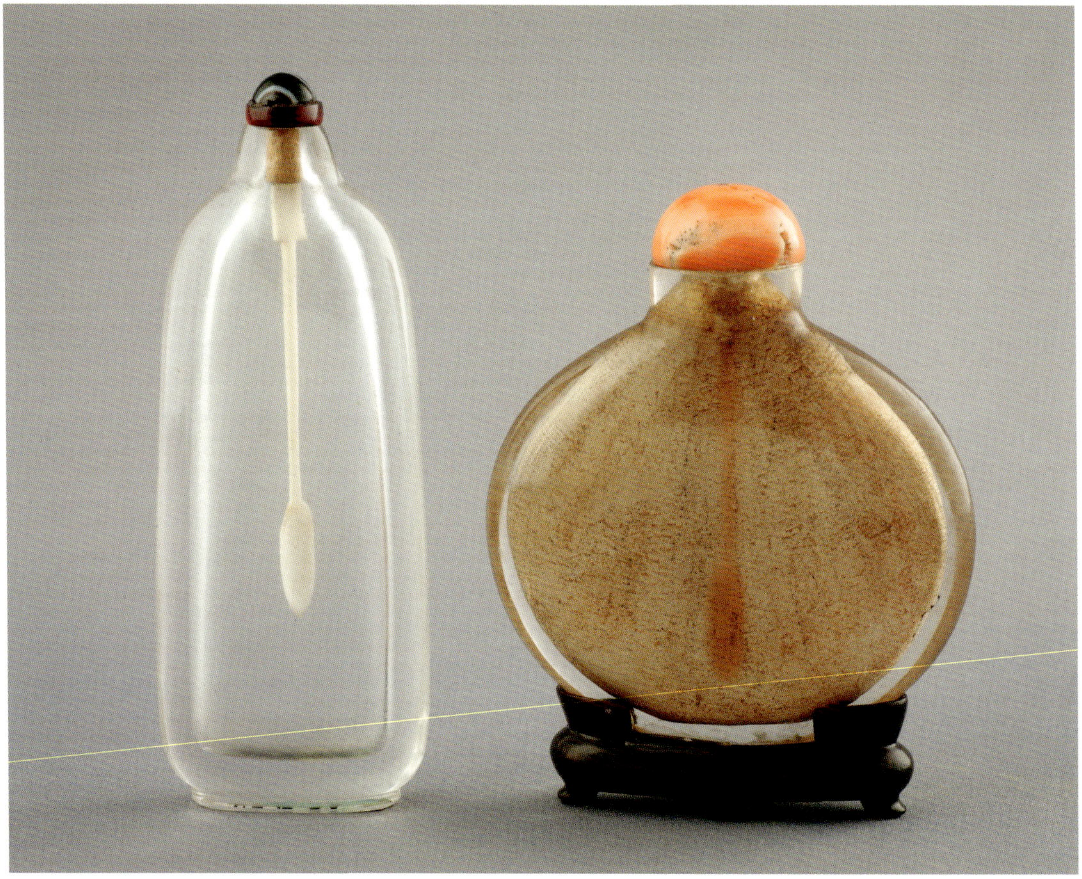

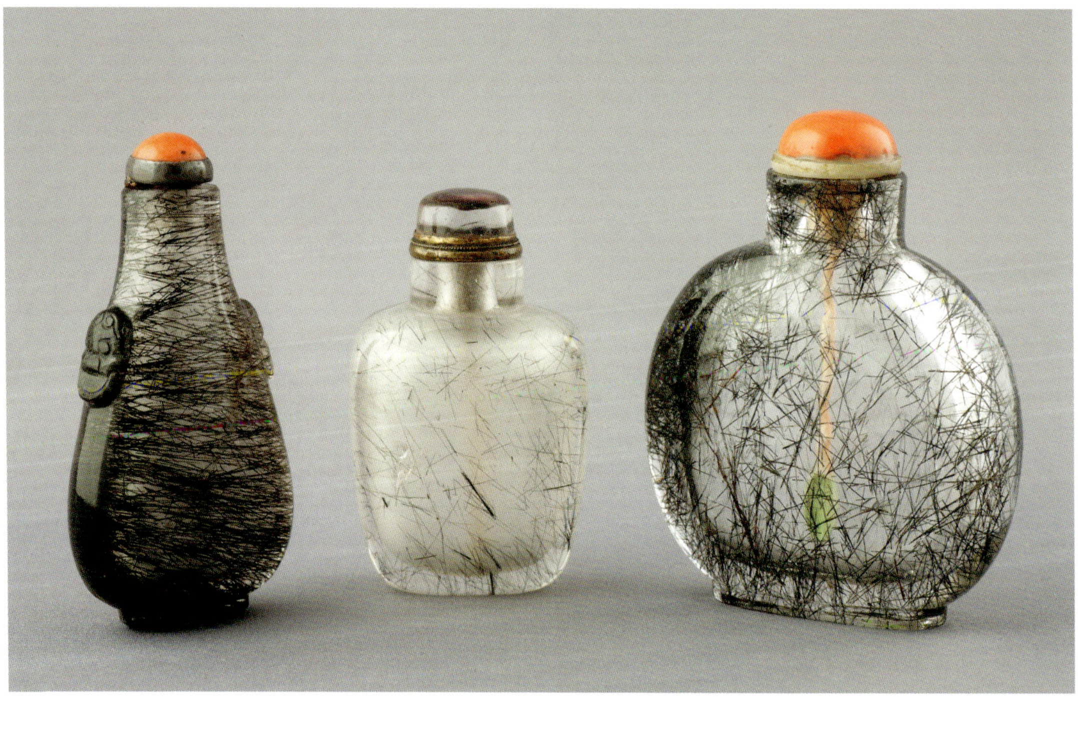

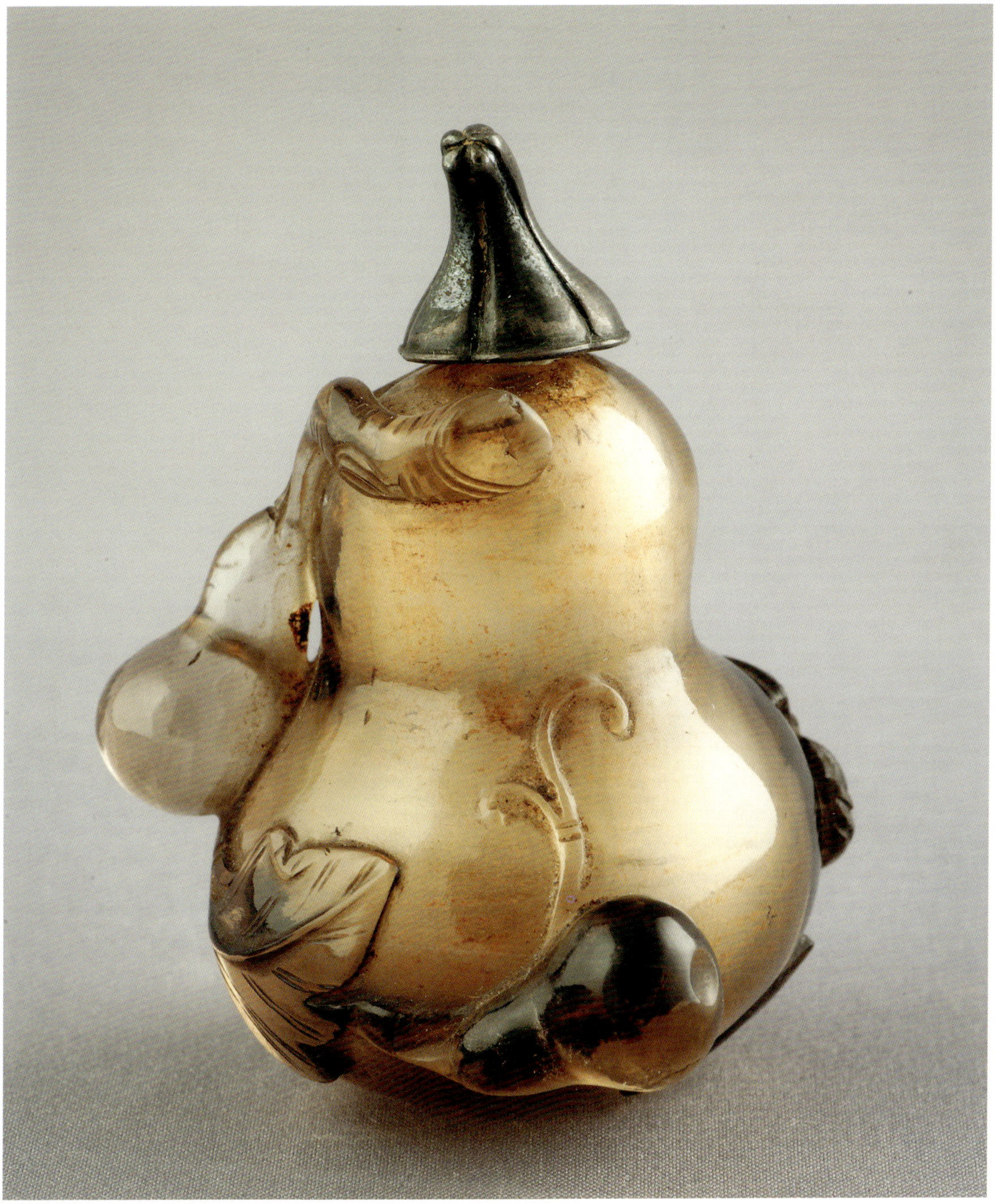

Snuff Bottles • Tabatières • Qing dynasty, 19th century • quartz/crystal • Gift of Helen Sawyer, AGGV 1995.012.028 • Gift of the Joy DeWeese-Wehen Estate, AGGV 2003.004.012

Snuff Bottles • Tabatières • Qing dynasty, 19th century • quartz/hair crystal • Gift of Helen Sawyer, AGGV 1995.012.005 , Gift of the Joy DeWeese-Wehen Estate, AGGV 2003.004.007, Private Collection, Intended Gift

Snuff Bottle in the form of a gourd with a relief of a bat • **Tabatière** en forme de gourde avec un relief de chauve-souris • Qing dynasty, 19th century • quartz/crystal • Given in Memory of John P. Nind (R.M.L.I. ret.) by his wife Mildred and their daughter Ann Neilson, AGGV 1974.144.001

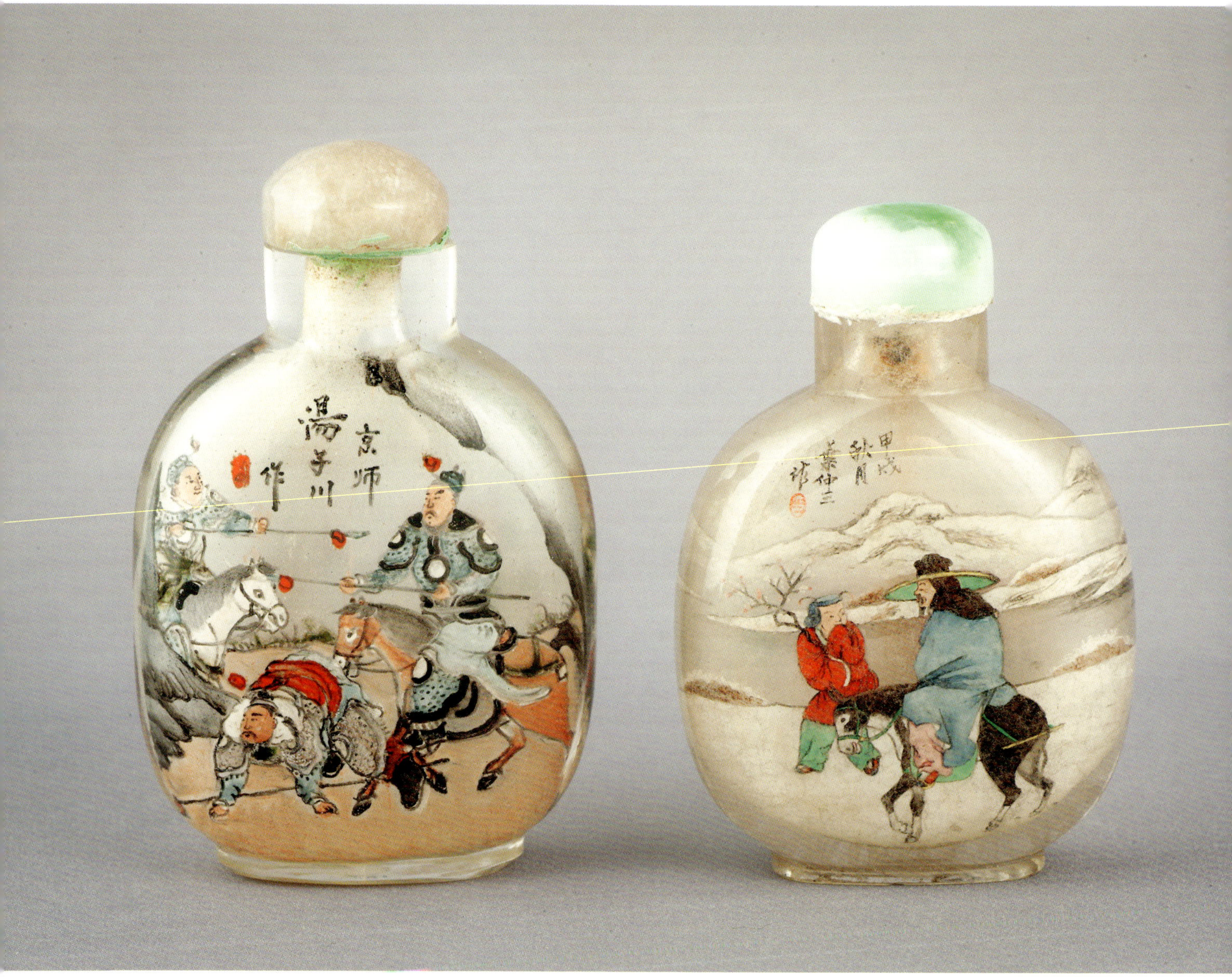

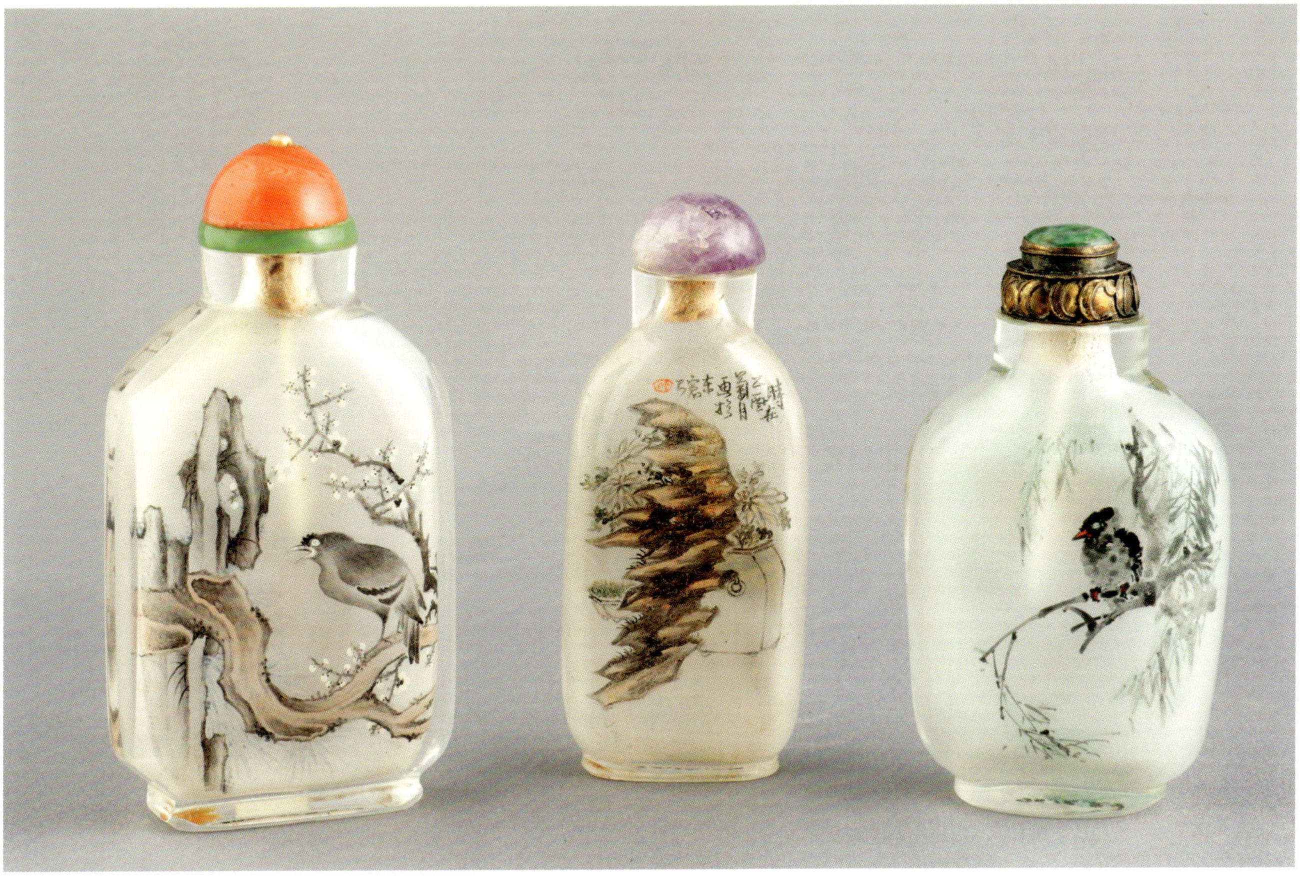

(left) **Snuff Bottle** painted inside with battle scene, signed Tang Zichuan, early 20th century • (à gauche) **Tabatière** avec scène de bataille peinte de l'intérieur, signée Tang Zichuan, début du 20e siècle • glass, pigments • Gift of Helen Sawyer, AGGV 1995.012.025 • (right) **Snuff Bottle** painted inside with man on donkey, archer on horse on verso, signed Ye Zhongsan, early 20th century • (à droite) **Tabatière** avec scène peinte de l'intérieur d'un homme sur un âne; archer sur un cheval au verso, signée Ye Zhongsan, début du 20e siècle • glass pigments • Gift of the Joy DeWeese-Wehen Estate, AGGV 2003.004.004

(left) **Snuff Bottle** painted inside with a bird on a blossoming branch, a corroded rock and a sprig of plum blossom next to a cauldron on verso, signed Guan Yutian, late 19th/early 20th century • (à gauche) **Tabatière** avec scène peinte de l'intérieur d'un oiseau sur une branche en fleurs; rocher corrodé et brindille de prunier en fleurs près d'un chaudron au verso, signée Guan Yutian, fin du 19e/début du 20e siècle • glass, pigments • Gift of Helen Sawyer, AGGV 2004.007.013 • (middle) **Snuff Bottle** painted inside with corroded rock, chrysanthemum, calligraphy, cricket and grass, signed Zhou Leyuan, early 20th century • (au milieu) **Tabatière** peinte de l'intérieur avec motifs de rocher corrodé, chrysanthèmes, caractères de calligraphie, cricket et herbe, signée Zhou Leyuan, début du 20e siècle • glass, pigments • Gift of Helen Sawyer, AGGV 1995.012.026 • (right) **Snuff Bottle** painted inside with bird on a willow and floral sprays, signed Jin Hua, early 20th century • (à droite) Tabatière peinte de l'intérieur avec oiseau sur une branche de saule et grappes de fleurs, signée Jin Hua, début du 20e siècle • glass, pigments • Gift of Helen Sawyer, AGGV 1995.012.024

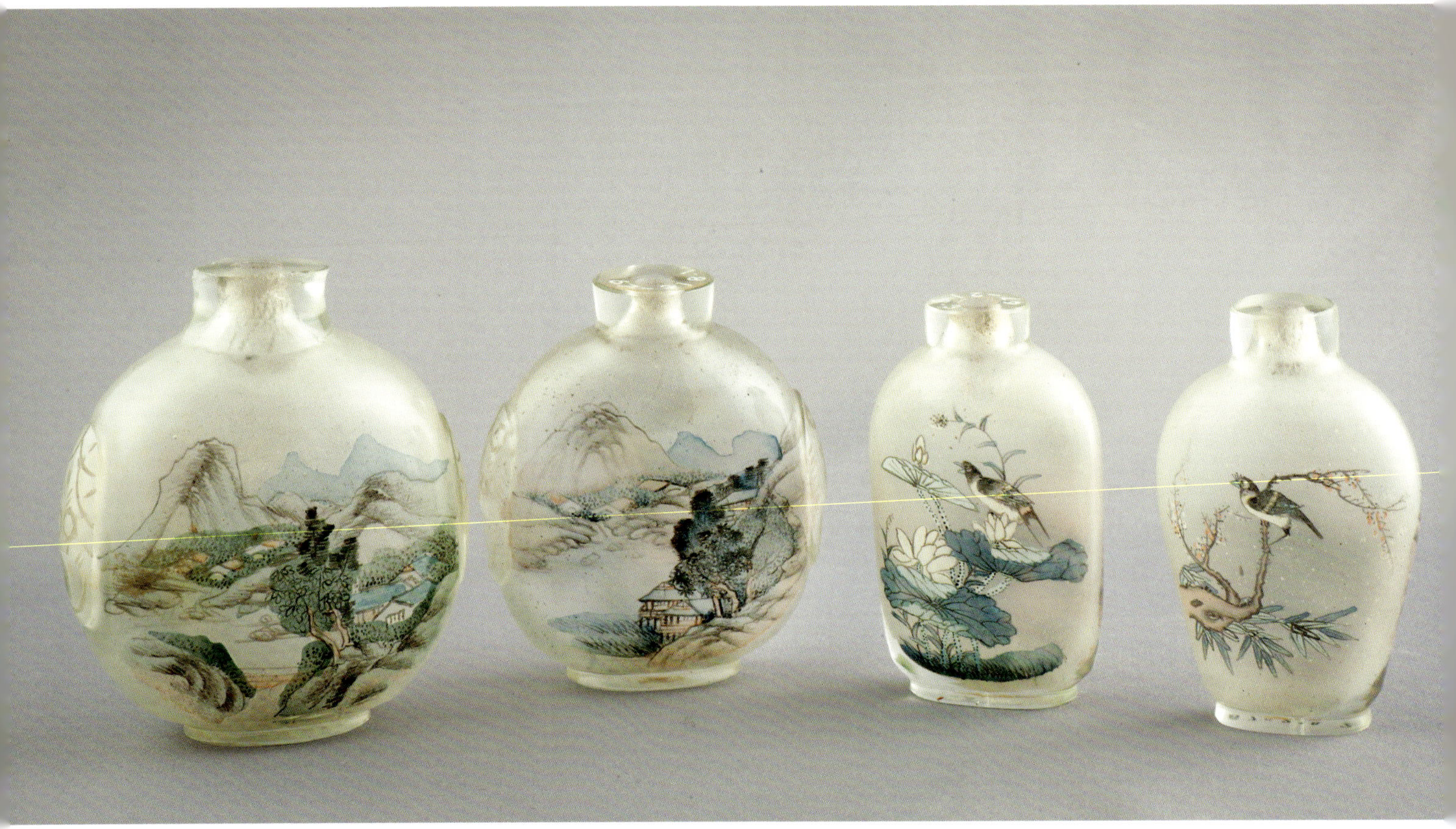

Four **Snuff Bottles** painted inside with landscapes with birds on a branch in verso • Quatre **tabatières** avec paysage peint de l'intérieur; oiseaux sur une branche au verso • first half of 20th century • glass, pigments • J.P.E. Klaverwyden Bequest, AGGV 1967.218.000 - .003

Snuff Bottle • Tabatière • Qing dynasty, late 19th/ early 20th century • brown glass with gold speckling • Given in memory of Woody (E.O.J.) Woodward by his wife Frances Woodward, AGGV 2006.003.002

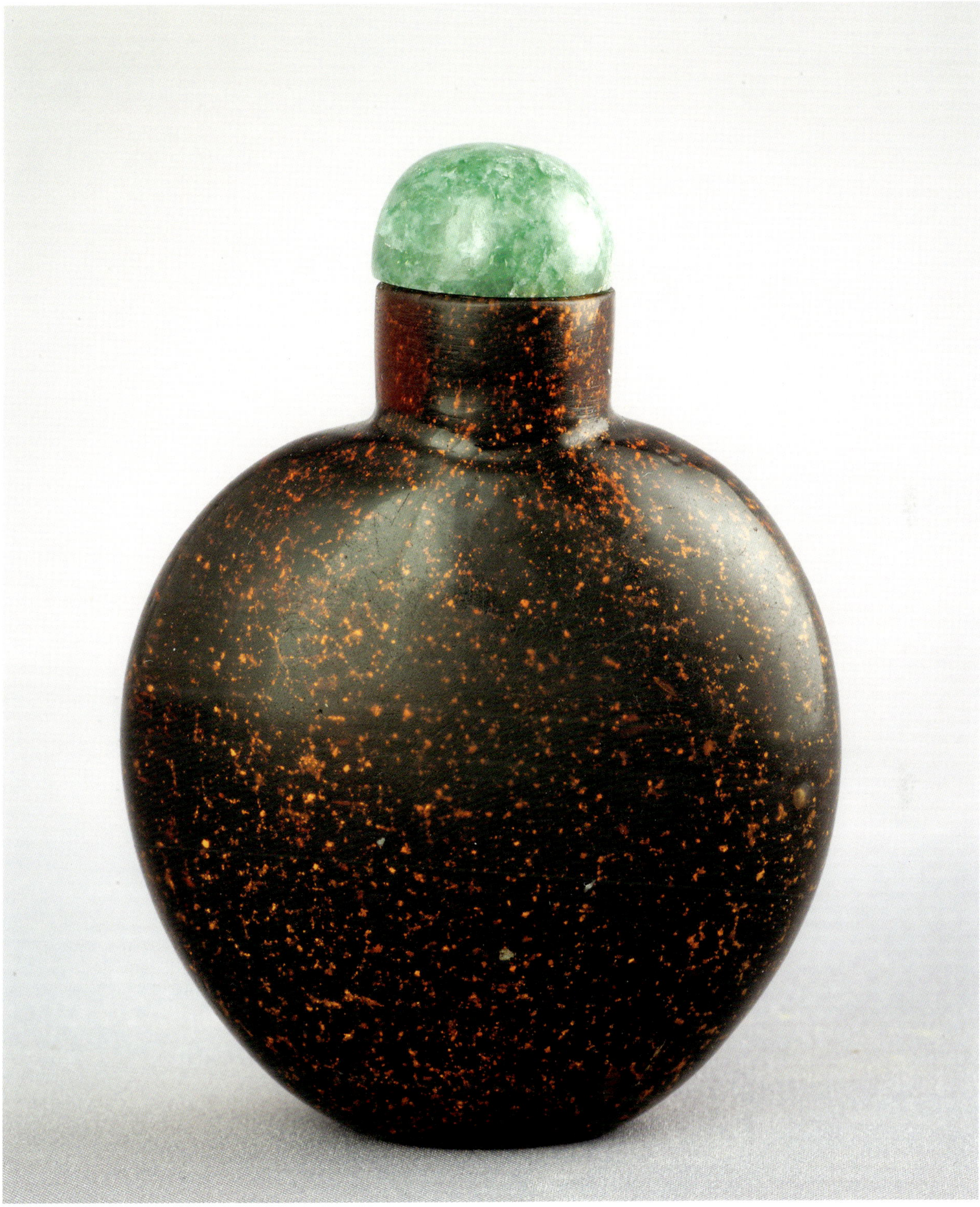

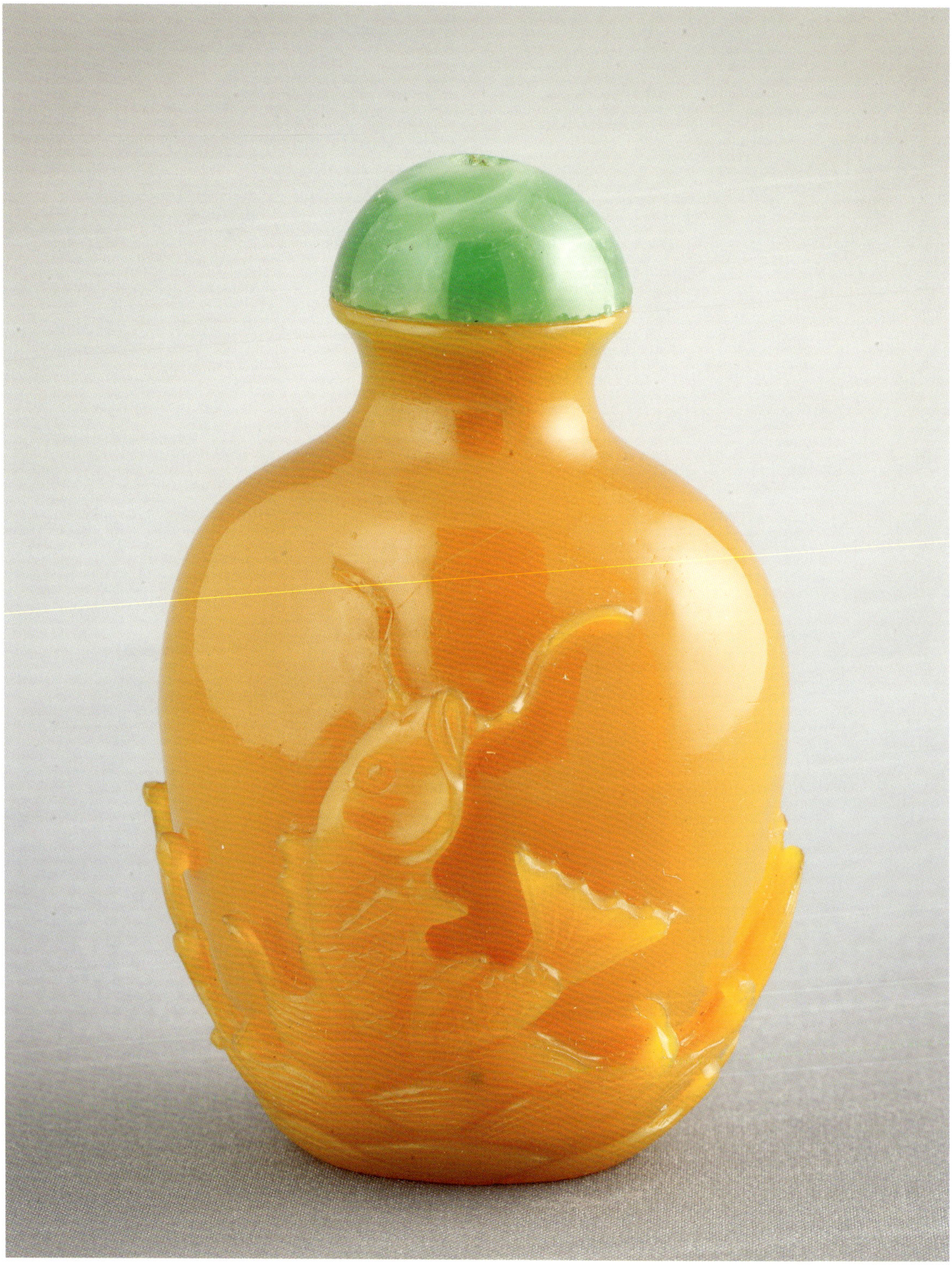

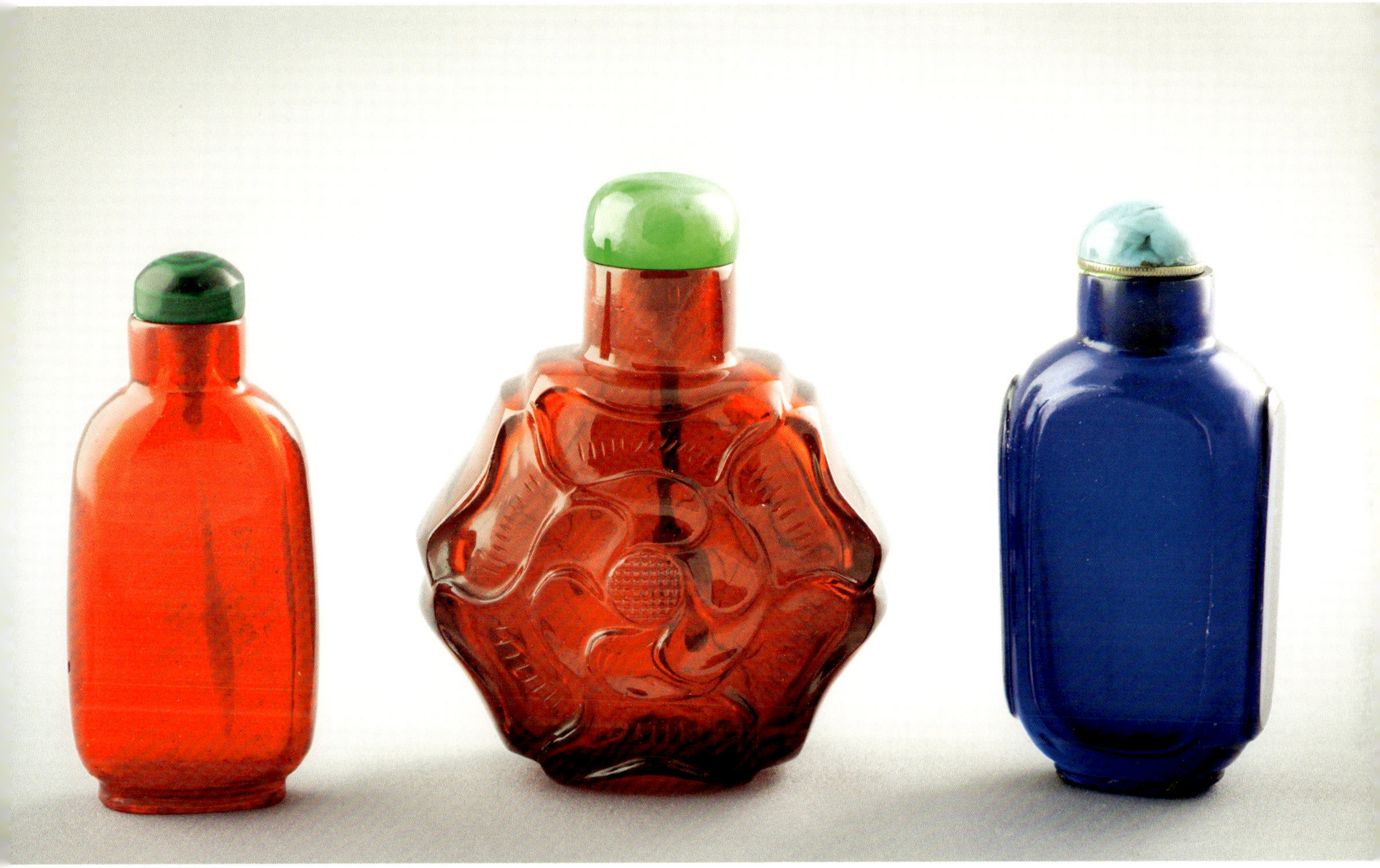

Snuff Bottle with design of carp above waves • **Tabatière** avec motif de carpe au-dessus des vagues • Qing dynasty, 19th century • yellow glass • Given by Mrs. Mary Irwin from the Estate of Miss Janet Gibson, AGGV 1976.090.004

Snuff Bottles two undecorated/one with design of a peony • **Tabatières** dont deux non décorées/une avec motif de pivoine • Qing dynasty, late 18th/19th century • red and blue glass • Gift of Helen Sawyer, AGGV 1995.012.061, Gift of the Joy DeWeese-Wehen Estate, AGGV 2003.004.026, Private Collection, Intended Gift

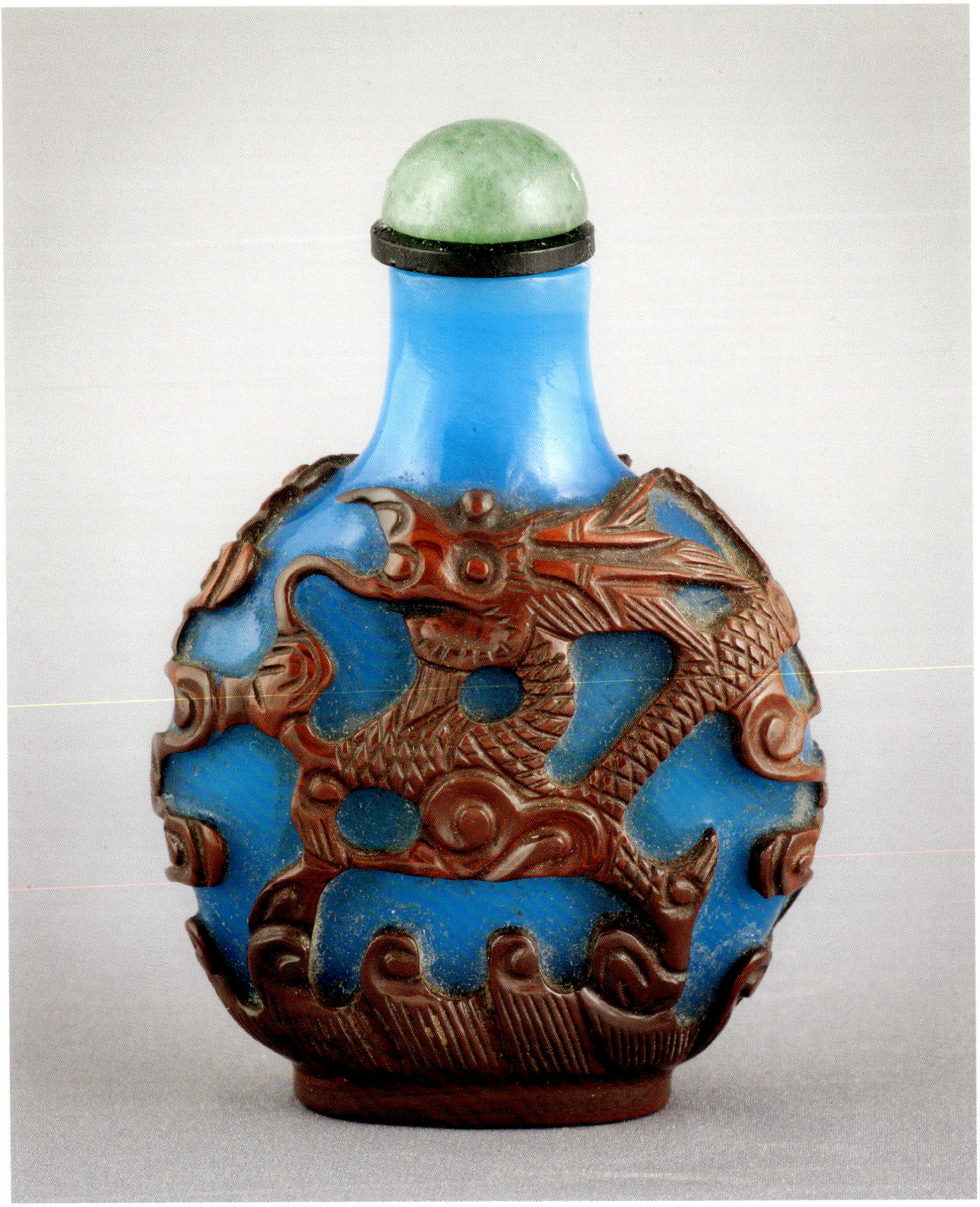

Snuff Bottle with design of coiling dragon amidst clouds over waves • **Tabatière** avec motif de dragon qui se tortille dans les nuages au-dessus des vagues • Qing dynasty, late 19th/early 20th century • blue glass with brown overlay • Given in memory of John P. Nind (R.M.L.I. ret.) by his wife Mildred and their daughter Ann Neilson, AGGV 1974.138.001

Snuff Bottle with design of a bird on a flowering branch and rock • **Tabatière** avec motif d'oiseau sur une branche en fleurs et un rocher • Qing dynasty, late 19th/early 20th century • blue glass with enamels • Given by Mrs. Mary Irwin from Estate of Miss Janet Gibson, AGGV 1976.090.006

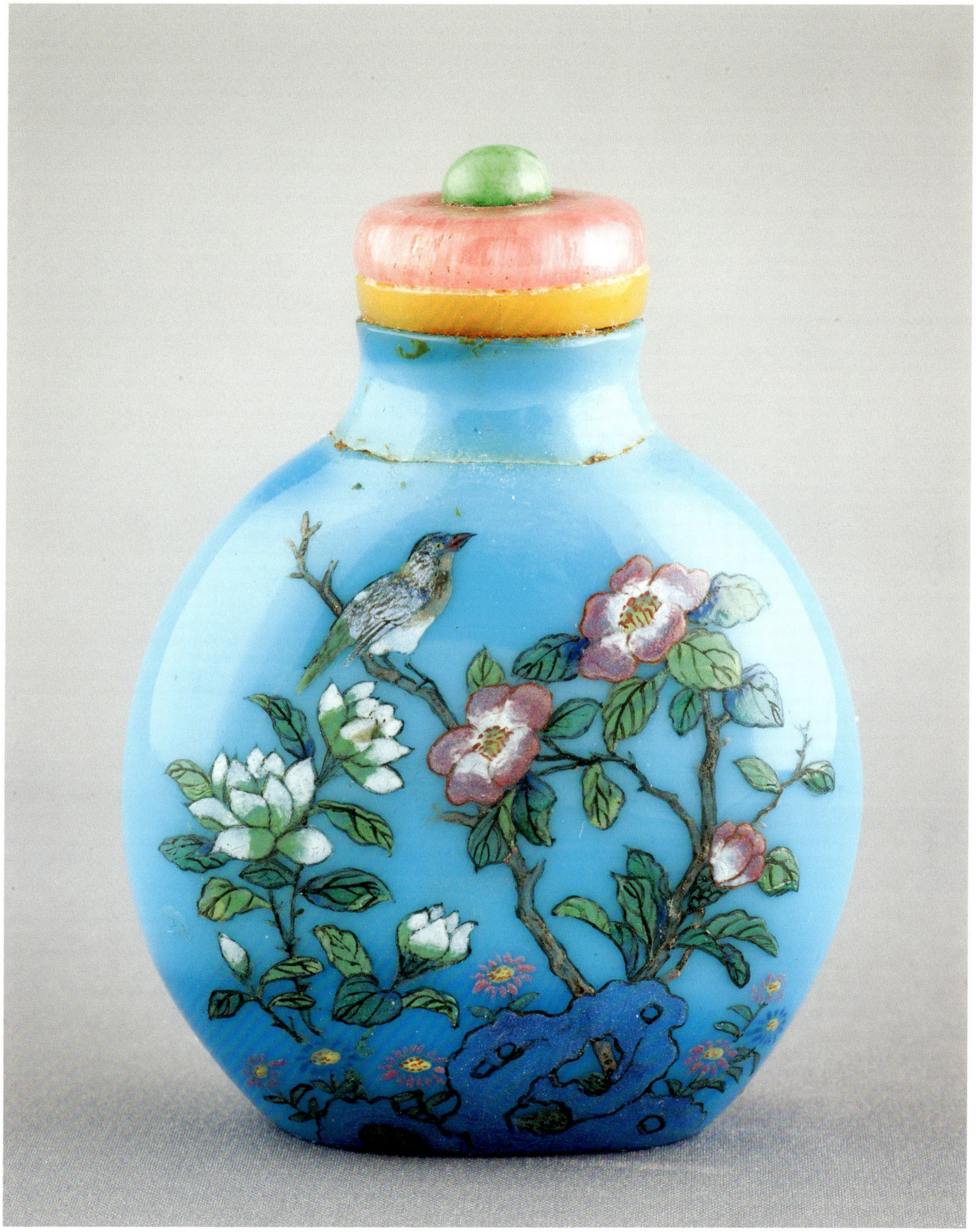

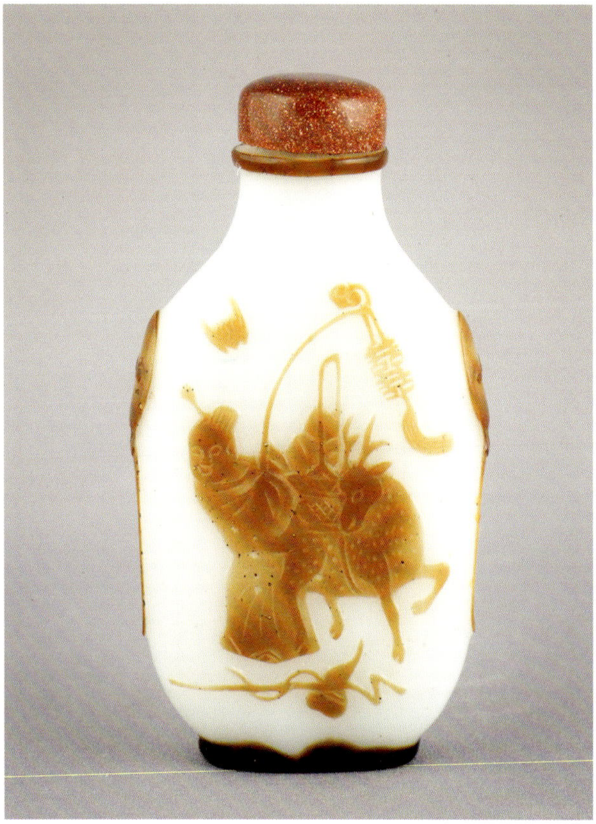

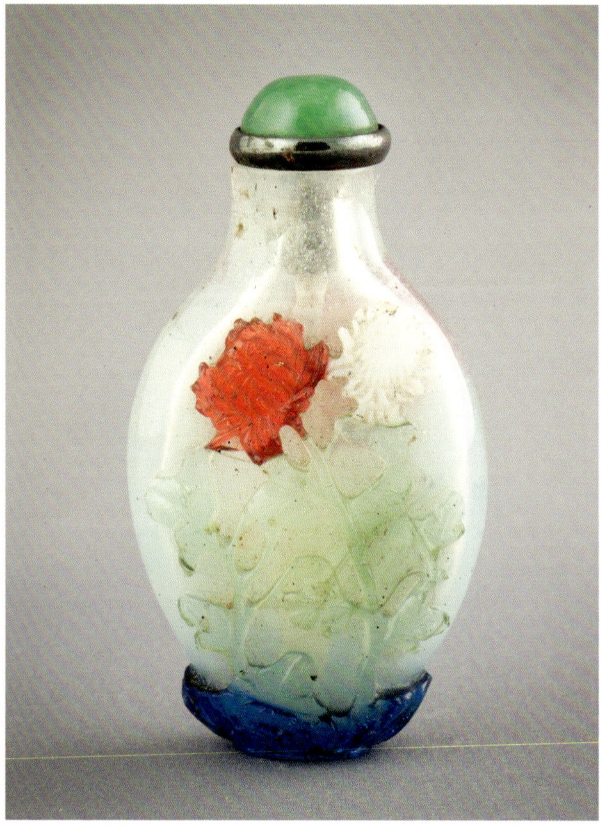

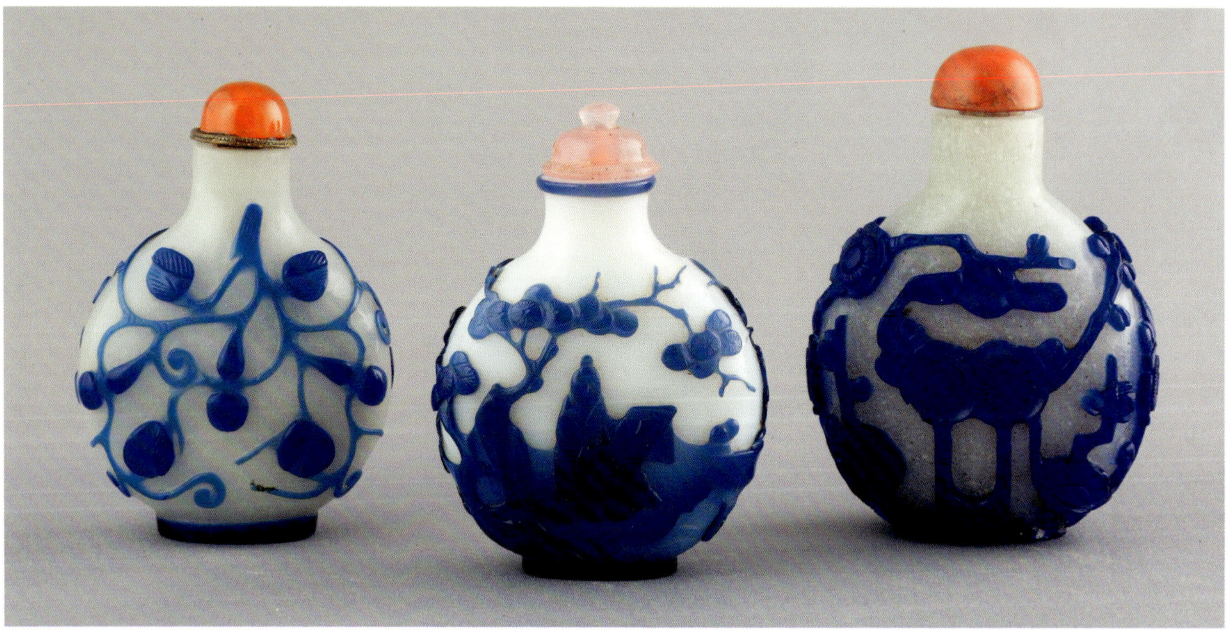

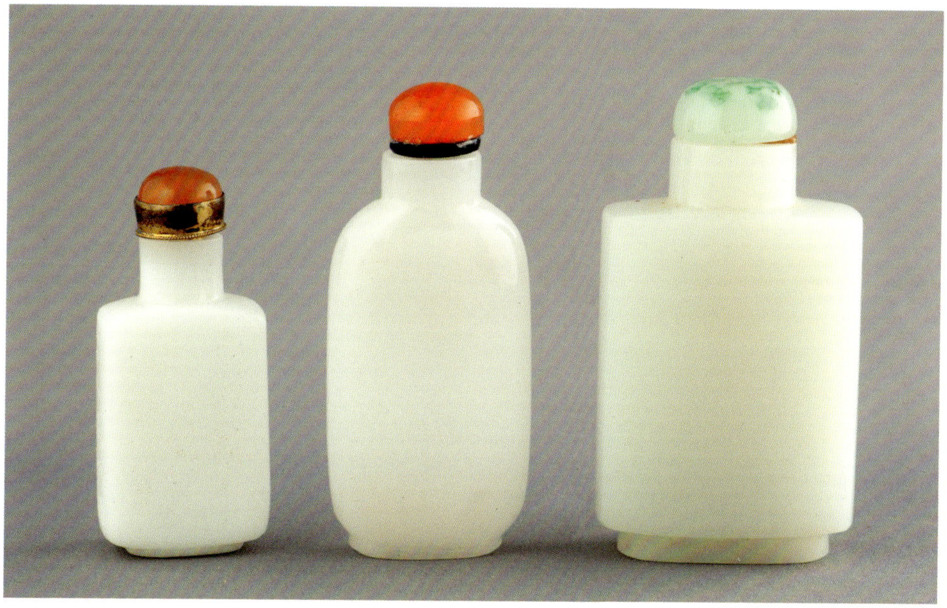

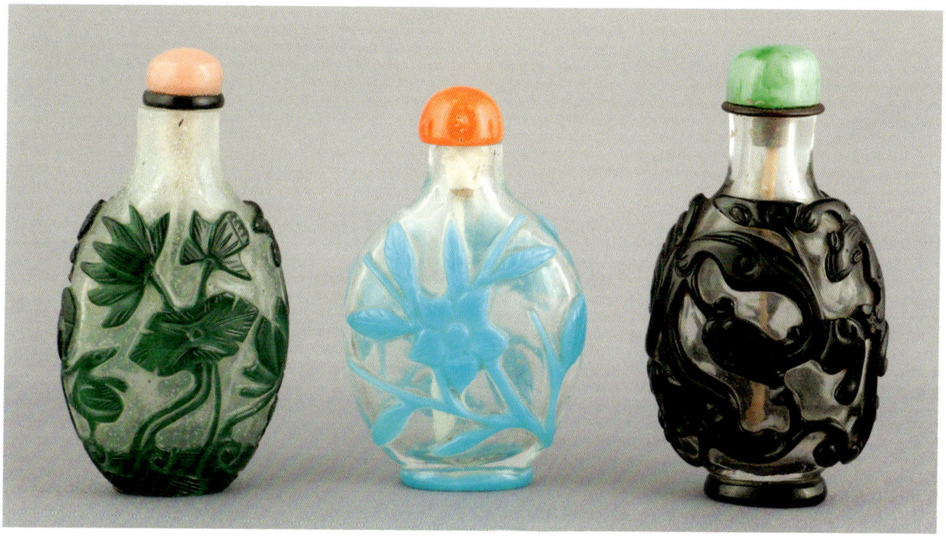

Snuff Bottle with scenes of Daoist figures • **Tabatière** avec scènes de personnages taoïstes • Qing dynasty, 19th century, (Yangzhou school style) • milky white glass with brown overlay • Gift of the Joy DeWeese-Wehen Estate, AGGV 2003.004.009

Snuff Bottle with design of chrysanthemums • **Tabatière** avec motif de chrysanthèmes • Qing dynasty, 19th century • glass with red, white, blue and light green overlay • Gift of the Joy DeWeese-Wehen Estate, AGGV 2003.004.010

Snuff Bottles with designs of gourds and vines/of a sage and attendants in a garden/of flowers • **Tabatières** avec motifs de gourdes et vignes/sage et ses disciples dans un jardin/fleurs • Qing dynasty, 19th century • white glass with blue overlay • Given in Memory of John P. Nind (R.M.L.I. ret.) by his wife Mildred and their daughter Ann Neilson, AGGV 1974.140.001, Gift of the Joy DeWeese-Wehen Estate, AGGV 2003.004.015, Gift of Helen Sawyer, AGGV 2004.007.003

Snuff Bottles with incised calligraphy and flower spray/two undecorated • **Tabatières** avec caractères de calligraphie gravés et grappe de fleurs/dont deux non décorées • Qing dynasty, 19th century • milky white glass • Gift of Helen Sawyer, AGGV 1995.012.057, 1995.012.059, Given by Mrs. Mary Irwin from the Estate of Miss Janet Gibson, AGGV 1976.090.002

Snuff Bottles with designs of lotus and birds/of a cherry branch and chrysanthemum spray/an elongated dragon • **Tabatières** avec motifs de lotus et d'oiseaux/branche de cerisier et grappe de chrysanthèmes/dragon allongé • Qing dynasty, 19th century • glass with green, turquoise and black overlay • Gift of Helen Sawyer, AGGV 1995.012.023, Given in Memory of John P. Nind (R.M.L.I. ret.) by his wife Mildred and their daughter Ann Neilson, AGGV 1974.142.001, Gift of Helen Sawyer, AGGV 1995.012.027

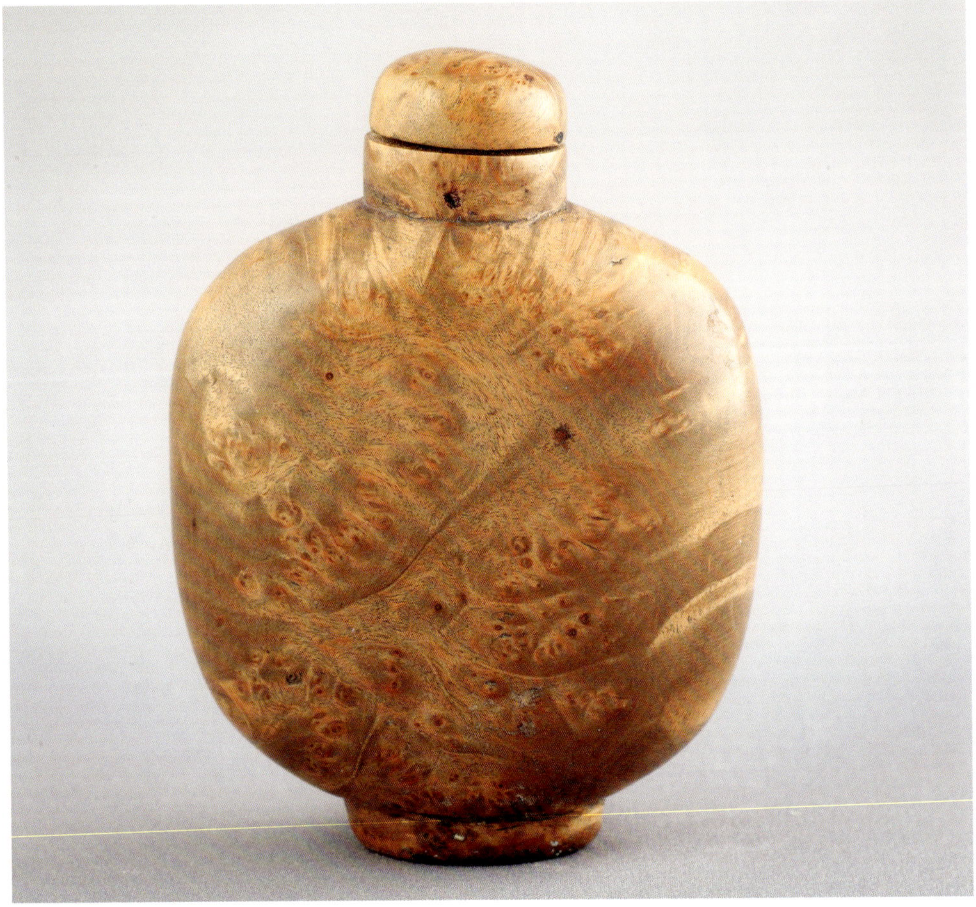

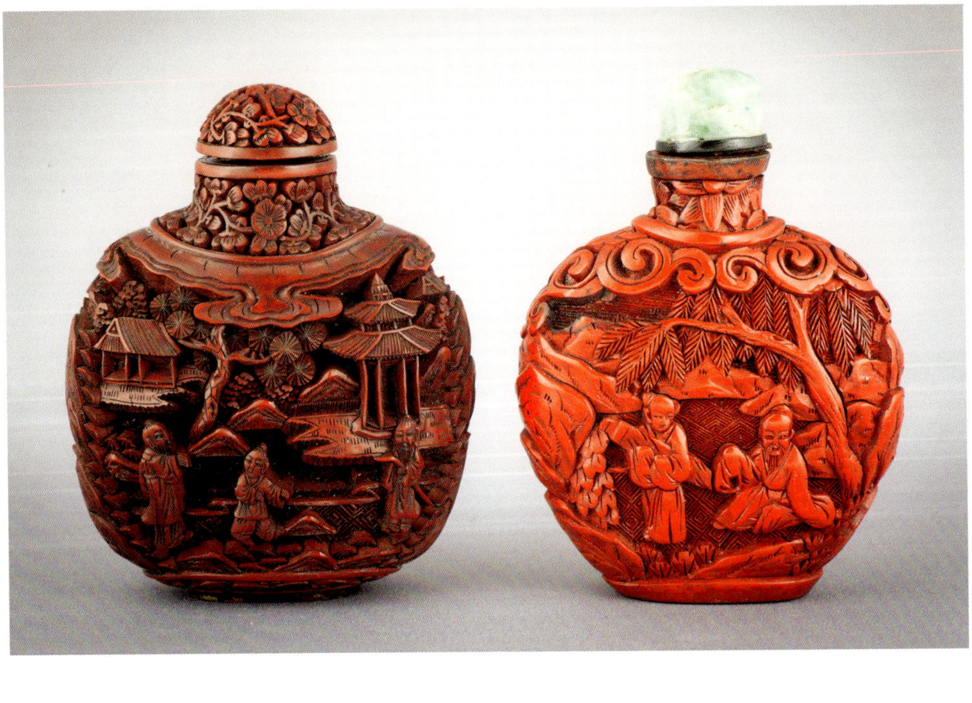

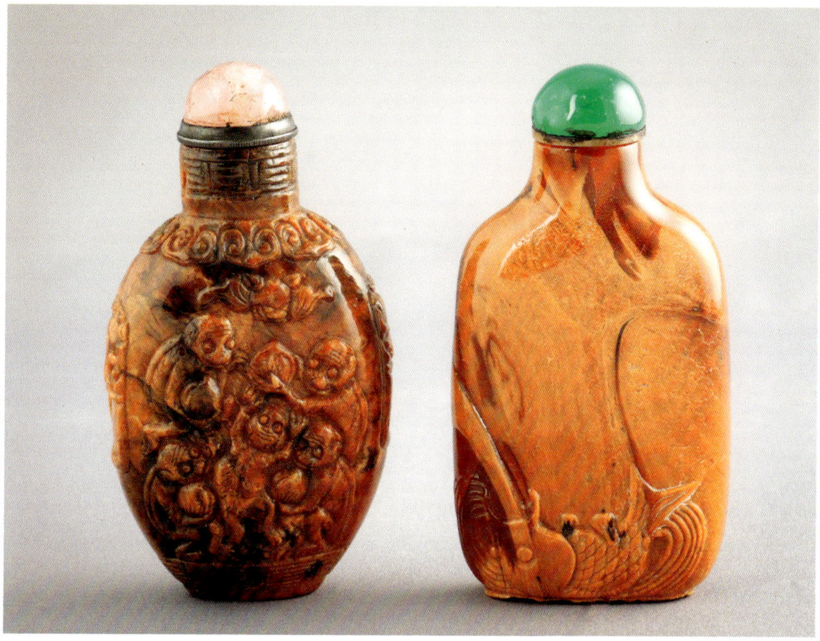

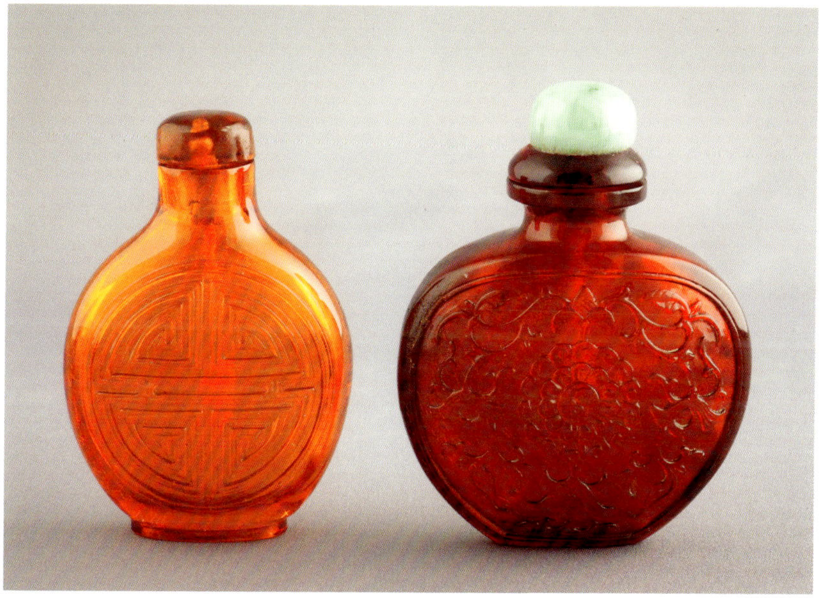

Snuff Bottle • Tabatière • late 19th/early 20th century • burl • Gift of Helen Sawyer, AGGV 1995.012.058

Snuff Bottles with carved design of figures amidst architectural structures and trees/figures in a garden • **Tabatières** avec motif sculpté de personnages au milieu d'arbres et de structures architecturales/personnages dans un jardin • Qing dynasty, 19th century • cinnabar lacquer • Gift of Arthur Menzies, AGGV 2003.029.050, Gift of Helen Sawyer, AGGV 1995.012.053

Snuff Bottles with design of monkeys on a peach tree with goats on verso/of carp in waves • **Tabatières** ornées de singes sur un pêcher; avec chèvres au verso/carpes dans les vagues • Qing dynasty, 18th/19th century • root amber • Francis and Kay Reif Collection, AGGV 1999.023.061, 1999.023.063

Snuff Bottles with design of the Chinese character for longevity *(shou)*/of *yin yang* symbol with floral sprays • **Tabatières** ornées du caractère chinois de la longévité *(shou)*/symbole du *yin* et du *yang* et grappes de fleurs • Qing dynasty, 18th/19th century • amber • Francis and Kay Reif Collection, AGGV 1999.023.054, 1999.023.058

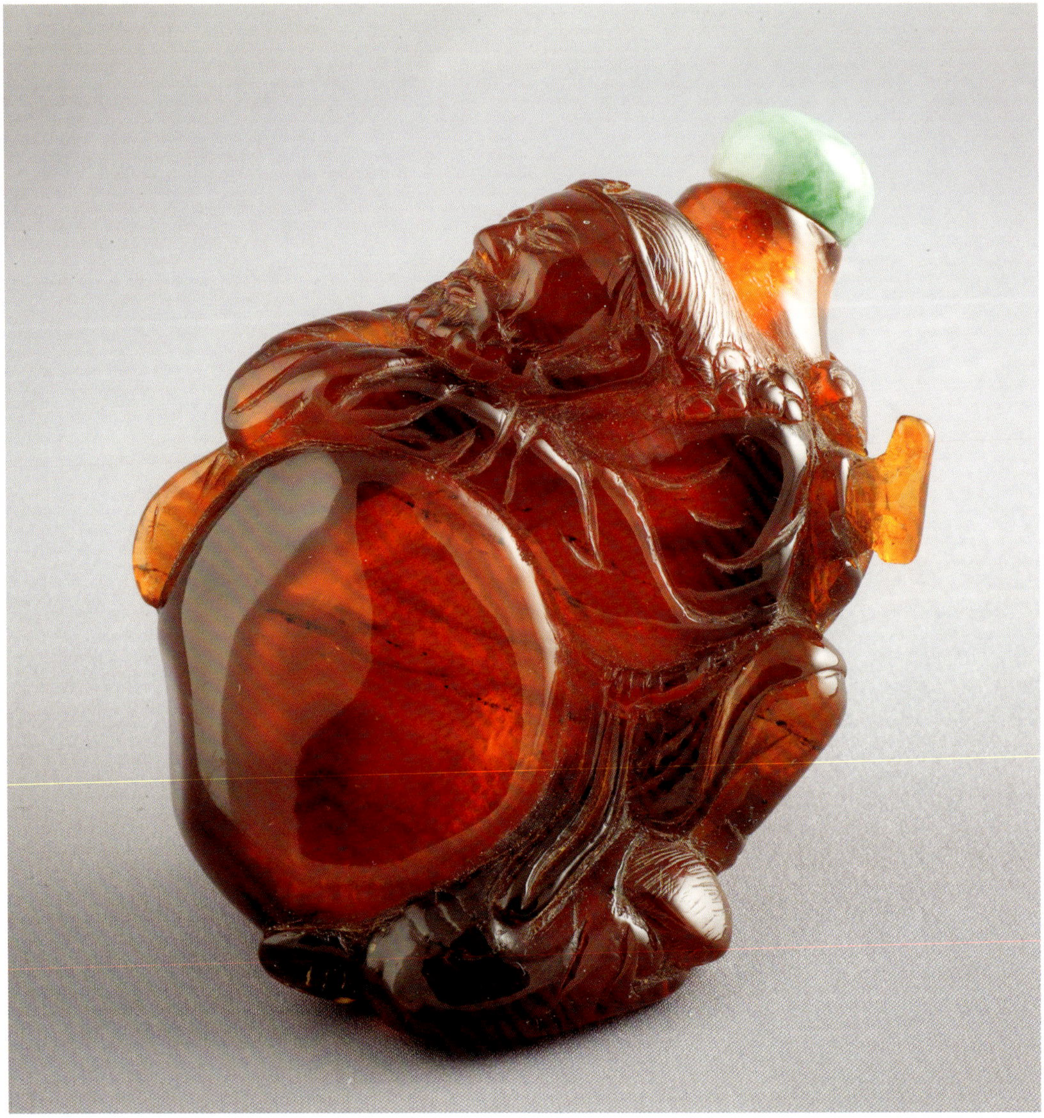

Snuff Bottle in the form of Budai resting his hands on his sack • **Tabatière** en forme de Bouddha riant avec les mains qui reposent sur son sac • Qing dynasty, 18th/19th century • amber • Francis and Kay Reif Collection, AGGV 1999.023.059

(left) **Snuff Bottle** with design of bats, monkeys, deer, butterfly, crane, bird and trees • (à gauche) **Tabatière** avec motif de chauves-souris, singes, cerfs, papillon, grue, oiseau et arbres • Qing dynasty, 18th/19th century • amber • Francis and Kay Reif Collection, AGGV 1999.023.062 • (middle) **Snuff Bottle** with design of plum tree, deer, goats, birds • (au milieu) **Tabatière** avec motif de prunier, cerf, chèvres et oiseaux • Qing dynasty, 18th/19th century • amber • Francis and Kay Reif Collection, AGGV 1999.023.052 • (right) **Snuff Bottle** with design of herons amidst lotus • (à droite) **Tabatière** avec motif de hérons dans les lotus • Qing dynasty, 18th/19th century • amber • Francis and Kay Reif Collection, AGGV 1999.023.060

(left) **Snuff Bottle** with design of *lingzhi* fungus stems • (à gauche) **Tabatière** ornée de tiges de champignons *lingzhi* • Qing dynasty, 18th/19th century • amber • Francis and Kay Reif Collection, AGGV 1999.023.047 • (right) **Snuff Bottle** with design of plant and large insect • (à droite) **Tabatière** ornée d'une plante et d'un gros insecte • Qing dynasty, 18th/19th century • amber • Francis and Kay Reif Collection, AGGV 1999.023.050

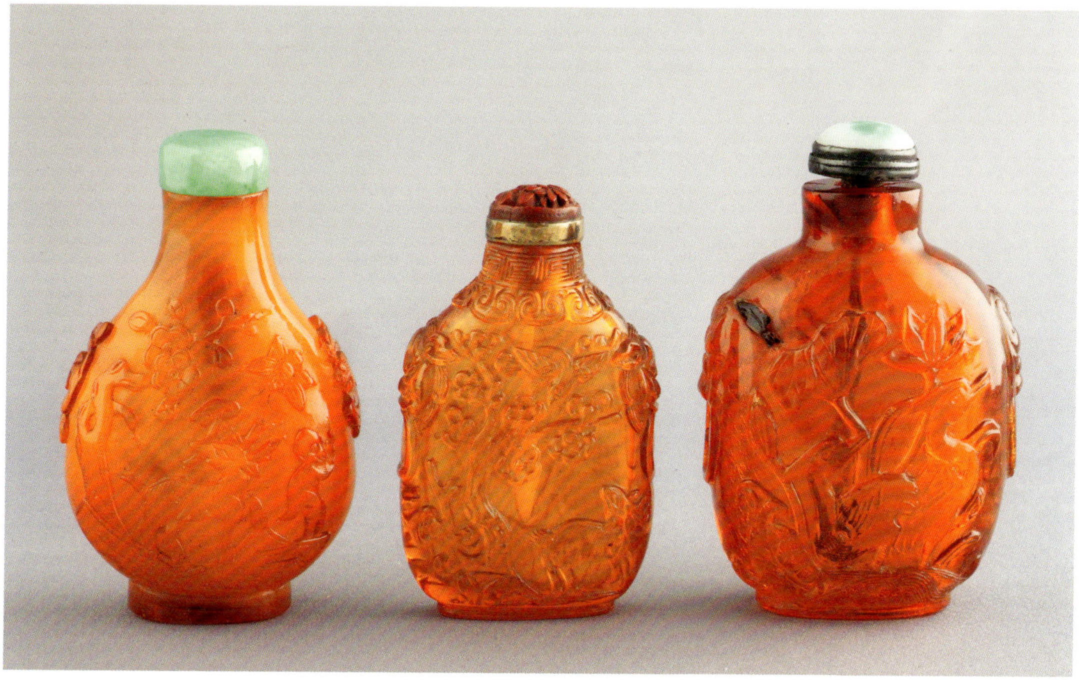

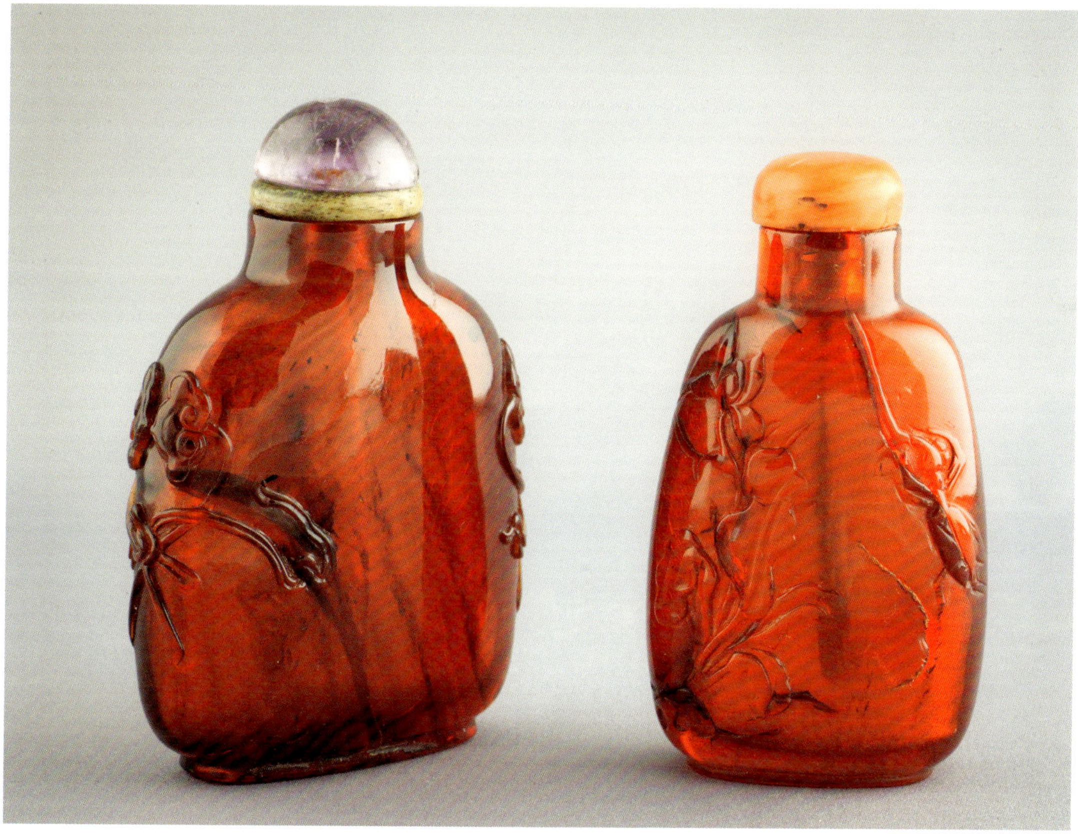

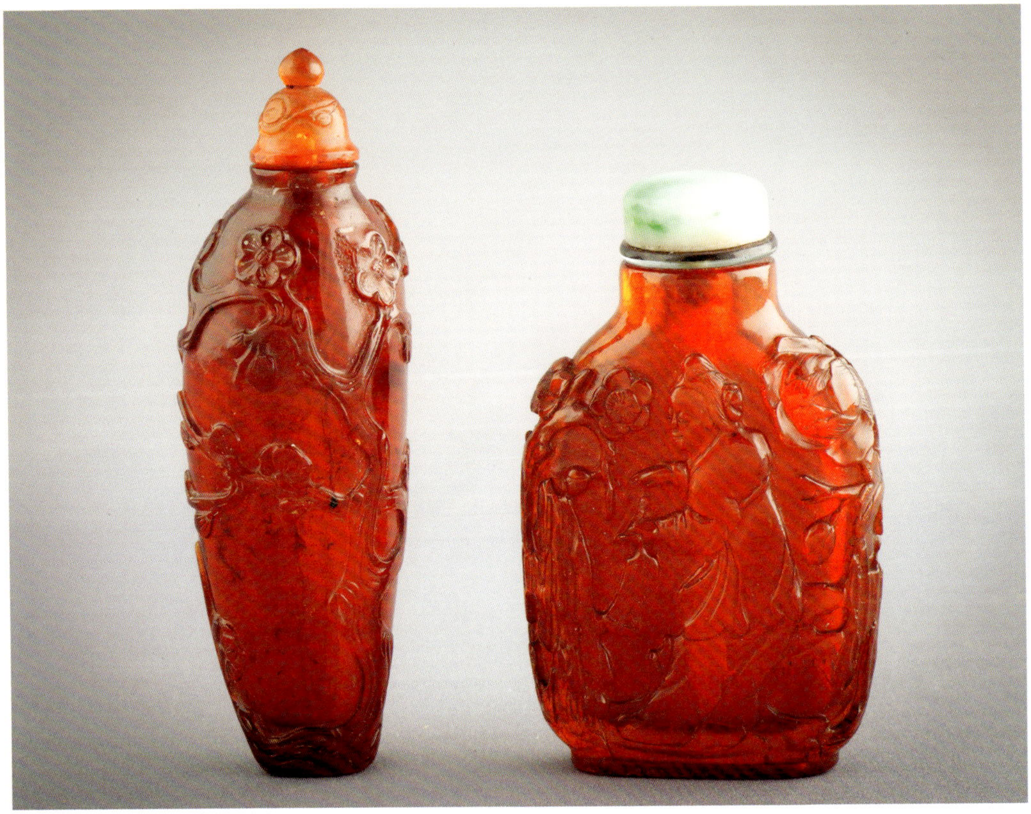

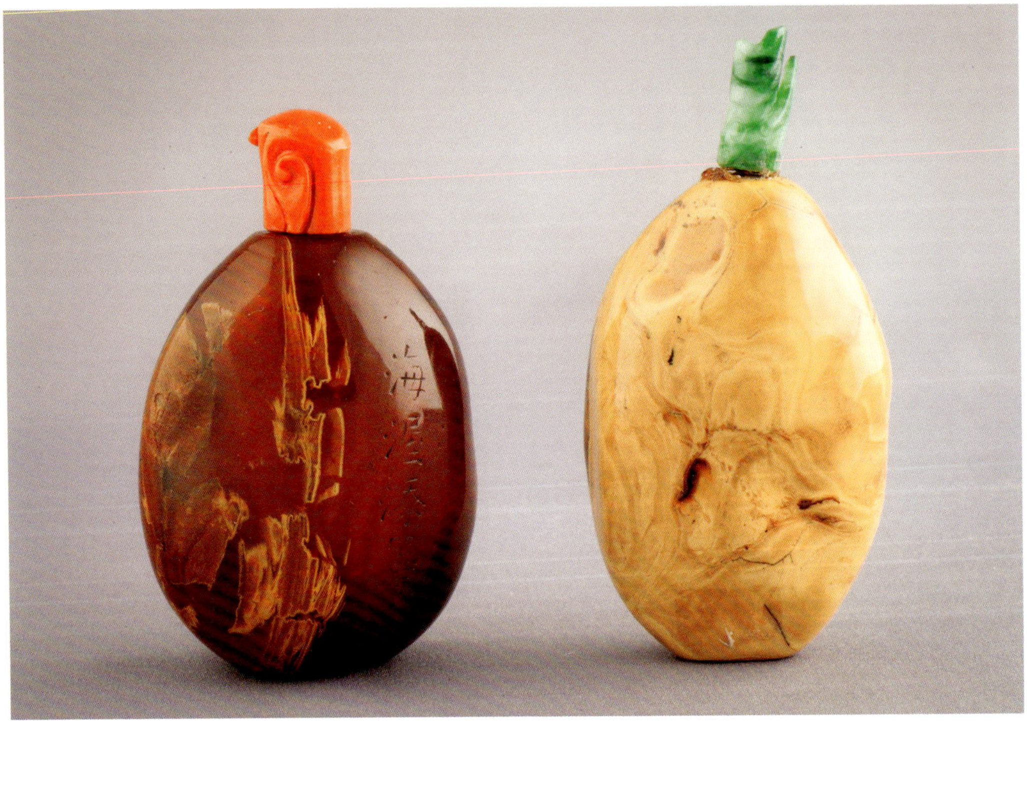

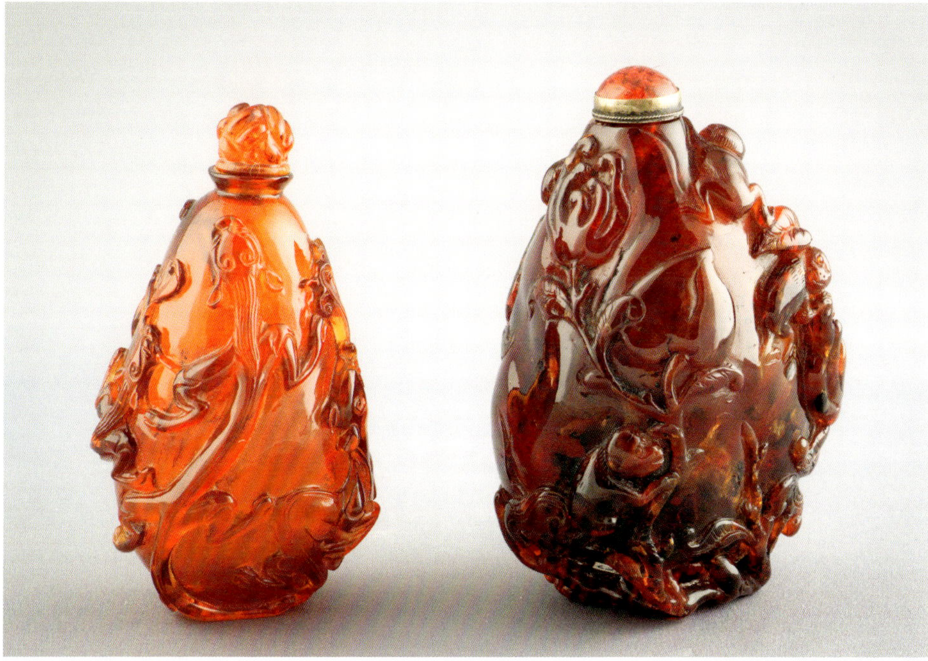

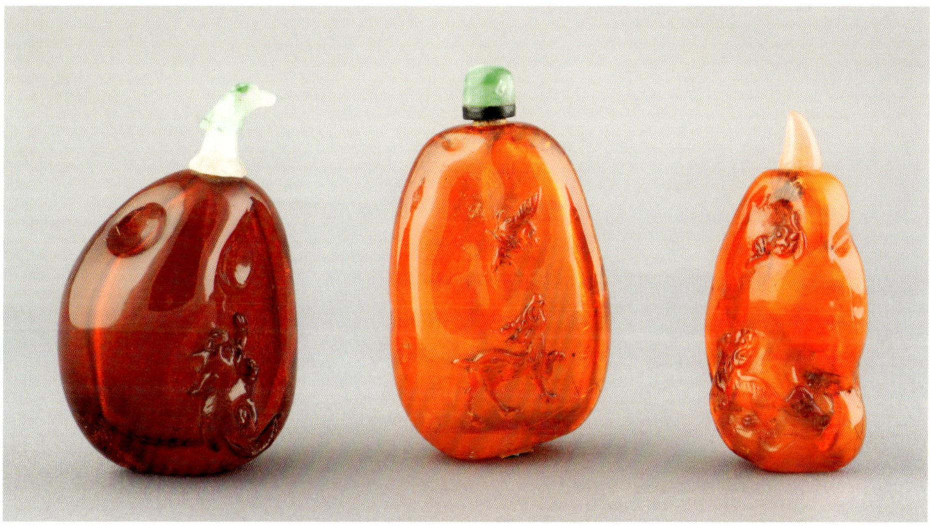

(left) **Snuff Bottle** with design of plum blossoms • (à gauche) **Tabatière** ornée de fleurs de prunier • Qing dynasty, 18th/19th century • amber • Francis and Kay Reif Collection, AGGV 1999.023.048 • (right) **Snuff Bottle** with design of a woman holding a bird with a man and boy on verso • (à droite) **Tabatière** avec motif représentant une femme tenant un oiseau; un homme et un garçon au verso • Qing dynasty, 18th/19th century • amber • Francis and Kay Reif Collection, AGGV 1999.023.049

Snuff Bottles in the form of pebbles, left has incised Chinese characters • **Tabatières** en forme de caillou; caractères chinois gravés du côté gauche • Qing dynasty, 18th/19th century • root amber • Francis and Kay Reif Collection, AGGV 2004.007.008, Gift of Helen Sawyer, AGGV 1995.012.001

Snuff Bottles in the form of a large pebble with design of coiling dragons/of monkeys climbing up a peach tree • **Tabatières** en forme d'un gros caillou avec motif de dragons qui se tortillent/singes qui grimpent dans un pêcher • Qing dynasty, 18th/19th century • amber • Francis and Kay Reif Collection, AGGV 1999.023.055, 1999.023.046

Snuff Bottles in the form of pebbles with design of a cat/of a deer and a bird/of a feline and a bat • **Tabatières** en forme de caillou avec motif de chat/cerf et oiseau/félin et chauve-souris • Qing dynasty, 18th/19th century • amber • Francis and Kay Reif Collection, AGGV 1999.023.053, 1999.023.051; 1999.023.056

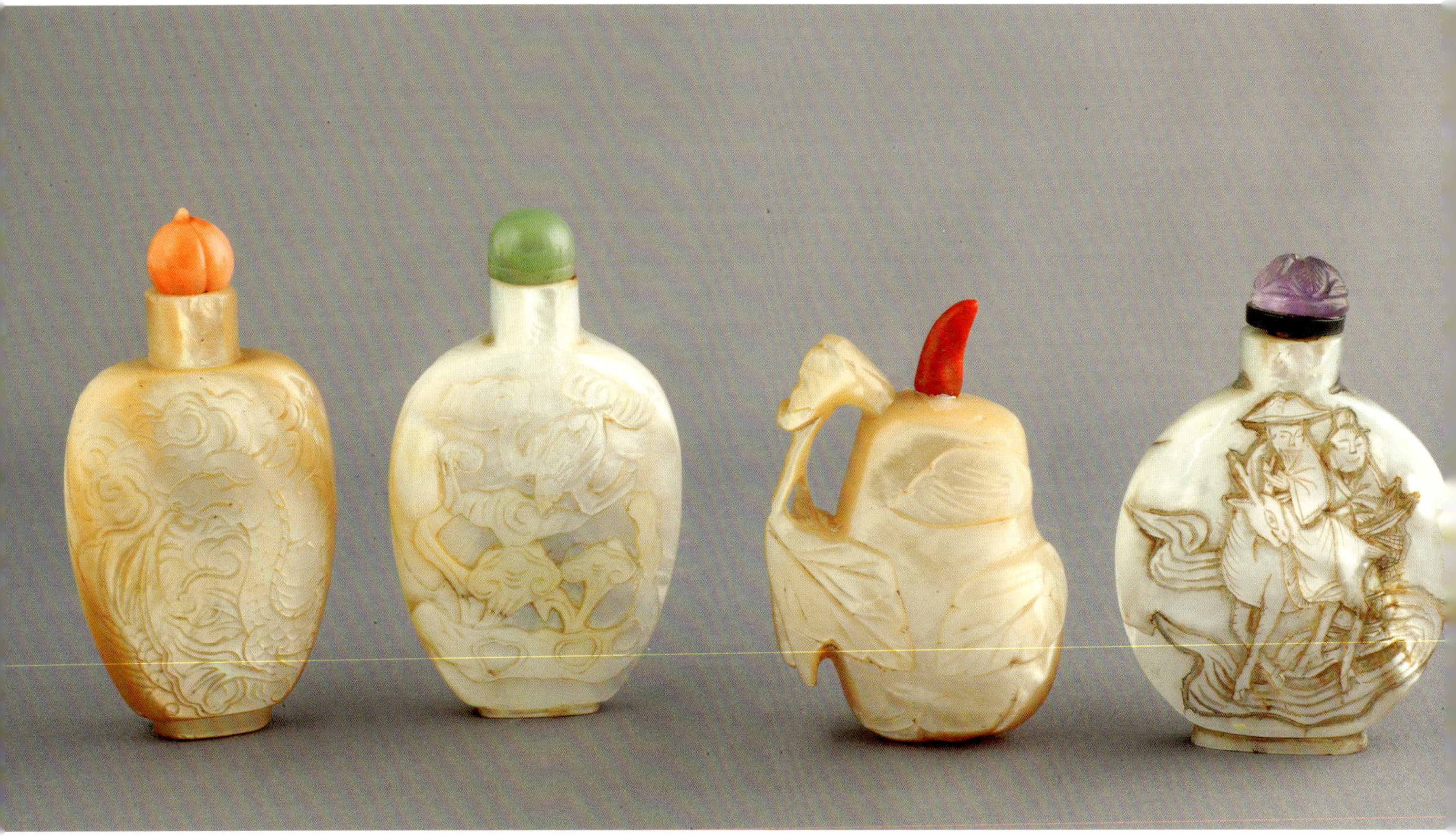

Snuff Bottles with design of dragon with bat on verso/of fungus and bats with dragon on verso/of leaves on a flattened gourd shape/of a man on horse with man on deer on verso • **Tabatières** avec motif de dragon; chauve-souris au verso/champignon et chauves-souris; dragon au verso/feuilles sur une gourde aplatie/cavalier à cheval; homme sur un cerf au verso • Qing dynasty, late 19th/early 20th century • mother-of-pearl • Gift of the Joy DeWeese-Wehen Estate, AGGV 2003.004.016, Gift of Helen Sawyer, AGGV 1995.012.060, 2004.007.007, Private Collection Intended Gift

Snuff Bottle with design of woman holding a fan with flowers and rock on verso • **Tabatière** avec motif représentant une femme tenant un éventail; fleurs et rocher au verso • early 20th century • mother-of-pearl, embellished with other stones • From the Collection of Bruce and Dorothy Brown, given by their son Tony Brown, AGGV 2005.034.003

Snuff Bottle with design of bat, ewers, plants and flowers • **Tabatière** avec motif de chauve-souris, aiguières, plantes et fleurs • Qing dynasty, late 19th/early 20th century • coral • Private Collection, Intended Gift

Snuff Bottles with relief design of bird on blossoming branch/of a pair of dragons on either side of the character for longevity *(shou)* • **Tabatières** avec motif en relief d'oiseau sur une branche en fleurs/ dragon de chaque côté du caractère de la longévité *(shou)* • late 19th/early 20th century • hornbill • Gift of Mrs. Shih Hua Chao and Mr. Shih Tsun Lee, AGGV 2007.009.006, 2007.009.005

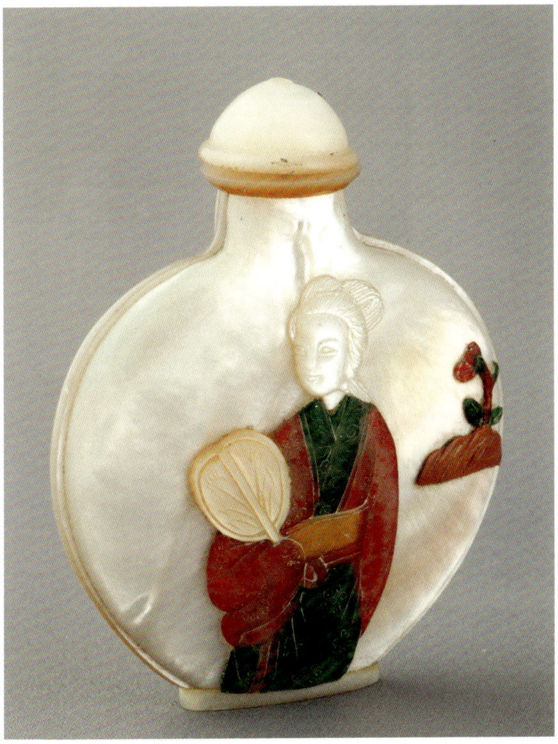

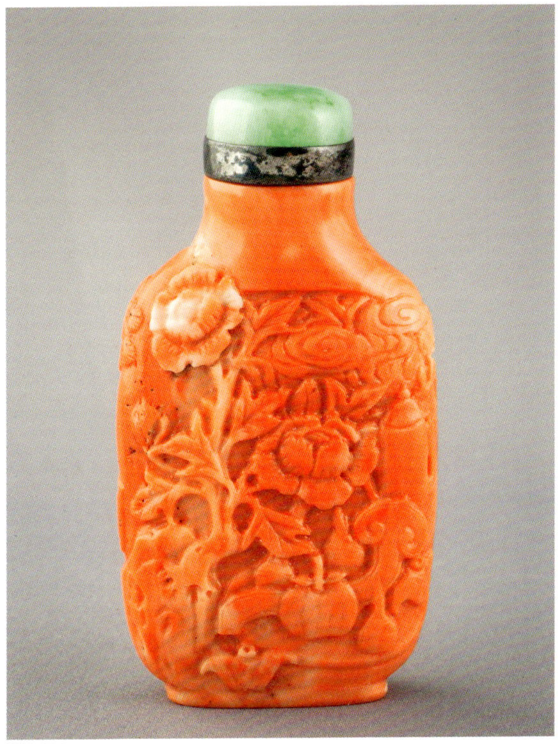

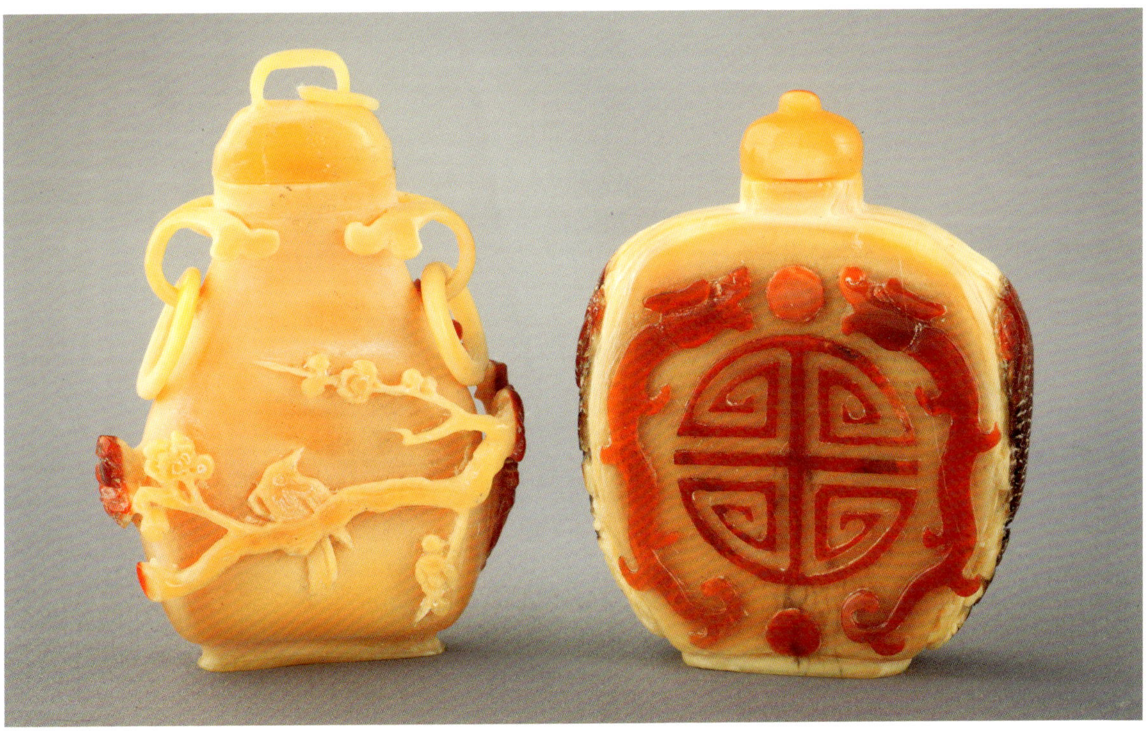

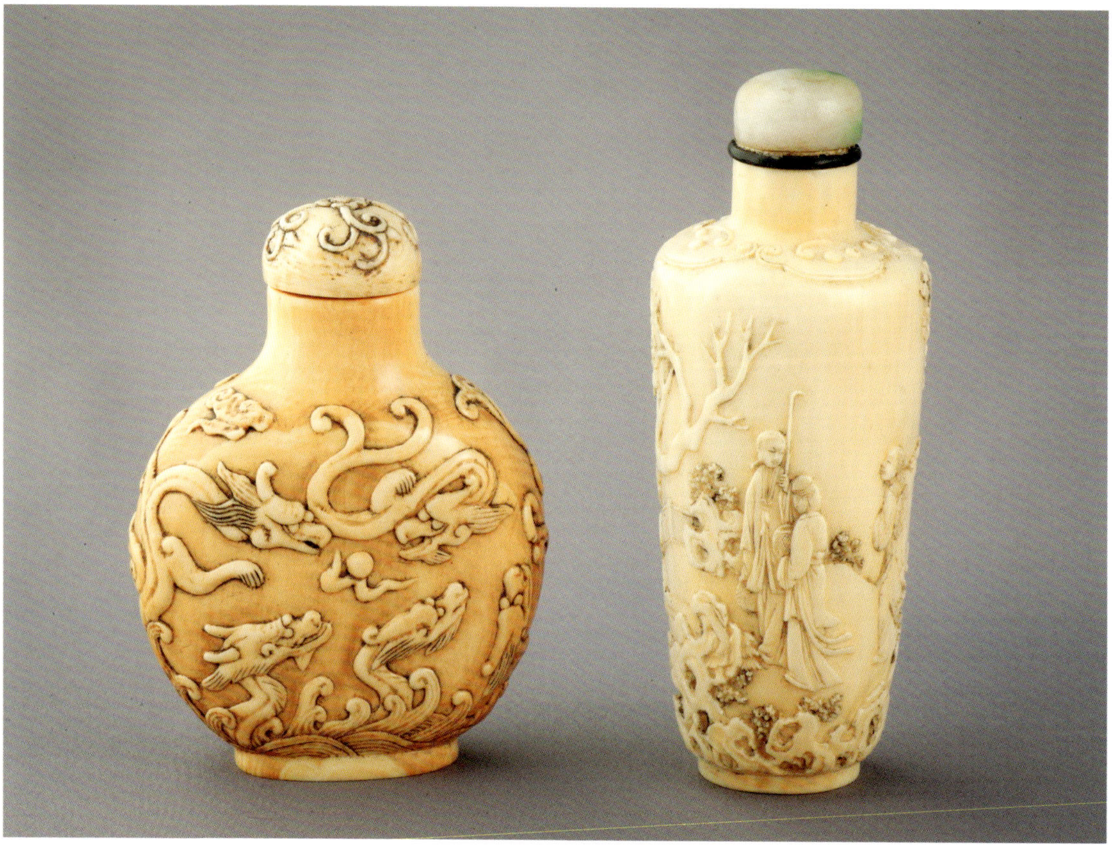

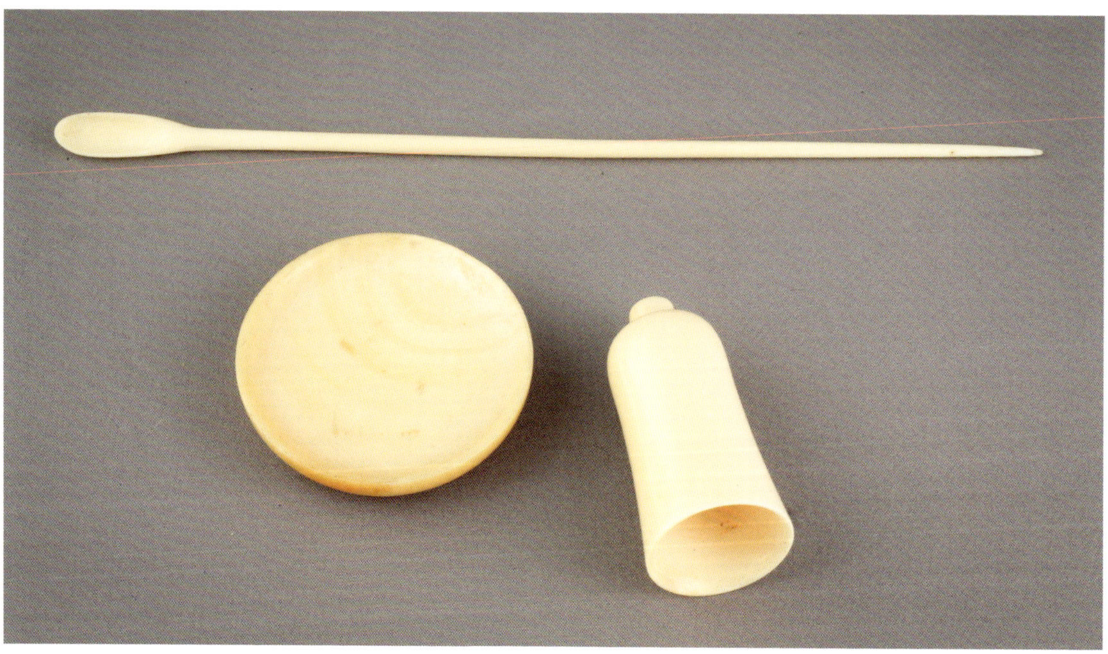

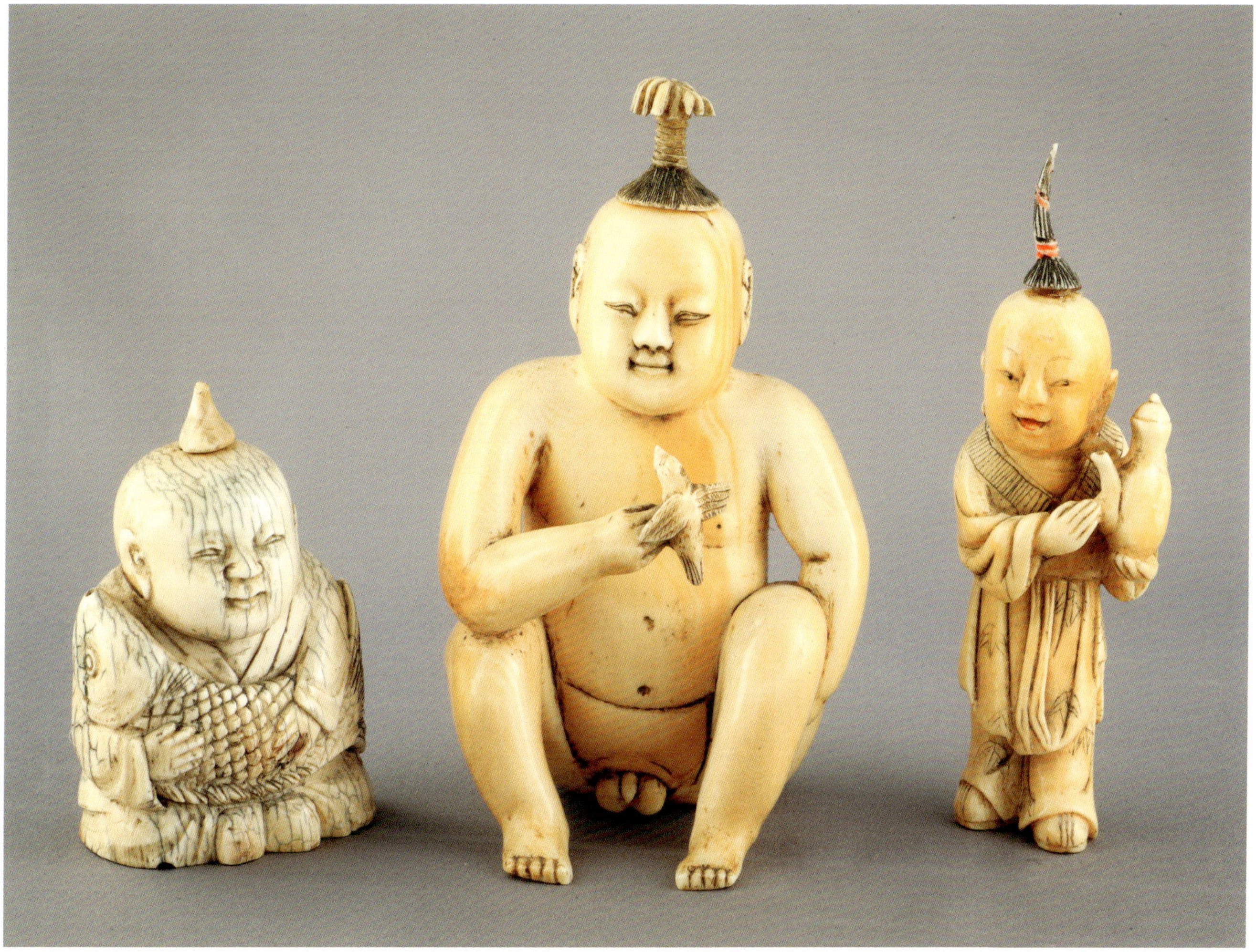

Snuff Bottles with designs of intertwined and elongated dragons/of figures in a garden • **Tabatières** avec motif de dragons allongés et entrelacés/personnages dans un jardin • Qing dynasty, 19th century • ivory • Francis and Kay Reif Collection, AGGV 2000.007.039 and .040

Set of Snuff Utensils – spoon, funnel and saucer • **Ensemble d'ustensiles à priser** : cuiller, entonnoir et soucoupe • Qing dynasty, 19th century • ivory • Francis and Kay Reif Collection, 2000.007.050.1

Snuff Bottles in the forms of seated and standing boys holding a carp, a bird and a ewer • **Tabatières** de la forme de garçons assis et debout tenant une carpe, un oiseau et une aiguière • Qing dynasty, 19th century • ivory • From the Collection of Bruce and Dorothy Brown, given by their son Tony Brown, AGGV 2005.034.002**,** Francis and Kay Reif Collection, AGGV 000.7.41, Rev. James M. Menzies Collection lent by his granddaughter, Nora Menzies

Japanese Snuff Bottles

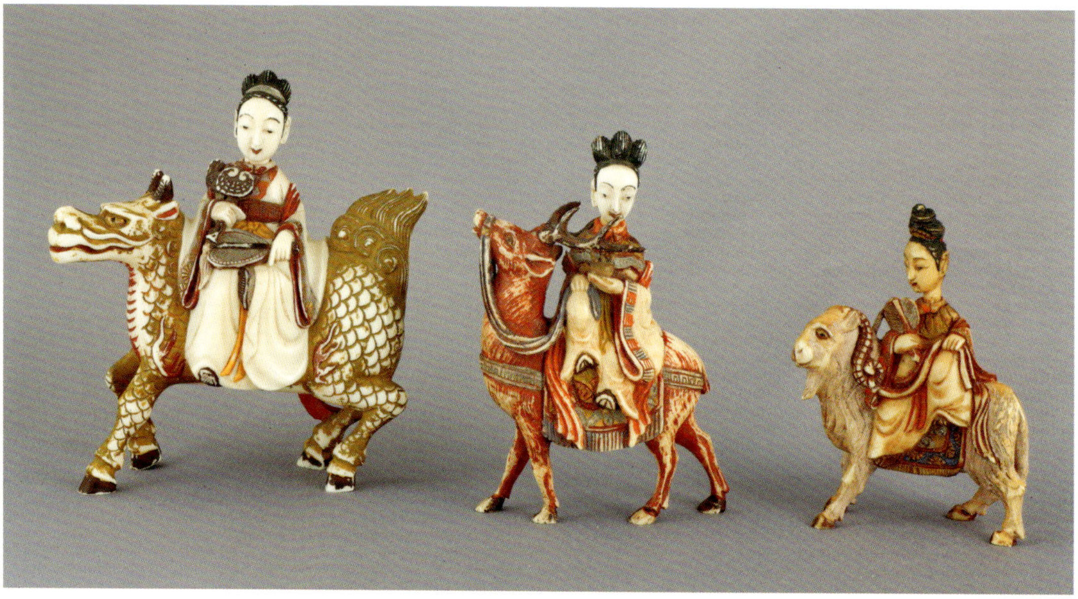

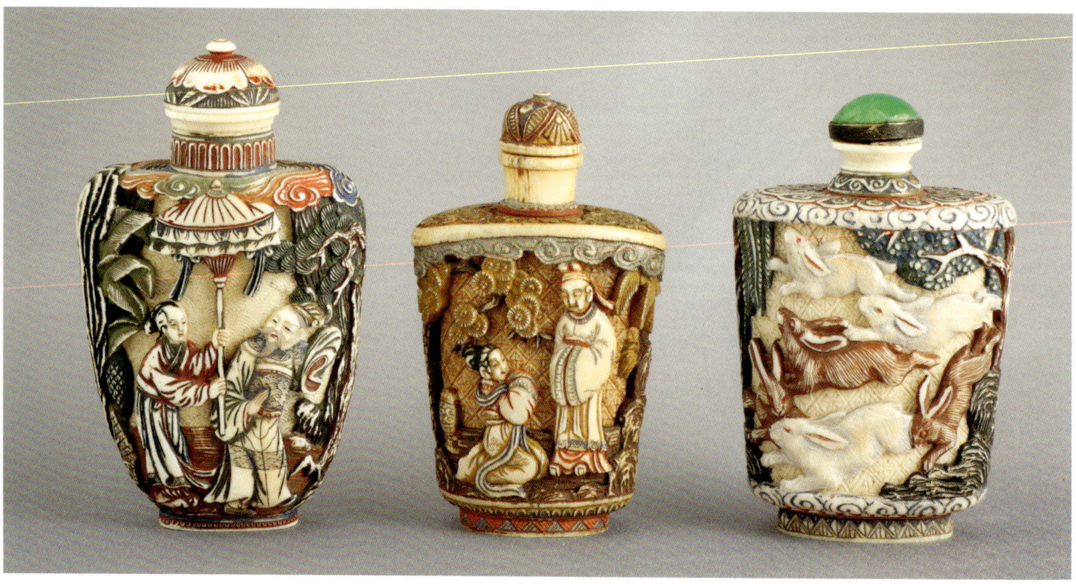

Snuff Bottles of women on a *kirin,* a stag and a goat Japanese • **Tabatières** ornées d'une femme sur un *kirin,* un cerf et une chèvre • Meiji period, late 19th century • ivory, pigments • Fred and Isbel Pollard Collection, AGGV 1965.098.001, Gift of Mrs. G. K. Roffey, AGGV 1975.034.001, Gift of Helen Sawyer, AGGV 1995.012.019

Snuff Bottles with a scene of courtiers/of figures in a garden/of rabbits • **Tabatières** ornées de scènes de courtisans/personnages dans un jardin/lapins • Japanese, Meiji period, late 19th century • carved ivory, pigments • Gift of the Joy DeWeese-Wehen Estate, AGGV 2003.004.002, Gift of Helen Sawyer, AGGV 1995.012.030, Gift of Kathleen Wilson Lambert Marpole, AGGV 1993.046.002

Snuff Bottle with a garden scene of two men drinking tea and a woman playing a stringed instrument • **Tabatière** ornée d'une scène représentant deux hommes qui prennent le thé et une femme qui joue d'un instrument à cordes dans un jardin • Japanese, Meiji period, late 19th century • ivory, red lacquer • Gift of Kathleen Wilson Lambert Marpole, AGGV 1993.046.001

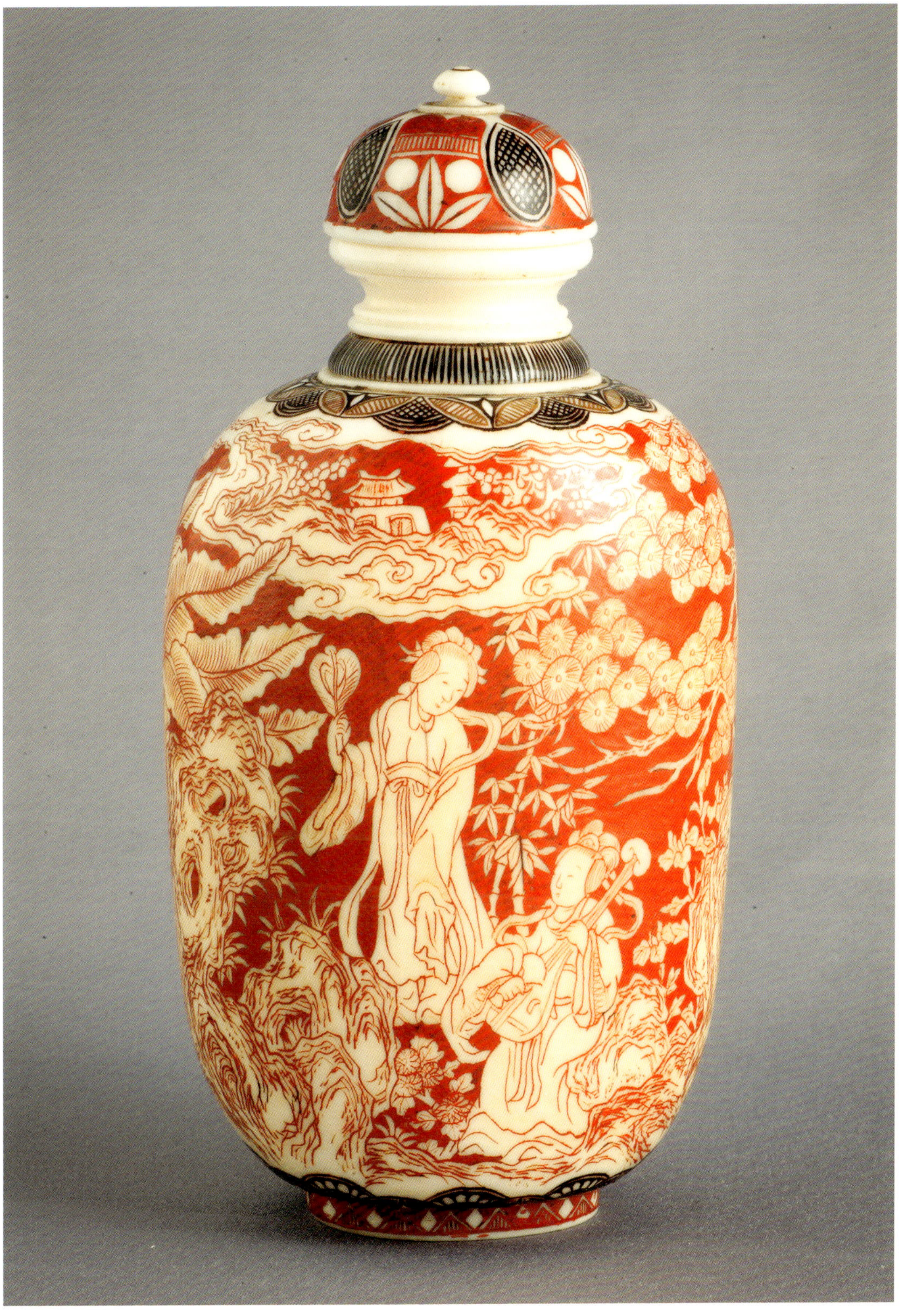

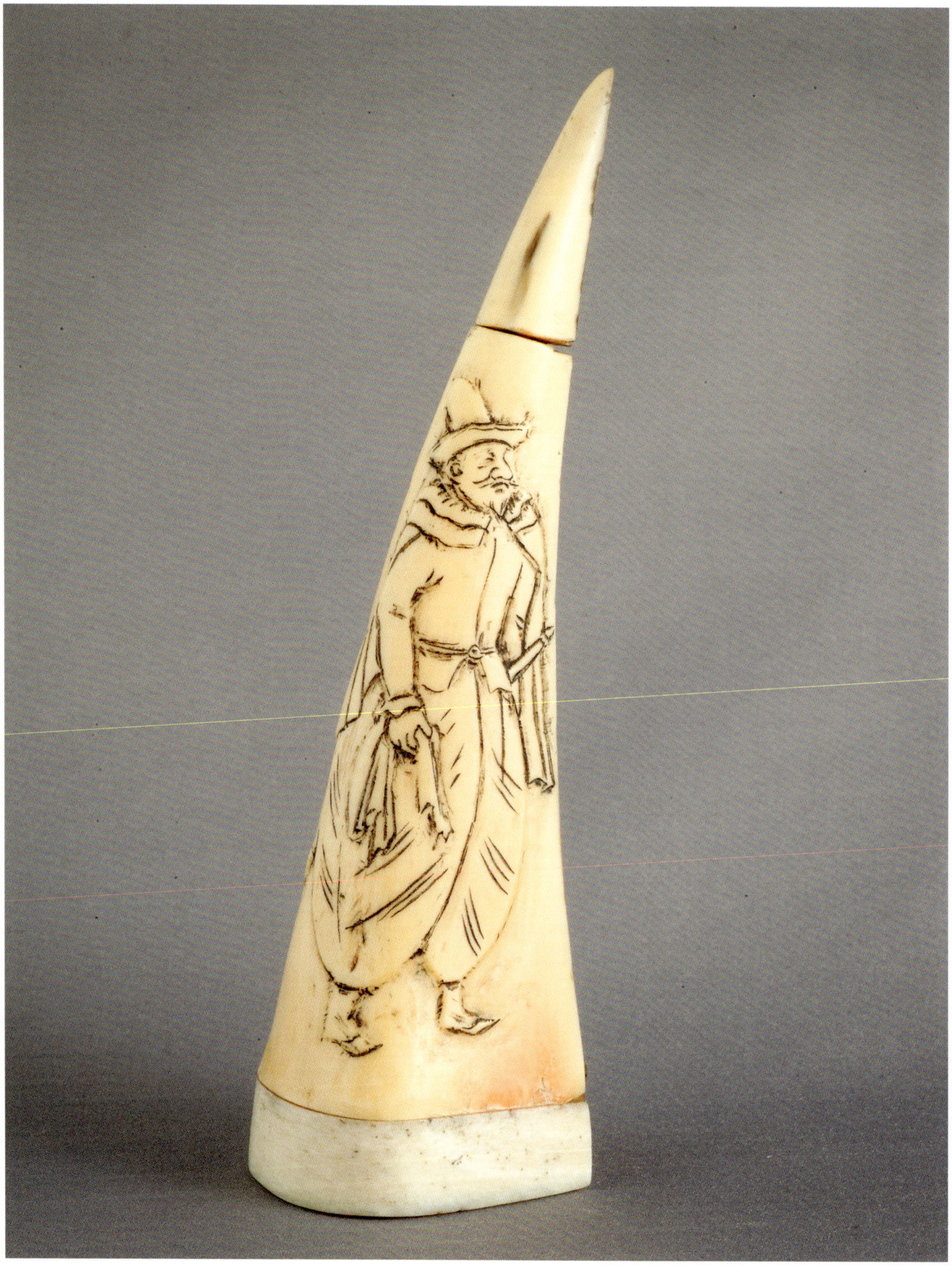

Snuff Bottle with design of a *Nanban* (foreign) trader • **Tabatière** avec motif de commerçant *Nanban* (étranger) • Japanese, Meiji period, late 19th century • Gift of Peggy Matheson and Family from the C.C. Knox Collection AGGV 2007.006.027

Chinese Opium Boxes

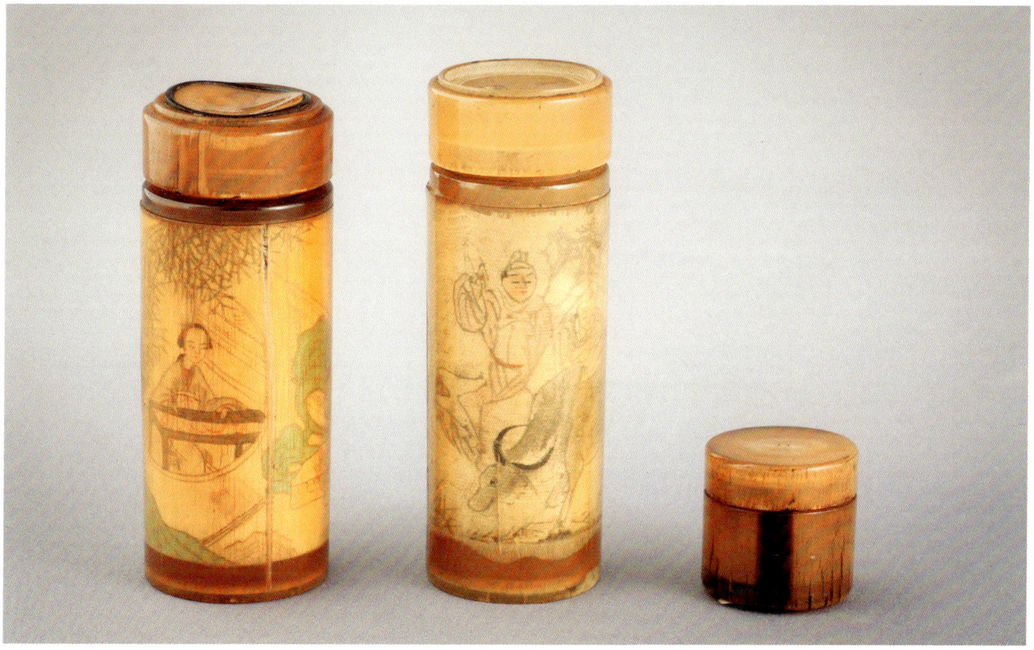

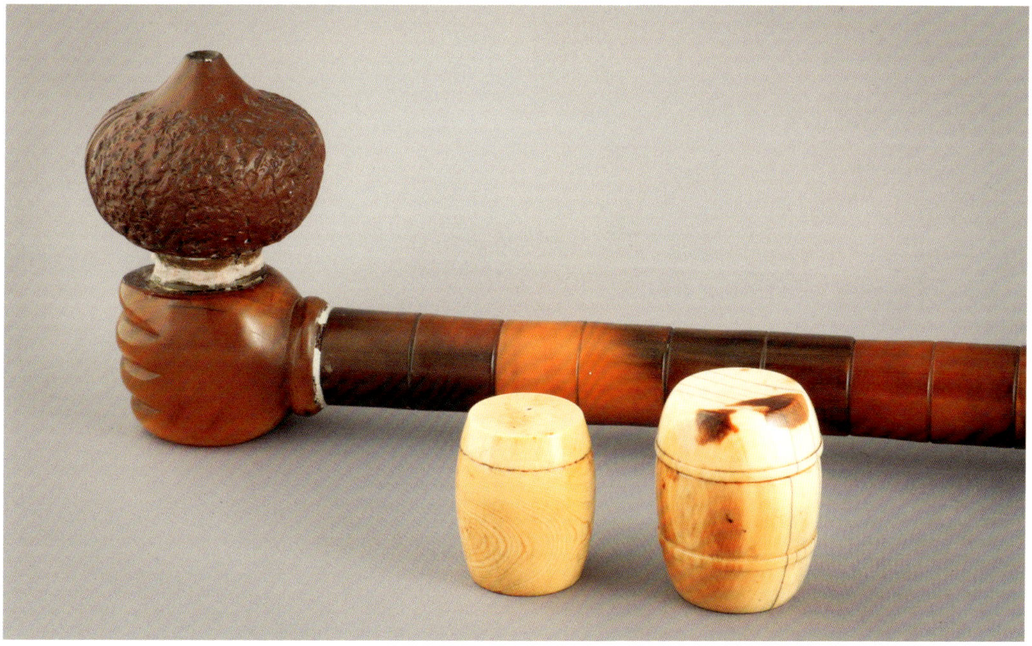

Opium Boxes with a painted design of figures and musicians in a garden/of a water buffalo and figures/ one undecorated • **Flacons à opium** avec motif peint représentant des personnages et des musiciens dans un jardin/boeuf d'Asie et personnages/dont un non décoré • Qing dynasty, 19th century • horn, painted paper • Gift of Hy Eiley, AGGV 2003.012.011, 2002.028.009 and 009

Opium Pipe • Pipe à opium • Qing dynasty, 19th century • amber, pottery • Francis and Kathleen Reif Collection, AGGV 1998.042.012 • **Opium Boxes • Flacons à opium** • Qing dynasty, 19th century • ivory • Francis and Kathleen Reif Collection, AGGV 2000.007.047 and .048

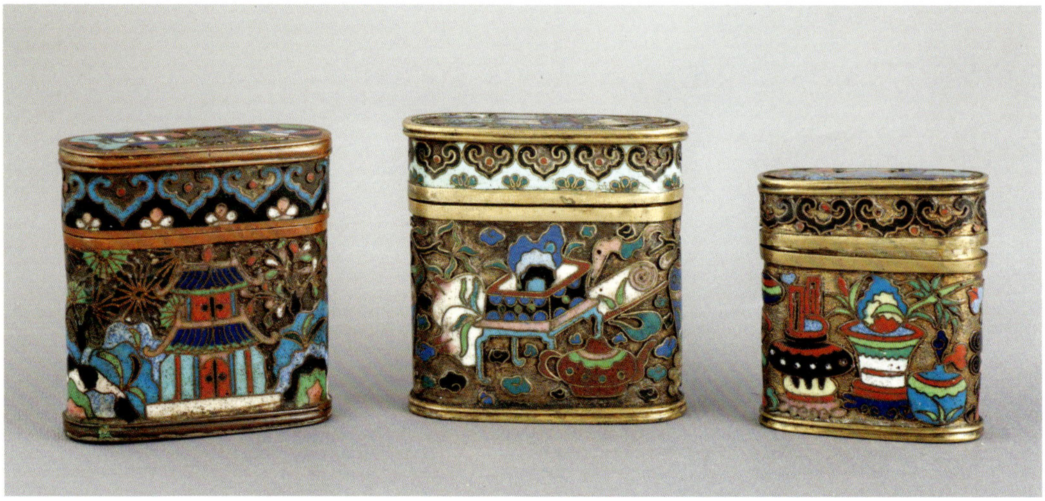

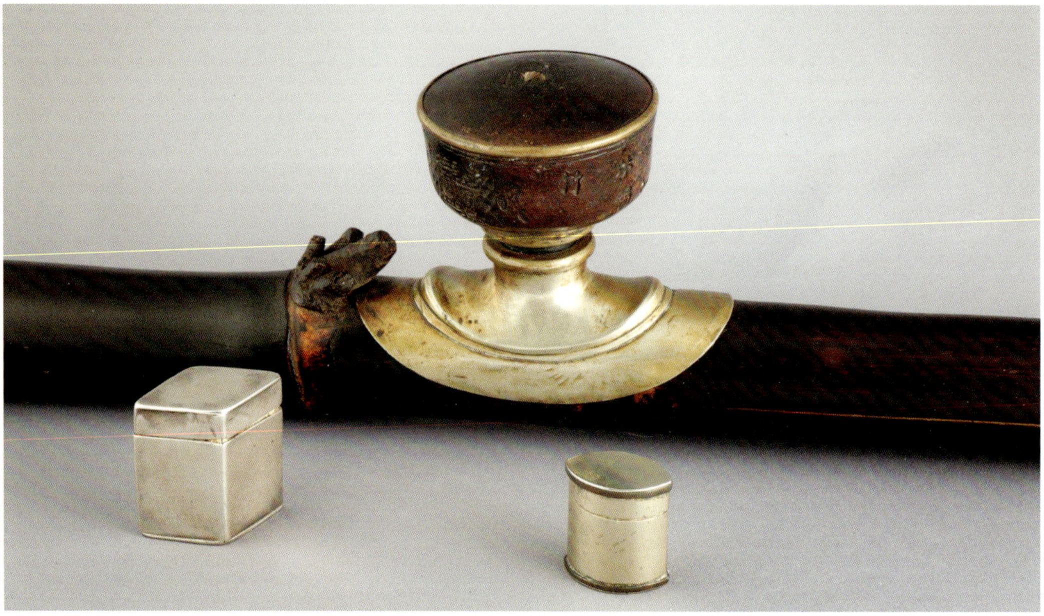

Opium Boxes with scene of pavilions/of objects for the scholar's desk • **Flacons à opium** ornés de pavillons/objets de pupitre de lettré • Qing dynasty, 19th century • cloisonné/champlevé • Gift of Hy Eiley, AGGV 2003.012.007 , 2003.012.006, 2003.012.001

Opium Pipe • **Pipe à opium** • Qing dynasty, 19th/early 20th century • bamboo, ivory, bronze • Gift of Bruce and Dorothy Brown, AGGV 2004.008.031 • **Opium Boxes** • **Flacons à opium** • Qing dynasty, 19th century • silver • Gift of Hy Eiley, AGGV 2003.012.016, 2003.012.008

Opium Boxes with relief design of intertwined flowers, leaves and a bat/of chrysanthemums • **Flacons à opium** avec motif en relief de fleurs enchevêtrées, feuilles et chauve-souris/chrysanthèmes • Qing dynasty, 19th century • silver, enamels • Gift of Hy Eiley, AGGV 2002.028.014, 2003.012.009

(left) **Opium Box** with porcupine quills (middle, right) • (à gauche) **Flacon à opium** orné d'aiguilles de porc-épic • **Opium Boxes** with scenes of architecture in landscape and geometric design/peony • (au milieu, à droite) **Flacons à opium** ornés de scènes d'architecture dans un paysage et d'un motif géométrique/pivoine, bambou et pin • Qing dynasty, 19th century • bamboo and pine niello ware • Gift of Hy Eiley, AGGV 2003.012.012, 2003.012.002, 2002.028.010

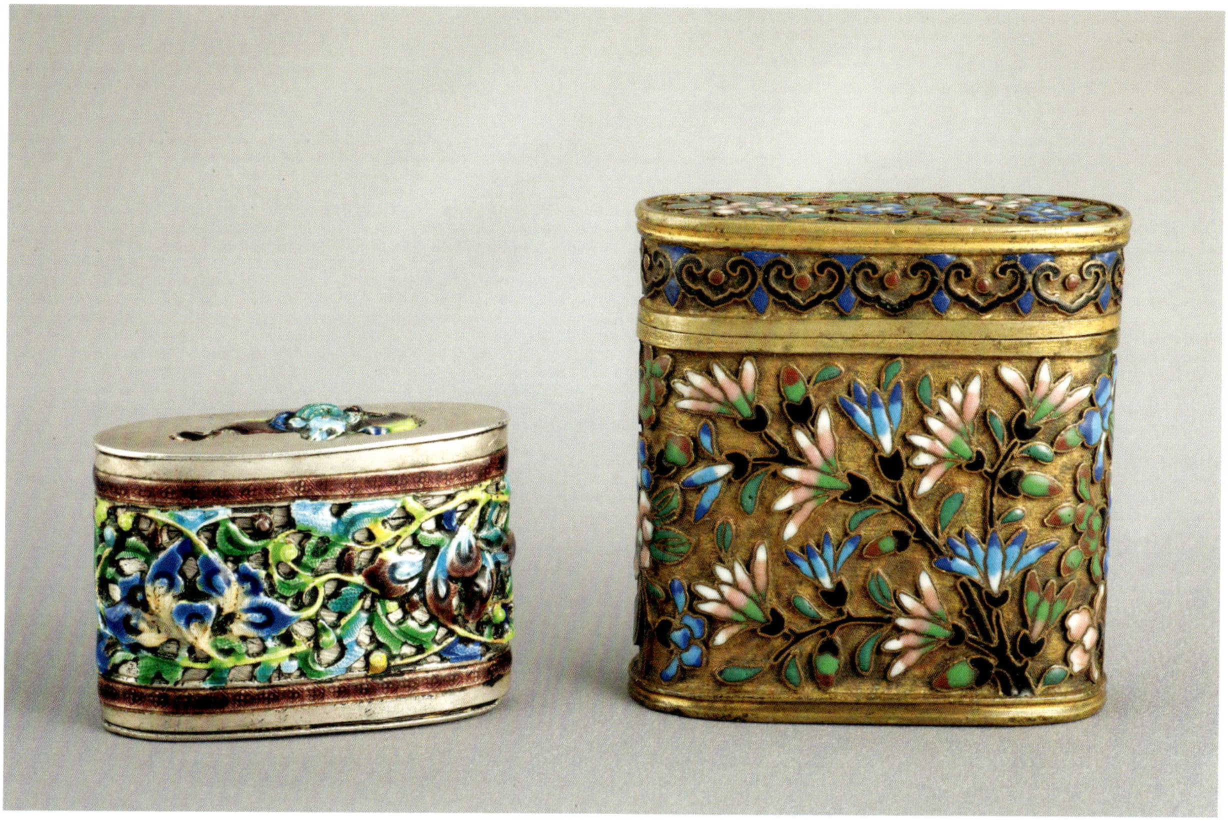

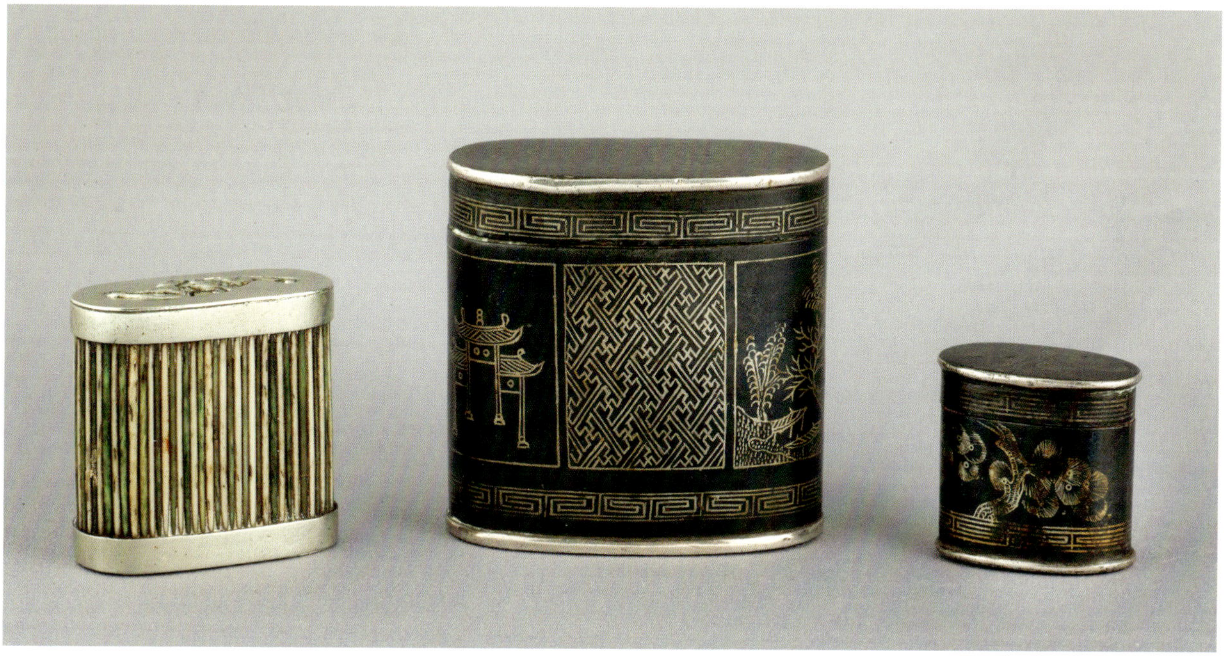

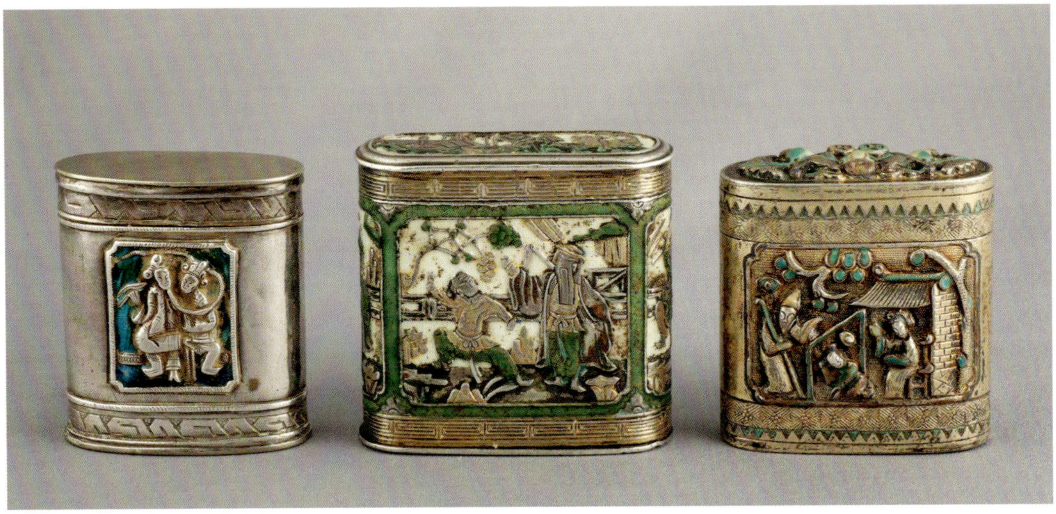

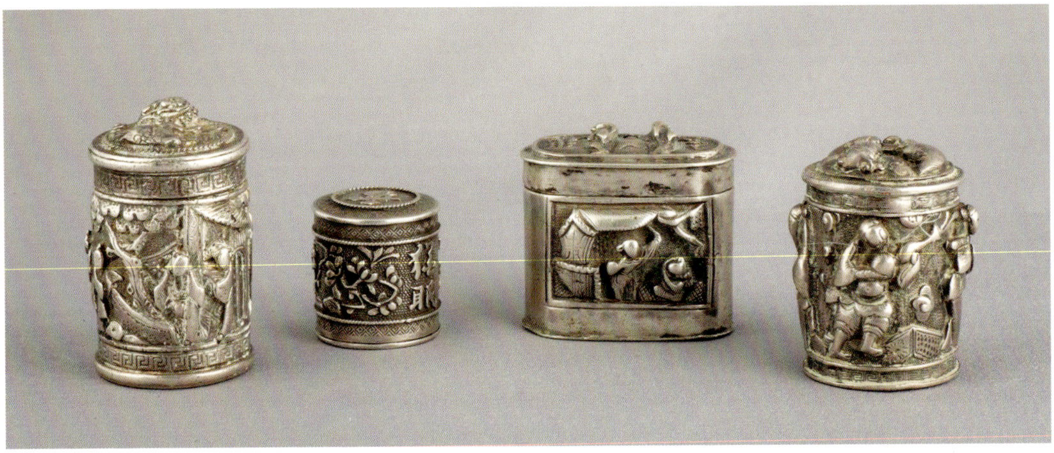

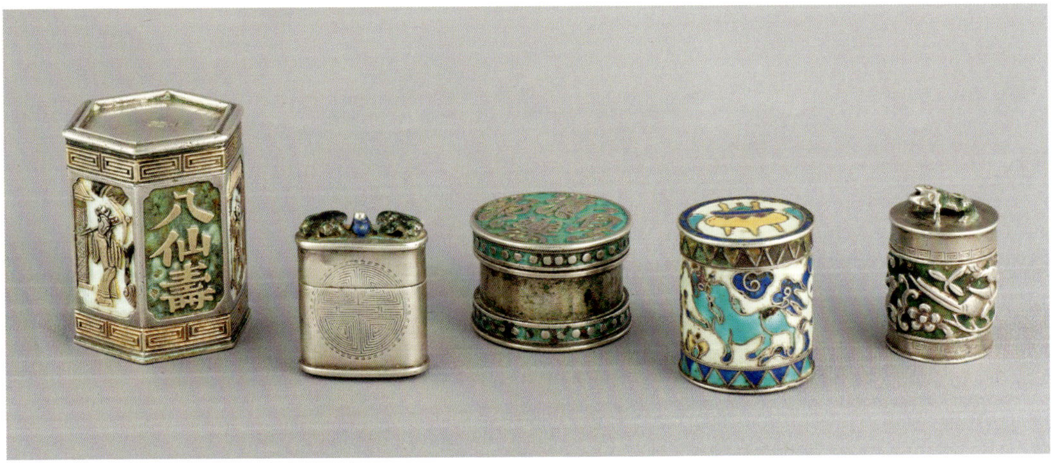
八仙壽

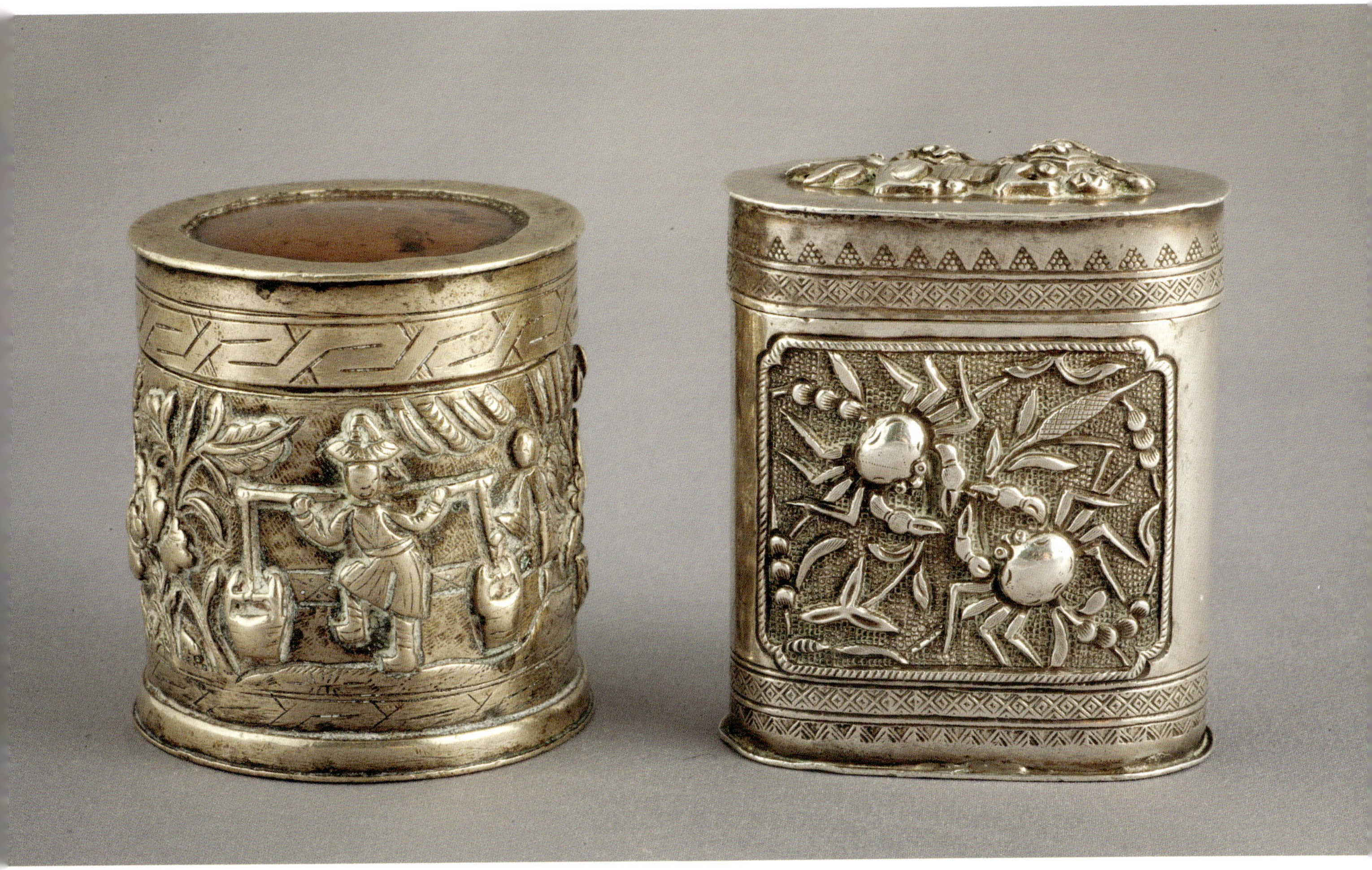

Opium Boxes with relief design of scenes from an opera/of figures in a garden • **Flacons à opium** avec motif en relief représentant des scènes d'un opéra/ personnages dans un jardin • Qing dynasty, 19th century • silver, enamel • Gift of Hy Eiley, AGGV 2003.012.004 and .018, 2002.028.007

Opium Boxes with relief design of figures and buildings in a garden/of Chinese characters and prunus branches/of figures near a building and playing chess/of four of the Eight Immortals • **Flacons à opium** avec motif en relief représentant des personnages et des édifices dans un jardin/caractères chinois et branches de cerisier/ personnages près d'un édifice jouant aux échecs/quatre des huit immortels • Qing dynasty, 19th century • silver • Gift of Hy Eiley, AGGV 2002.028.004, .011 and .012, 2003.028.007

Opium Boxes with scenes of figures in a garden alternating with Chinese characters and signed Yuan Feng/of frogs on top and a large incised character for long life (*shou*) with Chinese inscription – "In one breath the refined pill of immortality is used up. Use it and eat." on verso/of Chinese characters on top/of lion dogs and incense tripod/of a frog, birds and flowers • **Flacons à opium** ornés d'une scène représentant des personnages dans un jardin alternant avec des caractères chinois/grenouilles sur le dessus d'un gros caractère chinois de longévité gravé (*shou*) avec l'inscription suivante au verso : « Dans un souffle, la pilule raffinée de l'immortalité est utilisée. Utilise-la et mange. »/caractères chinois sur le dessus/chiens lions et trépied brûle-parfum/ grenouille, oiseaux et fleurs • Qing dynasty, 19th century • silver, enamel • Gift of Hy Eiley, AGGV 2002.028.002, 2003.012.017, 2003.012.013, 2003.012.010, 2003.012.014

Opium Boxes with relief design of a figure carrying water in a landscape/of two crabs, crane, deer by flowering plum tree • **Flacons à opium** avec motif en relief représentant un porteur d'eau dans un paysage/deux crabes, une grue, un cerf près d'un prunier en fleurs • Qing dynasty, 19th century • silver, one with copper • Gift of Hy Eiley, AGGV 2002.028.0013 and.003

Chinese Pith Painting

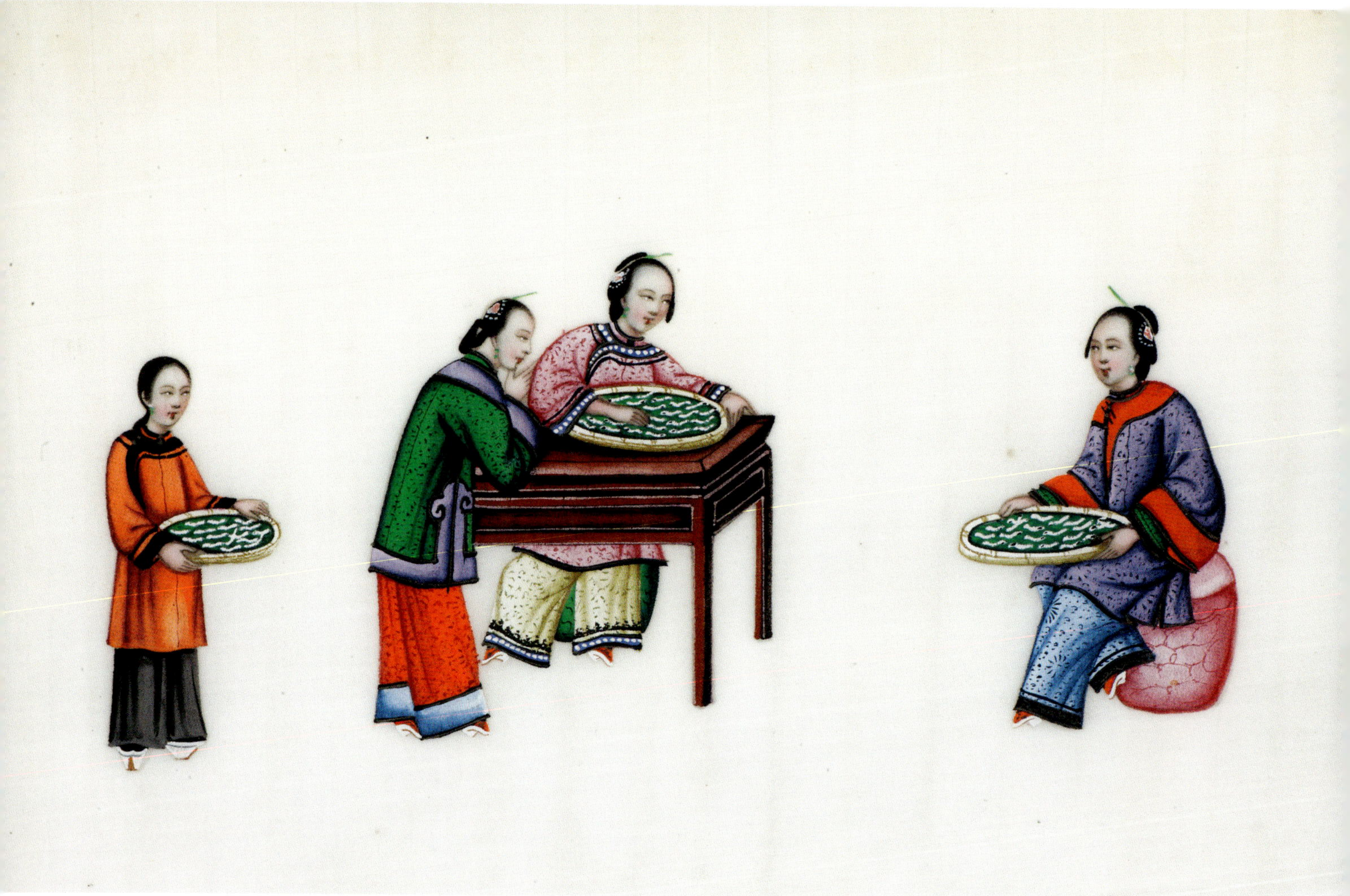

Chinese Pith Painting – Twelve Scenes showing the process of silk manufacture, four illustrated: 1. selecting the worms, 2. dying the cocoons, 3. winding the silk from the cocoons placed in boiling water, 4. preparing the warp • **Peintures chinoises sur papier de moelle** – Douze scènes représentant les étapes de la fabrication de la soie, Quatre illustrées : 1. Choix des vers, 2. Teinte des cocons, 3. Déroulement de la soie des cocons placés dans l'eau bouillante, 4. Préparation de la fibre • artist unknown, 19th century • ink and colours on pith paper • AGGV SC764.1-.12

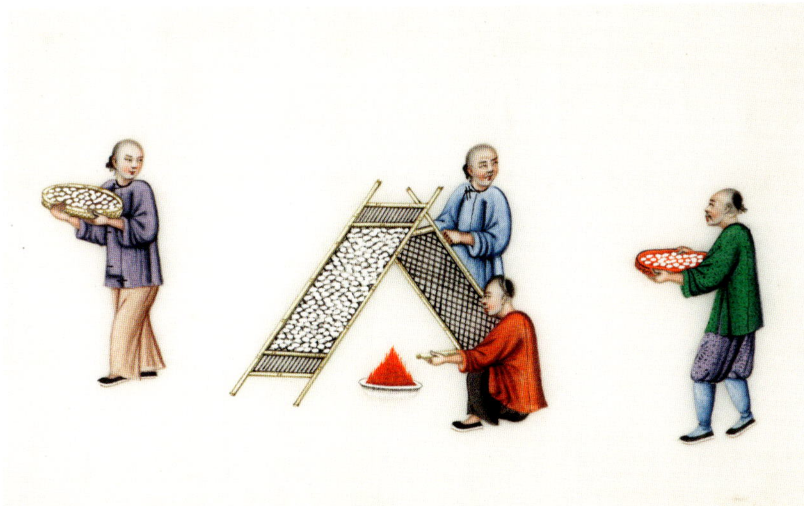

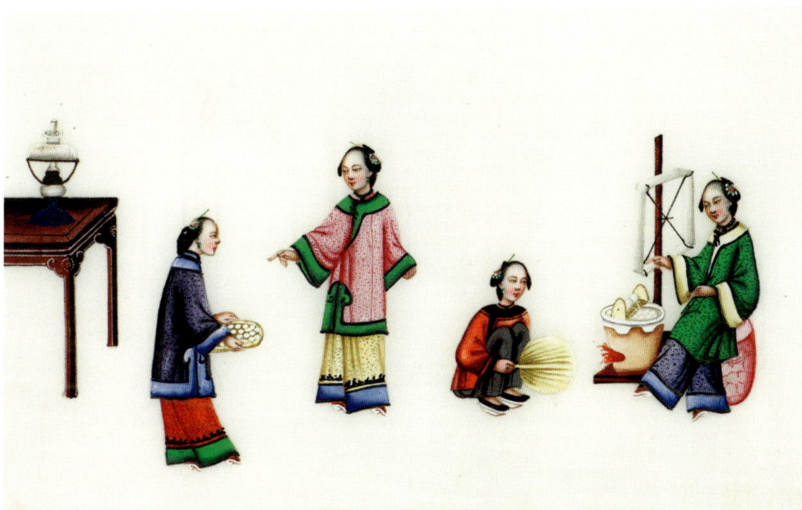

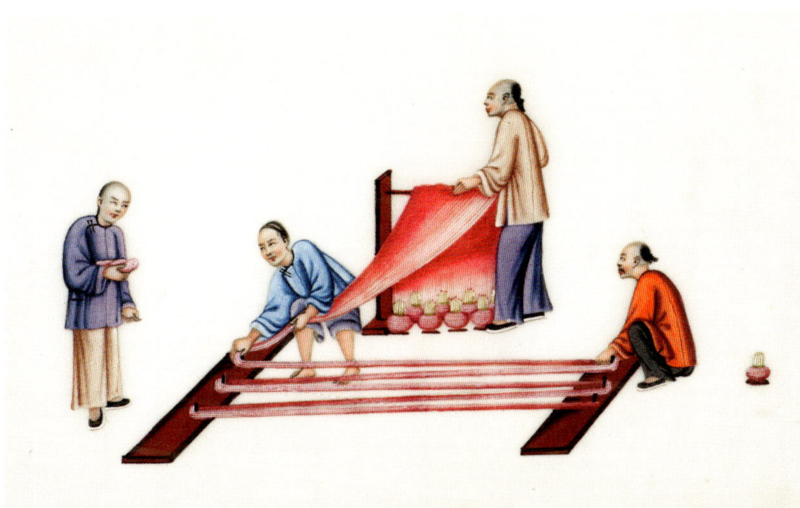

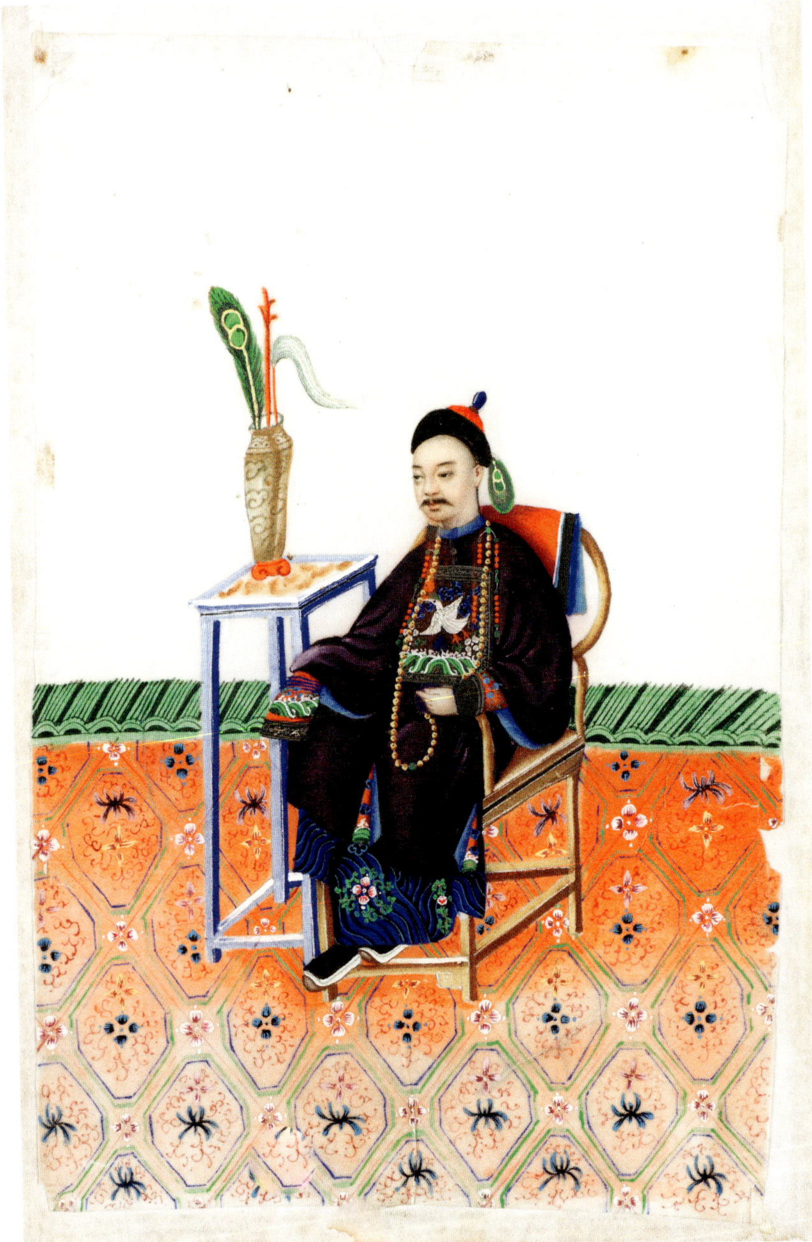

Chinese Pith Painting – Series of portraits of seated men and women, two illustrated • **Peintures chinoises sur papier de moelle** – Série de portraits de femmes et d'hommes assis, deux illustrés • artist unknown, 19th century • ink and colours on pith paper • Gift of Colin C. Graham, AGGV 2004.004.009

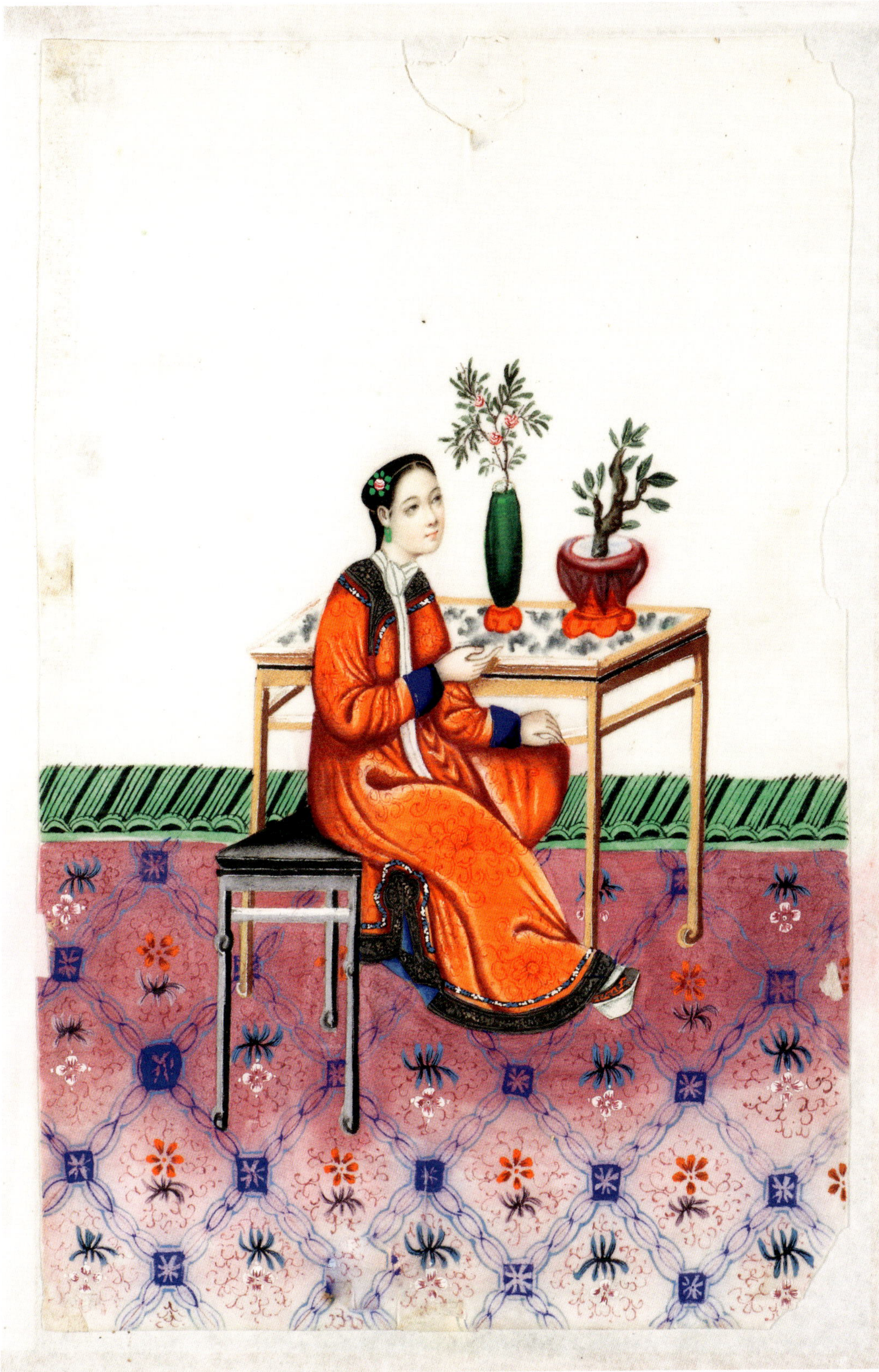

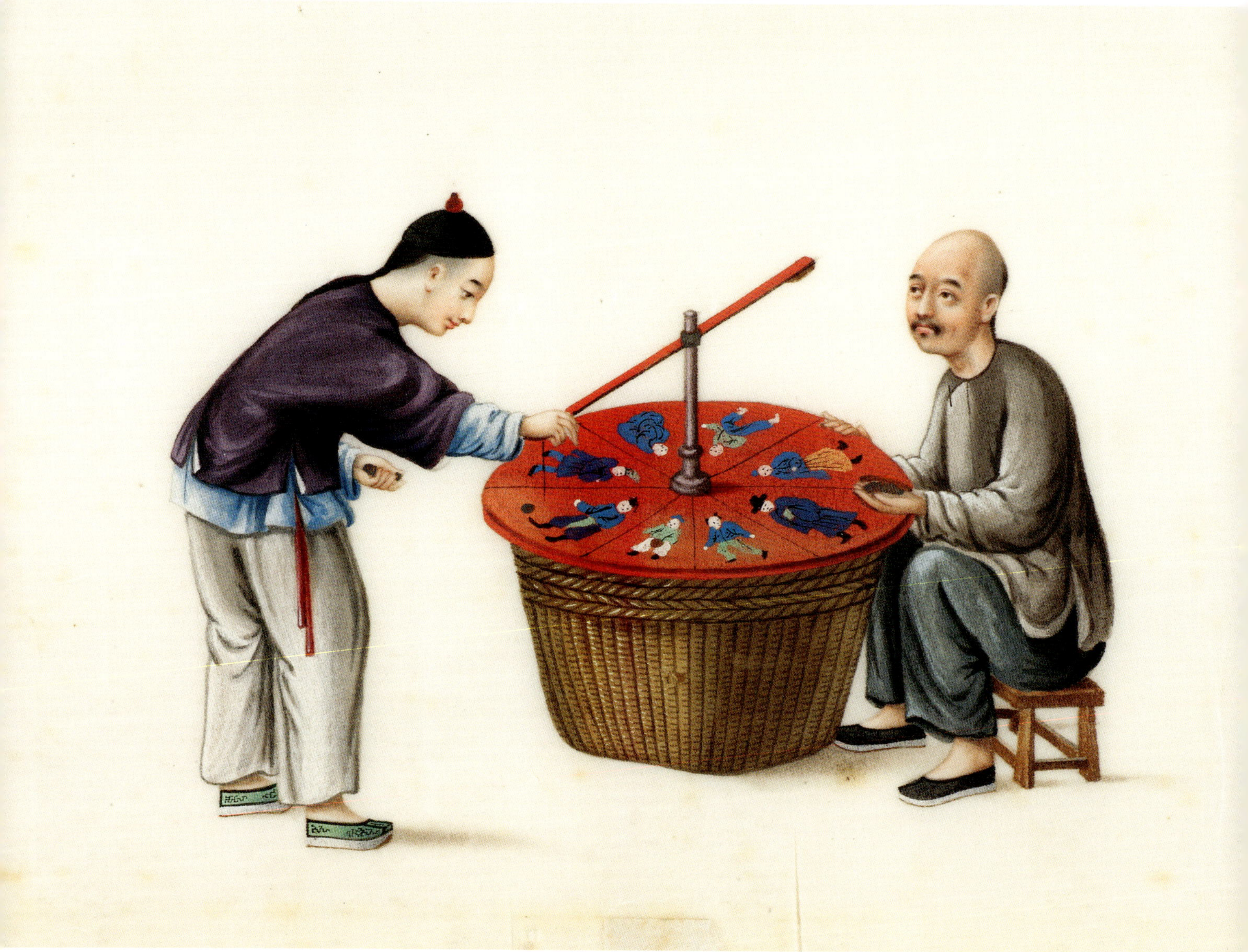

Chinese Pith Painting – Set of twelve traditional games. Illustrated: 1. two men with a spinning top, 2. two men with spinning apparatus, 3. two men involved with cricket fighting, 4. two men involved with quail fighting, Cricket and quail fighting were popular pastimes in old China and often associated with gambling, 5. two men playing chess (*xiangqi*), 6. two men playing dominoes, women, 7. one Manchu and one Han Chinese playing with fortune sticks on a bed, 8. women, one Manchu and one Han Chinese playing a game at a table • **Peintures chinoises sur papier de moelle** – Ensemble de douze jeux traditionnels. Illustrés : 1. Deux hommes avec une toupie, 2. Deux hommes avec un article servant à filer, 3. Deux hommes et un combat de crickets, 4. Deux hommes et un combat de cailles, les batailles de crickets et de cailles étaient un passe-temps populaire dans la Chine d'autrefois et étaient souvent associées aux gageures. 5. Deux hommes qui jouent aux échecs (*xiangqi*), 6. Deux hommes qui jouent aux dominos, 7. Femmes, une mandchoue et l'autre chinoise de la dynastie Han, qui jouent avec des bâtons de fortune sur un lit, 8. Femmes, une mandchoue et l'autre chinoise de la dynastie Han, qui jouent à un jeu à une table • artist unknown, 19th century • ink and colours on pith paper • Gift of Miss Keanes, SC125.1 - .12

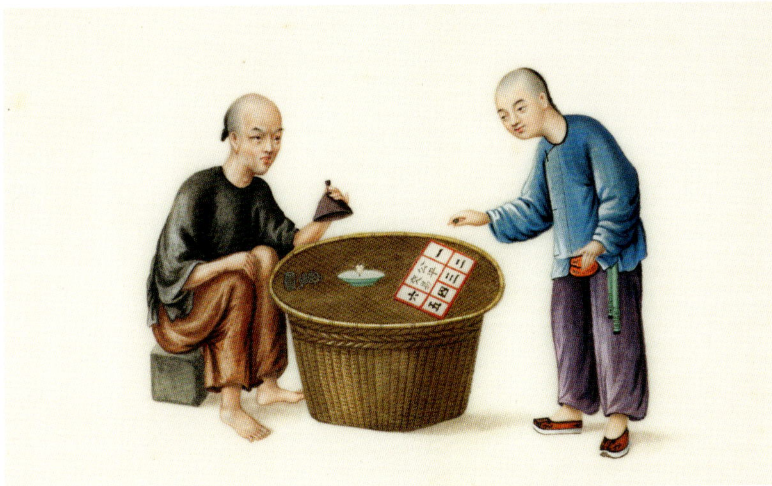
一
二
三
四
五
六

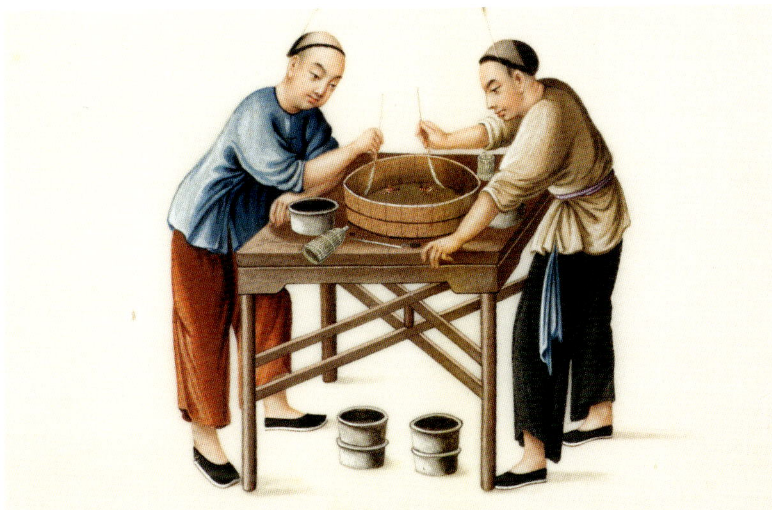

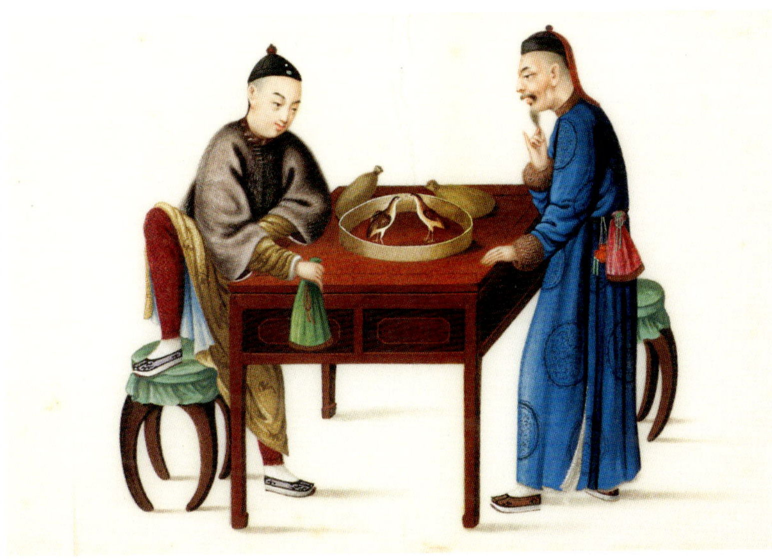

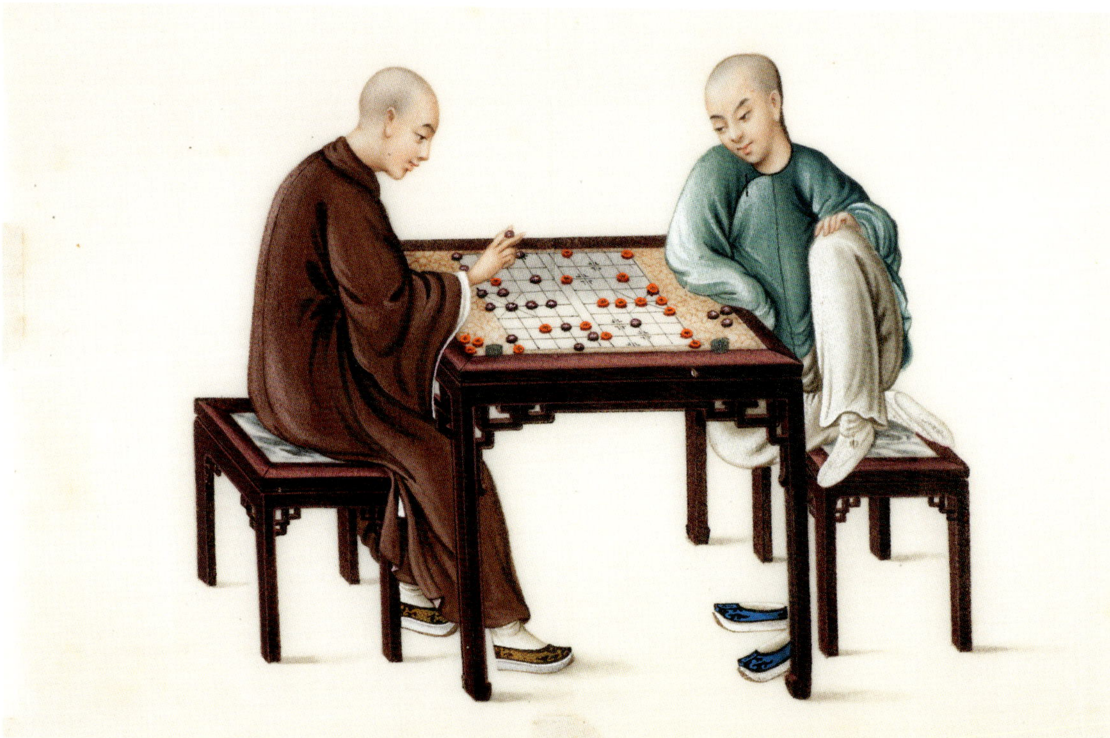

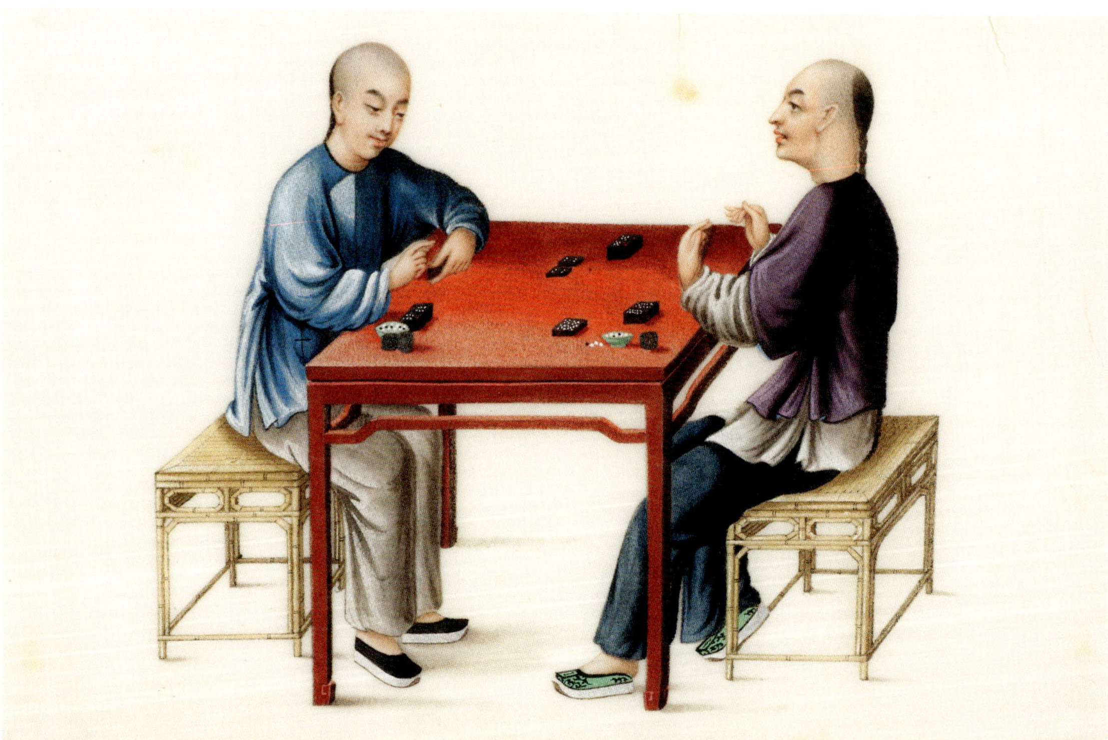

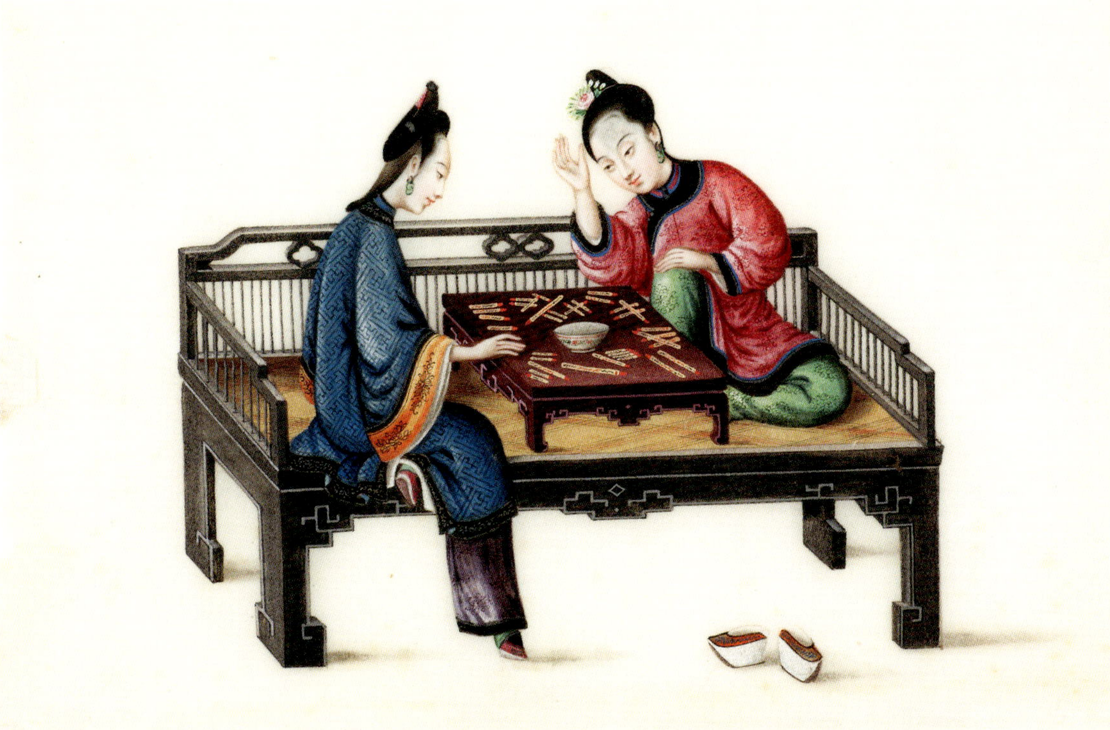

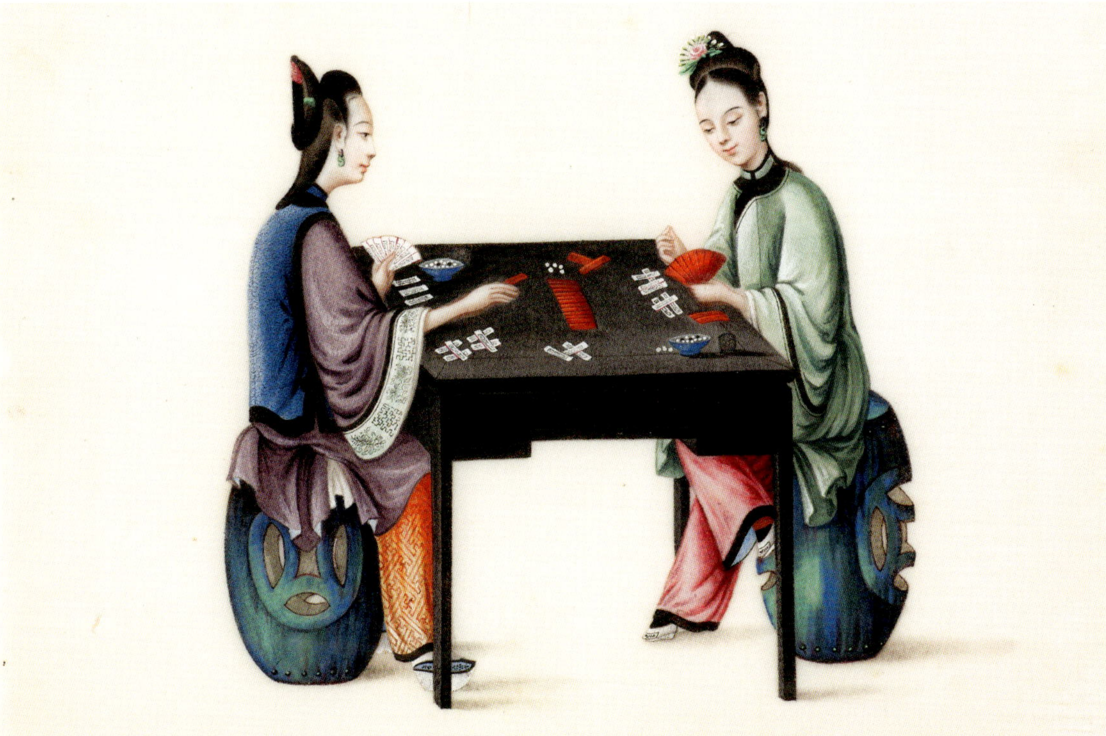

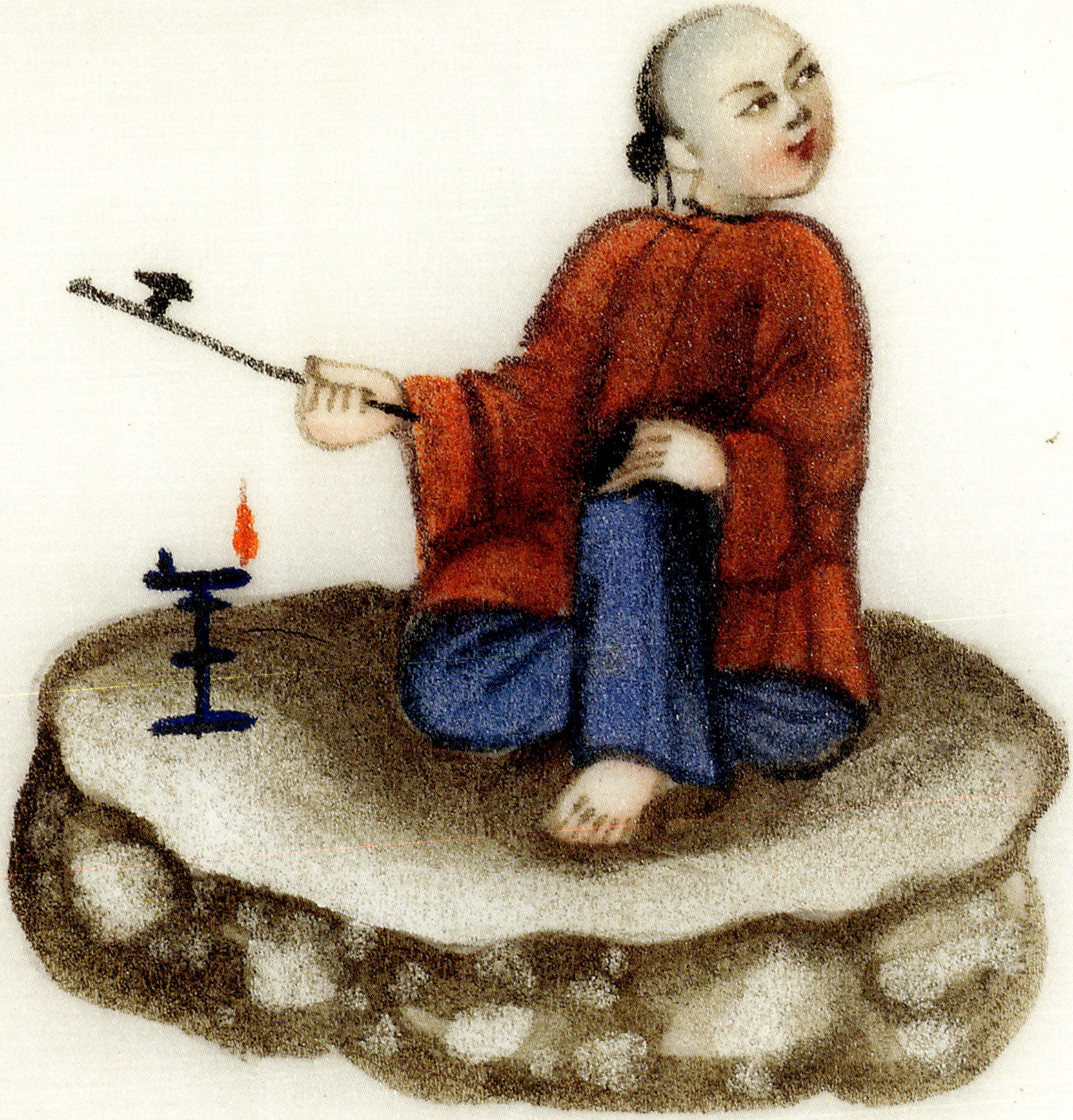

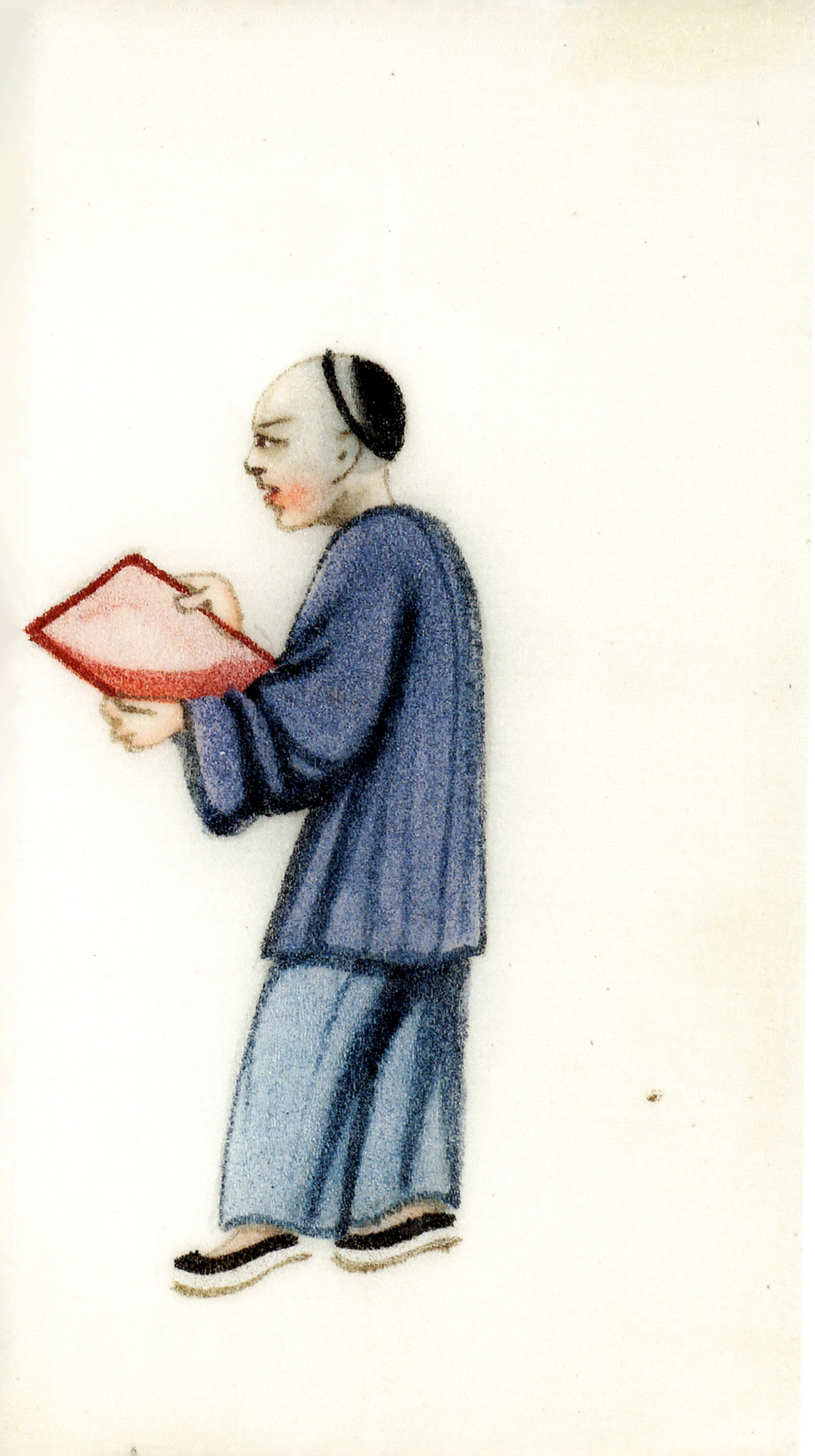

Chinese Pith Painting – Opium smoker • **Peintures chinoises sur papier de moelle** – Fumeur d'opium
• artist unknown, 19th century
• ink and colours on pith paper
• Gift of Trisha Glatthaar, AGGV 2010.015.001

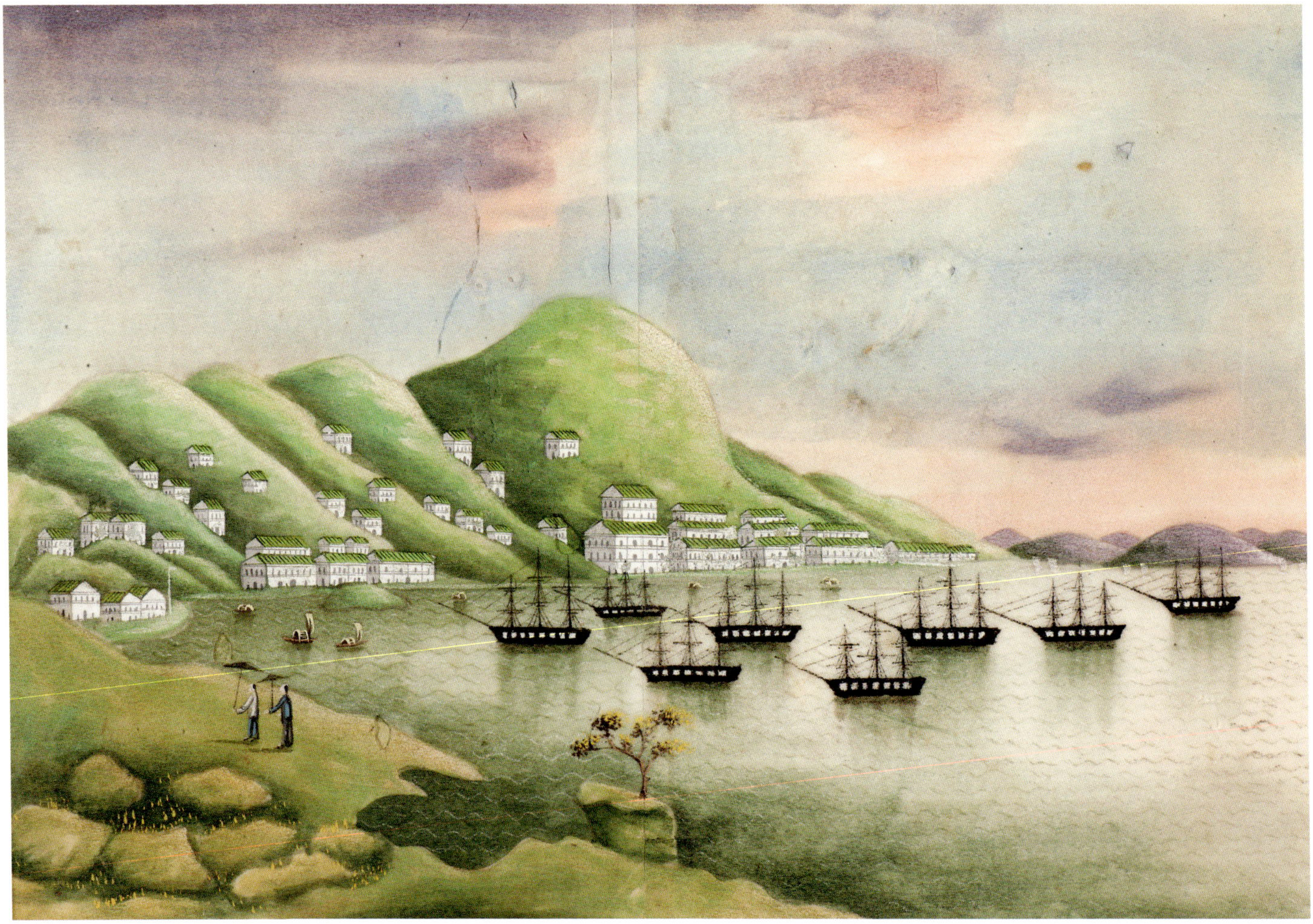

Chinese Pith Painting – Set of harbour scenes with tall ships and buildings • **Peintures chinoises sur papier de moelle** – Série de scènes portuaires avec grands navires et édifices • artist unknown, 19th century • ink and colours on pith paper • Gift of Colin C. Graham, 2004.004.004

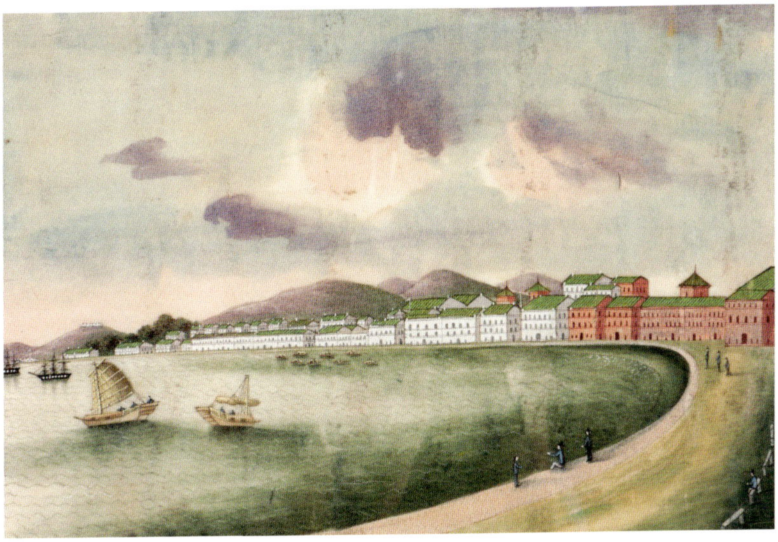
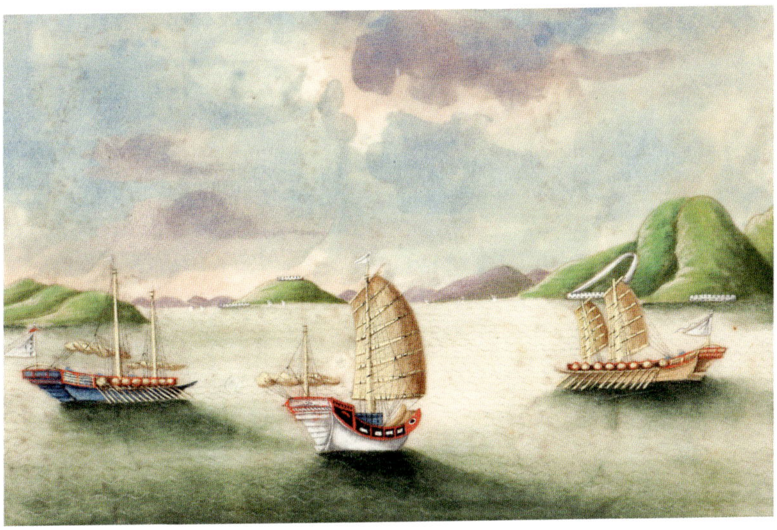
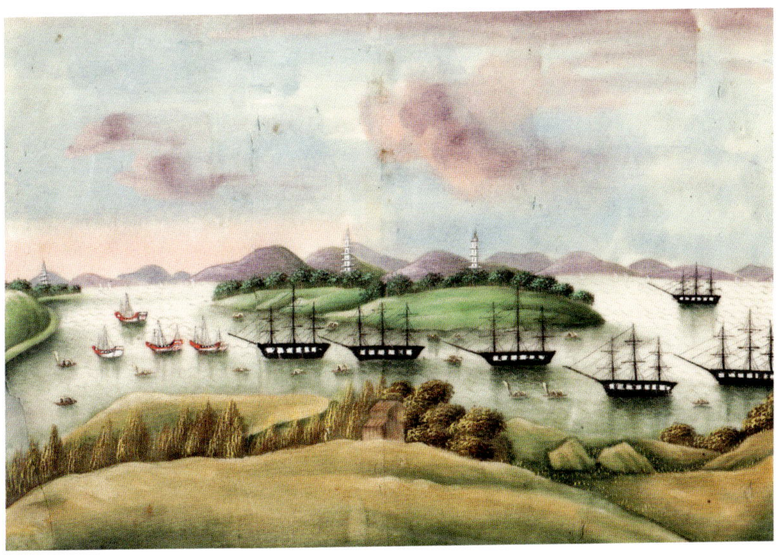

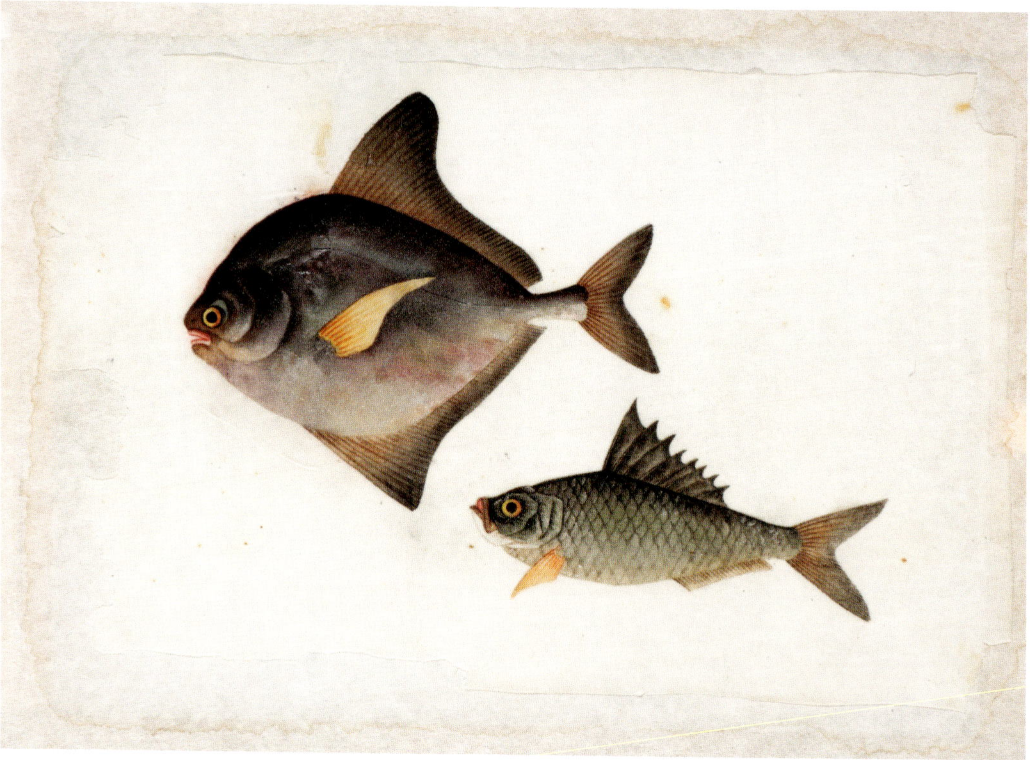

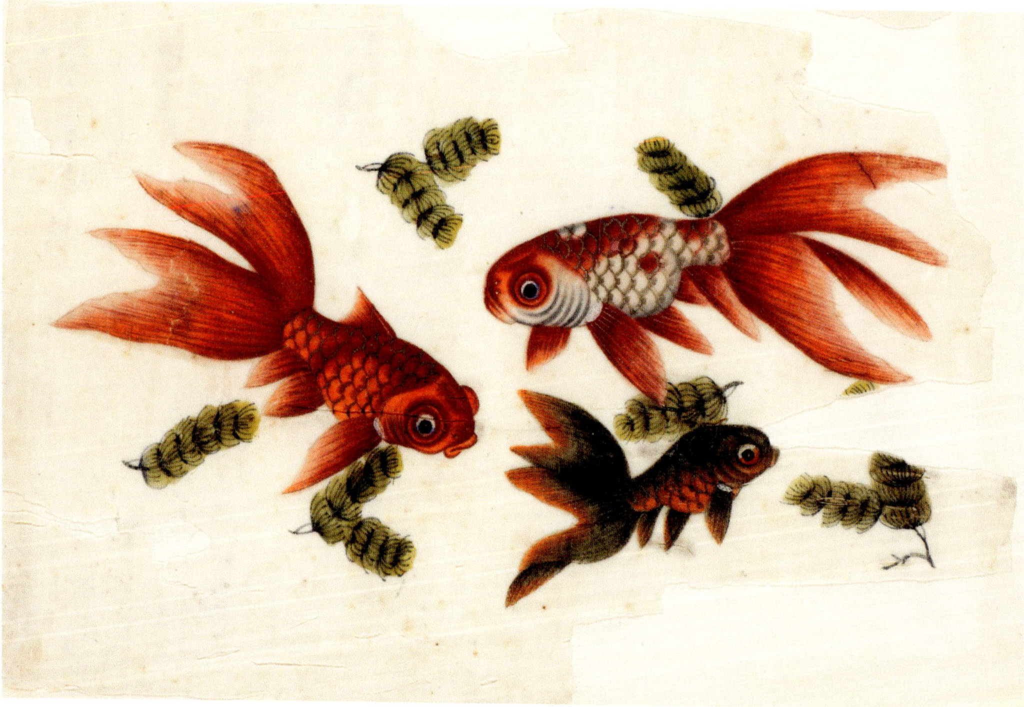

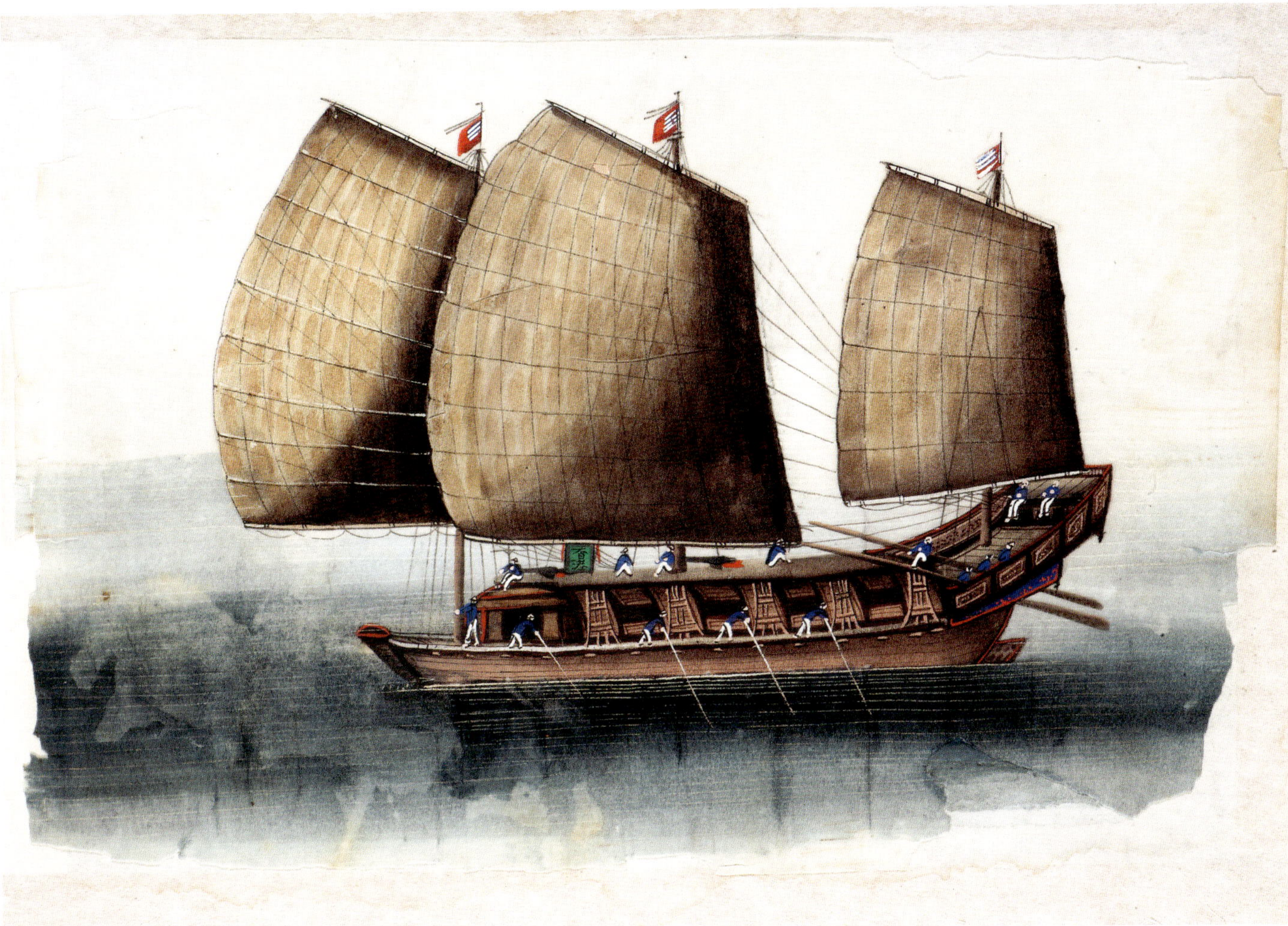

Chinese Pith Painting – Fish • **Peintures chinoises sur papier de moelle** – Poisson • artist unknown, 19th century • ink and colours on pith paper • Gift of Colin C. Graham, SC 115

Chinese Pith Painting – Goldfish • **Peintures chinoises sur papier de moelle** – Cyprin doré • artist unknown, 19th century • ink and colours on pith paper • Gift of Colin C. Graham, 2004.004.018

Chinese Pith Painting – Set of Chinese sailing vessels • **Peintures chinoises sur papier de moelle** – Série de voiliers chinois • (one illustrated) artist unknown, 19th century • ink and colours on pith paper • Gift of Colin C. Graham, SC 104.3

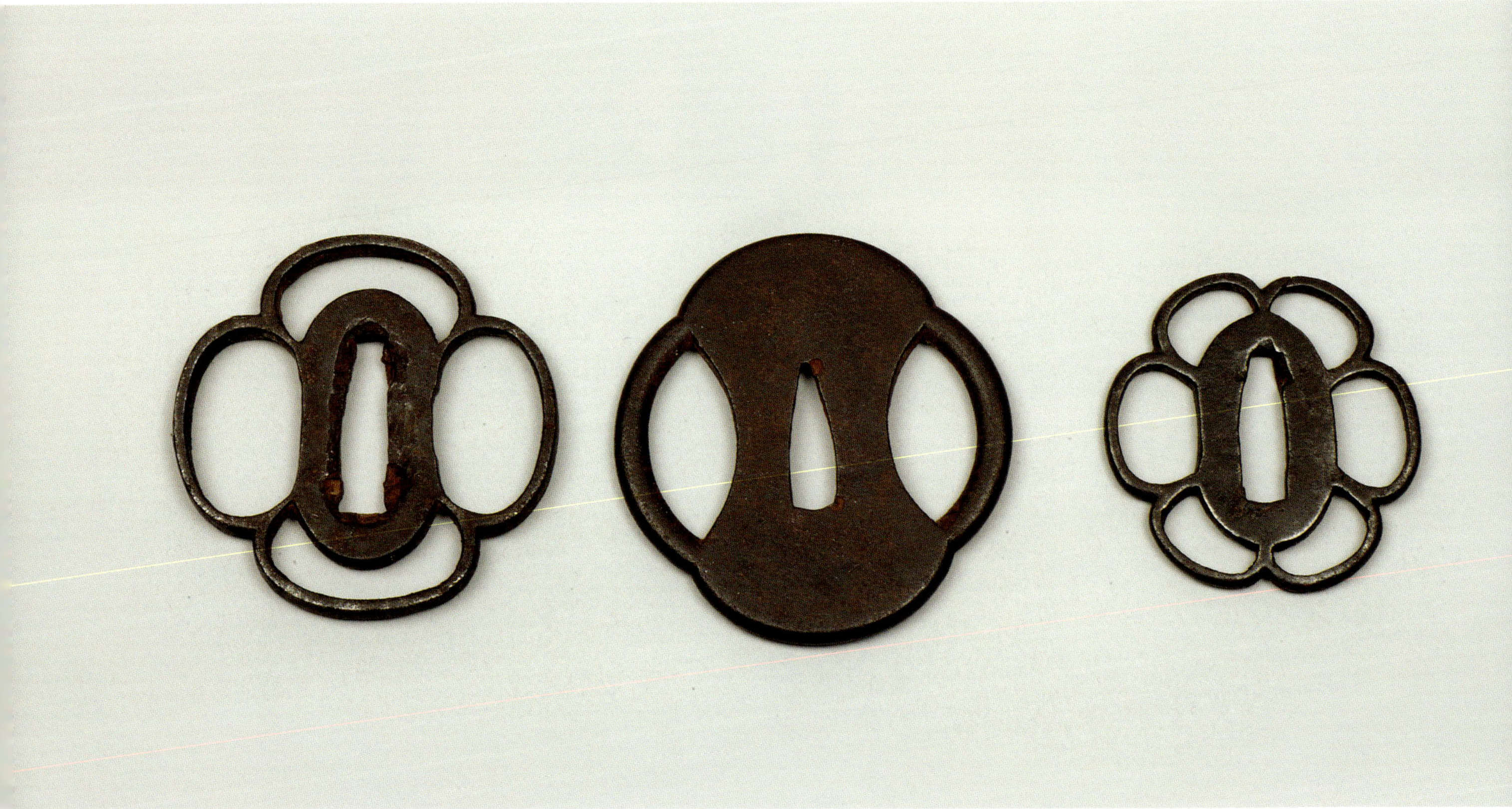

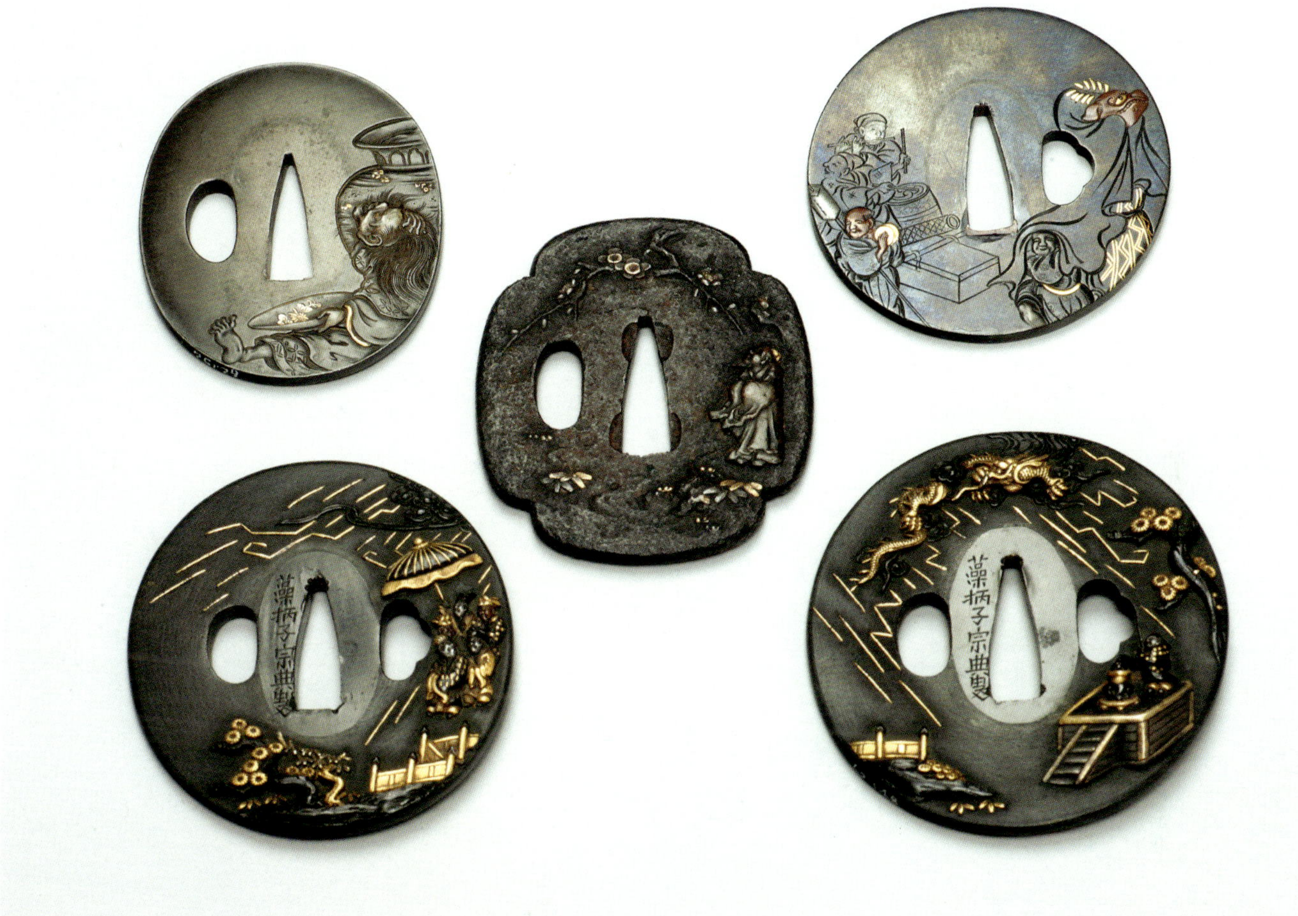

Three ***tsuba*** sword guards with openwork designs • Trois gardes ***tsuba*** de sabre japonais avec motifs ajourés • unsigned, Edo period (1603-1868) • iron • Collection of Frank Low-Beer, AGGV 2005.029.011- .016

Assortment of ***tsuba*** sword guards, Edo period (1603-1868) • Assortiment de gardes ***tsuba*** de sabre, période Edo (1603 à 1868) • (top left) ***tsuba*** with design of seated man with tray of flowers beside large jar; dipper and fan on verso, signed Tomonao (also Kosetsu Kan) • (en haut, à gauche) ***tsuba*** avec motif représentant un homme assis avec un plateau de fleurs à côté d'une grande jarre; louche et éventail au verso, signée Tomonao (aussi Kosetsu Kan) • *shibuichi* with gold details • (top right) ***tsuba*** with design of three musicians and masked dancer; rocks and flowers on verso, signed Kikuchi Joko • (en haut, à droite) ***tsuba*** avec motif représentant trois musiciens et un danseur masqué; rochers et fleurs au verso, signée Kikuchi Joko • *shakudo, shibuichi*, gold and brass inlay • (middle) ***tsuba*** with design of a scholar under a plum blossoming tree; blossoming branch on verso, unsigned • (au milieu) ***tsuba*** avec motif représentant un érudit sous un prunier en fleur; branche en fleurs au verso • iron, gold *numone* • (bottom) pair of ***tsuba*** with carved relief designs of dragon in thunderstorm and figure offering incense on altar and man with banner on verso; other with thunderstorm and five figures under umbrella; cloud, rain, blossoms on verso, signed Soheishi Soten • (en bas) Deux ***tsuba*** avec motifs of dragon durant un orage et personnage offrant de l'encens sur l'autel, homme et bannière au verso; autre personnage avec orage et cinq personnages sous un parapluie; nuage, pluie, fleurs au verso, signée Soheishi Soten • *shakudo*, gold • Fred and Isabel Pollard Collection, AGGV 1962.152.001, 1962,153.001, 1962.094.001, 1962.147.001, 1962.148.001

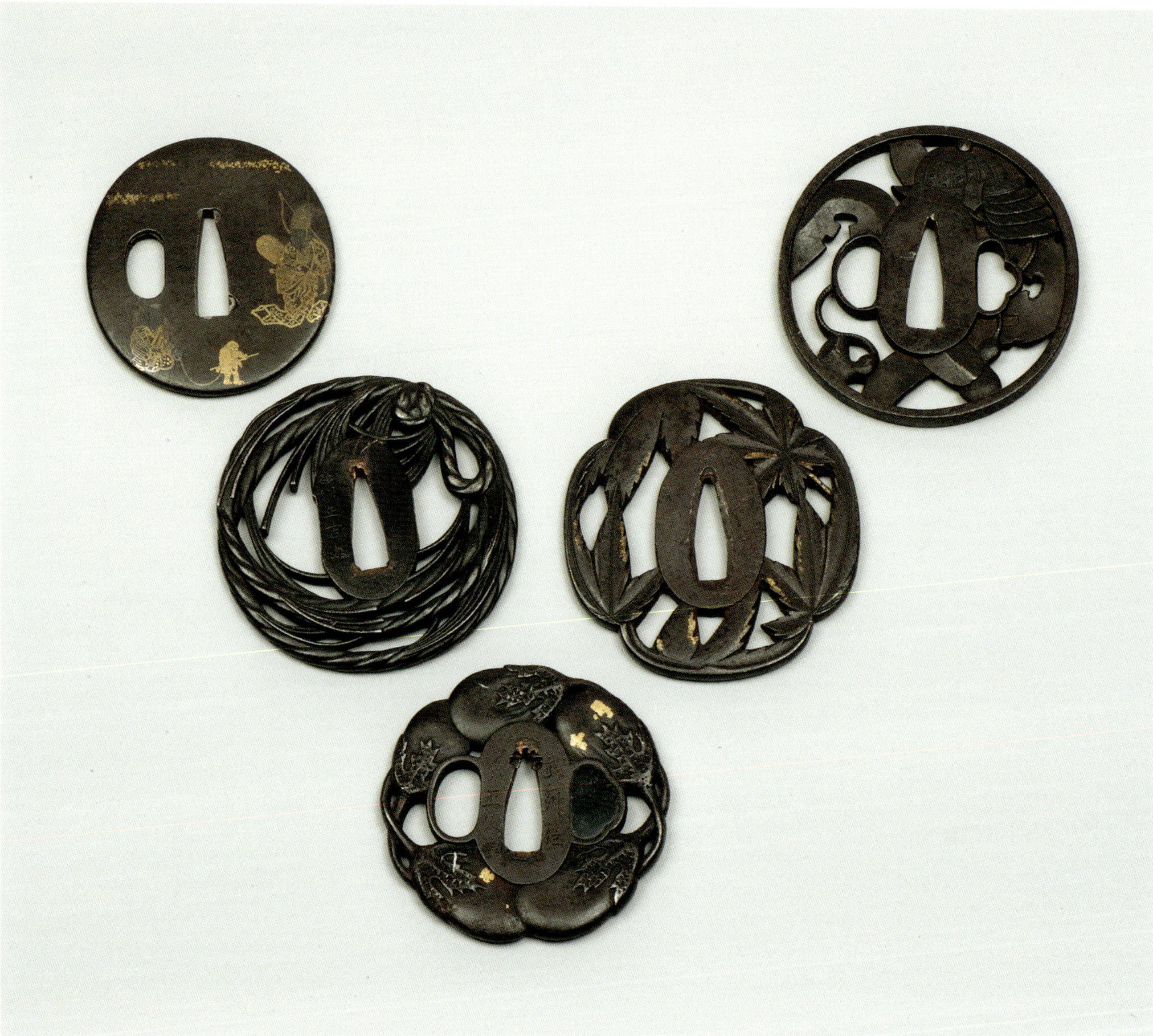

Assortment of ***tsuba*** sword guards, Edo period (1603-1868) • Assortiment de gardes ***tsuba*** de sabre, période Edo (1603 à 1868) • (top left) ***tsuba*** with design of archer and trainer with his monkey, unsigned • (en haut, à gauche) ***tsuba*** avec motif représentant un archer et un dompteur et ses singes, non signée • iron, gold inlay • (top right) ***tsuba*** with openwork and design of warrior helmet and saddle, unsigned • (en haut, à droite) ***tsuba*** ajourée et motif représentant un casque de guerrier et une selle, non signée • iron • (middle left) ***tsuba*** with openwork design of intertwined straw rope, signed Sunagawa Masayoshi • (au milieu, à gauche) ***tsuba*** ajourée avec motif représentant une corde de paille entrelacée, signée Sunagawa Masayoshi • iron • (middle right) ***tsuba*** with openwork design of leaves, signed Tatsunao • (au milieu, à droite) ***tsuba*** ajourée avec motif de feuilles, signée Tatsunao • iron, gold *numone* • (bottom) ***tsuba*** with design of eggplants, signed Bushu ju Masahisa • (en bas) ***tsuba*** avec motif d'aubergine, signée Bushu ju Masahisa • iron, gold *numone* • Given in memory of Ervin and Frances Newcombe by their son, Gordon Newcombe, AGGV 2001.001.001 -.005

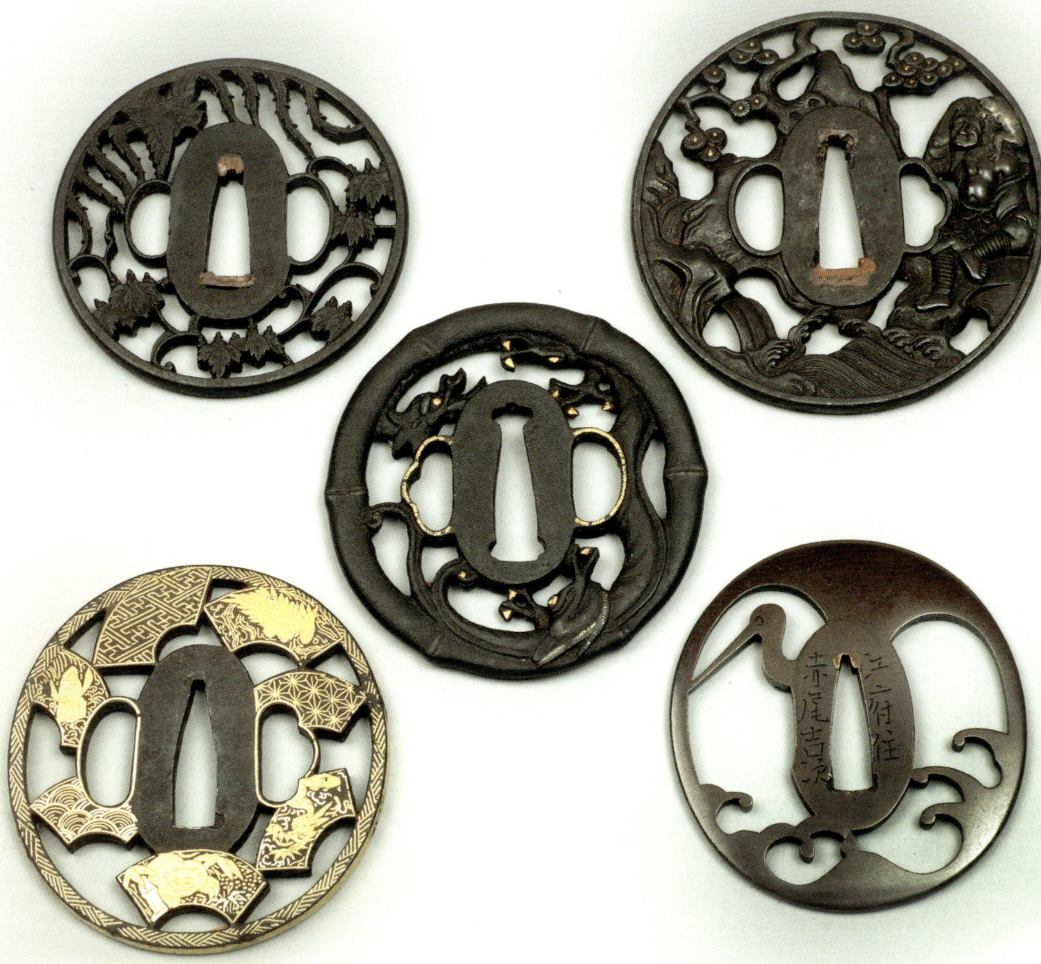

Assortment of ***tsuba*** sword guards, Edo period (1603-1868) • Assortiment de gardes ***tsuba*** de sabre, période Edo (1603 à 1868) • (top left) ***tsuba*** with openwork design of a phoenix and leaves • (En haut, à gauche) ***tsuba*** ajourée avec motif de phœnix et de feuilles • iron • (top right) ***tsuba*** with openwork design of the *sennin* Gama with a three legged toad beside a stream and a tree possibly the work of Shoami ca. 1625 • (En haut, à droite) ***tsuba*** ajourée avec motif représentant le *sennin* Gama et un crapaud à trois pattes près d'un ruisseau et d'un arbre, peut-être l'œuvre de Shoami, vers 1625 • iron, gold *numone* • (middle) ***tsuba*** with openwork design of an elongated dragon • (en bas, à gauche) ***tsuba*** ajourée avec motif d'éventails • iron, gold *numone* • (bottom left) ***tsuba*** with openwork design of fans • iron, gold • (bottom right) ***tsuba*** with openwork design of a crane, signed Kofu ju Akao Yoshitsugu ca. 1775 • (en bas, à droite) ***tsuba*** ajourée avec motif de grue, signée Kofu ju Akao Yoshitsugu, vers 1775 • iron • Intended Gift, Private Collection

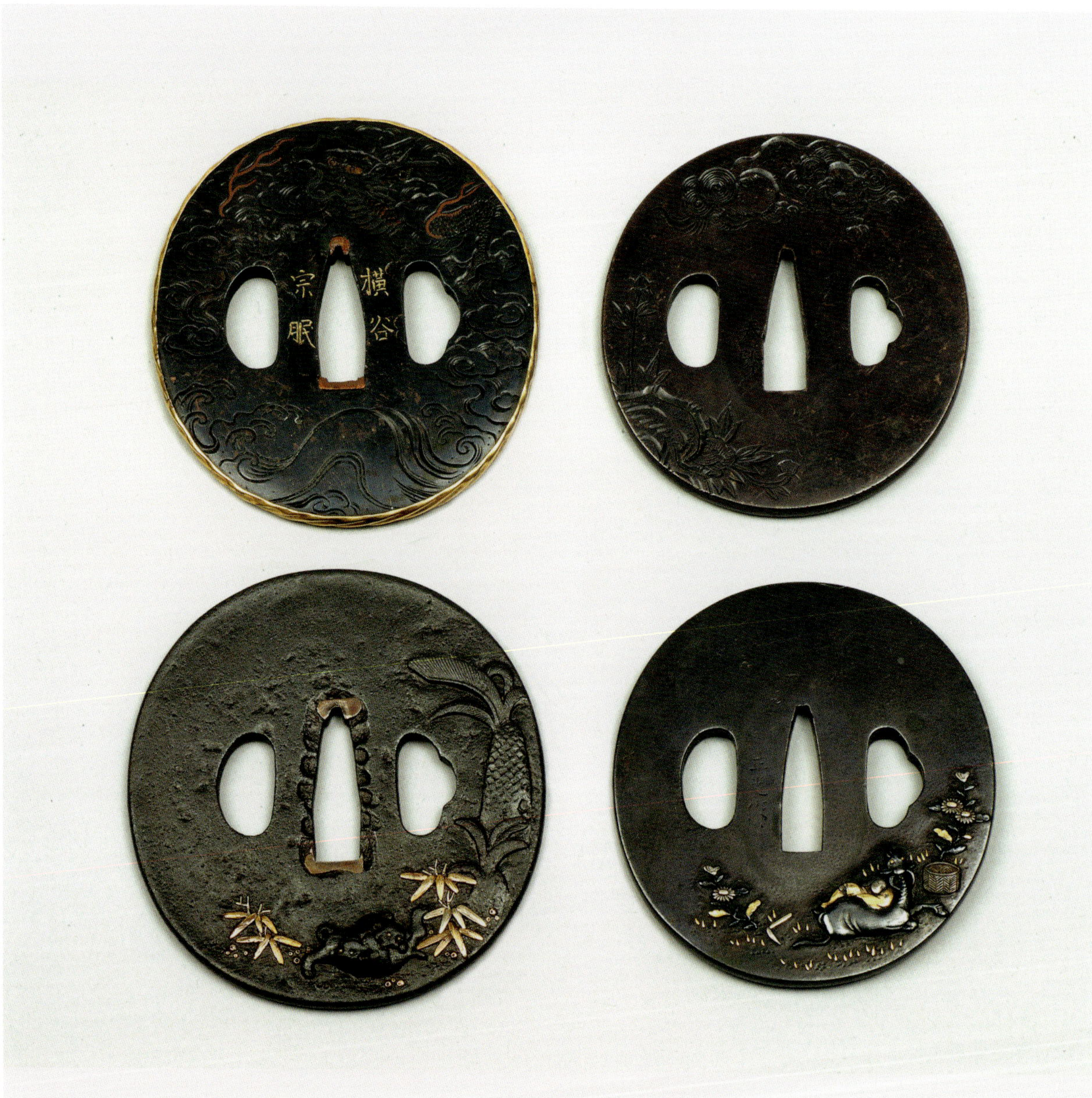
横谷
宗眠

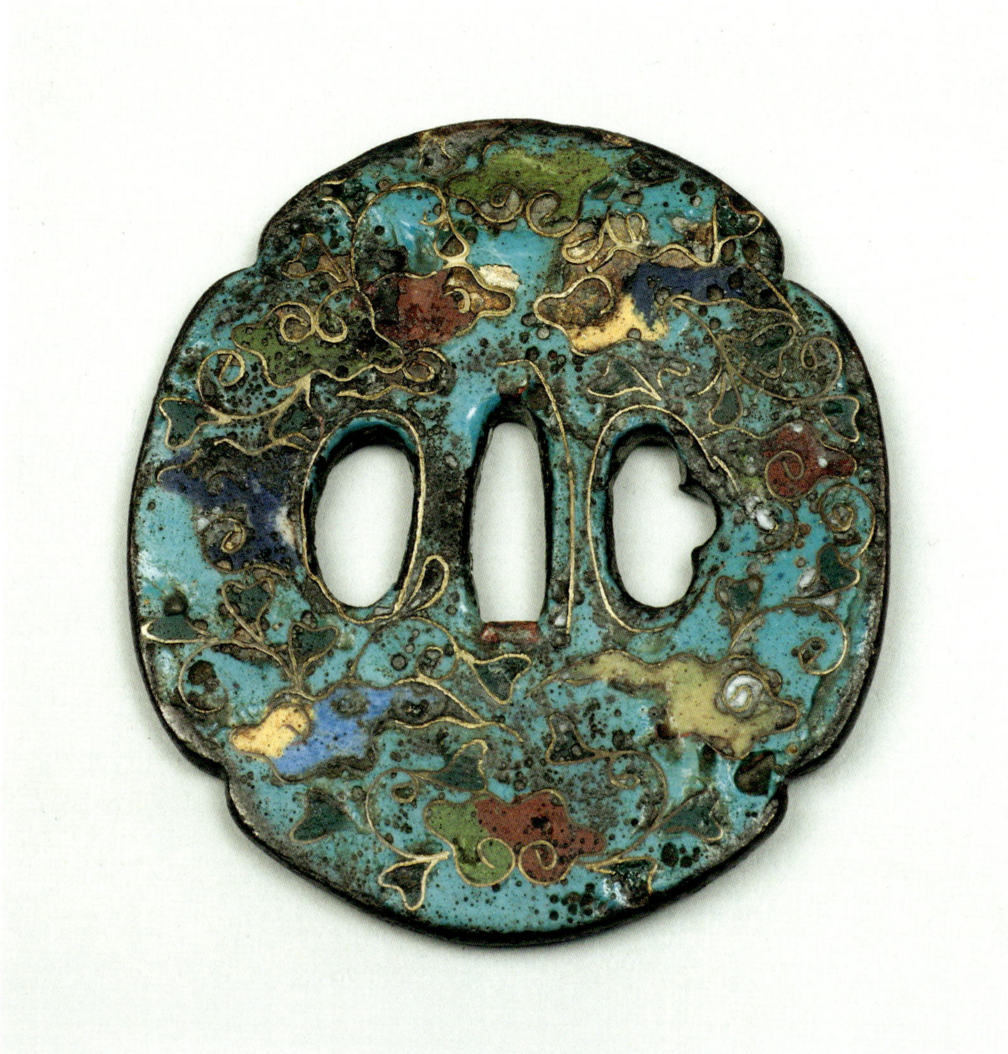

Assortment of ***tsuba*** sword guards, Edo period (1603-1868) • Assortiment de gardes ***tsuba*** de sabre, période Edo (1603 à 1868) (top left) ***tsuba*** with design of a dragon amidst clouds, signed Yokotani Somin • (en haut, à gauche) ***tsuba*** avec motif de dragon dans les nuages; bordure dorée, signée Yokotani Somin • iron, gold rim • (top right) *tsuba* with design of *shishi* lion dog with flower and rock; rock and flowers on verso, signed Shunrin • (en haut, à droite) ***tsuba*** agrémentée d'un motif de chien lion *shishi*, avec fleur et rocher; rocher et fleurs au verso, signée Shunrin • iron • (bottom left) ***tsuba*** with carved relief design of puppies playing by a tree; flowers and stream on verso • (en bas, à gauche) ***tsuba*** avec motif de chiots jouant près d'un arbre; fleurs et ruisseau au verso • unsigned • iron, gold • (bottom right) ***tsuba*** with carved relief design of boy on ox amidst flowers; flowers on verso, signed Shoko or Masamitsu? • (en bas à droite) ***tsuba*** avec motif représentant un garçon sur un bœuf au milieu des fleurs; fleurs au verso, signée Shoko ou Masamitsu? • iron, gold • Intended Gift, Private Collection

tsuba, made in China for Japanese market, Ming dynasty, ca. 1600 • ***tsuba***, fabriquée en Chine pour le marché japonais, Fabriquée en Chine sous la dynastie Ming vers 1600 • cloisonné • Gift of Lady Stuart Taylor, AGGV 62.293

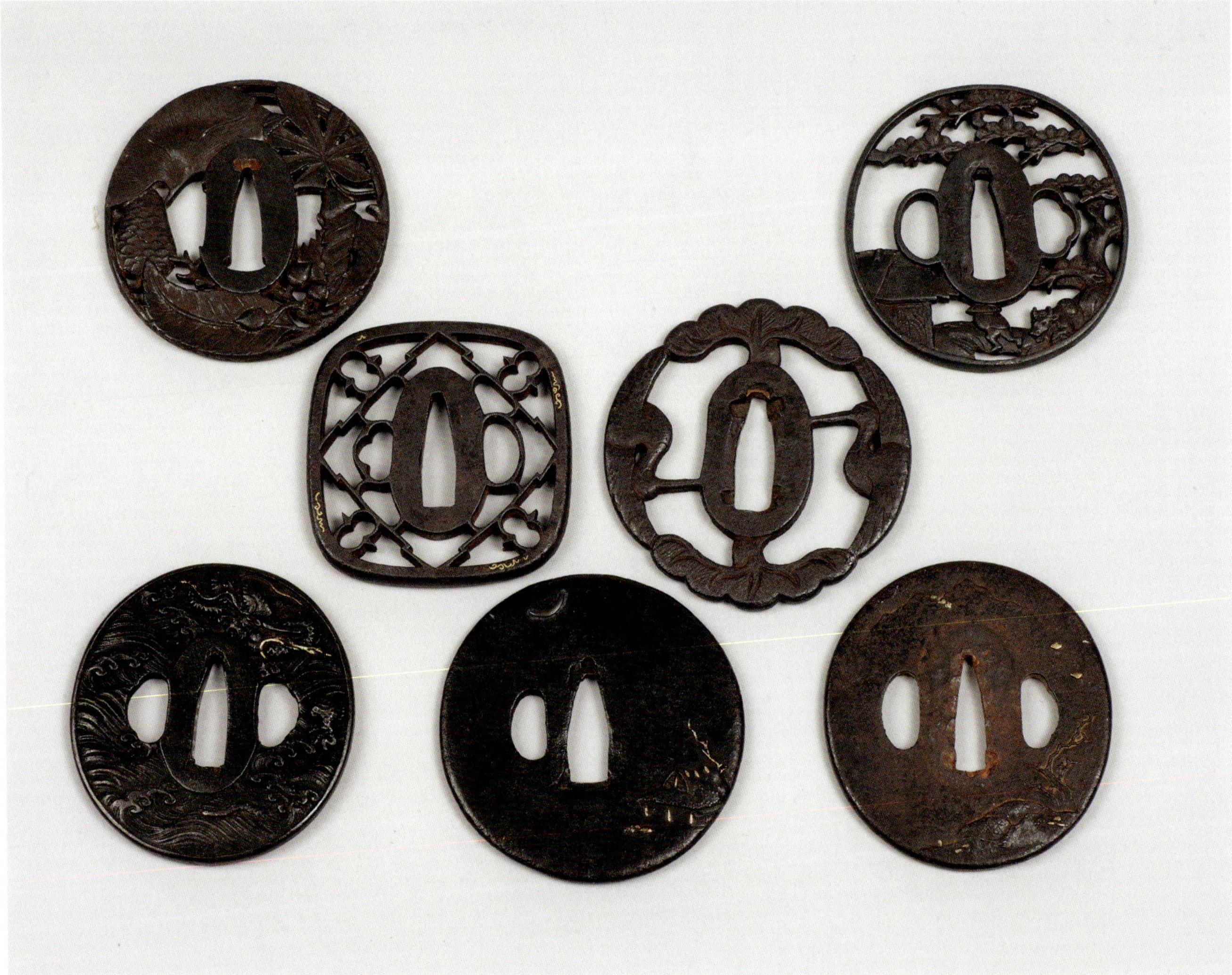

Assortment of ***tsuba*** sword guards, Edo period (1615-1868) • Assortiment de gardes ***tsuba*** de sabre, période Edo (1615 à 1868) • (top left) ***tsuba*** with openwork design of leaves and pine cones and chestnuts • (en haut, à gauche) ***tsuba*** ajourée avec motif de feuilles, pommes de conifère et châtaignes • unsigned, iron • Gift of Patricia Butler, AGGV 2004.041.031 • (top right) ***tsuba*** with openwork design of pine trees, man with ox headed to a house, signed Nobumasa • (en haut, à droite) ***tsuba*** ajourée *avec* motif représentant des pins, un homme avec un bœuf se dirigeant vers une maison, signée Nobumasa • Gift of Arden and Judy Schnee, 1999.035.006 • (middle left) ***tsuba*** with openwork fret design, unsigned, iron, gold *numone* • (au milieu, à gauche) ***tsuba*** ajourée avec motif découpé Gift of Arden and Judy Schnee, AGGV 2000.017.002 • (middle right) ***tsuba*** with openwork design of two cranes and two pines • (En bas, au milieu) *tsuba* avec maison et croissant de lune • unsigned • iron • Gift of Arden and Judy Schnee, AGGV 2000.017.001 • (bottom left) ***tsuba*** with design of dragon and waves on both sides • (au milieu, à droite) ***tsuba*** ajourée avec motif représentant deux grues et deux pins • unsigned • iron, gold *numone* • Gift of Mr. J.N. Anderson, AGGV 1962.035.001 • (bottom middle) ***tsuba*** with house and crescent moon • (En bas, à gauche) ***tsuba*** avec motif de dragon et de vagues des deux côtés • unsigned, iron, gold *numone* • Gift of Mr. J.N. Anderson, AGGV 1962.036.001 • (bottom right) ***tsuba*** with design of mountains, rocks and a tree with two small flowers on verso • (en bas, à droite) ***tsuba*** avec motif de montagnes, rochers; arbre avec deux petites fleurs au verso • unsigned, iron, gold *numone* • Gift of Judge Montague Tyrwhitt-Drake, AGGV 2000.005.002

tsuba with design of Shoki, the demon queller with an *oni* demon, floral design on verso, signed Masanari, early 19th century • ***tsuba*** avec motif représentant Shoki, le démon queller, avec un démon *oni*; motif floral au verso, signée Masanari • iron, gold *numone* • Gift of Brian S. McElney, AGGV 1992.002.024

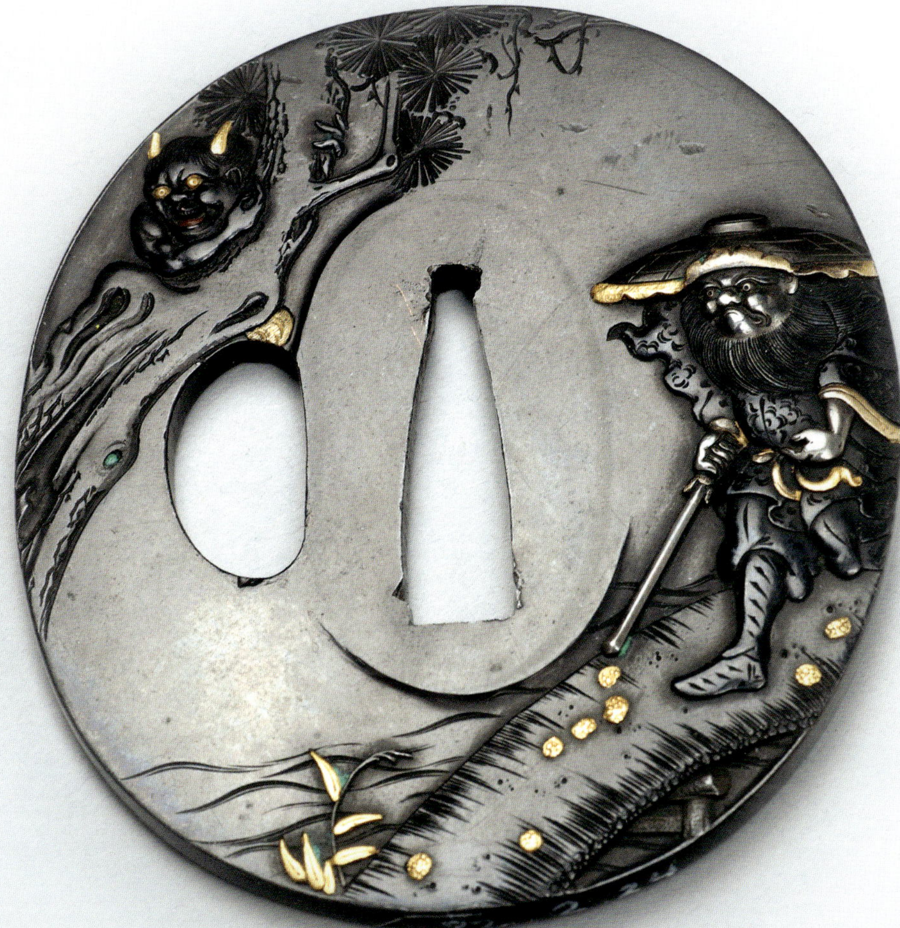

Japanese Netsuke Toggles, Ojime Beads and Inro Containers

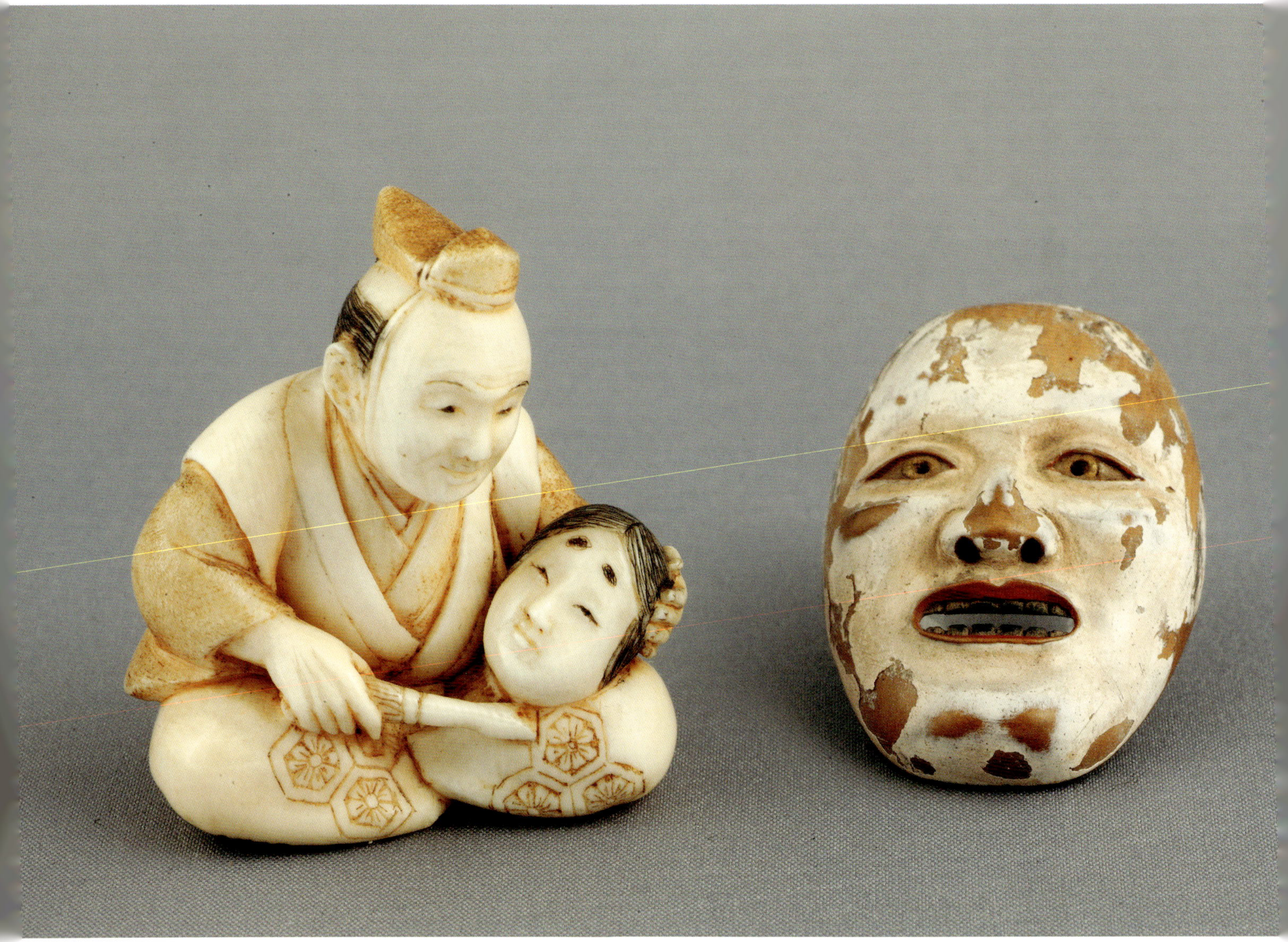

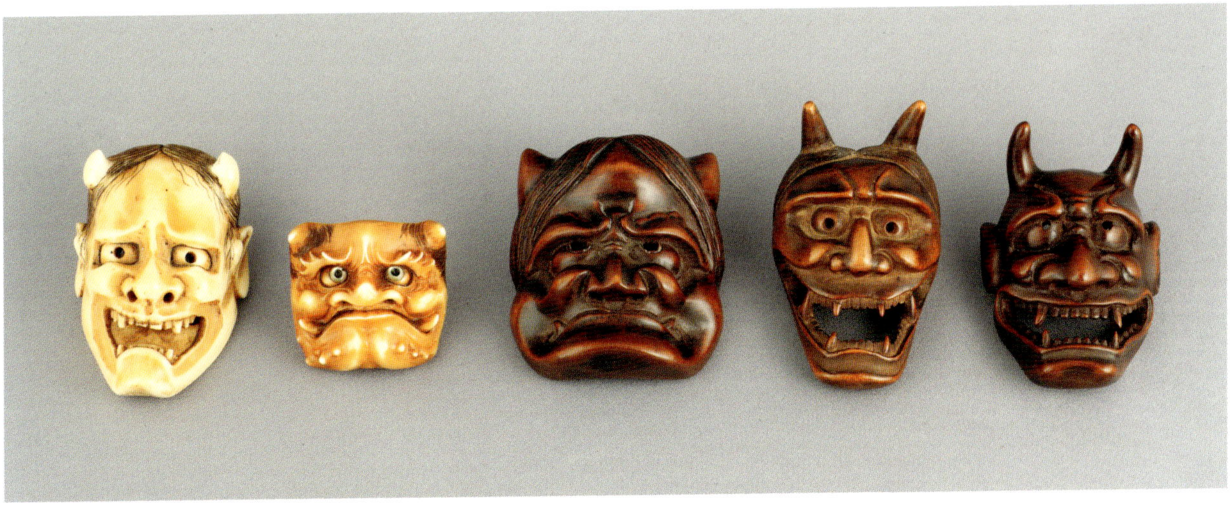

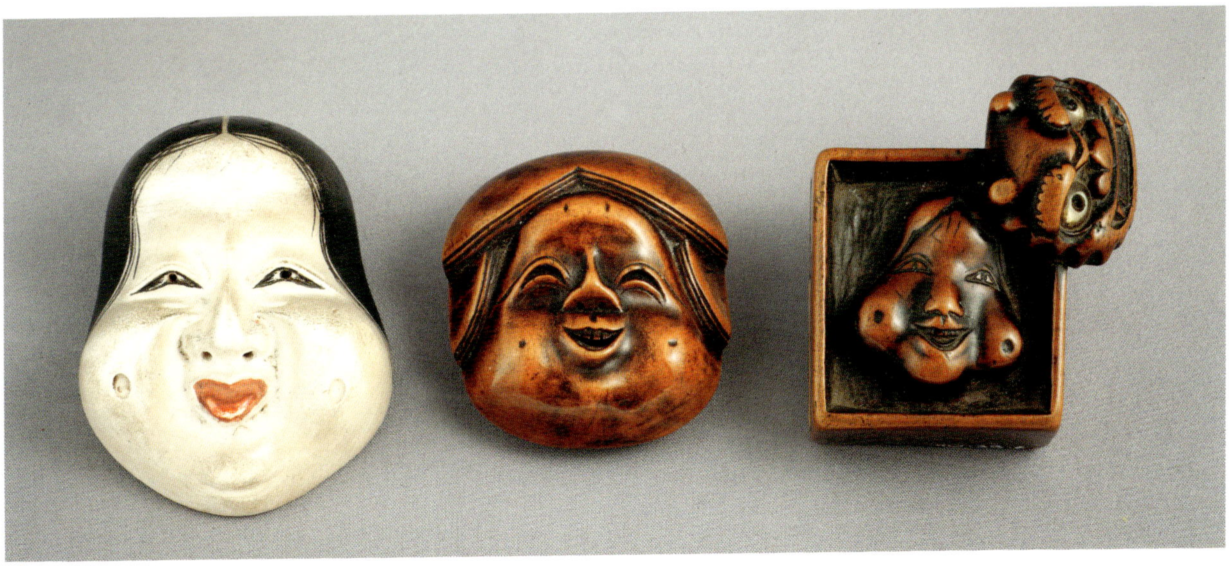

(left) ***netsuke*** of a man holding *Noh* theatre mask, signed Shozan • (à gauche) ***netsuke***, homme tenant un masque du théâtre *Nô*, signé Meisho • early 20th century • ivory • Gift of the Estate of Elizabeth Stewart, 2009.029.033 • (right) ***netsuke*** in form of a *Noh* mask • (à droite) ***netsuke*** en forme de masque *Nô* • 18th/19th century • wood, lacquer • Fred and Isabel Pollard Collection, AGGV 1967.140.001

netsuke in the form of demon masks • ***netsuke*** en forme de masques de démon • (left) Hannya, female demon mask, signed Kogetsu To, 19th century • (à gauche) Hannya, masque de démon féminin, signé Kogetsu To, 19e siècle • ivory • Gift of James and Joanna Davidson, AGGV 2006.002.022 • (second left) demon mask, signed Naokasu or Tadakazu or Masakazu, 19th century • (deuxième à gauche) Masque de démon, signé Naokazu ou Tadakazu ou Masakazu, 19e siècle • ivory • Edith Low-Beer Collection, AGGV 1990.038.007 • (middle) demon mask, 19th century • (au milieu) Masque de démon, 19e siècle • wood • Edith Low-Beer Collection, AGGV 1990.038.002 • (two on right) Hannya, female demon mask, 18th/19th century • (deux à droite) Hannya, masque de démon féminin, 18e/19e siècle • wood • Fred and Isabel Pollard Collection, AGGV 1974.209.001, 1974.208.001

netsuke in the form of Kyogen masks • ***netsuke*** en forme de masques de Kyogen • (left) Okame mask, 19th century • (à gauche) Masque d'Okame, 19e siècle • wood, lacquer • Fred and Isabel Pollard Collection, AGGV 1967.182.000 • (middle) Okame mask, signed Gyoku, late 18th/early 20th century • (au milieu) Masque d'Okame, signé Gyoku, fin du 18e/début du 20e siècle • wood • Gift of James and Joanna Davidson, AGGV 2006.002.021 • (right) Okame mask in a box with demon mask on lip, 19th century • (à droite) Masque d'Okame dans une boîte avec masque de démon sur la lèvre, 19e siècle • wood, ivory, abalone • Edith Low-Beer Collection, AGGV 1990.038.006

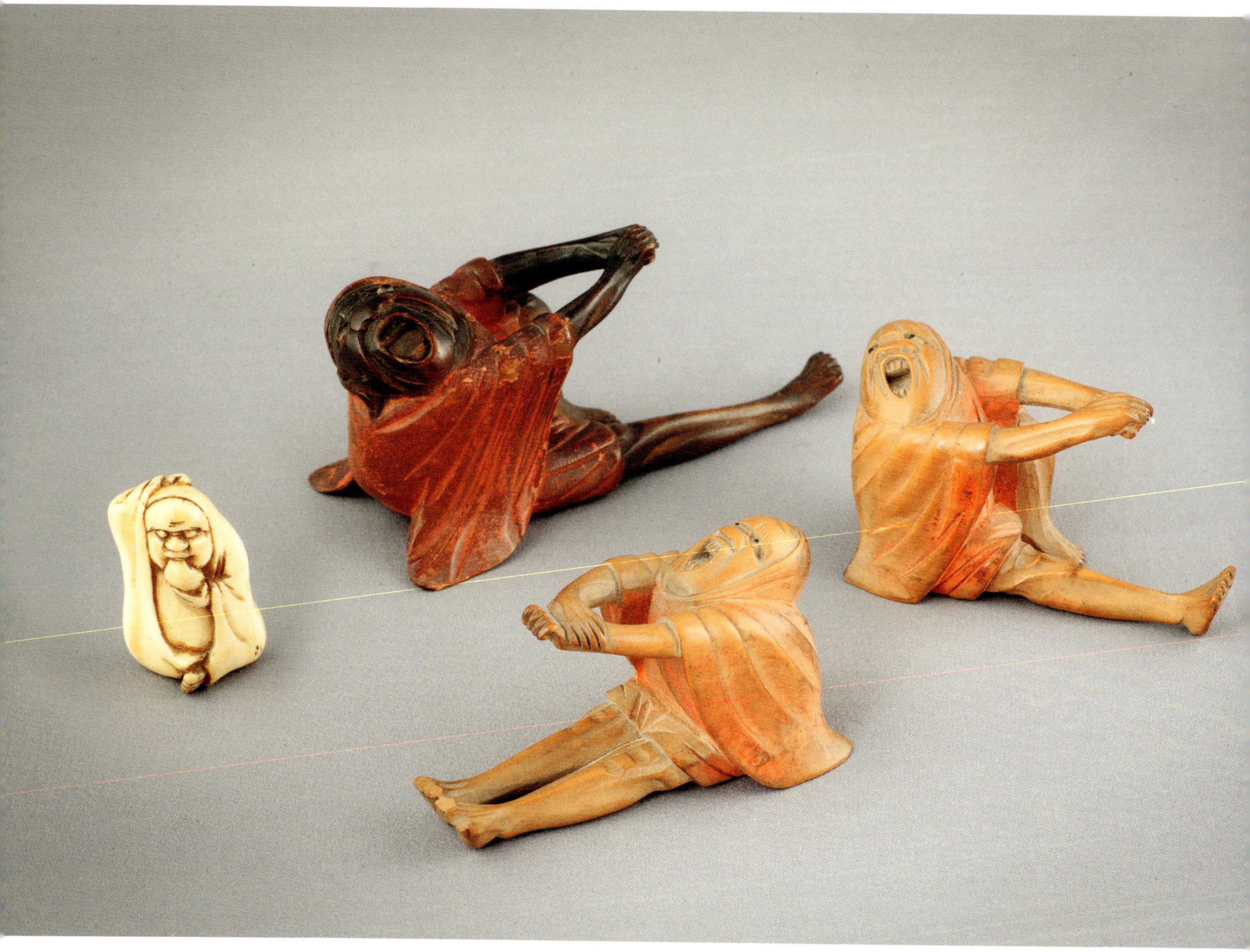

(left) ***netsuke*** of Daruma with a Peach • (à gauche) ***netsuke***, Daruma avec une pêche •early 19th century • ivory • Gift of James and Joanna Davidson, AGGV 2006.002.011 • (remaining) ***netsuke*** of Daruma awakening • (les autres) ***netsuke***, Daruma se réveillant • 19th century • wood, pigments • Gift of the Lewis and Ruth Sherman Foundation, AGGV 2007.016.007, (two on right) Gift of James and Joanna Davidson, AGGV 2006.002.037, 2006.002.038

(left) ***netsuke*** in the form of Hotei • (à gauche) ***netsuke*** en forme de Hotei • 19th century • ivory • Fred and Isabel Pollard Collection AGGV 1974.217.001• (right) ***netsuke*** of Hotei in a Boat, signed Yoshikazu, 19th century • (à droite) ***netsuke***, Hotei dans une embarcation, signé Yoshikazu, 19e siècle • ivory • Gift of James and Joanna Davidson, AGGV 2006.002.018

(left) ***netsuke*** of Okame with a fan, signed Mitsuyuki, 19th century • (à gauche) ***netsuke***, Okame avec un éventail, signé Mitsuyuki, 19e siècle • ivory • Gift of James and Joanna Davidson, AGGV 2006.002.026 • (right) ***netsuke*** of Okame in a basket with sake, signed Hositsu • (à droite) ***netsuke***, Okame dans un panier avec du saké, signé Hositsu, 19e siècle • ivory • Gift of James and Joanna Davidson, AGGV 2006.002.008

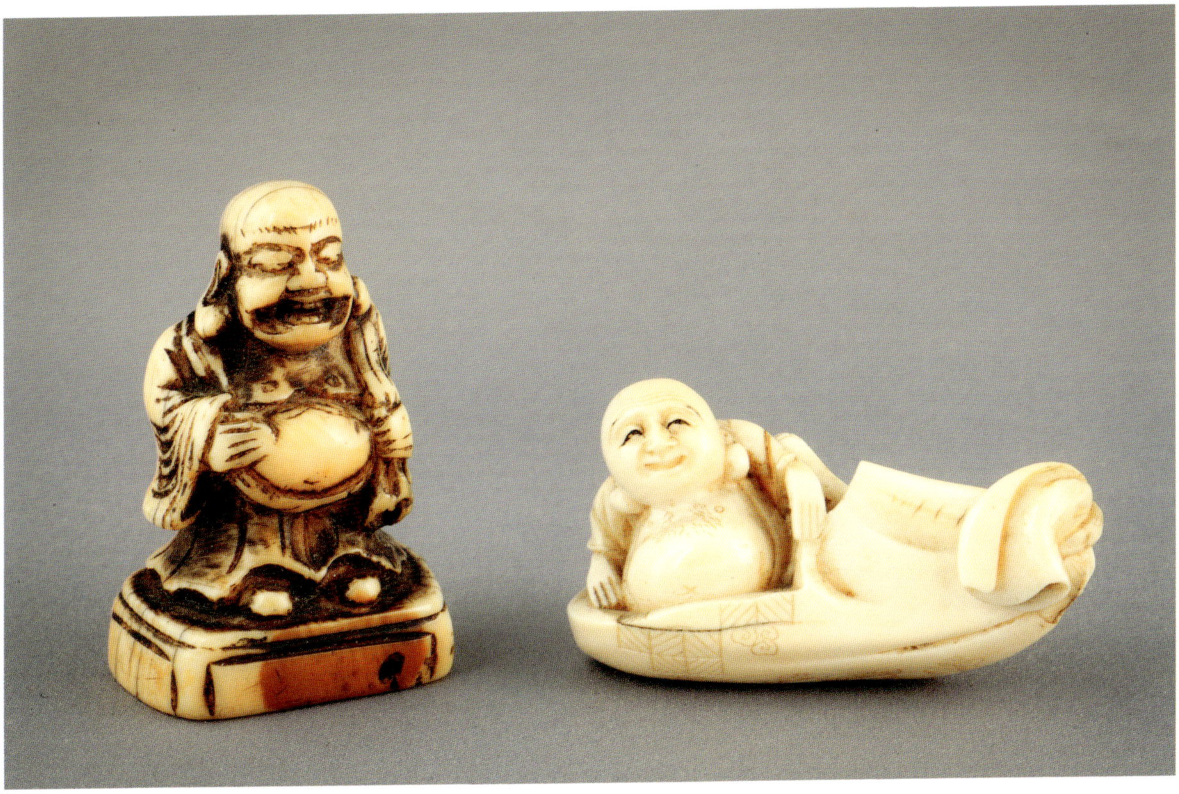

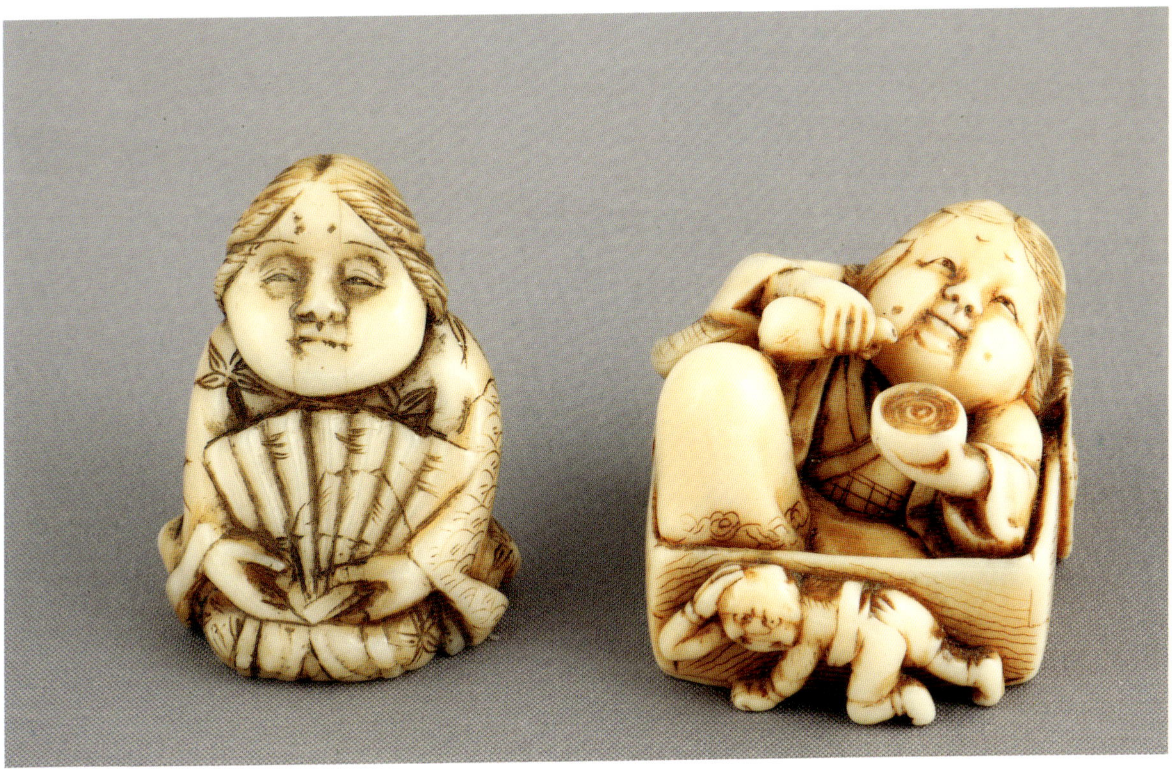

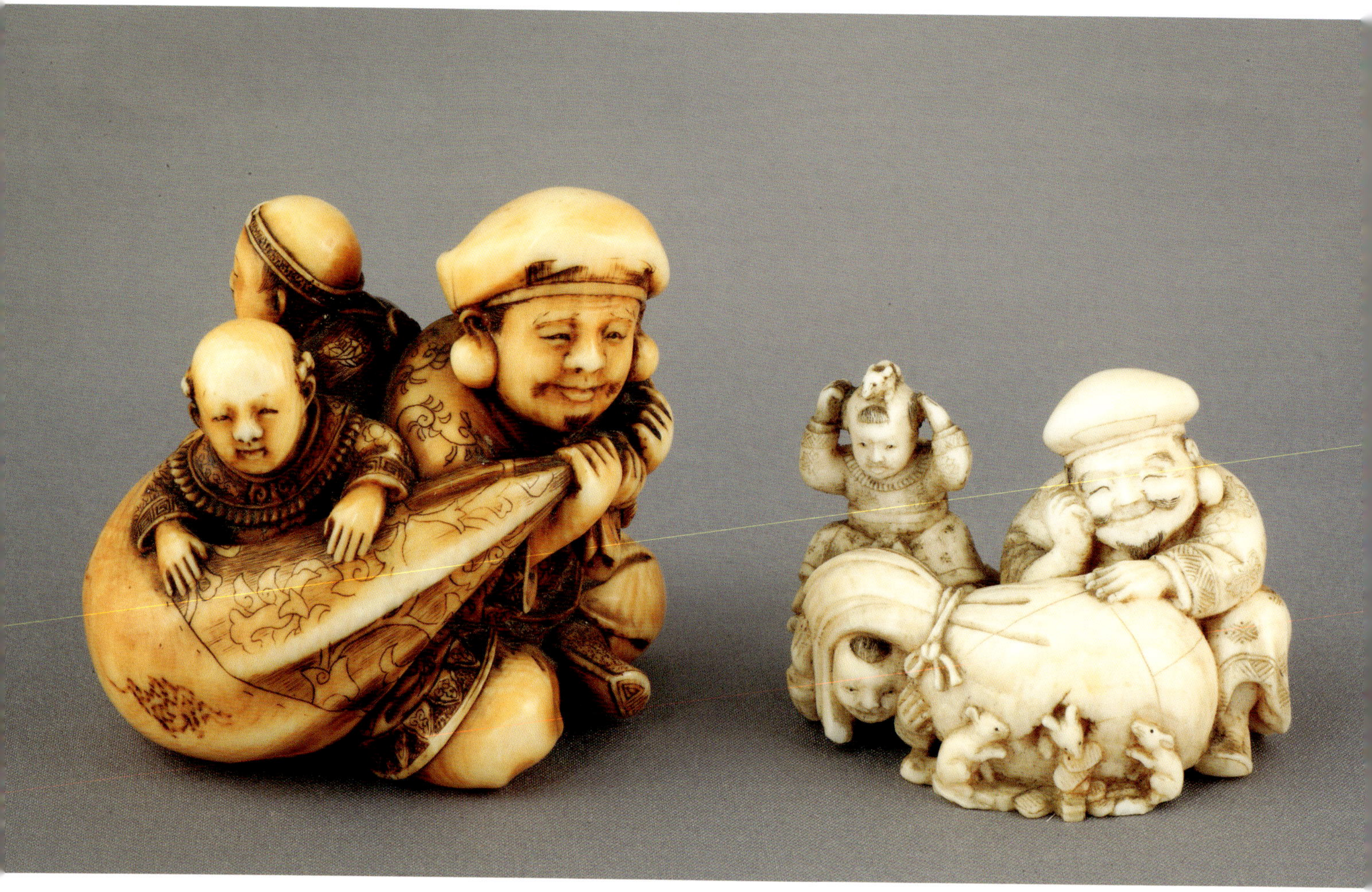

netsuke depicting Daikokuten with children playing with his sack, signed Toshimitsu (left) and signed Omura Ryoraku (right), 19th century • ***netsuke***, Daikokuten avec des enfants qui jouent avec son sac , signé Toshimitsu (à gauche) et signé Omura Ryoraku (à droite), 19e siècle • ivory • Gift of Mrs. E. C. Lewis, AGGV 1964.124.001, Gift of the Lewis and Ruth Sherman Foundation, AGGV 2007.016.027

netsuke of Shoki, the Demon Queller • ***netsuke***, Shoki, le démon queller • 19th century • wood • Fred and Isabel Pollard Collection, AGGV 1974.199.001

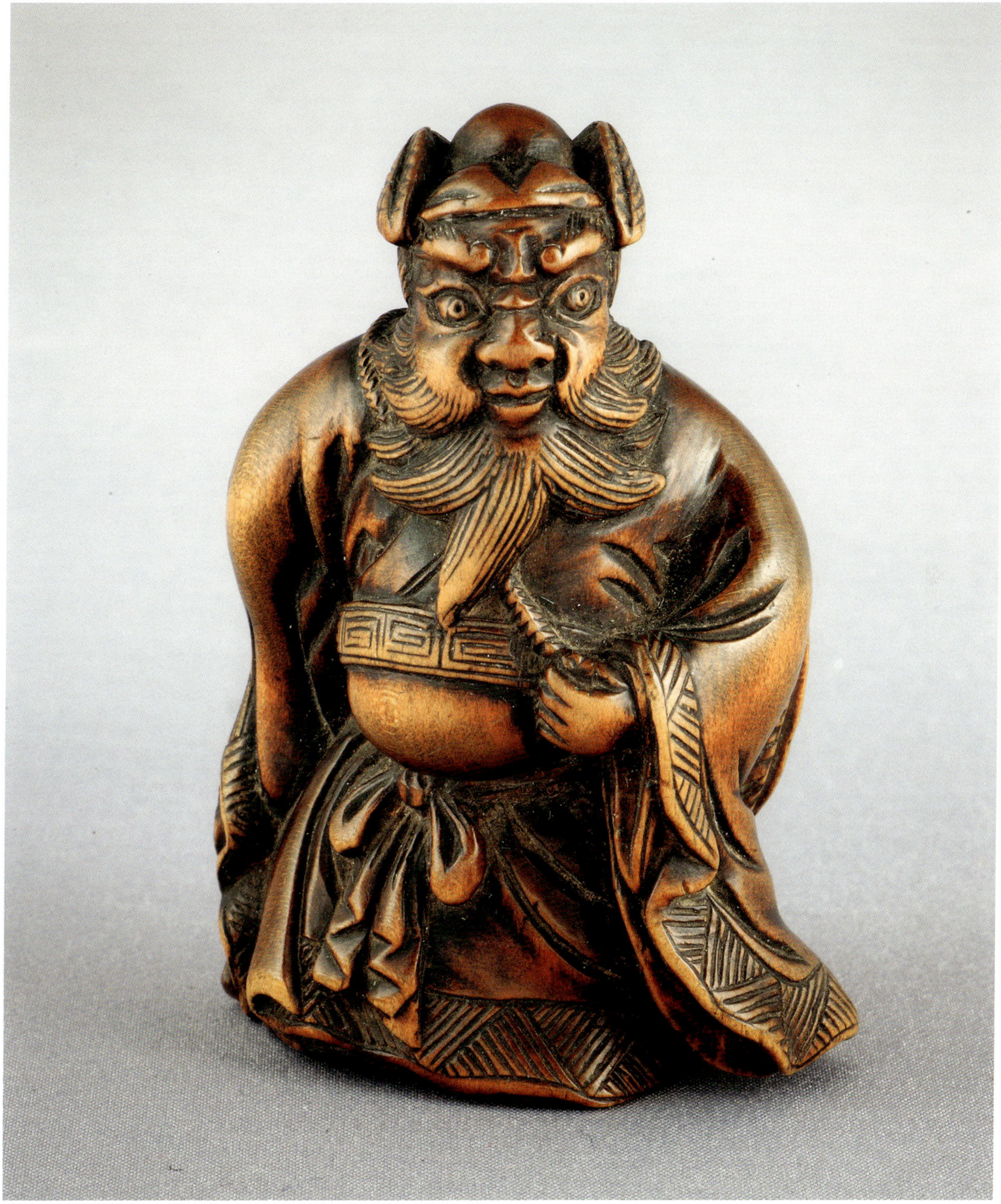

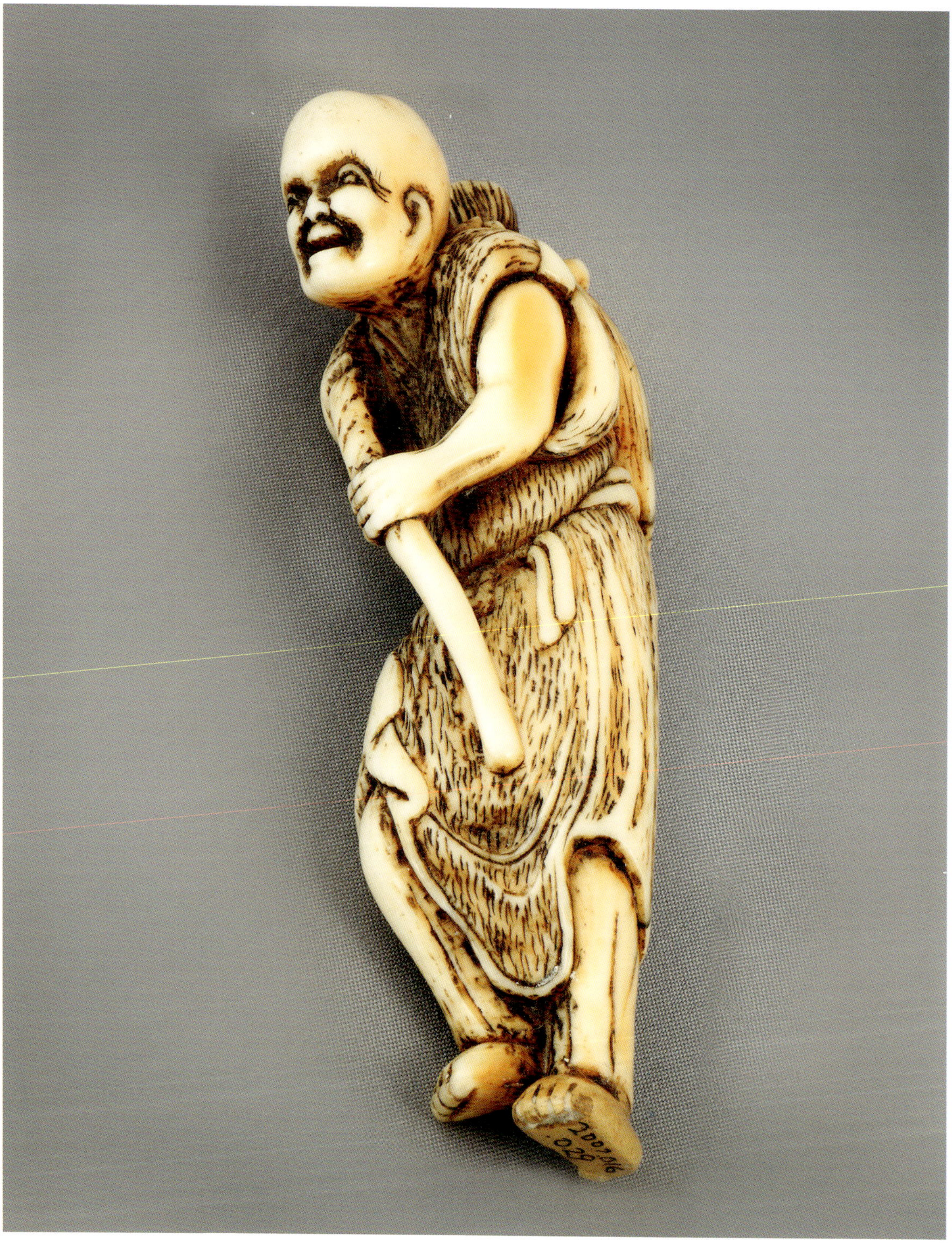

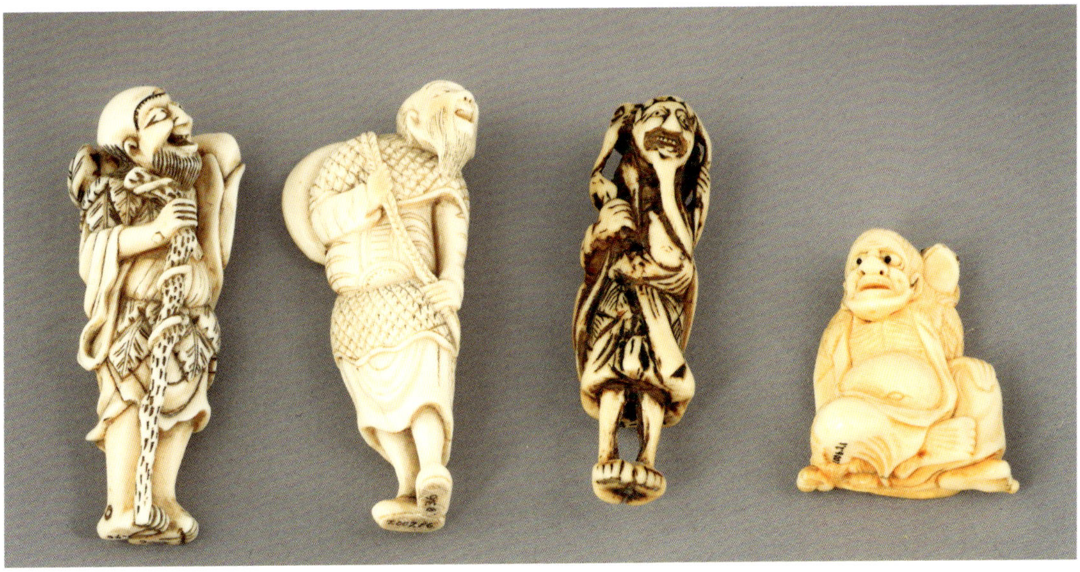

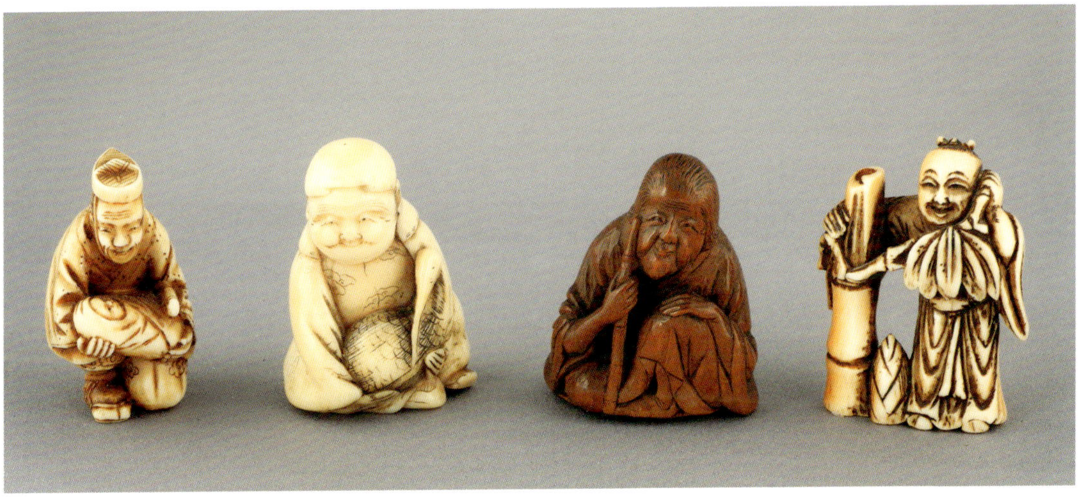

netsuke of a farmer carrying a rice sheaf • ***netsuke***, fermier transportant une gerbe de riz • 18th century • ivory • Gift of the Lewis and Ruth Sherman Foundation, AGGV 2007.016.029

(left) ***netsuke*** of a *sennin* with a peach and a staff • (à gauche) ***netsuke***, *sennin* avec une pêche et un bâton • 19th century • ivory • Gift of James and Joanna Davidson, AGGV 2006.002.040 • (second left) ***netsuke*** of *sennin* with hat slung over shoulder (deuxième à gauche) ***netsuke***, *sennin* avec chapeau à l'épaule • 19th century • ivory • Gift of the Lewis and Ruth Sherman Foundation, AGGV 2007.016.036 • (second right) ***netsuke*** of *sennin* Gama and toad, signed Nagamachi Shuzan, 19th century • (deuxième à droite) ***netsuke***, *sennin* Gama et crapaud, signé Nagamachi Shuzan, 19e siècle • bone • Fred and Isabel Pollard Collection, AGGV 1974.211.001 • (right) ***netsuke*** of *sennin* Gama and his toad • (à droite) ***netsuke***, *sennin* Gama et son crapaud • late 18th/early 19th century • ivory • Gift of James and Joanna Davidson, AGGV 2006.002.001

(left) ***netsuke*** of Taketori no Okina and Moon Child Baby • (à gauche) ***netsuke***, Taketori no Okina et bébé de la lune • late 18th/early 19th century • ivory • Gift of James and Joanna Davidson, AGGV 2006.002.004 • (second left) ***netsuke*** of man holding a crane • (deuxième à gauche) ***netsuke***, homme tenant une grue • early 19th century • ivory • Gift of James and Joanna Davidson, AGGV 2006.002.007 • (second right) ***netsuke*** of seated man with staff • (deuxième à droite) ***netsuke***, homme assis avec un bâton • 19th century • wood • Edith Low-Beer Collection, AGGV 1990.038.004 • (right) ***netsuke*** of Moso with Bamboo • (à droite) ***netsuke***, Moso et bambou • 19th century • ivory • Gift of the Lewis and Ruth Sherman Foundation, AGGV 2007.016.031

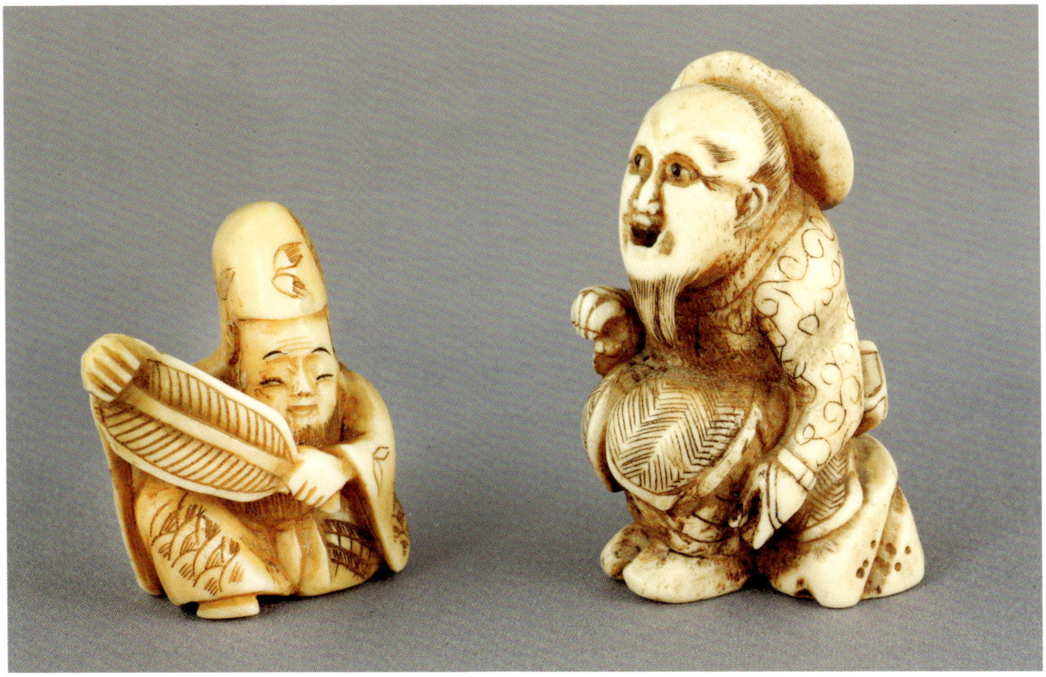

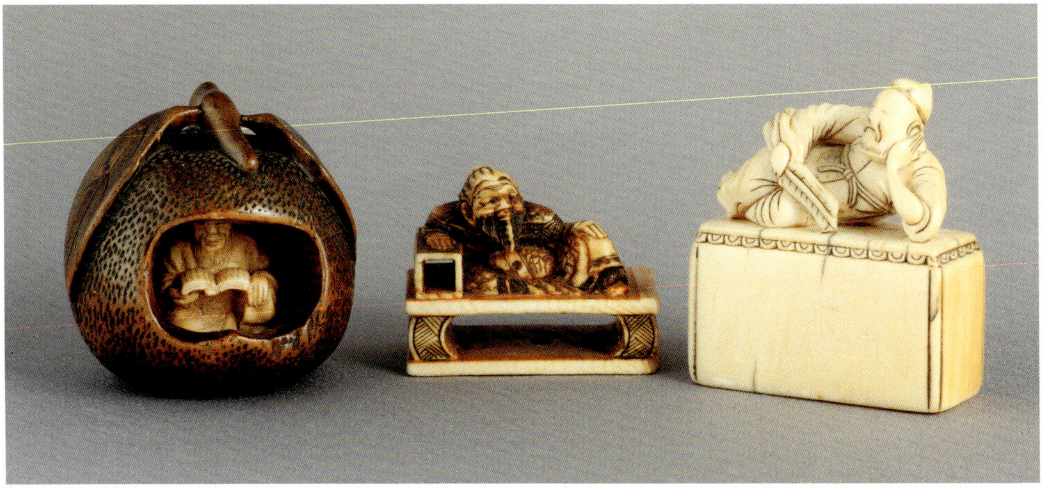

(left) ***netsuke*** of a figure (Fukurokuju?) with a fan, signed Gyokuichi, 19th century • (à gauche) ***netsuke***, personnage (Fukurokuju?) avec un éventail, signé Gyokuichi, 19e siècle • ivory • Fred and Isabel Pollard Collection, AGGV 1965.097.001 • (right) ***netsuke*** of archer seated on a rock, signed Kawamata Tsunemasa, 18th century • (à droite) ***netsuke***, archer assis sur un rocher, signé Kawamata Tsunemasa, 18e siècle • ivory • Fred and Isabel Pollard Collection, AGGV 1974.204.001

(left) ***netsuke*** depicting a sage inside a tangerine • (à gauche) ***netsuke***, sage assis dans une mandarine • 19th century • ivory, wood • Fred and Isabel Pollard Collection, AGGV 1974.216.001 • (middle) ***netsuke*** of a reclining scholar, signed Masahiro, 19th century • (au milieu) ***netsuke***, érudit étendu, signé Masahiro, 19e siècle • ivory • Gift of Ines Mottershead in memory of her father Col. H.C.Carey, C.M.G. AGGV 1978.194.001 • (right) ***netsuke*** of a Chinese sage with a fan on a rectangle dais • (à droite) ***netsuke***, sage chinois avec un éventail sur une estrade rectangulaire • 18th century • ivory • Gift of the Lewis and Ruth Sherman Foundation, AGGV 2007.016.091

(left) ***netsuke*** of *shishimai* lion dancer with mask • (à gauche) ***netsuke***, *shishimai*, danseur lion avec masque • 18th century • ivory • Gift of James and Joanna Davidson, AGGV 2006.002.028 • (right) ***netsuke*** of *shishimai* lion dancer • (à droite) ***netsuke***, danseur lion *shishimai* • 19th century • boxwood, lacquer • Gift of James and Joanna Davidson, AGGV 2006.002.045

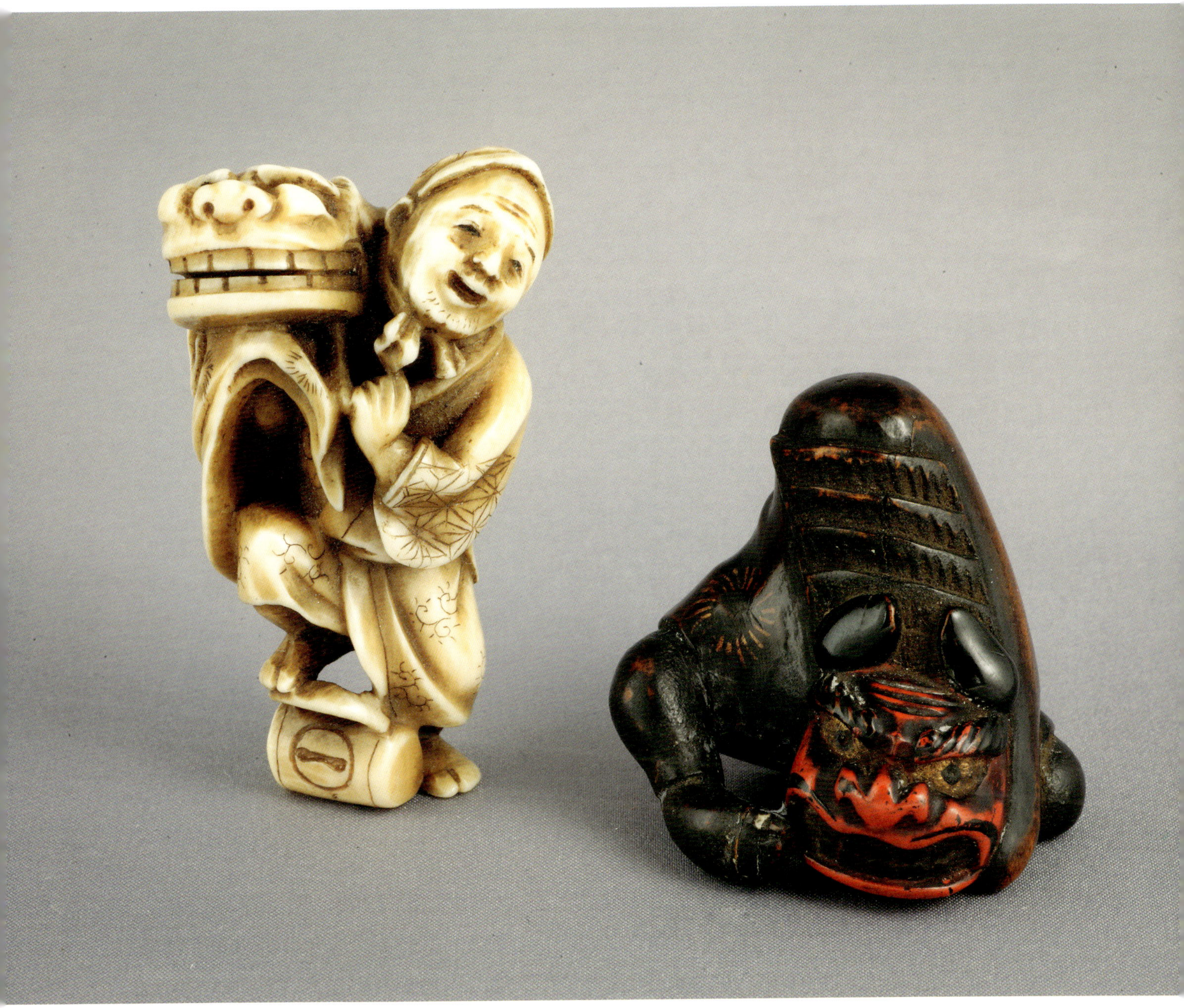

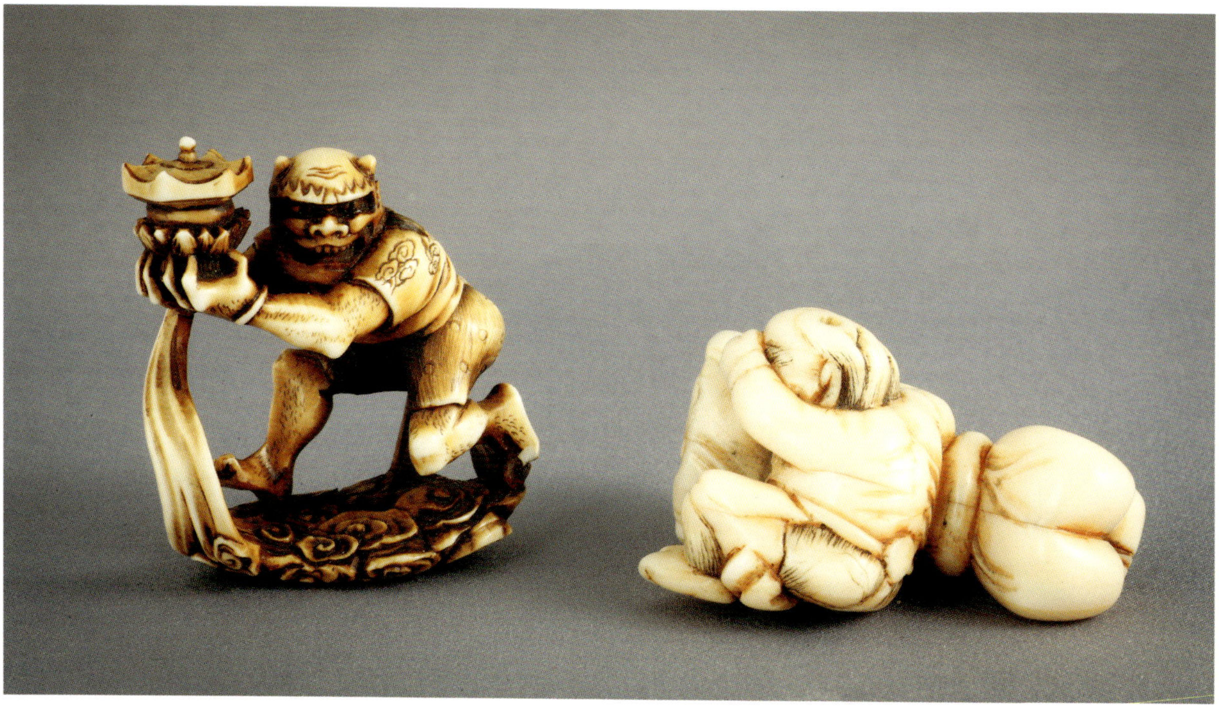

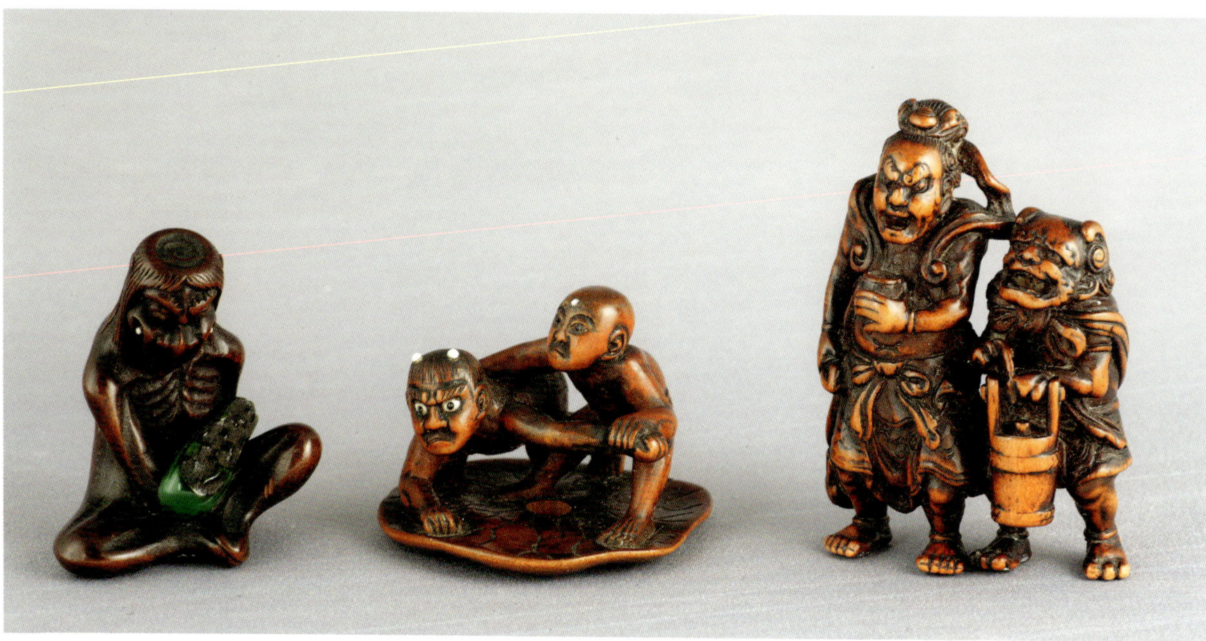

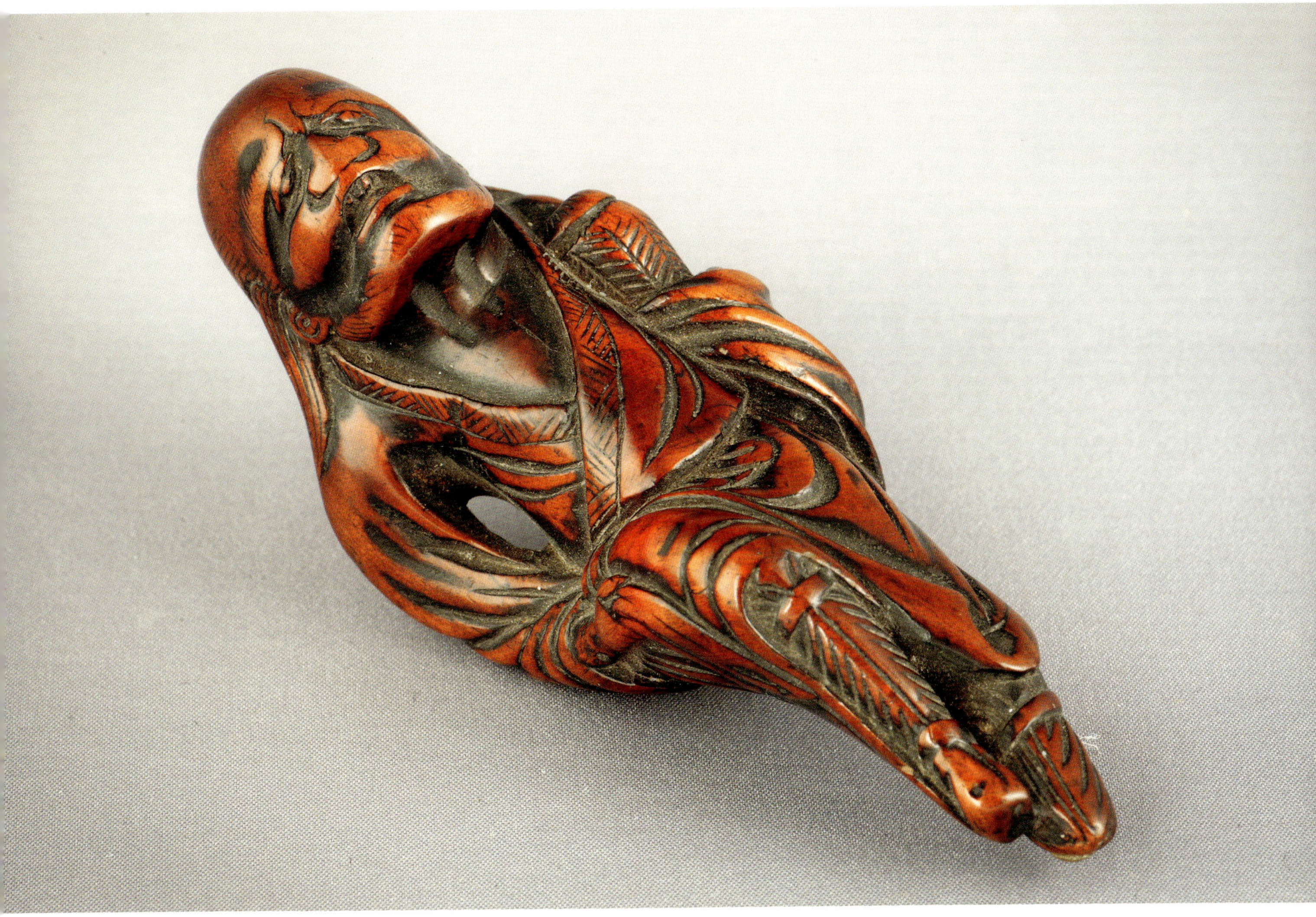

(left) ***netsuke*** of an *oni* lantern bearer • (à gauche) ***netsuke***, porteur de lanterne *oni* • 19th century • ivory • Fred and Isabel Pollard Collection, AGGV 1974.221.001 • (right) ***netsuke*** of small *oni* demon with large severed arm • (à droite) ***netsuke***, petit démon *oni* avec grand bras coupé • early 20th century • ivory • Gift of the Lewis and Ruth Sherman Foundation, AGGV 2007.016.048

(left) ***netsuke*** of *kappa* holding a cucumber signed Ryusai, late 19th century • (à gauche) ***netsuke***, *kappa* tenant un concombre, signé Ryusai, fin du 19e siècle • fruitwood, ivory, horn • Gift of the Lewis and Ruth Sherman Foundation, AGGV 2007.016.045 • (middle) ***netsuke*** of the Buddhist deity Jizo and an *oni* wrestling • (au milieu) ***netsuke***, lutte de la déité bouddhiste Jizo ave un *oni* • 19th century • boxwood, ivory, mother-of-pearl • Gift of the Lewis and Ruth Sherman Foundation, AGGV 2007.016.006 • (right) ***netsuke*** of a Nio and Raijin the Thunder God sharing a cup of sake, signed Ikkosai, 19th century • (à droite) ***netsuke***, Nio et Raijin, le dieu du tonnerre, partageant une tasse de saké, signé Ikkosai, 19e siècle • boxwood • Gift of the Lewis and Ruth Sherman Foundation, AGGV 2007.016.041

netsuke of ghostly figure • ***netsuke***, personnage fantomatique 19th century • wood • Given in Memory of John P. Nind by his Wife and Daughter 1974.148.001

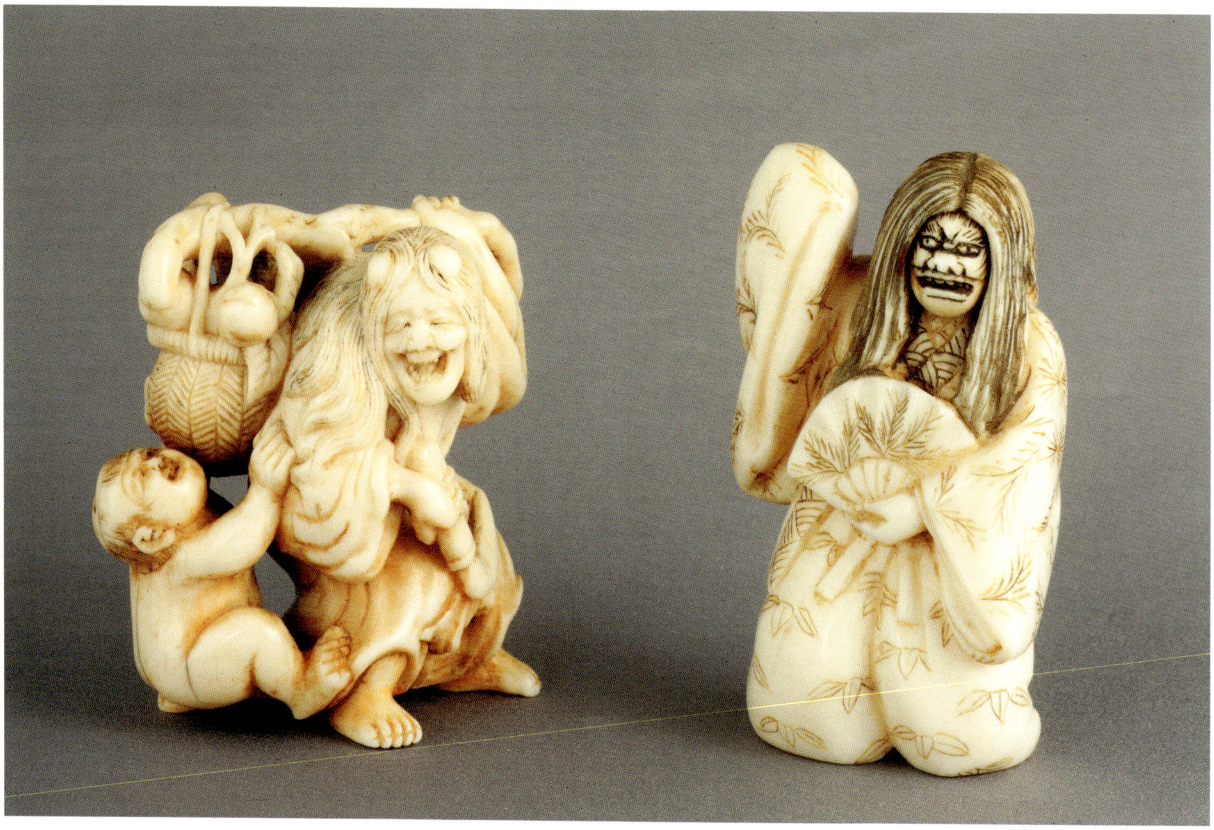

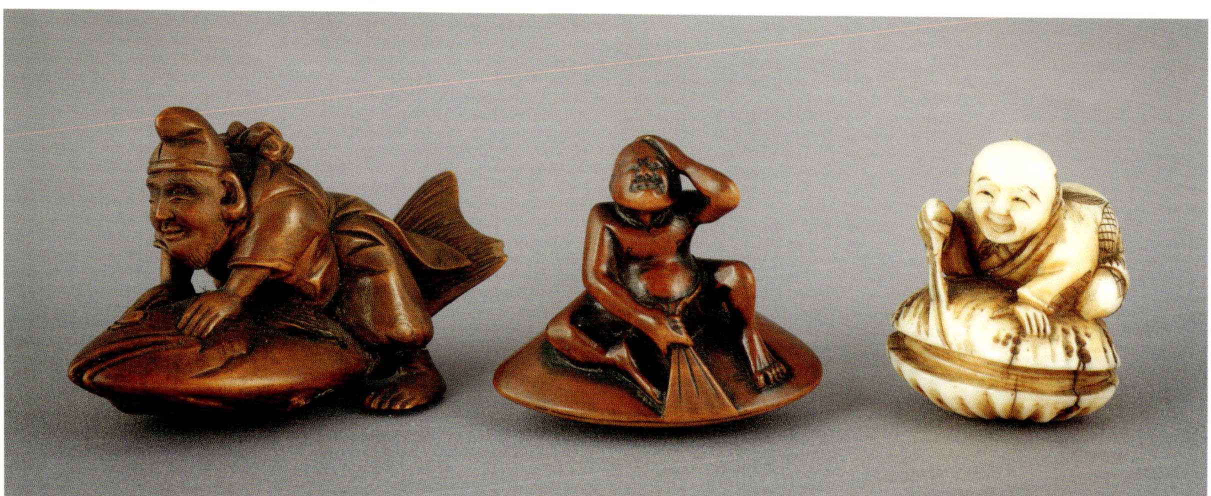

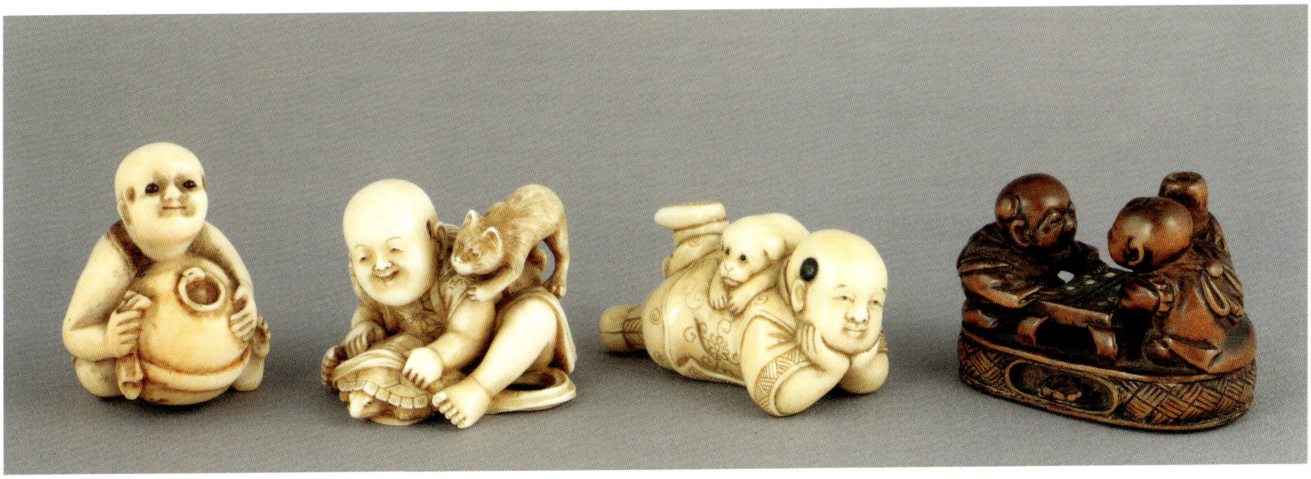

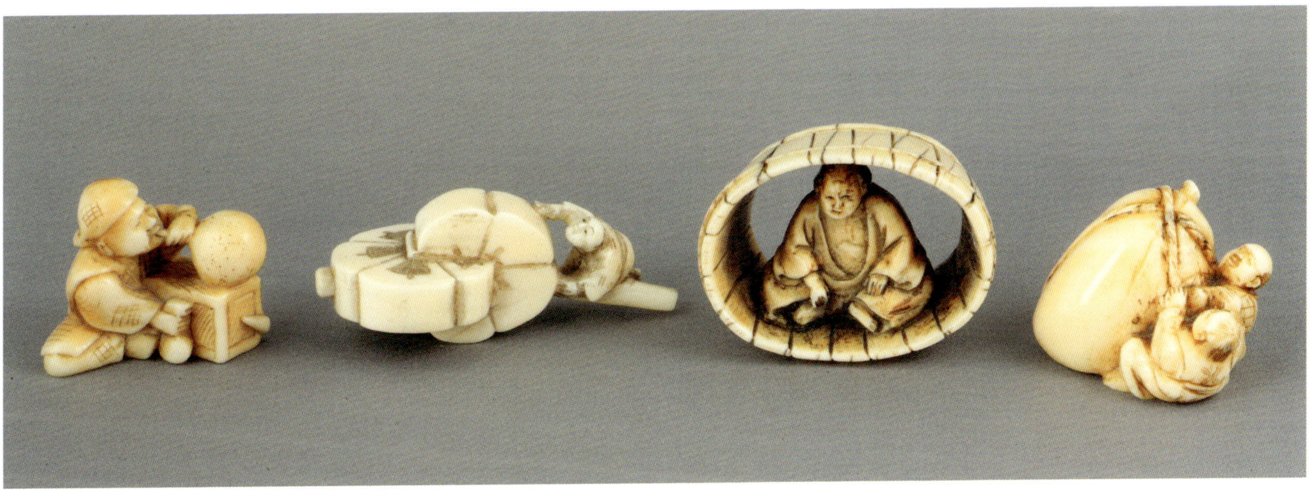

(left) ***netsuke*** depicting Yamauba and her son Kintaro harvesting peaches • (à gauche) ***netsuke***, Yamauba et son fils Kintaro récoltant les pêches • late 19th century • ivory • Gift of the Lewis and Ruth Sherman Foundation, AGGV 2007.016.022 • (right) ***netsuke*** of *Noh* actor with rotating faces • (à droite) ***netsuke***, masque d'un acteur *Nô* avec rotation des visages • early 20th century • ivory • Given in memory of J.E. (Ted) Browne by his wife Cora, AGGV SC1028

(left) ***netsuke*** of Ebisu with a large fish • (à gauche) ***netsuke***, Ebisu avec un gros poisson • early 20th century • wood • Gift of Mrs. Ruth McCuaig, SC1128 • (middle) ***netsuke*** of fisherman on a large clam • (au milieu) ***netsuke***, pêcheur sur une grosse palourde • 19th century • boxwood • Gift of the Lewis and Ruth Sherman Foundation, AGGV 2007.016.063 • (right) ***netsuke*** of man on giant clam • (à droite) ***netsuke***, homme sur une palourde géante • 19th century • ivory • Gift of James and Joanna Davidson, AGGV 2006.002.017

(left) ***netsuke*** of a glassblower • (à gauche) ***netsuke***, souffleur de verre • early 20th century • ivory • Gift of Glwladys Downes, AGGV SC441 • (second left) ***netsuke*** depicting a man and a rice mill, signed Umeichi, 19th century • (deuxième à gauche) ***netsuke***, un homme et une rizerie, signé Umeichi, 19e siècle bone • Fred and Isabel Pollard Collection, AGGV 1974.202.001 • (second right) ***netsuke*** of man in a barrel, signed Gyokushi, 19th century • (deuxième à droite) ***netsuke,*** homme dans un baril, signé Gyokushi, 19e siècle • ivory • Gift of James and Joanna Davidson, AGGV 2006.002.025 • (right) ***netsuke*** of two men with a giant marrow • (à droite) ***netsuke***, deux hommes avec une courge géante • 19th century • ivory • Gift of James and Joanna Davidson, AGGV 2006.002.033

(left) ***netsuke*** of a boy polishing a *mokugyo* bell, signed Masatami, 19th century • (à gauche) ***netsuke***, garçon polissant une cloche *mokugyo*, signé Masatami, 19e siècle • ivory • Gift of James and Joanna Davidson. AGGV 2006.002.019 • (second left) ***netsuke*** of happy boy with turtle and cat, signed Toranemu, 19th century • (deuxième à gauche) ***netsuke***, garçon joyeux avec une tortue et un chat, signé Toranemu, 19e siècle • ivory • Fred and Isabel Pollard Collection, AGGV 1974.210.001 • (second right) ***netsuke*** of a Chinese boy with a puppy • (deuxième à droite) ***netsuke***, garçon chinois avec un chiot • 19th century • ivory • Gift of the Lewis and Ruth Sherman Foundation, AGGV 2007.016.001 • (right) ***netsuke*** of two boys playing *go* • (à droite) ***netsuke***, deux garçons jouant au jeu de *go* • 19th century • wood • Fred and Isabel Pollard Collection, AGGV 1964.002.001

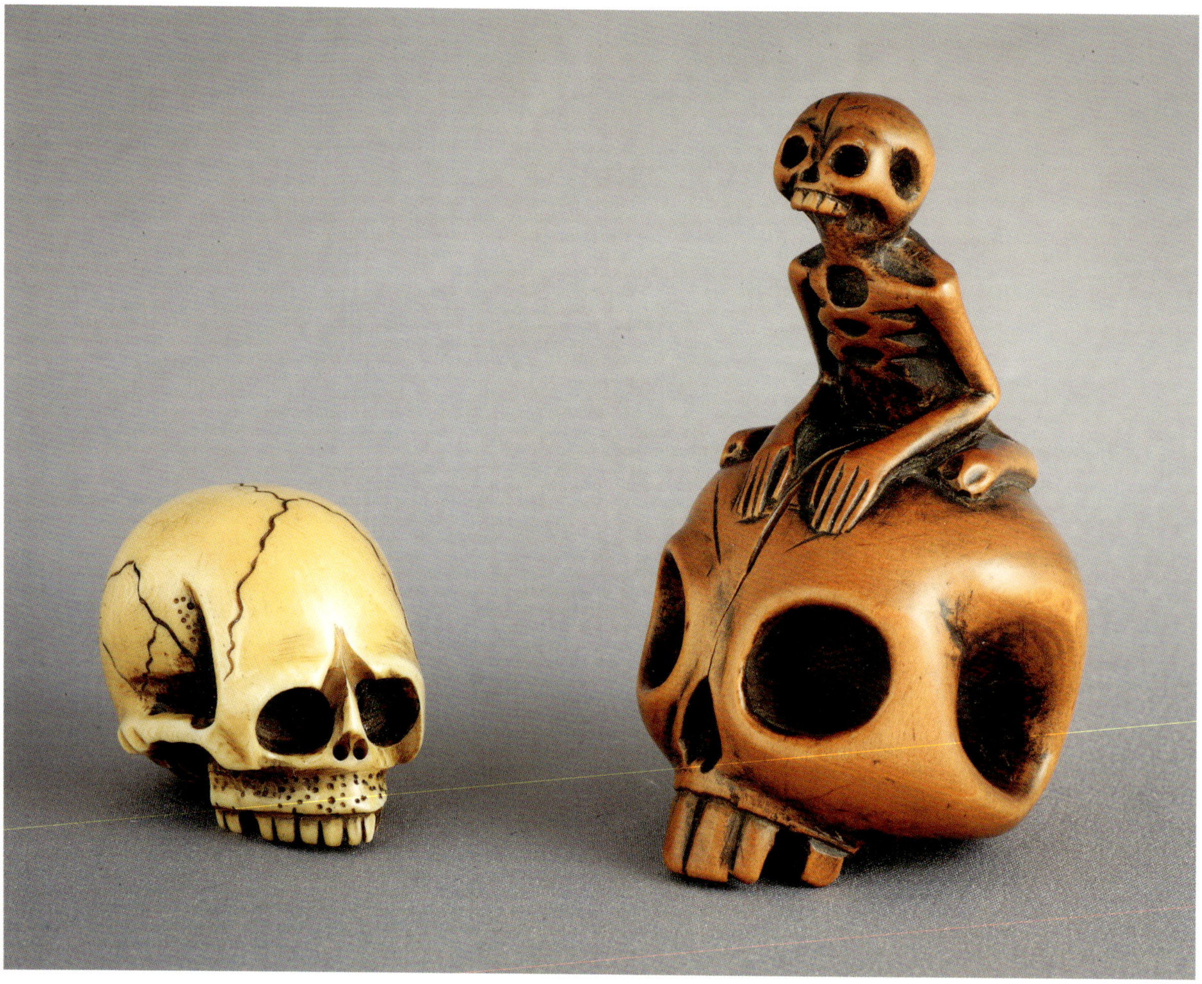

(left) ***netsuke*** of a skull • (à gauche) ***netsuke***, crâne • 19th century • ivory • Gift of Philip and Georgina Steel, SC898 • (right) ***netsuke*** of a skeleton on a skull • (à droite) ***netsuke***, squelette sur un crâne • 19th century • boxwood • Gift of the Lewis and Ruth Sherman Foundation, AGGV 2007.016.046

(left) ***netsuke*** a court lady wearing a kimono with a puppy in a fold, signed Hidemasa, late 18th century • (à gauche) ***netsuke***, courtisane en kimono avec un chiot dans un pli, signé Hidemasa, fin du 18e siècle • ivory • Gift of James and Joanna Davidson, AGGV 2006.002.009 • (second left) ***netsuke*** of a woman wearing a kimono, signed Shunei, 19th century • (deuxième à gauche) ***netsuke***, femme en kimono, signé Shunei, 19e siècle • ivory • Fred and Isabel pollard Collection, AGGV 1974.195.001 • (second right) ***netsuke*** a woman wearing a kimono casting beans with an *oni*, signed Shuraku, 19th century • (deuxième à droite) ***netsuke***, femme en kimono lançant des haricots avec un *oni*, signé Shuraku, 19e siècle • ivory • Gift of James and Joanna Davidson, AGGV 2006.002.010 • (right) ***netsuke*** of a woman trimming her toenails, signed Yoshihide, ca. 1920 • (à droite) ***netsuke***, femme coupant ses ongles d'orteil, signé Yoshihide, vers 1920 • fruitwood, persimmon, pigment, ivory • Gift of the Lewis and Ruth Sherman Foundation, AGGV 2007.016.025

(left) ***netsuke*** of Oguri Hangan persuading his horse to kneel on a *go* board, signed Mitsutoshi, early 20th century • (à gauche) ***netsuke***, Oguri Hangan essayant de persuader son cheval de s'agenouiller sur une planche du jeu de *go*, signé Mitsutoshi, début du 20e siècle • ivory • Gift of the Lewis and Ruth Sherman Foundation, AGGV2007.016.035 • (right) ***netsuke*** of woman seated on her servant examining plum blossoms, signed Keiun, early 20th century • (à droite) ***netsuke***, femme assise sur domestique examinant les fleurs de prunier, signé Keiun, début du 20e siècle • ivory, pigment • Gift of the Lewis and Ruth Sherman Foundation, AGGV 2007.016.014

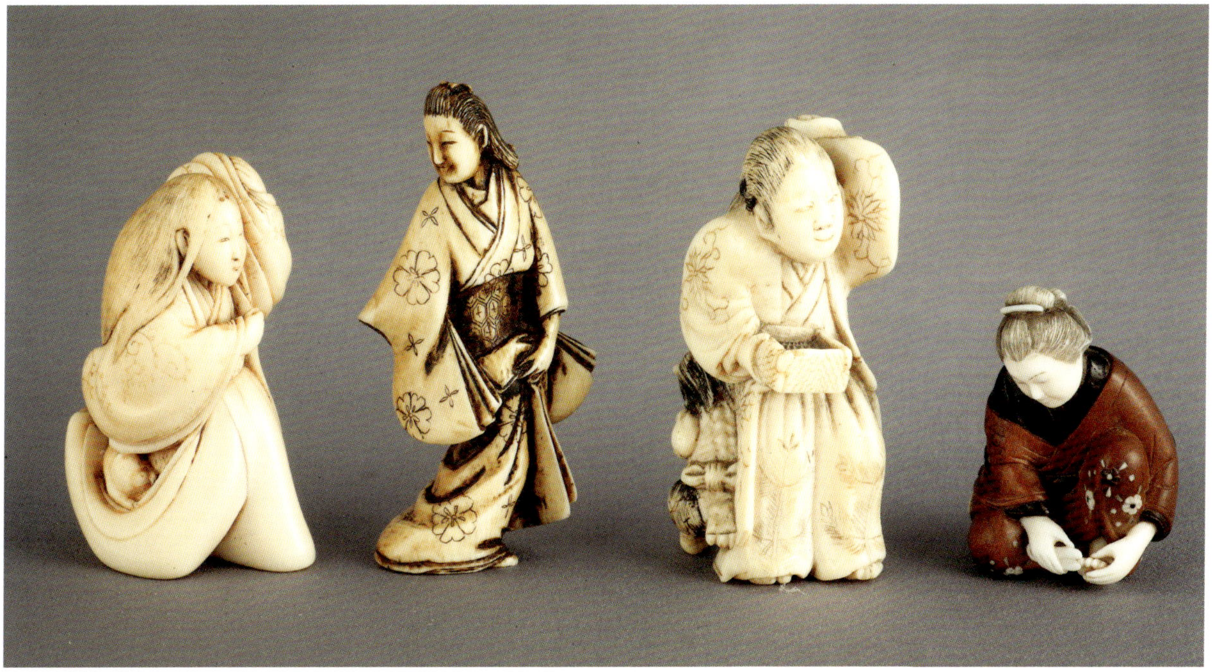

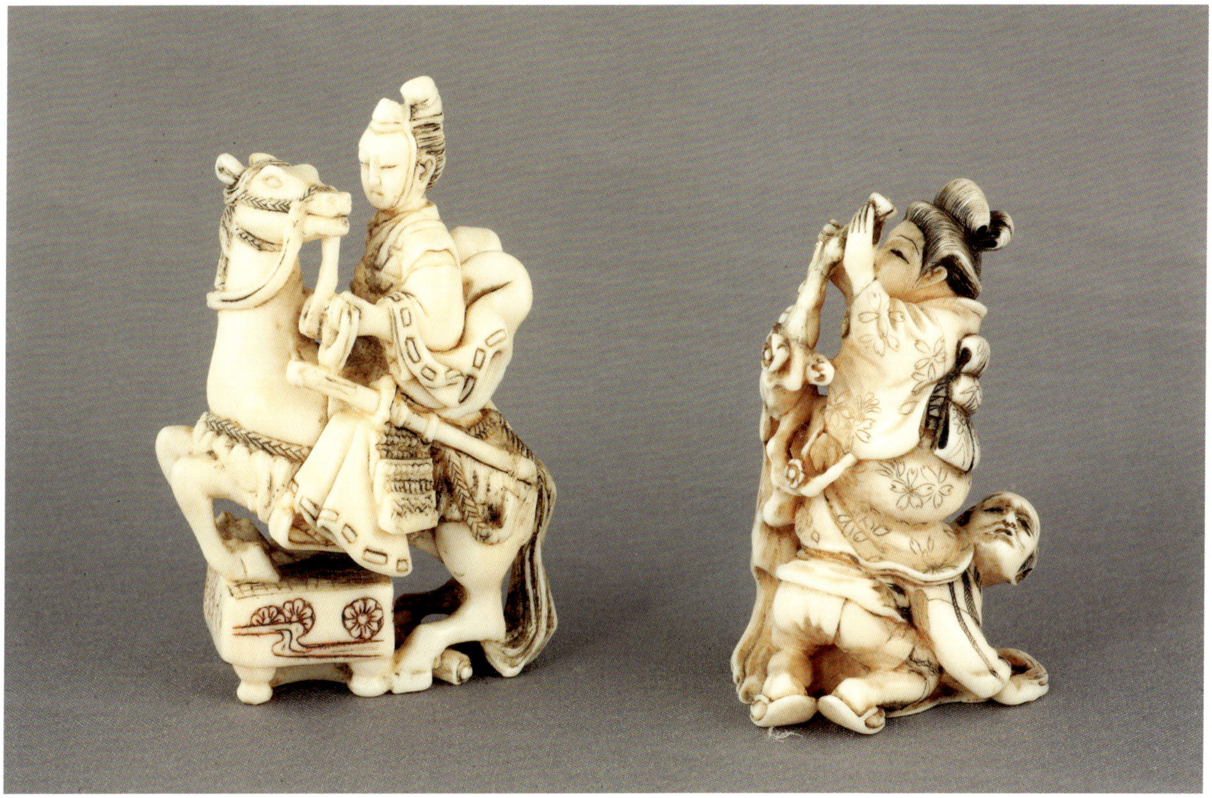

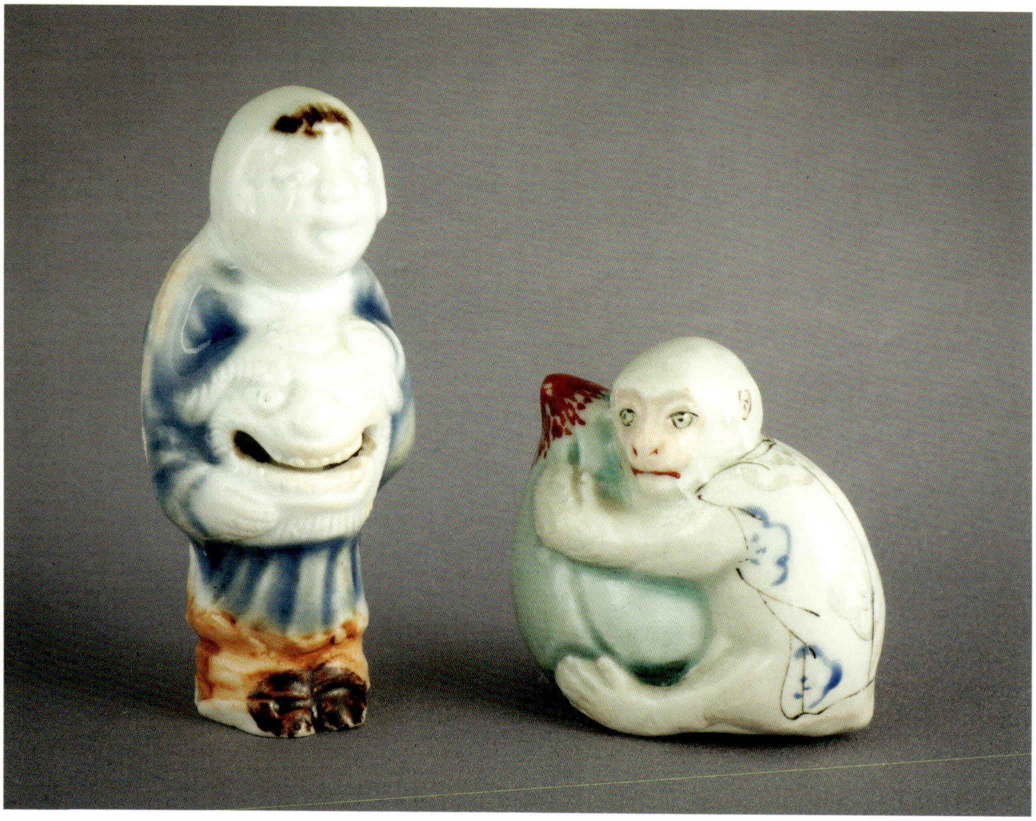

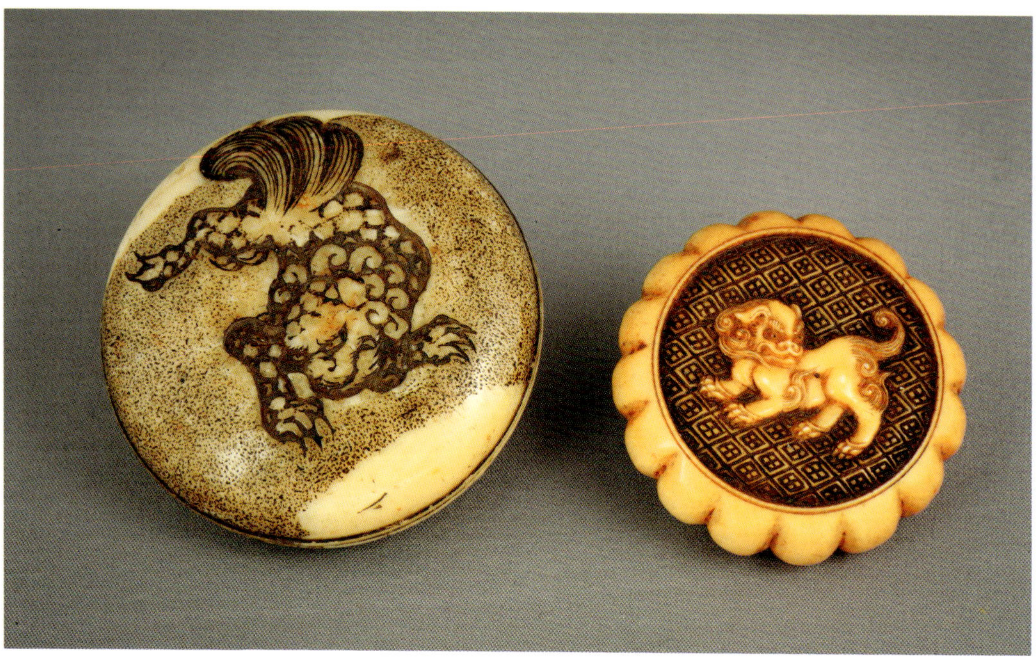

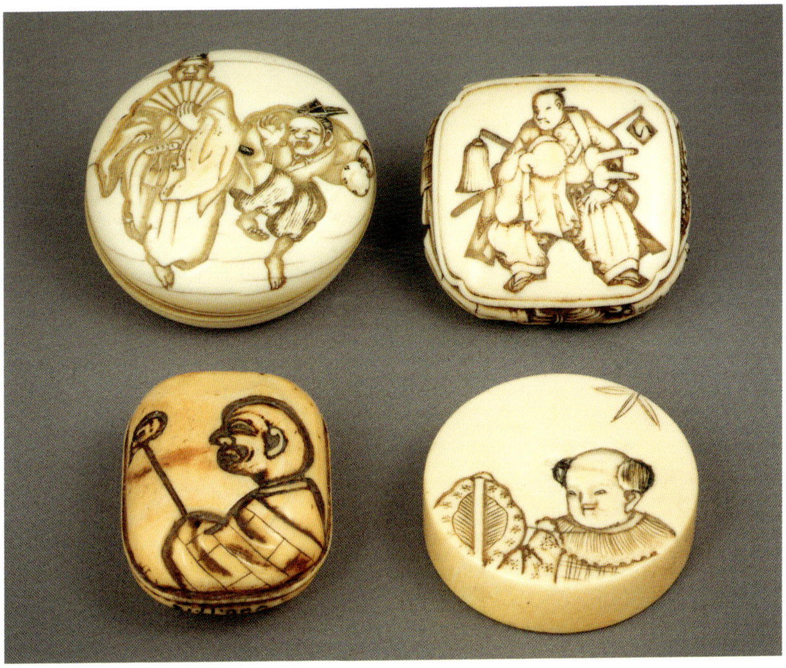

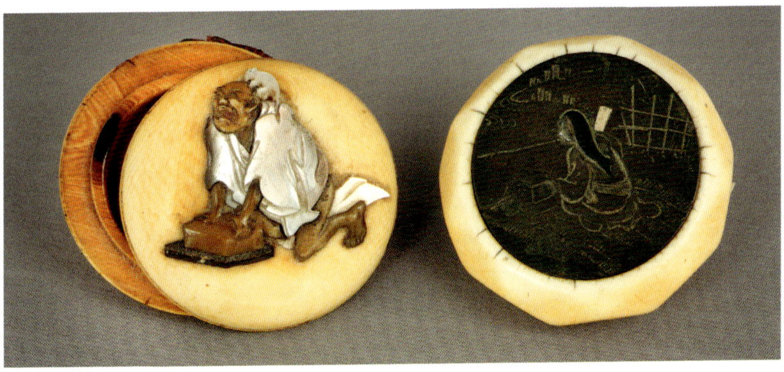

netsuke of Karako holding a lion dance mask/of a monkey with peach • ***netsuke***, Karako tenant un masque de la danse du lion/singe avec une pêche • 19th century • Hirado ware, porcelain • Gift of the Lewis and Ruth Sherman Foundation, AGGV 2007.016.013, 2007.016.081

(left) ***netsuke*** with design of a *shishi* lion • (à gauche) ***netsuke***, motif de lion *shishi* • 19th century • ivory • Gift of Arden and Judy Schnee, AGGV 200.017.0016 • (right) *manju* type ***netsuke*** with design of a *shishi* lion • (à droite) ***netsuke*** de type manju avec motif de lion *shishi* • 19th century • ivory • Gift of James and Joanna Davidson, AGGV 2006.002.043

(top left) *manju* type ***netsuke*** with *manzai* dancers, items for New Year's celebration on verso, Signed Koshu or Koju, 19th century • (En haut, à gauche) ***netsuke*** de type *manju* avec danseurs *manzai*, articles pour la célébration du Nouvel An au verso, signé Koshu ou Koju, 19e siècle • ivory • Gift of the Lewis and Ruth Sherman Foundation, AGGV 2007.016.098 • (top right) *manju* type ***netsuke*** with Leader of 47 Ronin, signed Gyokuho, 19th century • (En haut, à droite) ***netsuke*** de type *manju* avec chef des 47 Ronin, signé Gyokuho, 19e siècle • ivory • Gift of the Lewis and Ruth Sherman Foundation, AGGV 2007.016.034 • (bottom left) ***netsuke*** of Zen monk Ikkyu with skull on wand • (En bas, à gauche) ***netsuke***, moine zen Ikkyu avec un crâne sur une baguette • late 19th century • ivory • Gift of Arden and Judy Schnee, AGGV 2000.017.015 • (bottom right) ***netsuke*** of Karako with a Fan • (En bas, à droite) ***netsuke***, Karako avec un éventail • late 19th century • ivory • Gift of the Lewis and Ruth Sherman Foundation, AGGV 2007.016.033

(left) ***netsuke*** with inlay design of a rat catcher, signed Shoichi, early 20th century • (à gauche) ***netsuke***, motif incrusté représentant un attrapeur de rats, signé Shoichi, début du 20e siècle • ivory, mother-of-pearl • Gift of the Lewis and Ruth Sherman Foundation, AGGV 2007.016.028 • (right) *kagamibuta* ***netsuke*** with scene of a woman folding cloth • (à droite) ***netsuke*** *Kagamibuta*, scène représentant une femme pliant un linge •19th century • ivory, *shibuichi* alloy, *shakudo* alloy, gold, silver • Gift of the Lewis and Ruth Sherman Foundation, AGGV 2007.016.032

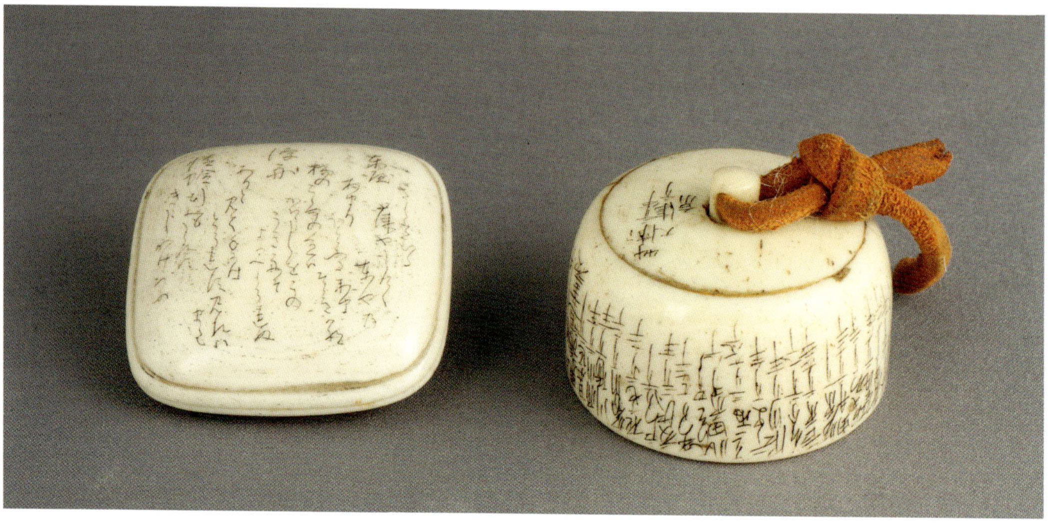

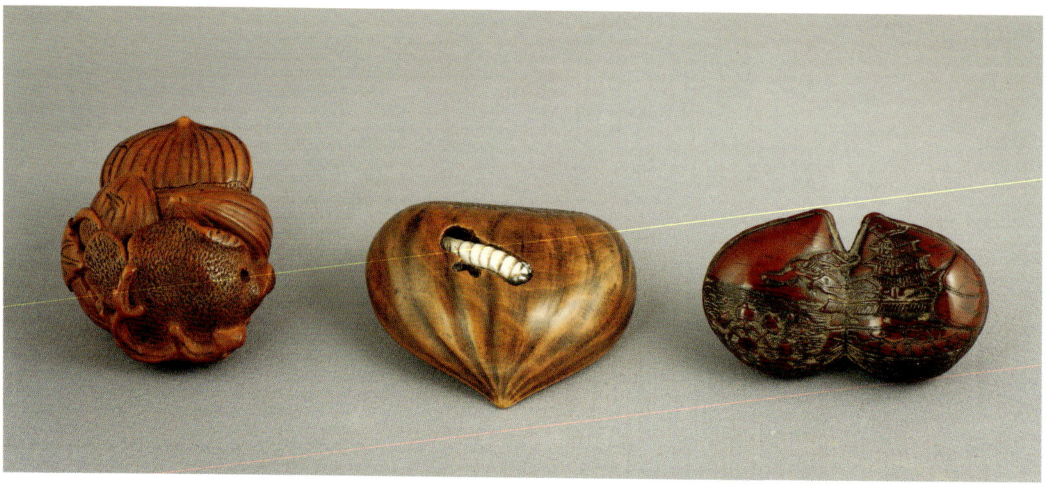

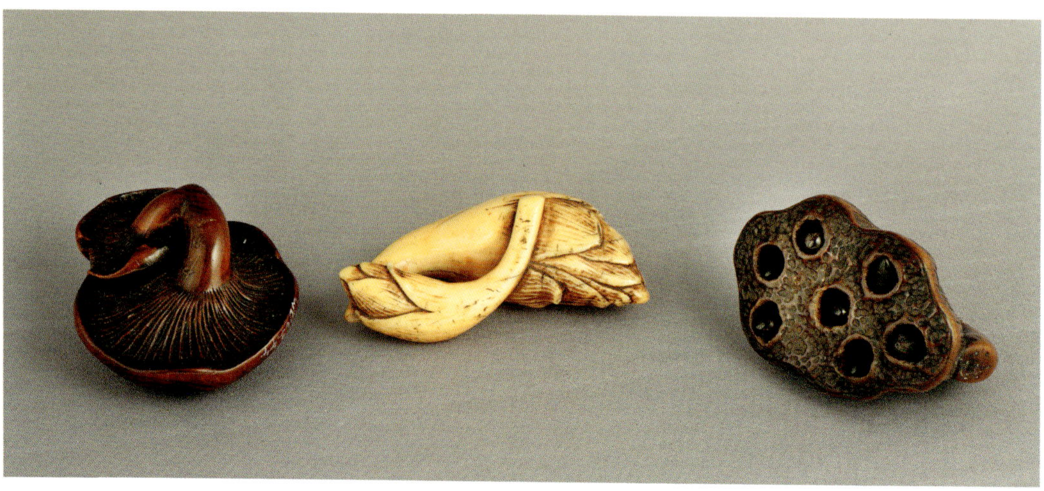

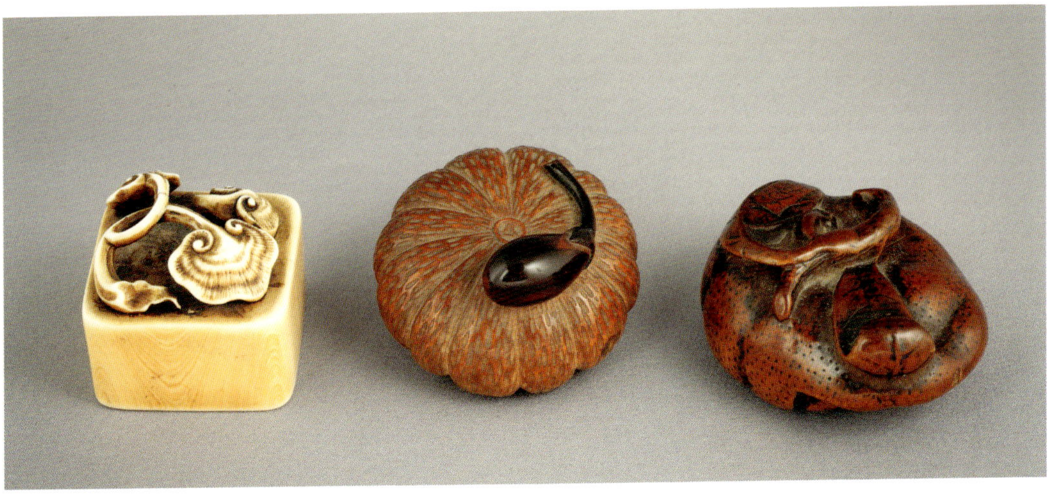

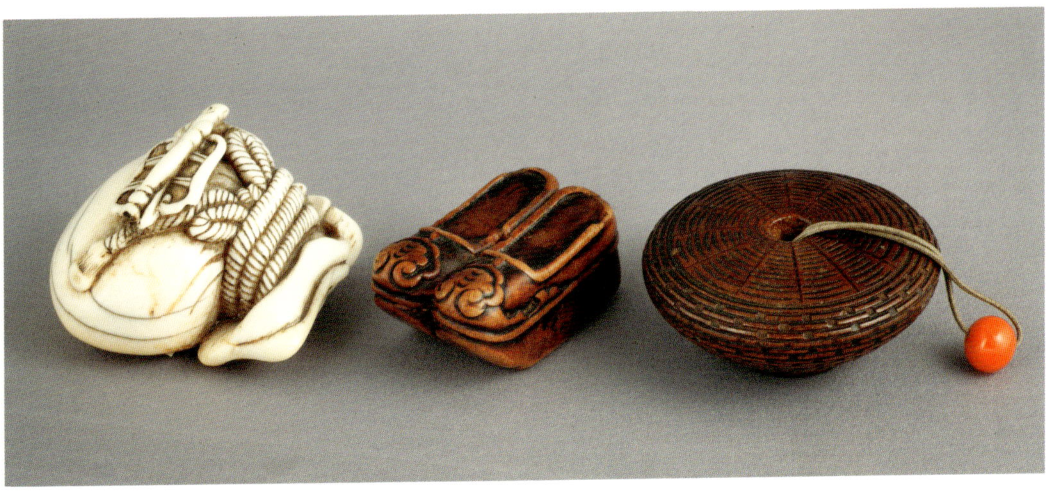

157

(left) *manju* type ***netsuke*** with calligraphy • (à gauche) ***netsuke*** de type *manju* avec caractères de calligraphie • 19th century • ivory • Gift of the Lewis and Ruth Sherman Foundation, AGGV 2007.016.097 • (right) ***netsuke*** in form of a bell with inscriptions listing the 53 Stations of the Tokaido Road • (à droite) ***netsuke*** en forme de cloche avec inscriptions • mid 19th century • ivory • Gift of James and Joanna Davidson, AGGV 2006.002.020

(left) ***netsuke*** of a chestnut, signed Suyo, 19th century • (à gauche) ***netsuke***, châtaigne, signé Suyo, 19e siècle • wood • Edith Low-Beer Collection, AGGV 1990.038.005 • (middle) ***netsuke*** in the shape of a chestnut with maggot • (au milieu) ***netsuke*** en forme de châtaigne et asticot • early 19th century • wood, ivory • Gift of James and Joanna Davidson, AGGV 2006 002.042 • (right) ***netsuke*** of two nuts with engraved landscape scene • (à droite) ***netsuke***, deux noix avec paysage gravé • 19th century • wood, lacquer • Gift of James and Joanna Davidson, AGGV 2006.002.027

(left) ***netsuke*** of two mushrooms • (à gauche) ***Nesuke***, deux champignons • 19th century • wood • Gift of James and Joanna Davidson, AGGV 2006.002.044 • (middle) ***netsuke*** of a spring vegetable • (au milieu) ***netsuke***, légume printanier • 19th century • ivory • Fred and Isabel Pollard Collection, AGGV 1967.182.004 • (right) ***netsuke*** of a lotus pod • (à droite) ***netsuke***, cosse de lotus • 19th century • wood • Fred and Isabel Pollard Collection, AGGV 1967.182.002

(left) ***netsuke*** of a fungus of immortality • (à gauche) ***netsuke***, champignon de l'immortalité • 19th century • ivory • Fred and Isabel Pollard Collection, AGGV 1974.203.001 • (middle) ***netsuke*** of a squash • (au milieu) ***netsuke***, courge • 19th century • wood • Given in Memory of John P. Nind by his Wife and Daughter, AGGV 1974.150.001 • (right) ***netsuke*** of mandarin orange, signed Tomonobu, early 19th century • (à droite) ***netsuke***, mandarine, signé Tomonobu, début du 19e siècle • wood • Gift of James and Joanna Davidson, AGGV 2006.002.041

(left) ***netsuke*** of Hotei's bag of good fortune • (à gauche) ***netsuke***, sac de Hotei symbolisant la bonne fortune • early 19th century • ivory • Gift of the Lewis and Ruth Sherman Foundation, AGGV 2007.016.030 • (middle) ***netsuke*** of monk's shoes • (au milieu) ***netsuke***, chaussures de moine • 19th century • wood • Fred and Isabel Pollard Collection, AGGV 1974.212.001 • (right) ***netsuke*** of fisherman's basket • (à droite) ***netsuke***, panier de pêcheur • 19th century • wood • Fred and Isabel Pollard Collection, AGGV 1974.214.001

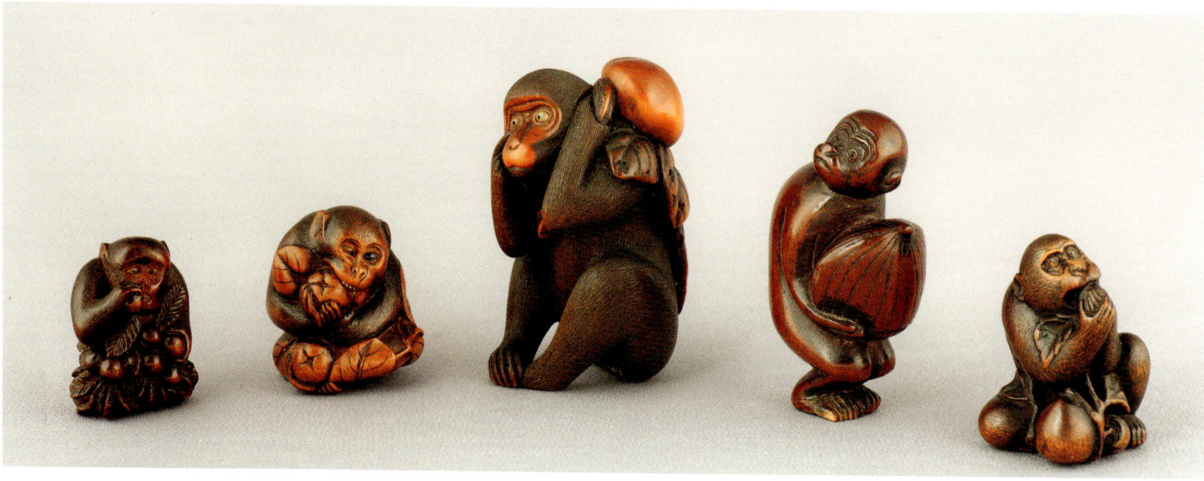

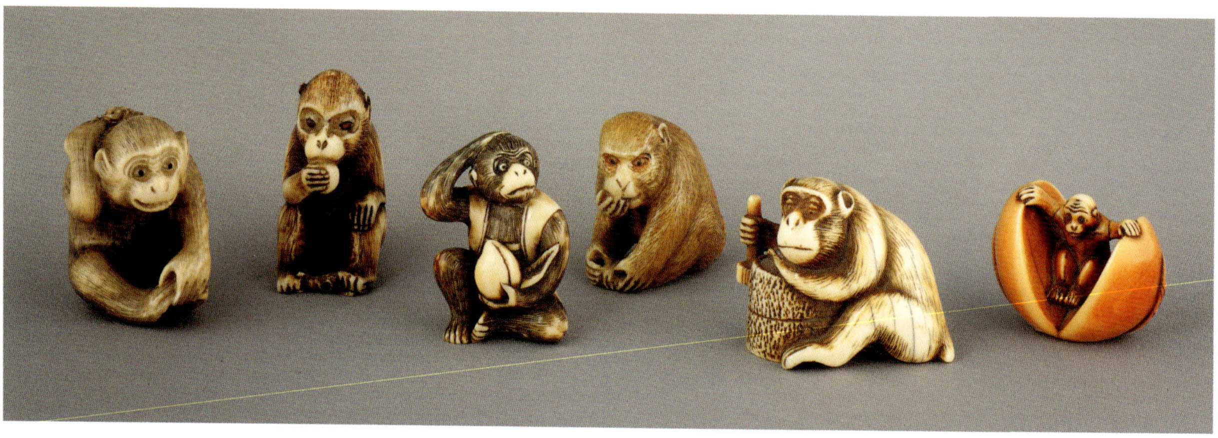

netsuke in form of monkeys • ***netsuke*** en forme de singes • (left) Monkey crouching • (à gauche) Singe en position accroupie • 19th century • wood • Gift of the Lewis and Ruth Sherman Foundation, AGGV 2007.016.054 • (second left) Monkey biting into a persimmon • (deuxième à gauche) Singe mordant dans un kaki • late 19th century • fruitwood, horn, ivory • Gift of the Lewis and Ruth Sherman Foundation, AGGV 2007.016.056 • (middle) Monkey eating from a branch of persimmon, signed Gyokuzan, late 19th century • (au milieu) Singe se nourrissant d'une branche de kaki, signé Gyokuzan, fin du 19e siècle • boxwood, horn • Gift of the Lewis and Ruth Sherman Foundation, AGGV 2007.016.069 • (middle) Monkey holding a branch with persimmons on its back, signed Koichu, early 20th century • (au milieu) Singe avec une branche de kaki sur le dos, signé Koichu, début du 20e siècle • boxwood, horn • Gift of the Lewis and Ruth Sherman Foundation, AGGV 2007.016.053 • (second right) Monkey with large chestnut • (deuxième à droite) Singe avec grosse châtaigne • 19th century • fruitwood • Gift of the Lewis and Ruth Sherman Foundation, AGGV 2007.016.010 • (right) Seated monkey eating a persimmon, signed Tomokazu, 19th century • (à droite) Singe assis mangeant un kaki, signé Tomokazu, 19e siècle • fruitwood • Gift of the Lewis and Ruth Sherman Foundation, AGGV 2007.016.021

netsuke in form of monkeys • ***netsuke*** en forme de singes • (left) Monkey with lobster • 19th/early 20th century • ivory • Gift of James and Joanna Davidson, AGGV 2006.002.032 • (second left) Monkey eating a peach, signed Rankwa, late 19th century • (Deuxième, à gauche) Singe mangeant une pêche, signé Rankwa, fin du 19e siècle • ivory, agate • Gift of James and Joanna Davidson, AGGV 2006.002.014 • (middle left) Seated monkey wearing a vest holding a peach • (au milieu, à gauche) Singe assis portant une veste et tenant une pêche • 19th century • ivory • Gift of the Lewis and Ruth Sherman Foundation, AGGV 2007.016.005 • (middle right) Seated monkey with right hand to mouth, signed Yoshihisa • (au milieu, à droite) Singe assis portant la main droite à la bouche, signé Yoshihisa • ivory • Fred and Isabel Pollard Collection, AGGV 1975.017.001 • (second right) Monkey holding mallet in right hand with left hand on mill • (Deuxième, à droite) Singe tenant un maillet dans la main droite et tenant la main gauche sur un moulin • 19th century • ivory • Fred and Isabel Pollard Collection, AGGV 1974.218.001 • (right) Monkey seated inside giant split peach • (à droite) Singe assis dans une pêche géante ouverte • 19th century • ivory • Fred and Isabel Pollard Collection, AGGV 1964.003.001

(left) ***netsuke*** of fans in openwork, signed Gyokuzan ?, 19th century • (à gauche) ***netsuke***, ajouré avec éventails, signé Gyokuzan ?, 19e siècle • ivory • Edith Low-Beer Collection, AGGV 1990.038.009 • (right) ***netsuke*** of an openwork cushion with chrysanthemum design • (à droite) ***netsuke***, coussin ajouré avec motif de chrysanthème • 19th century • ivory • Fred and Isabel Pollard Collection, AGGV 1974.206.001

164. (left) ***netsuke*** in shape of a clam with a scene of a Chinese legend • (à gauche) ***netsuke*** en forme de palourde orné d'une scène représentant une légende chinoise • 19th century • cinnabar lacquer on wood • Gift of the Lewis and Ruth Sherman Foundation, AGGV 2007.016.049 • (right) ***netsuke*** of a clam and octopus, signed Bokusan, early 19th century • (à droite) ***netsuke***, palourde et pieuvre, signé Bokusan, début du 19e siècle • ivory • Gift of James and Joanna Davidson, AGGV 2006.002.003

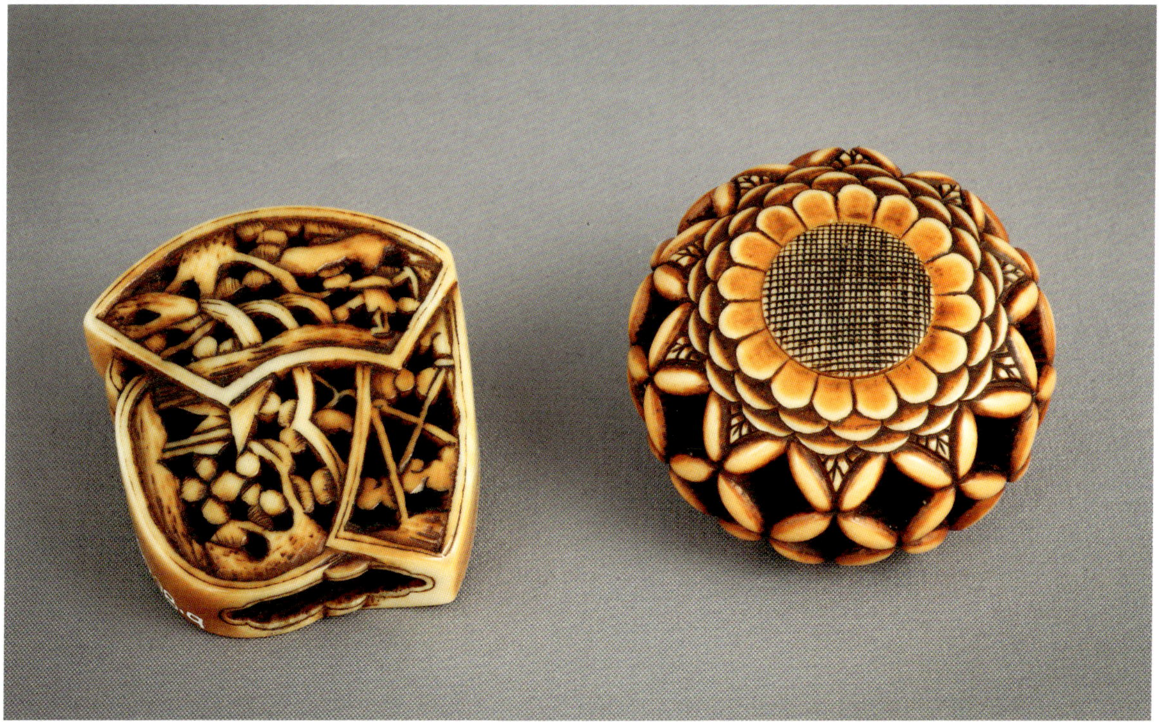

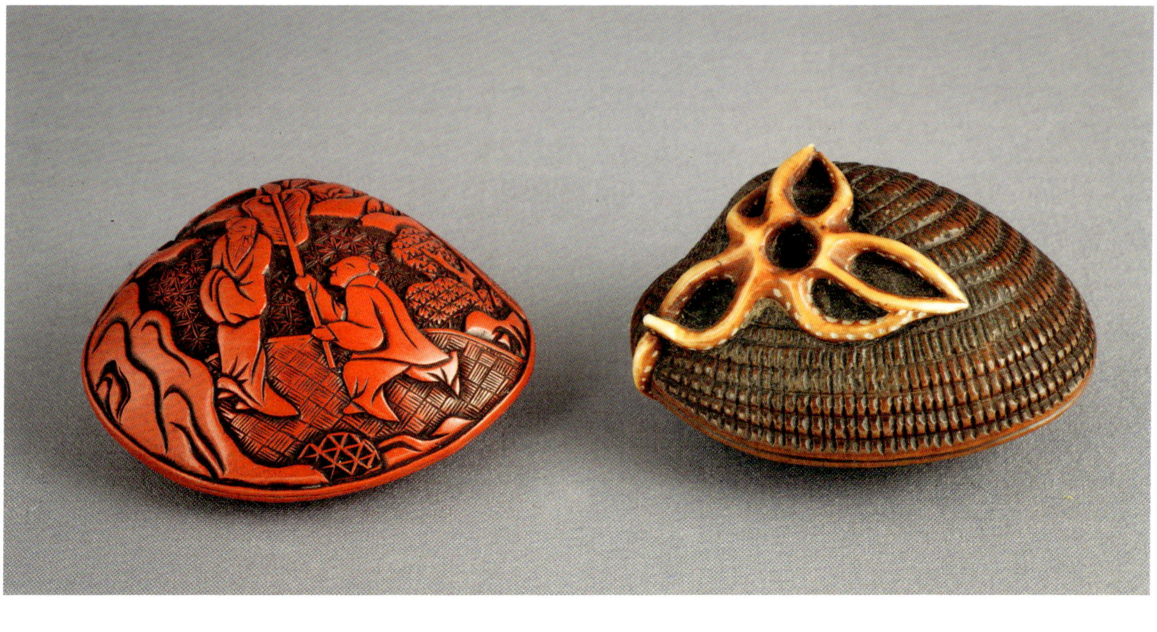

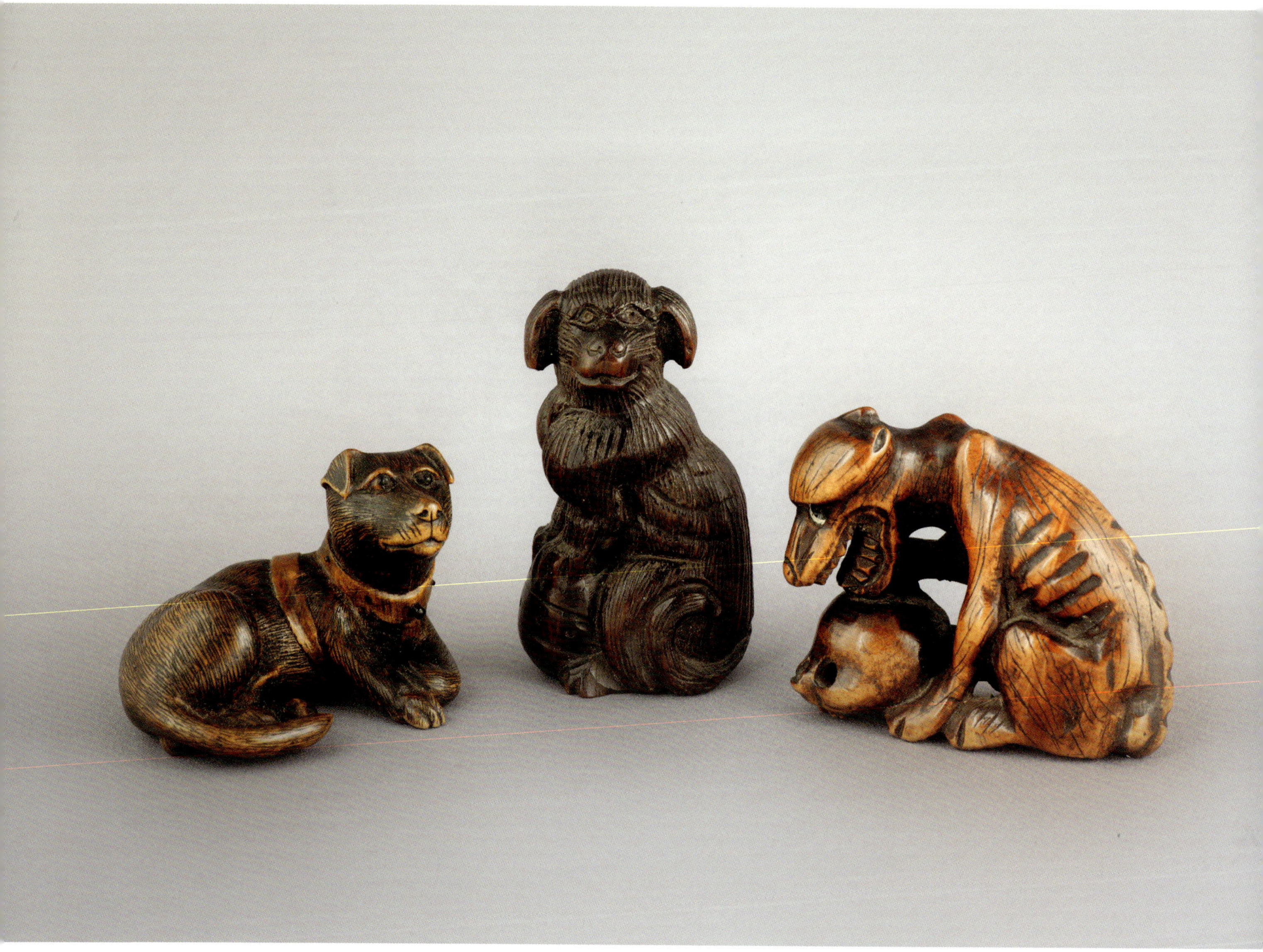

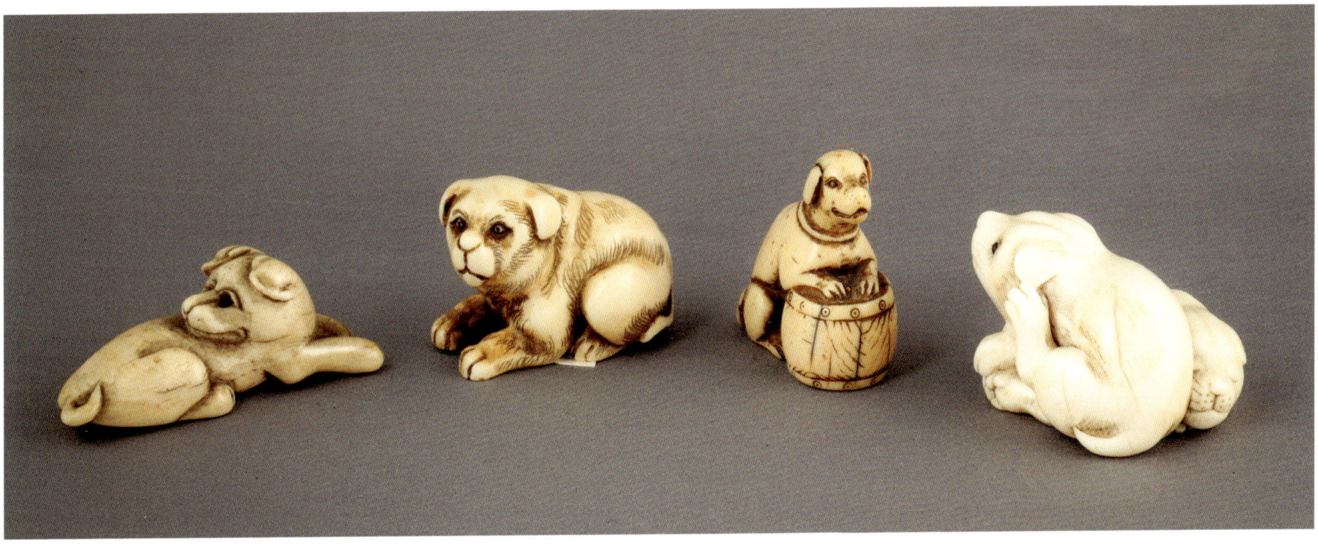

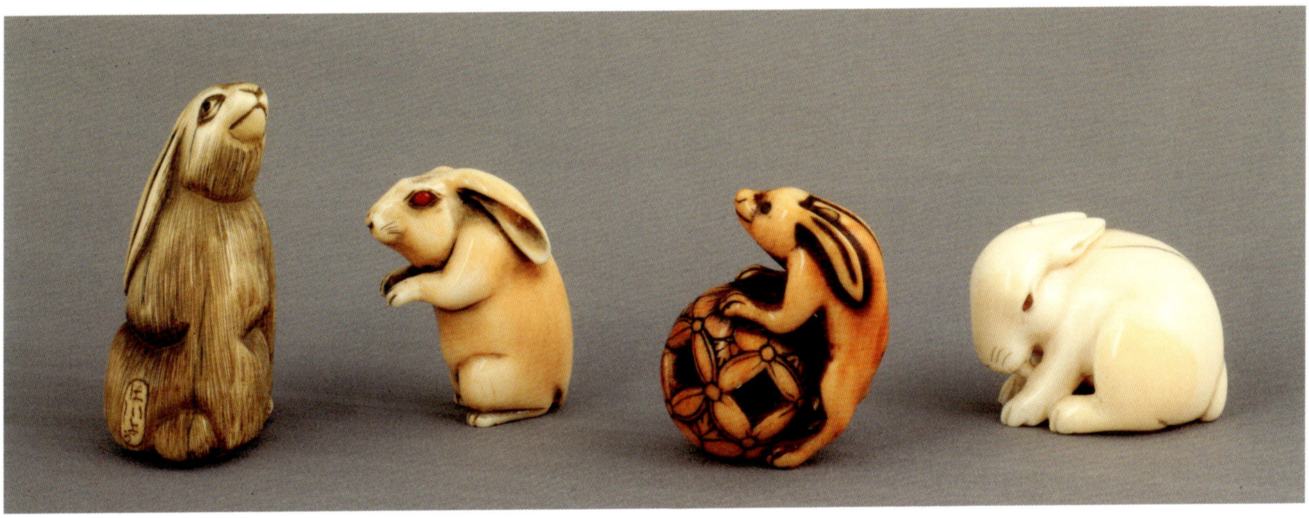

netsuke in the form of a dog • ***netsuke*** en forme de chien • (left) Reclining dog wearing a harness, signed Masanao Shinzan • (à gauche) Chien étendu portant un harnais, signé Masanao Shinzan • wood, lacquer • Fred and Isabel Pollard Collection, AGGV 1974.201.001 • (middle) Seated dog with ball, signed Gyokushi, 19th century • (au milieu) Chien assis avec balle, signé Gyokushi, 19e siècle • wood • Gift of James and Joanna Davidson, AGGV 2006.002.030 • (right) Starving dog with paw on a skull • (à droite) Chien affamé avec une patte sur un crâne • 19th century • wood • Fred and Isabel Pollard Collection, AGGV 1974.197.001

netsuke in the form of a dog • ***netsuke*** en forme de chien • (left) Reclining dog with head facing back over his body • (à gauche) Chien étendu avec la tête regardant vers l'arrière par-dessus son corps • ca. 1900 • ivory • Given in Memory of John P. Nind by his Wife and Daughter, AGGV 1974.153.001 • (second left) Reclining Dog, signed Toshiyuki, 19th century • (deuxième à gauche) Chien étendu, signé Toshiyuki, 19e siècle • ivory • Fred and Isabel Pollard Collection AGGV 1975.018.001 • (second right) Seated dog has forepaws on drum • (deuxième à droite) Chien assis avec les pattes de devant sur un tambour • ca. 1900 • ivory • Fred and Isabel Pollard Collection, AGGV 1974.227.001 • (right) Two puppies, one sleeping and the other scratching, signed Issan, late 19th century • (à droite) Deux chiots, dont un endormi et l'autre se grattant, signé Issan, fin du 19e siècle • ivory • Gift of the Lewis and Ruth Sherman Foundation, AGGV 2007.016.044

netsuke in the form of a hare • ***netsuke*** en forme de lièvre • (left) Hare, signed Haiyoshiu, 19th century • (à gauche) Lièvre, signé Haiyoshiu, 19e siècle • ivory • Gift of James and Joanna Davidson, AGGV 2006.002.031 • (second left) Hare sitting up on its haunches, signed Okatomo, 19th century • (deuxième à gauche) Lièvre assis sur son arrière-train, signé Okatomo, 19e siècle • ivory, glass • Fred and Isabel Pollard Collection, AGGV 1974.200.001 • (second right) Hare on a decorative pierced ball • (deuxième à droite) Lièvre sur une balle décorative percée • early 19th century • ivory • Gift of the Lewis and Ruth Sherman Foundation, AGGV 2007.016.089 • (right) Hare, signed Ranichi, mid 20th century • (à droite) Lièvre, signé Ranichi, milieu du 20e siècle • ivory, horn • Gift of the Lewis and Ruth Sherman Foundation, AGGV 2007.016.023

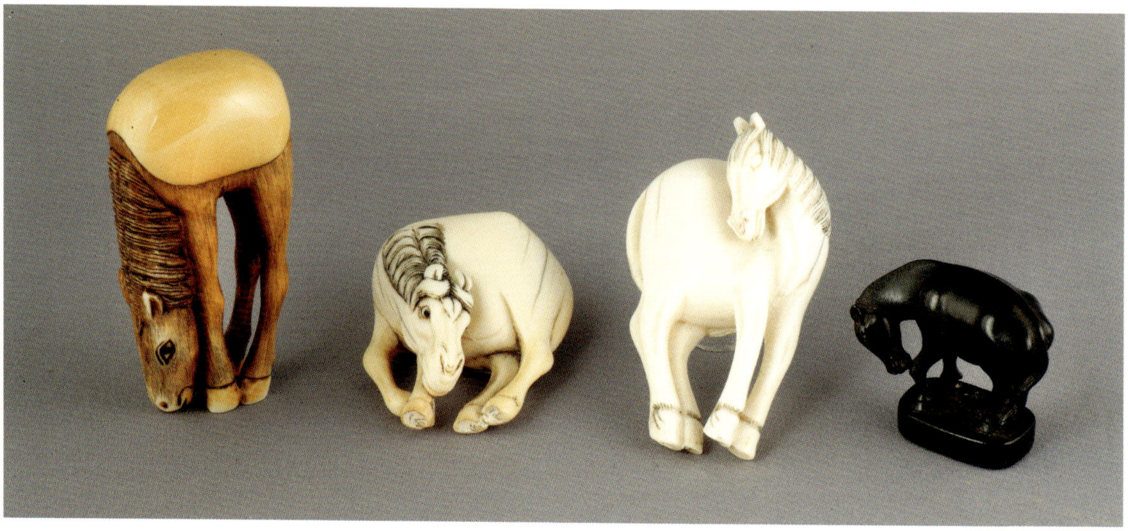

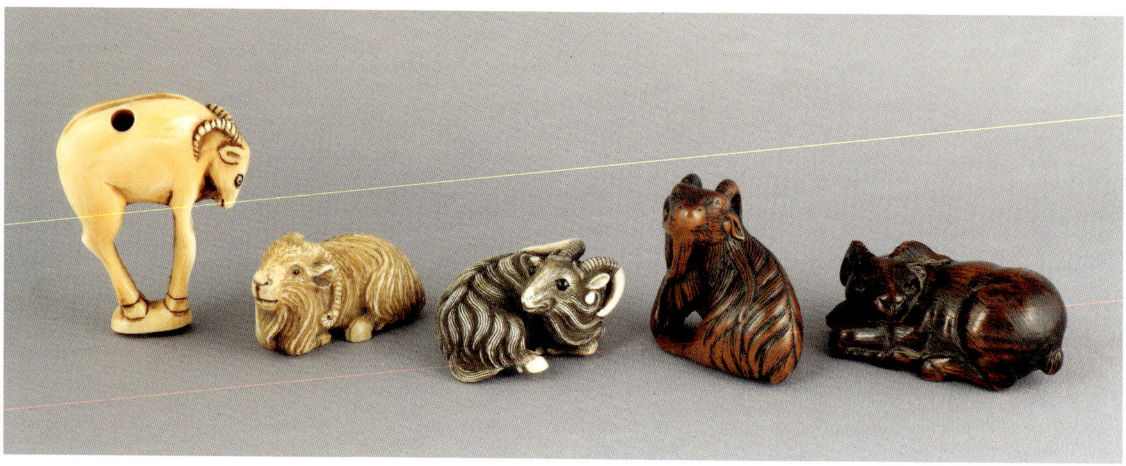

netsuke in the form of a horse • ***netsuke*** en forme de cheval • (left) Grazing horse, signed Tomomasa • (à gauche) Cheval broutant, signé Tomomasa • 19th century • ivory • Gift of James and Joanna Davidson, AGGV 2006.002.034 • (second left) Grazing horse • (deuxième à gauche) Cheval broutant • late 18th/early 19th century • ivory • Gift of the Lewis and Ruth Sherman Foundation, AGGV 2007.016.024 • (second right) Standing horse • (deuxième à droite) Cheval debout • 19th century • ivory • Gift of the Lewis and Ruth Sherman Foundation, AGGV 2007.016.043 • (right) Standing horse, signed Tametoma, 19th century • (à droite) Cheval debout, signé Tametoma, 19e siècle • wood • Fred and Isabel Pollard Collection, AGGV 1964.001.001

netsuke in the form of a goat • ***netsuke*** en forme de chèvre • (left) Standing goat, signed Kogetsu, 19th century • (à gauche) Chèvre debout, signé Kogetsu, 19e siècle • ivory • Gift of James and Joanna Davidson, AGGV 2006.002.015 • (second left) Reclining goat, signed Yoshihisa, 19th century • (deuxième à gauche) Chèvre étendue, signé Yoshihisa, 19e siècle • ivory • Fred and Isabel Pollard Collection, AGGV 1975.015.001 • (middle) Reclining goat • (au milieu) Chèvre étendue • late 18th/early 19th century • ivory • Gift of James and Joanna Davidson, AGGV 2006.002.005 • (second right) Goat • (deuxième à droite) Chèvre • 19th century • wood • Fred and Isabel Pollard Collection, AGGV 1974.219.001• (right) Goat, signed Gyokuzan, 19th century • (à droite) Chèvre, signé Gyokuzan, 19e siècle • wood • Gift of James and Joanna Davidson, AGGV 2006.002.039

netsuke in the form of lion dog • ***netsuke*** en forme de chien lion • (left) *shishi* lion-dog with ball, signed Mitsuhina Gyokuyo, 19th century • (à gauche) chien lion *shishi* avec balle, signé Mitsuhina Gyokuyo, 19e siècle • ivory • Given in Memory of John P. Nind by his Wife and Daughter, AGGV 1974.146.001 • (middle) Two *shishi* lion-dogs on large sphere • (au milieu) Deux chiens lions *shishi* sur une grande sphère • late 18th/early 19th century • ivory • Gift of James and Joanna Davidson, AGGV 2006.002.023 • (right) *shishi* lion-dog grasping a large ball • (à droite) chien lion *shishi* saisissant une grosse balle • 19th century • ivory • Given in Memory of John P. Nind by his Wife and Daughter, AGGV 1974.147.001

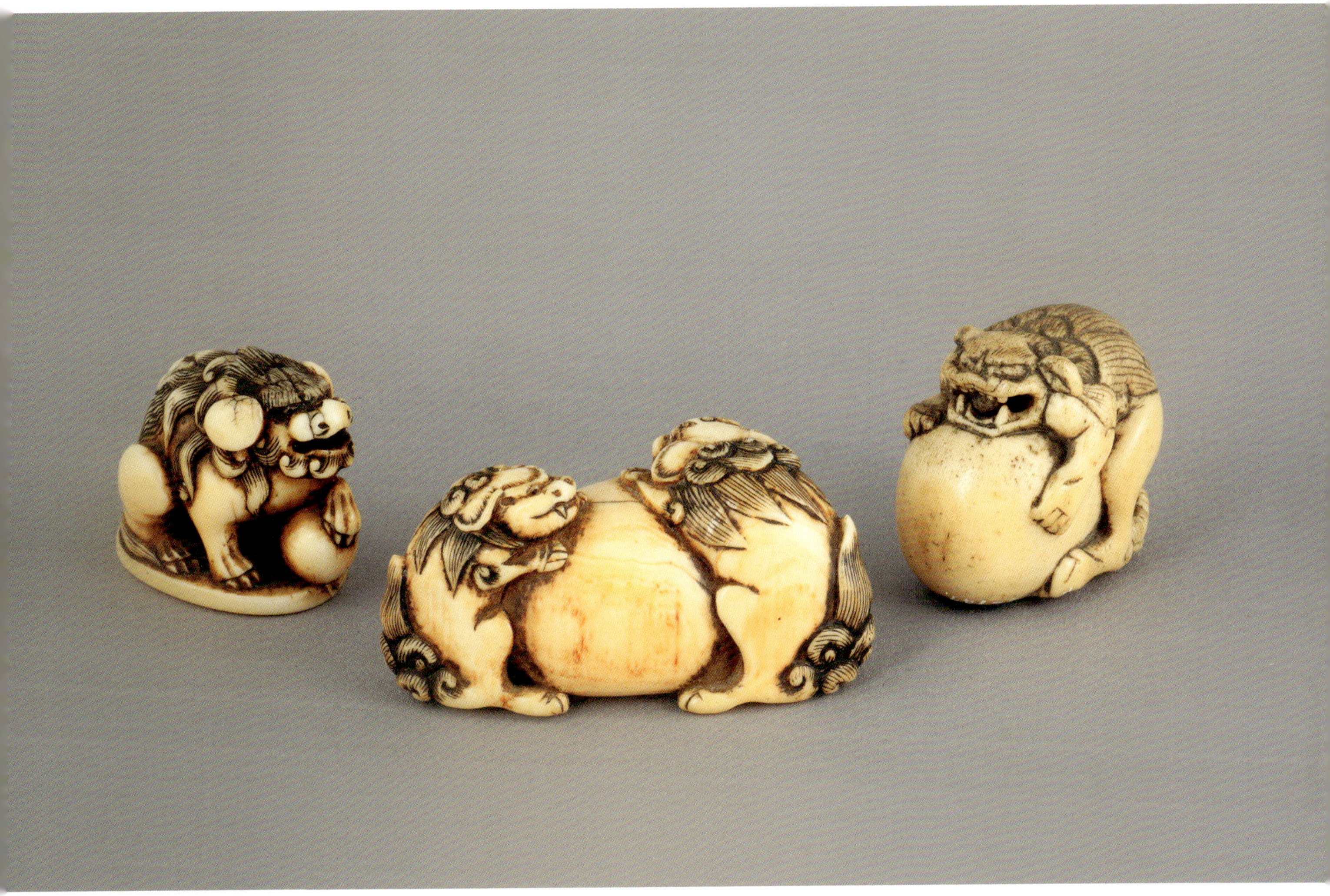

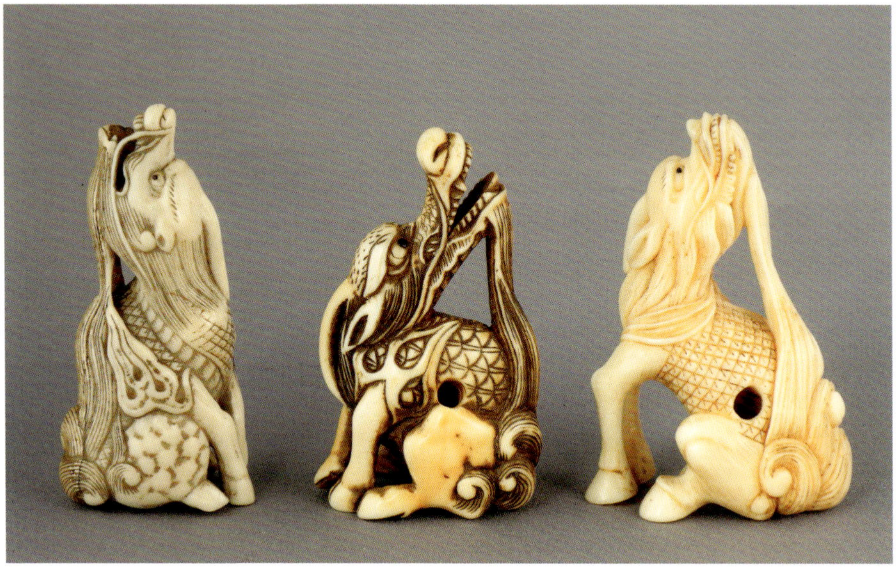

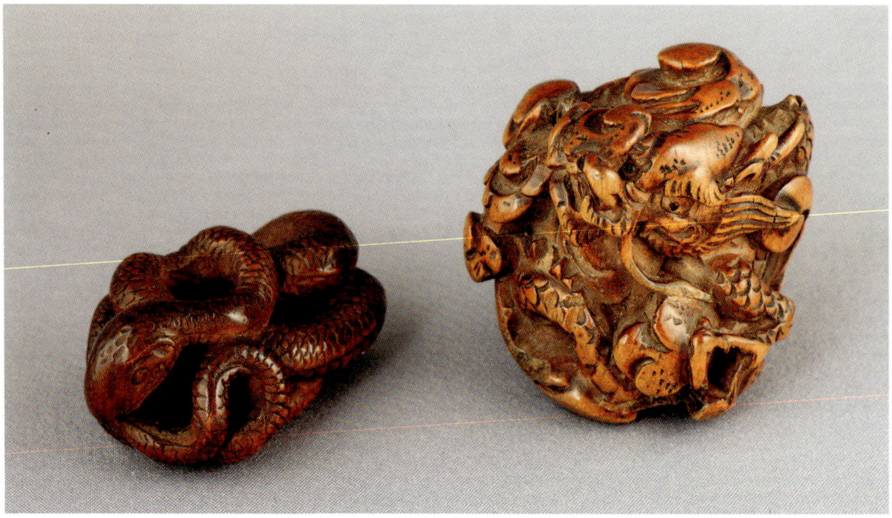

netsuke in the form of *kirin* mythical creature • ***netsuke*** en forme de créature mythique *kirin* • (left) *kirin* • (à gauche) *kirin* • 18th century • ivory • Gift of James and Joanna Davidson, AGGV 2006.002.012 • (middle, right) *kirin* • (au milieu, à droite) *kirin* • 18th/19th century • ivory • Gifts of Mr. and Mrs. Lewis and Ruth Sherman, AGGV 2007.016.003, 2007.016.090

(left) ***netsuke*** in the form of a serpent • (à gauche) ***netsuke*** en forme de serpent • 19th century • wood • Fred and Isabel Pollard Collection, AGGV 1974.215.001 • (right) ***netsuke*** in the form of a coiled dragon • (à droite) ***netsuke*** en forme de dragon se tortillant • 19th century • wood • Fred and Isabel Pollard Collection, AGGV 1974.196.001

netsuke in the form of a salmon • ***netsuke*** en forme de saumon • 19th century • ivory • Fred and Isabel Pollard Collection, AGGV 1967.182.003

netsuke in the form of a rat • ***netsuke*** en forme de rat • (left) Six rats on a bean pod and leaf, signed Masamitsu, 19th century • (à gauche) Six rats sur une cosse de haricots et une feuille, signé Masamitsu, 19e siècle • ivory • Gift of James and Joanna Davidson, AGGV 2006.002.029 • (middle) Rat eating • (au milieu) Rat en train de manger • 19th century • ivory • Given in Memory of John P. Nind by his Wife and Daughter, AGGV 1974.151.001 • (right) Rat with a candle stub, signed Ranichi, mid 20th century • (à droite) Rat avec un bout de chandelle, signé Ranichi, milieu du 20e siècle • ivory, ruby • Gift of the Lewis and Ruth Sherman Foundation, AGGV 2007.016.017

netsuke in the form of a rat • ***netsuke*** en forme de rat • (left) Seated rat • (à gauche) Rat assis • ca. 1900 • wood • Fred and Isabel Pollard Collection, AGGV 1974.207.001 • (middle) Rat, signed Masume, 18th century • (au milieu) Rat, signé Masume, 18e siècle • wood, horn • Gift of James and Joanna Davidson, AGGV 2006.002.013 • (right) Rat sitting atop a rice winnowing basket filled with mushrooms • (à droite) Rat assis sur un van de riz rempli de champignons • ca. 1900 • hardwood; horn • Gift of the Lewis and Ruth Sherman Foundation, AGGV 2007.016.064

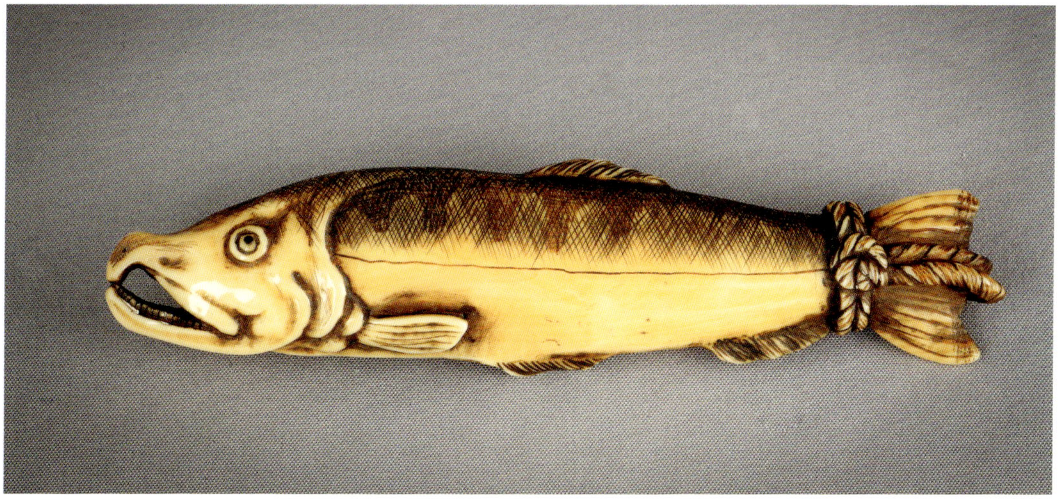

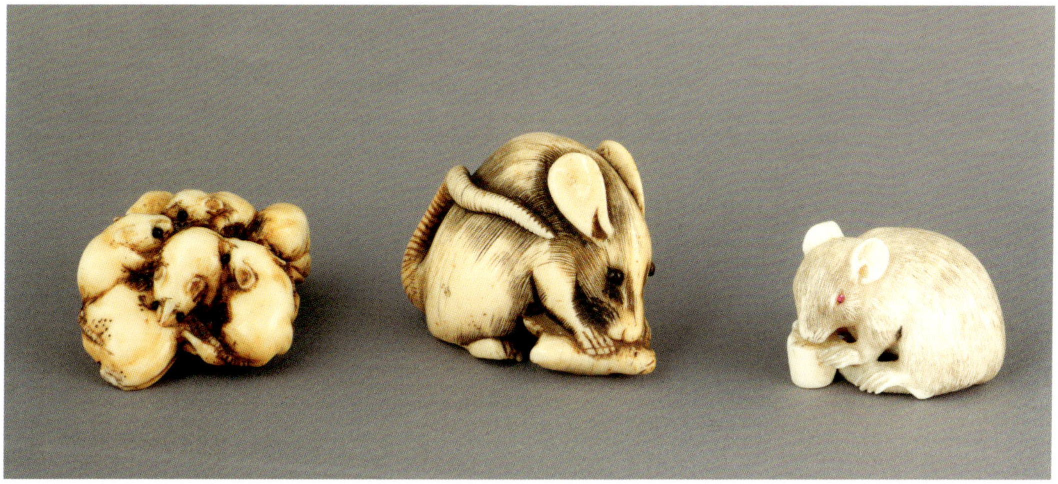

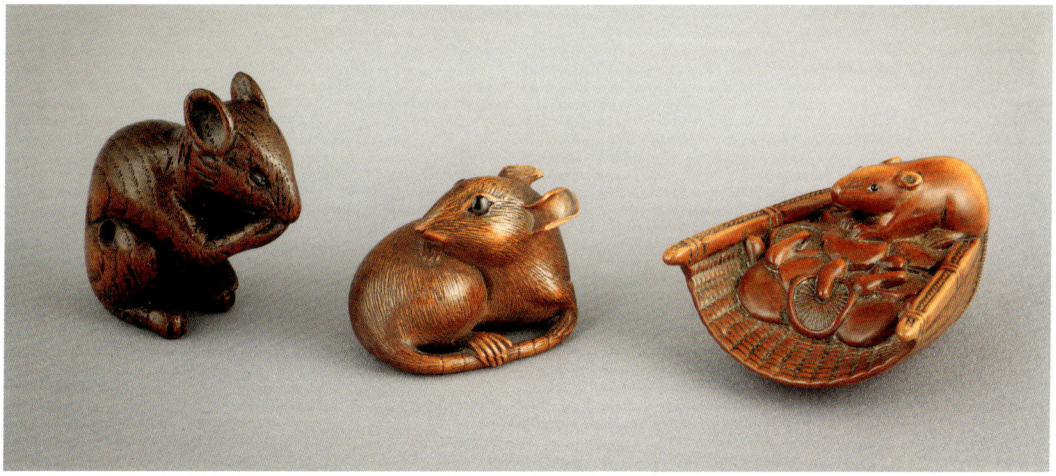

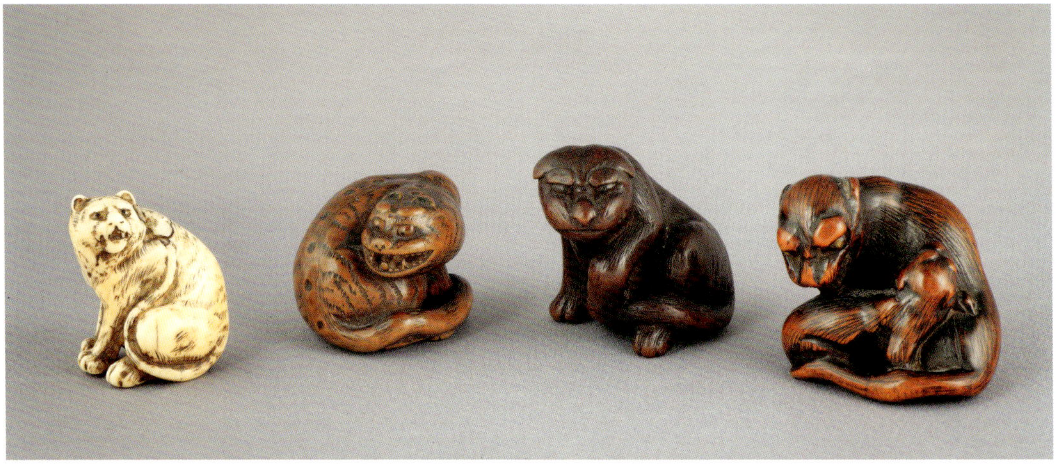

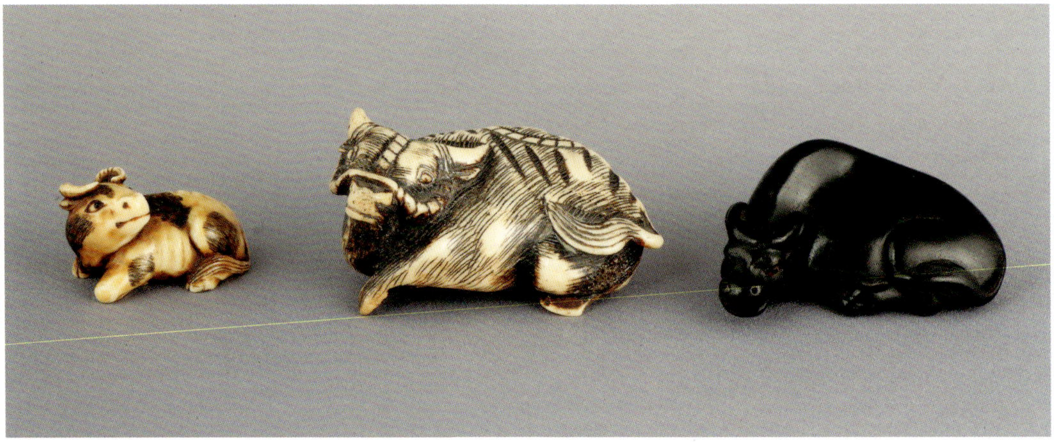

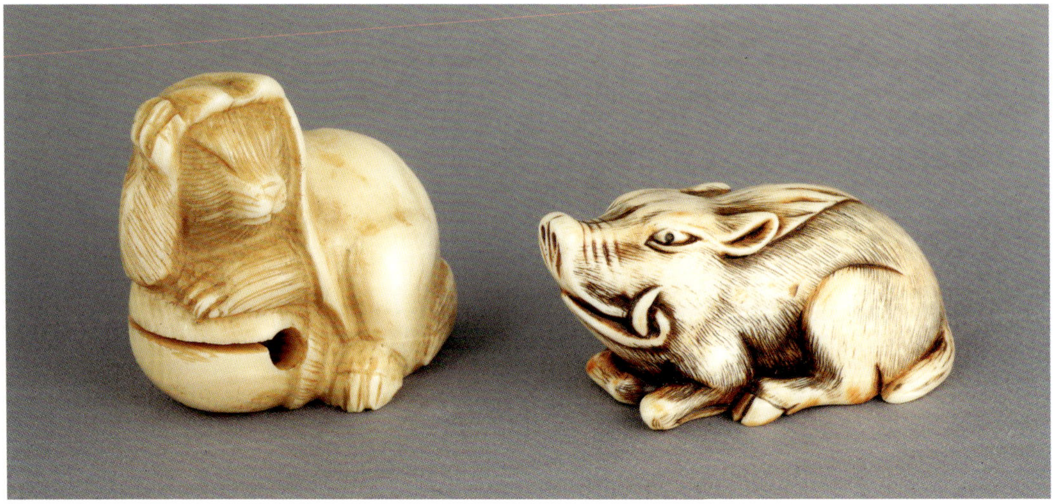

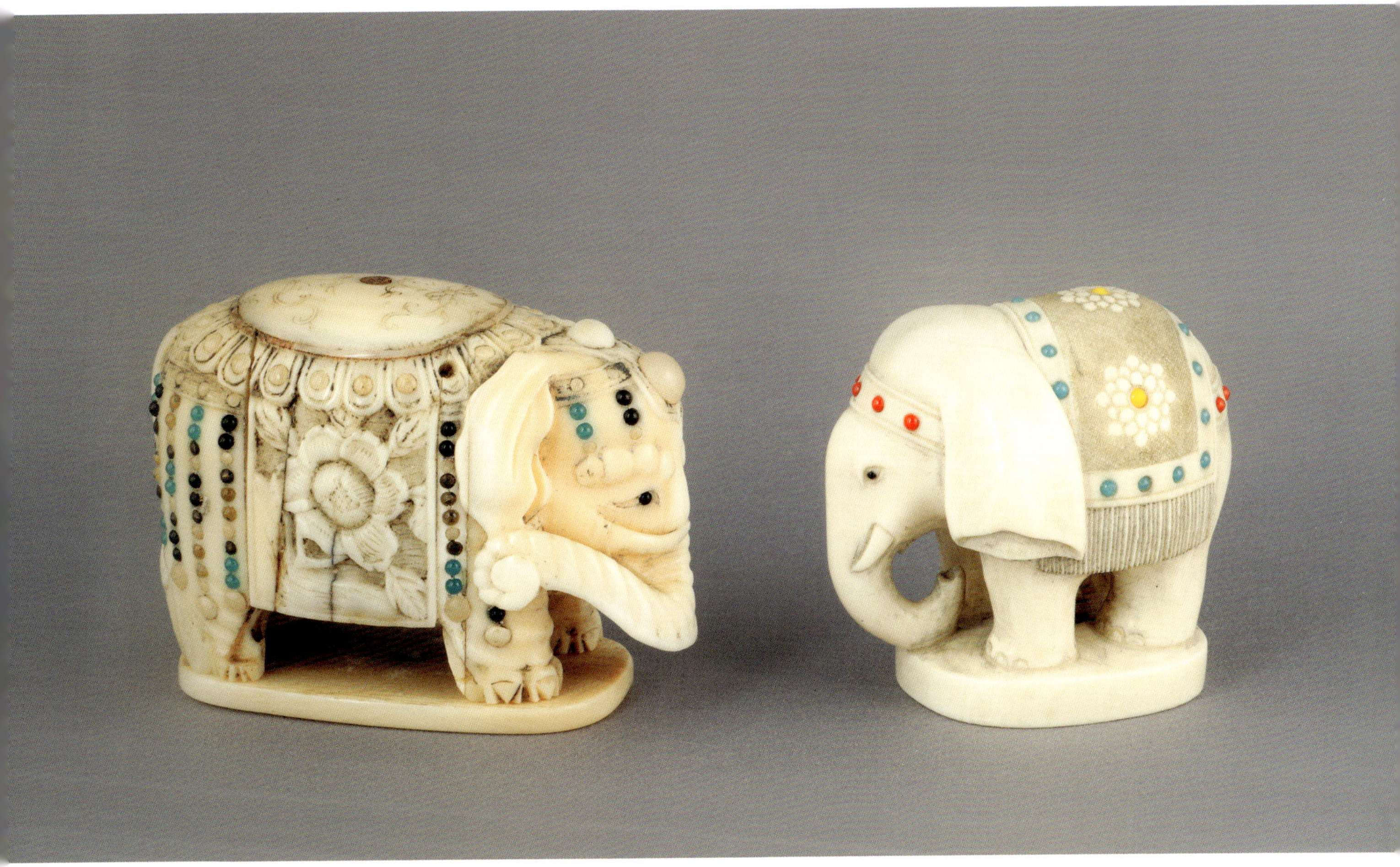

netsuke in the form of a tiger • ***netsuke*** en forme de tigre • (left) Seated tiger • (à gauche) Tigre assis • 19th century • ivory • Fred and Isabel Pollard Collection, AGGV 1974.213.001 • (second left) Crouching Tiger, signed Hirokazu, 19th century • (deuxième à gauche) Tigre accroupi, signé Hirokazu, 19e siècle • boxwood, horn • Gift of the Lewis and Ruth Sherman Foundation, AGGV 2007.016.047 • (second right) Seated tiger, signed Sari, 18th century • (deuxième à droite) Tigre assis, signé Sari, 18e siècle • cherrywood • Gift of the Lewis and Ruth Sherman Foundation, AGGV 2007.016.018 • (right) Seated tigress licking her cub • (à droite) Tigresse assise léchant ses petits • 19th century • boxwood, ivory • Gift of the Lewis and Ruth Sherman Foundation, AGGV 2007.016.092

netsuke in the form of an ox • ***netsuke*** en forme de boeuf • (left) Reclining Ox, signed Tomatada, 19th century • (à gauche) Boeuf étendu, signé Tomatada, 19e siècle • ivory • Gift of James and Joanna Davidson, AGGV 2006.002.016 • (middle) Reclining Ox • (au milieu) Boeuf étendu • 19th century • ivory • Fred and Isabel Pollard Collection, AGGV 1974.220.001 • (right) Reclining Ox, signed Masayoshi, 19th century • (à droite) Boeuf étendu, signé Masayoshi, 19e siècle • wood • Gift of the Lewis and Ruth Sherman Foundation, AGGV 2007.016.065

(left) ***netsuke*** in the form of a badger leaning on a wooden percussion instrument, signed Gyokuzan, 19th century • (à gauche) ***netsuke*** en forme de blaireau appuyé sur un instrument à percussion en bois, signé Gyokuzan, 19e siècle • ivory • Gift of James and Joanna Davidson. AGGV 2006.002.035 • (right) ***netsuke*** of a boar, signed Masatomo, 19th century • (à droite) ***netsuke***, sanglier, signé Masatomo, 19e siècle • ivory • Fred and Isabel Pollard Collection, AGGV 1974.198.001

netsuke in the form of an elephant • ***netsuke*** en forme d'éléphant • (left) Caparisoned elephant, signed Masaharu?, ca. 1900 • (à gauche) éléphant caparaçonné, signé Masaharu ?, vers 1900 • ivory, glass beads • Edith Low-Beer Collection, AGGV 1990.038.008 • (right) Caparisoned elephant, signed Nanshu?, mid 20th century • (à droite) éléphant caparaçonné, signé Nanshu? • ivory, glass • Gift of the Lewis and Ruth Sherman Foundation, AGGV 2007.016.015

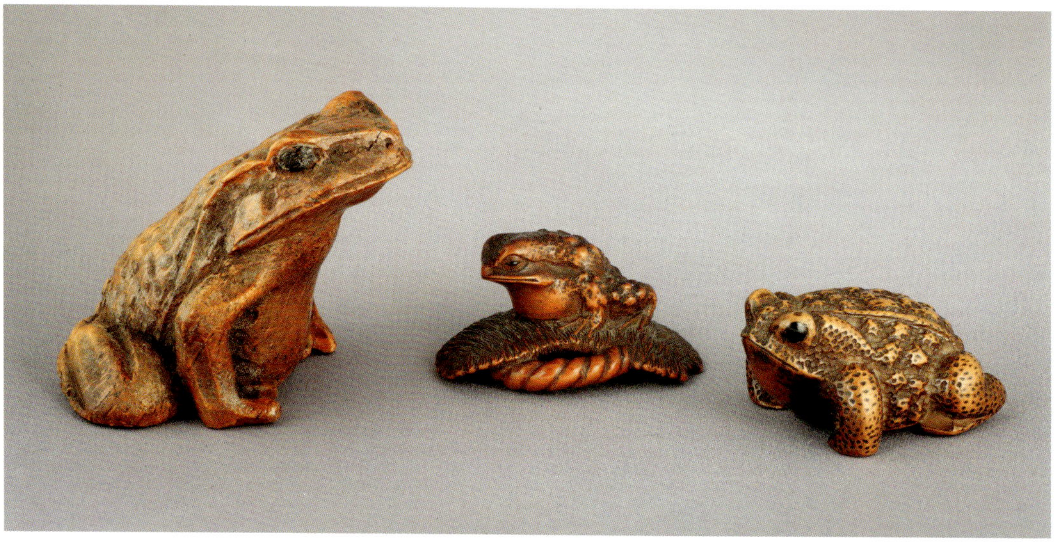

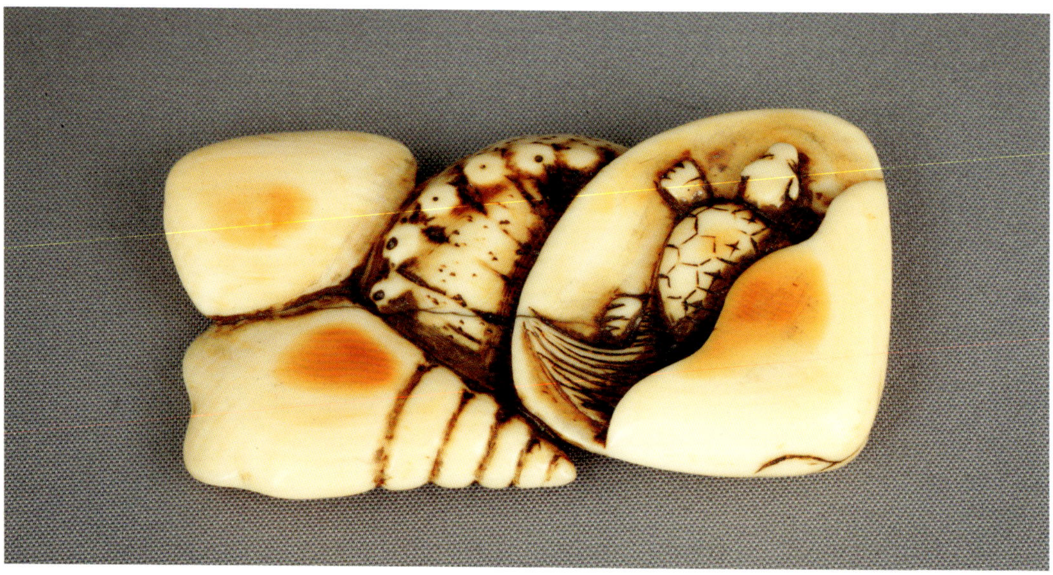

168

netsuke of frog/toad • ***netsuke***, grenouille/crapaud • (left) Frog • (à gauche) Grenouille • late 19th century • wood • Fred and Isabel Pollard Collection, AGGV 1973.153.001 • (middle) Toad on a sandal, signed Masanao Susuki, 19th century • (au milieu) Crapaud sur une sandale, signé Masanao Susuki, 19e siècle • wood • Gift of James and Joanna Davidson, AGGV 2006.002.002 • (right) Toad • (à droite) Crapaud • 19th century • wood • Fred and Isabel Pollard Collection, AGGV 1974.205.001

netsuke of a longevity turtle and shells • ***netsuke***, tortue de longévité et carapaces • early 19th century • ivory • Gift of the Lewis and Ruth Sherman Foundation, AGGV 2007.016.087 184

(left) ***netsuke*** in the form of a bird on a branch, signed Toyomasa, 19th century • (à gauche) ***netsuke*** en forme d'oiseau sur une branche, signé Toyomasa, 19e siècle • boxwood, ivory, horn • Gift of the Lewis and Ruth Sherman Foundation, AGGV 2007.016.055 • (right) ***netsuke*** of a chicken, signed Yoshihisa, late 19th century • (à droite) ***netsuke***, poulet, signé Yoshihisa, fin du 19e siècle • ivory • Fred and Isabel Pollard Collection, AGGV 1975.016.001

netsuke of two quails facing opposing directions seated on a coil of millet seeds • ***netsuke***, deux cailles en directions opposées, assises sur une spirale de graines de millet • (left) signed Okatomo, 18th century • (à gauche) signé Okatomo, 18e siècle • ivory • Gift of James and Joanna Davidson, AGGV 2006.002.006 • (right) signed Okatomo • (à droite) Deux cailles, signé Okatomo • wood • Gift of Mrs. Ruth McCuaig, AGGV 2001.021.001

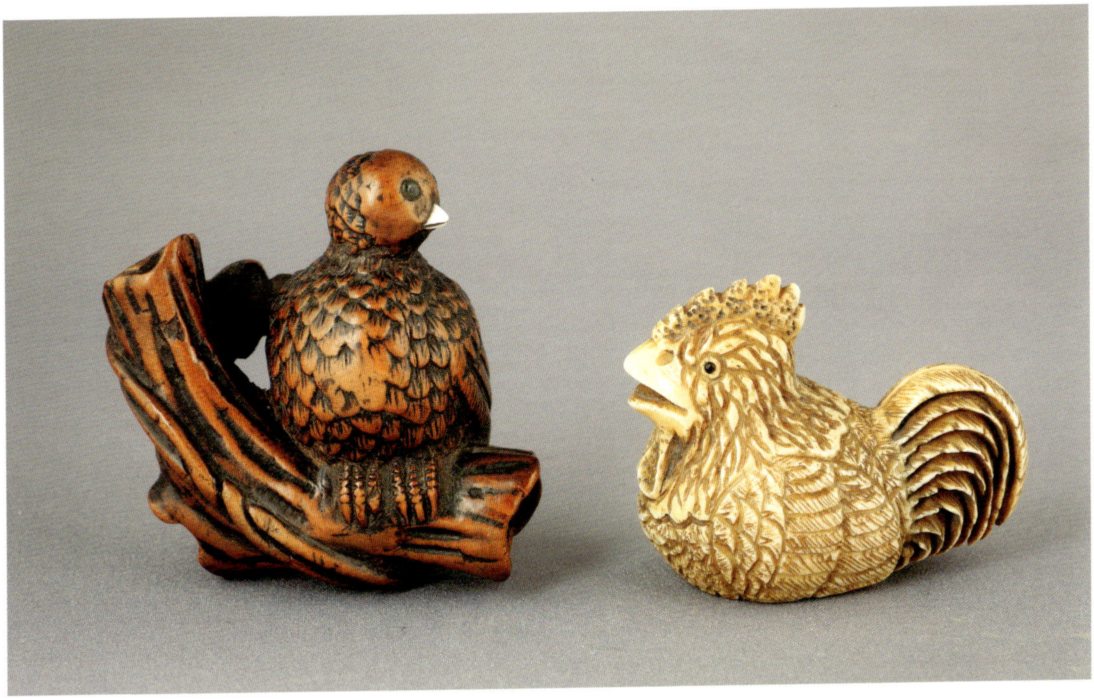

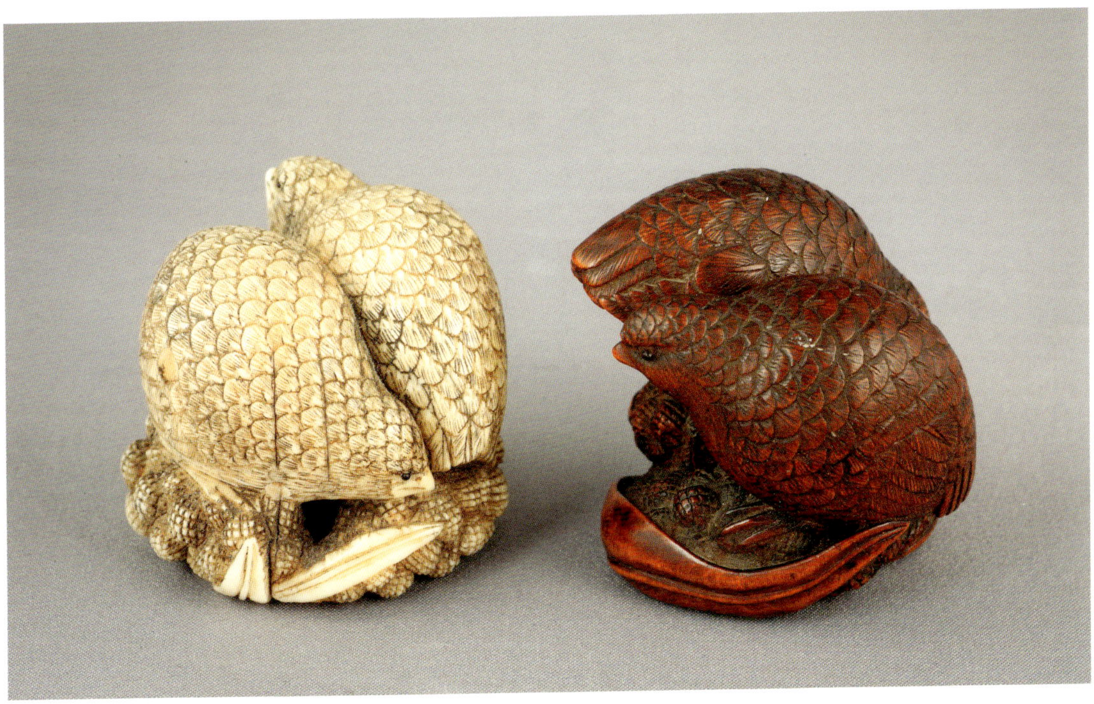

Contemporary and International netsuke

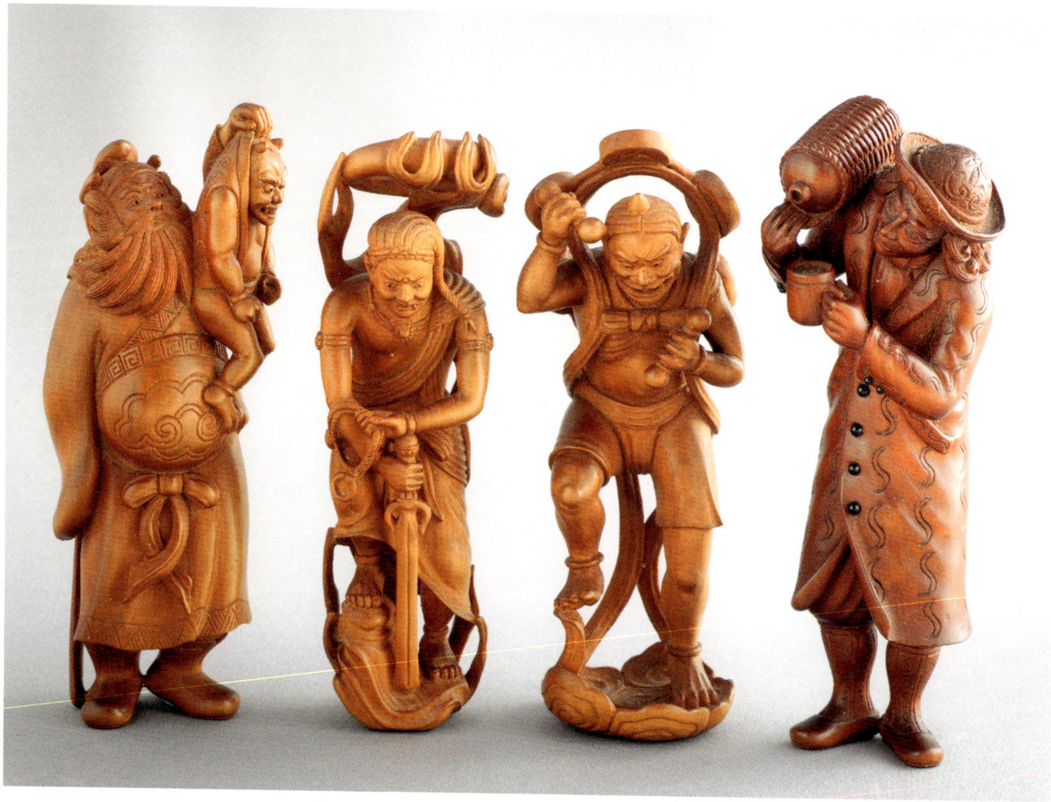

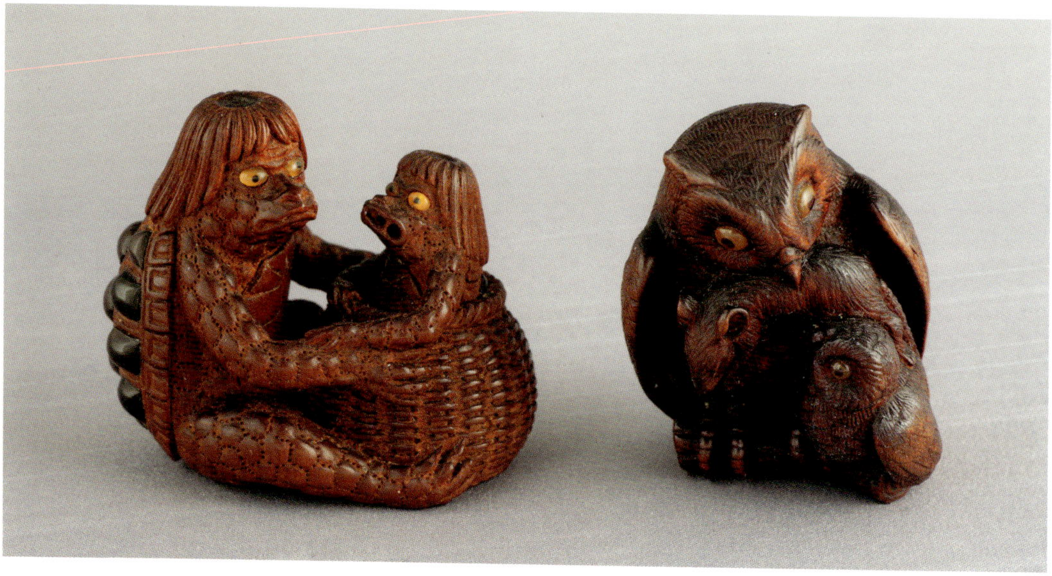

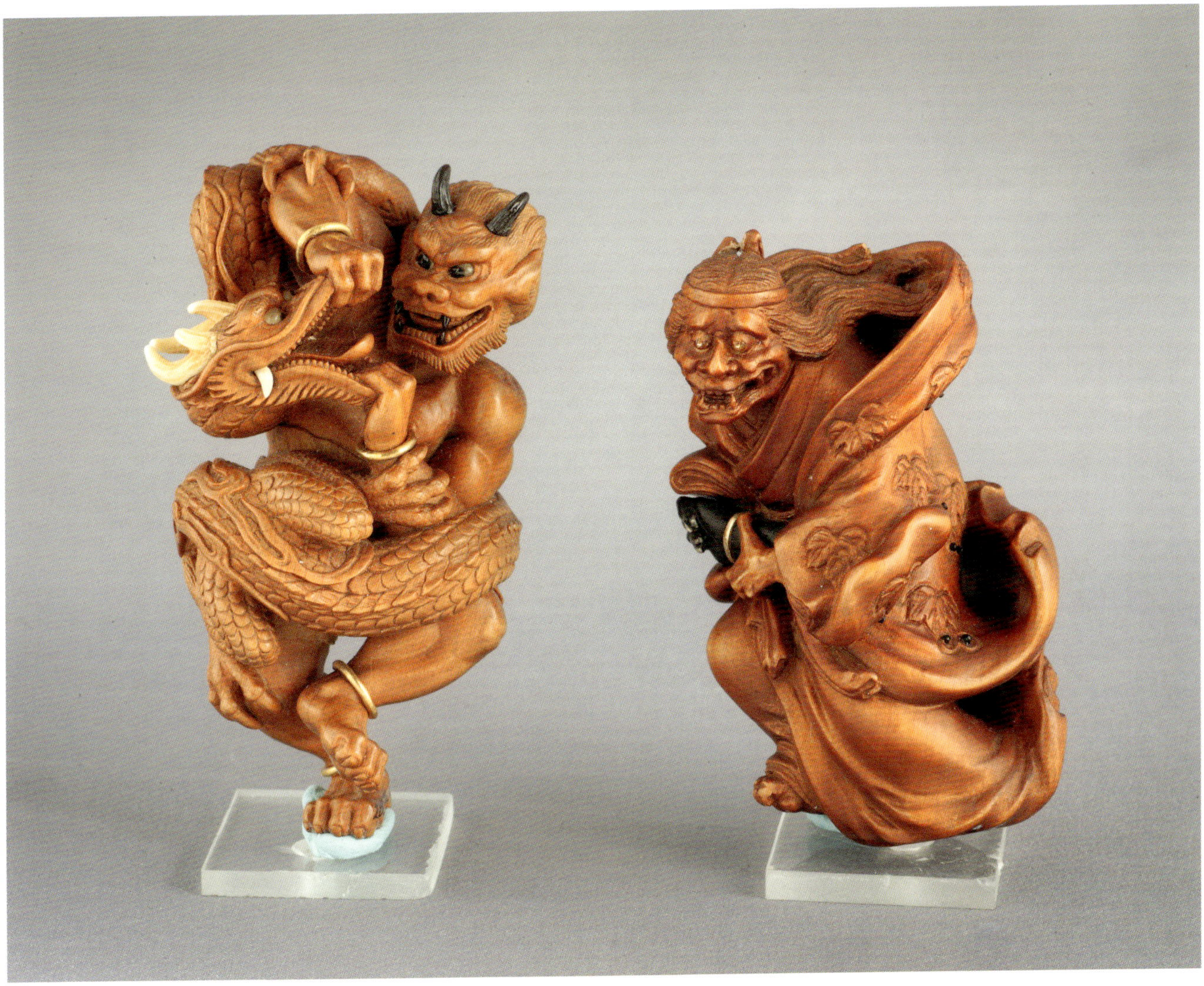

a. *netsuke* of the Demon Queller Shoki / of Fudo Myo-O, Buddhist Guardian / of Raijin the Thunder God/of Dutchman pouring a drink • ***netsuke***, démon queller Shoki/Fudo Myo-O, gardien bouddhiste/Raijin, le dieu du tonnerre/Hollandais versant une boisson • **b. *netsuke*** of *kappa* with it's child in a basket/ owl and chick with mouse • ***netsuke***, *kappa* avec son enfant dans un panier/Hibou et bébé avec souris • all signed Akihide, contemporary Japanese • tous signés Akihide, japonais contemporain • wood • Gift of the Lewis and Ruth Sherman Foundation, AGGV 2007.016.058, .040, .057, .042, .038, .004

(left) ***netsuke*** of demon wrestling with a dragon, signed Meikei, contemporary Japanese • (à gauche) ***netsuke***, démon luttant avec un dragon, signé Meikei, japonais contemporain • boxwood, ivory, gold, horn, glass • Gift of the Lewis and Ruth Sherman Foundation, AGGV 2007.016.078 • (right) ***netsuke*** of the Demon of Rashomon Gate carrying severed hand, signed Seiho, contemporary Japanese • (à droite) ***netsuke***, démon de la porte Rashomon transportant une main coupée, signé Seiho, japonais contemporain • boxwood, ebony, gold, silver, horn, glass • Gift of the Lewis and Ruth Sherman Foundation, AGGV 2007.016.077

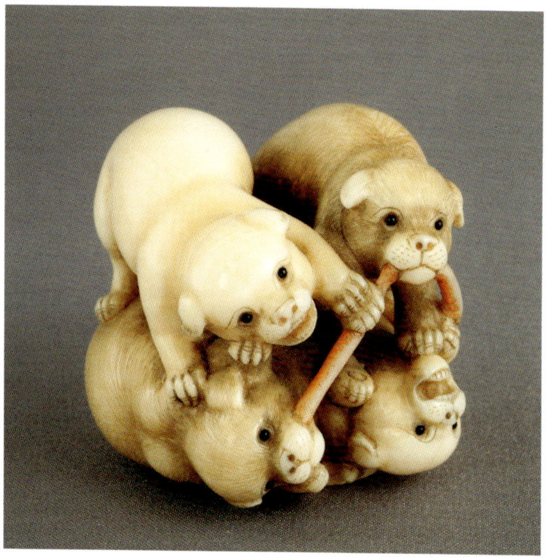
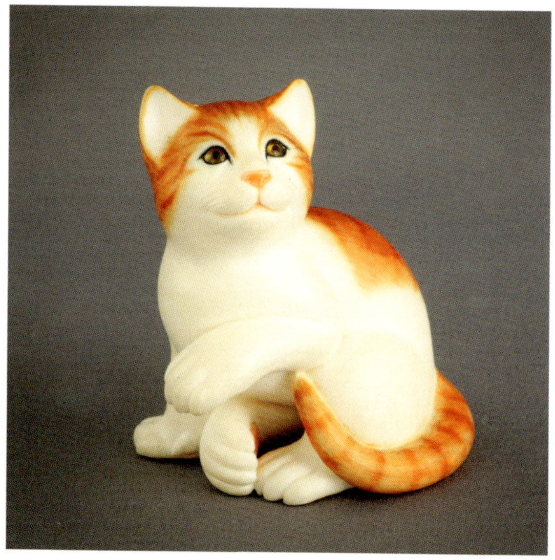
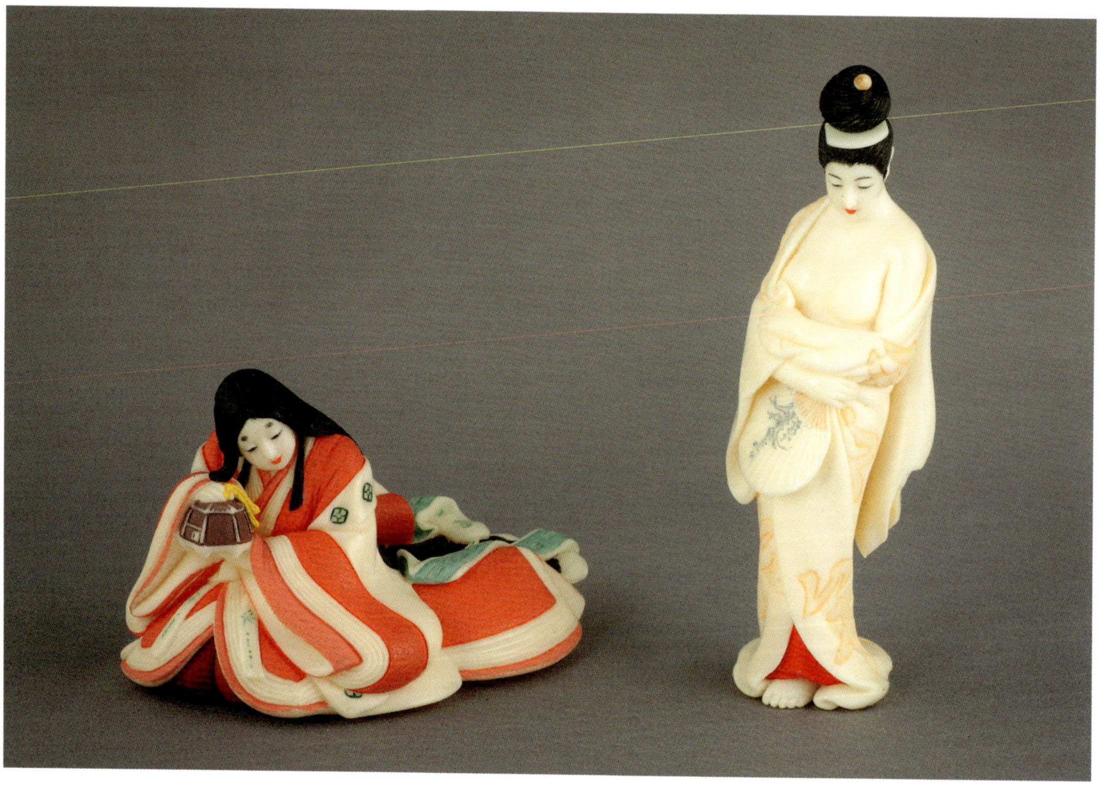

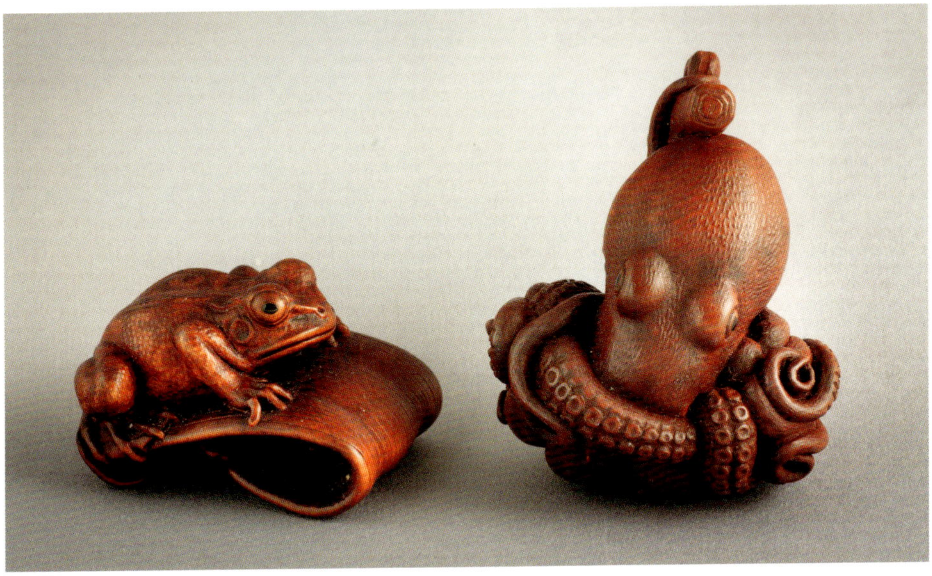

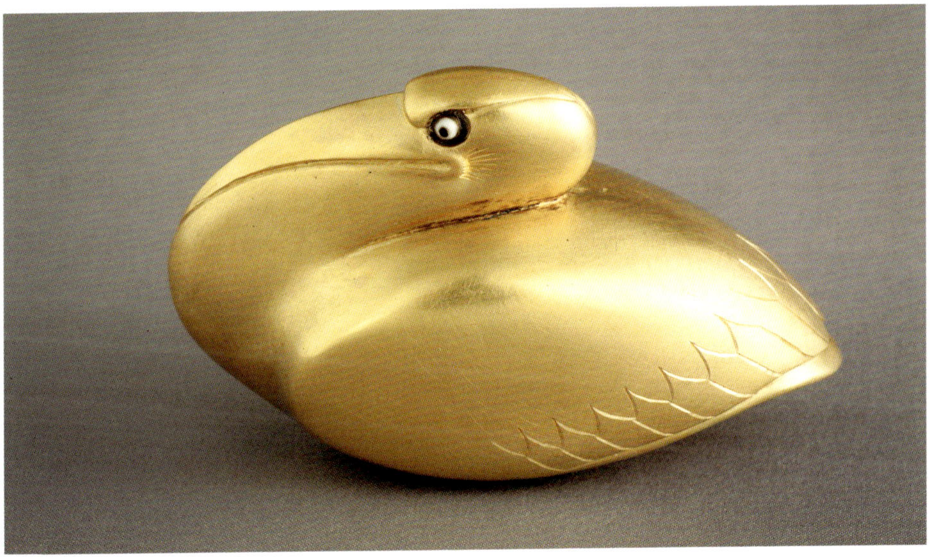

netsuke of five puppies, signed Kangyoku III, contemporary Japanese • ***netsuke***, cinq chiots, signé Kangyoku III, japonais contemporain • ivory, horn, coral • Gift of the Lewis and Ruth Sherman Foundation, AGGV 2007.016.037

netsuke of orange tabby cat, signed Shingetsu, contemporary Japanese • ***netsuke***, chat domestique marbré orange, signé Shingetsu, japonais contemporain • ivory, glass, pigments • Gift of the Lewis and Ruth Sherman Foundation, AGGV 2007.016.083

netsuke of seated court lady holding lantern / of woman with chest partially bared, signed Ryushi, contemporary Japanese • ***netsuke***, courtisane assise tenant une lanterne/femme avec la poitrine partiellement dénudée, signé Ryushi, japonais contemporain • ivory, pigments • Gift of the Lewis and Ruth Sherman Foundation, AGGV 2007.016.061, 2007.016.067

netsuke of frog on a leaf / octopus and anchor, signed Michael Webb (contemporary British) • ***netsuke***, grenouille sur une feuille/pieuvre et ancre, signé Michael Webb (britannique contemporain) • boxwood, horn • Gift of the Lewis and Ruth Sherman Foundation, AGGV 2007.016.026, 2007.016.051

netsuke of stylized pelican, signed George Weil (contemporary Israeli) • ***netsuke***, pélican stylisé signé George Weil (israélien contemporain) • gold • Gift of the Lewis and Ruth Sherman Foundation, AGGV 2007.016.068

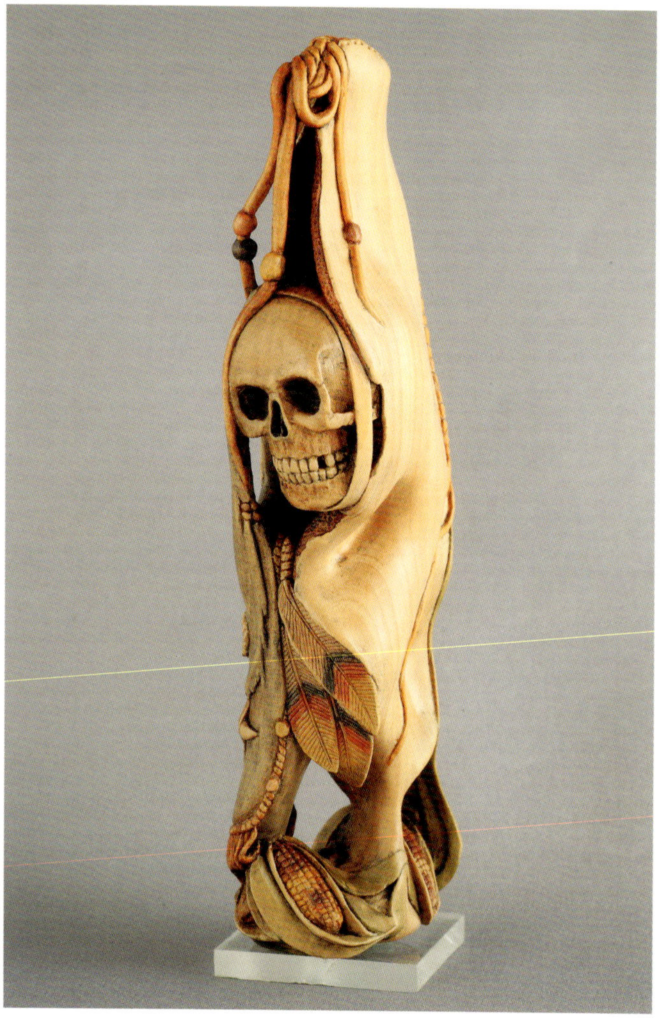

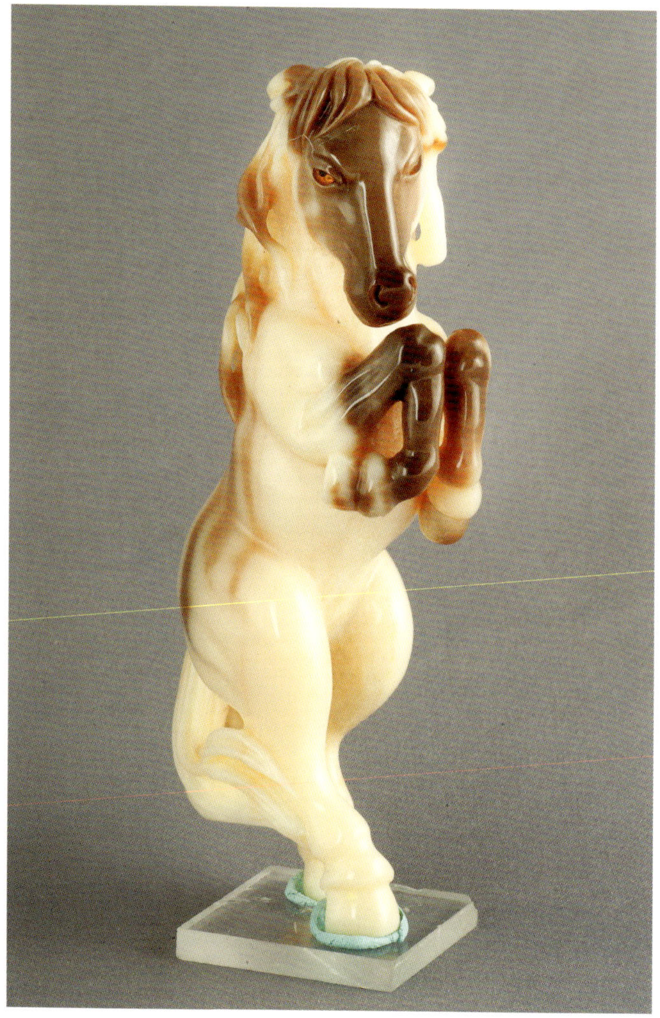

netsuke of a shaman's skull and corn, signed David Carlin (contemporary American) • ***netsuke***, crâne de shamane et maïs, signé David Carlin (américain contemporain) • boxwood, ivory, pigments • Gift of the Lewis and Ruth Sherman Foundation, AGGV 2007.016.084

netsuke of a horse, signed Greg Stradiotto (contemporary American) • ***netsuke***, cheval signé Greg Stradiotto (américain contemporain) • ivory, walrus fossil • Gift of the Lewis and Ruth Sherman Foundation, AGGV 2007.016.085

netsuke of anglefish / of mandarin ducks (symbol of fidelity), signed Guy Shaw (contemporary British) • ***netsuke***, baudroie/canards mandarins (symbole de fidélité), signé Guy Shaw (britannique contemporain) • ebony, moonstone, mother-of-pearl; (right) hardwood, horn • Gift of the Lewis and Ruth Sherman Foundation, AGGV 2007.016.071, 2007.016.072

Ojime

ojime of a plover signed Kaigyoku/of theatrical masks/of a flower design, late 19th century • ***ojime***, pluvier signé Kaigyoku/masques de théâtre/motif floral, fin du 19e siècle • ivory • Fred and Isabel Pollard, AGGV 1975.112.001, AGGV 9999.078, Given in Memory of John P. Nind by his Wife and Daughter, AGGV 1974.154.001

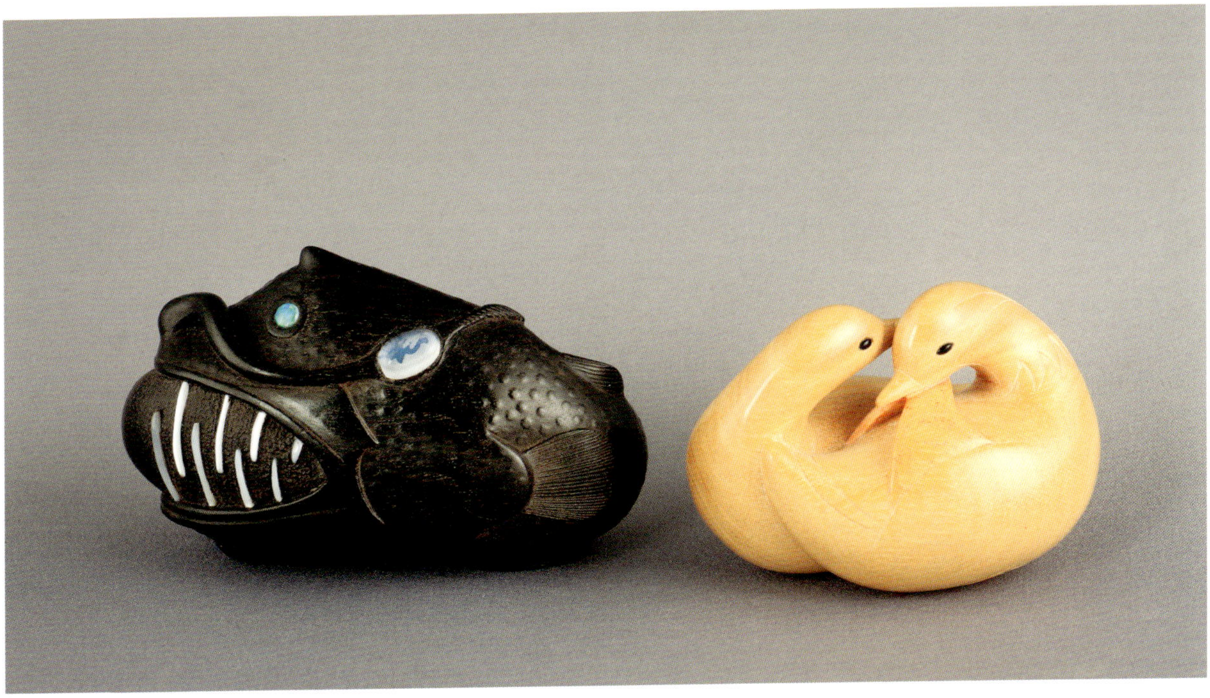

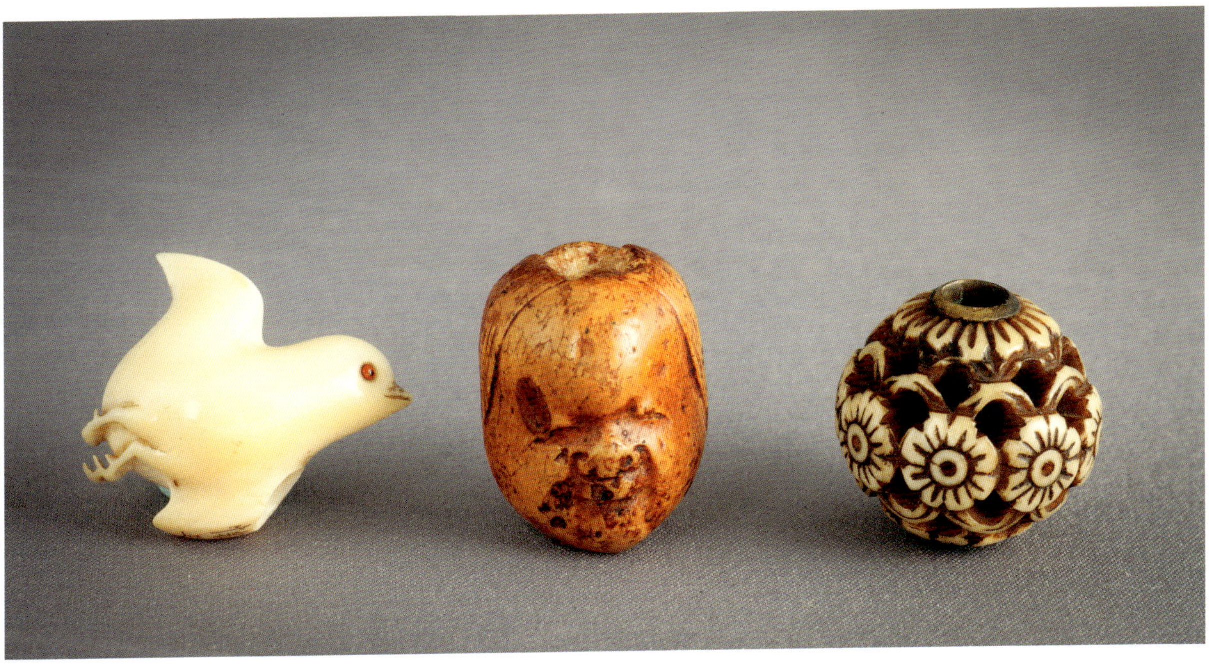

Inro, Ojime and Netsuke

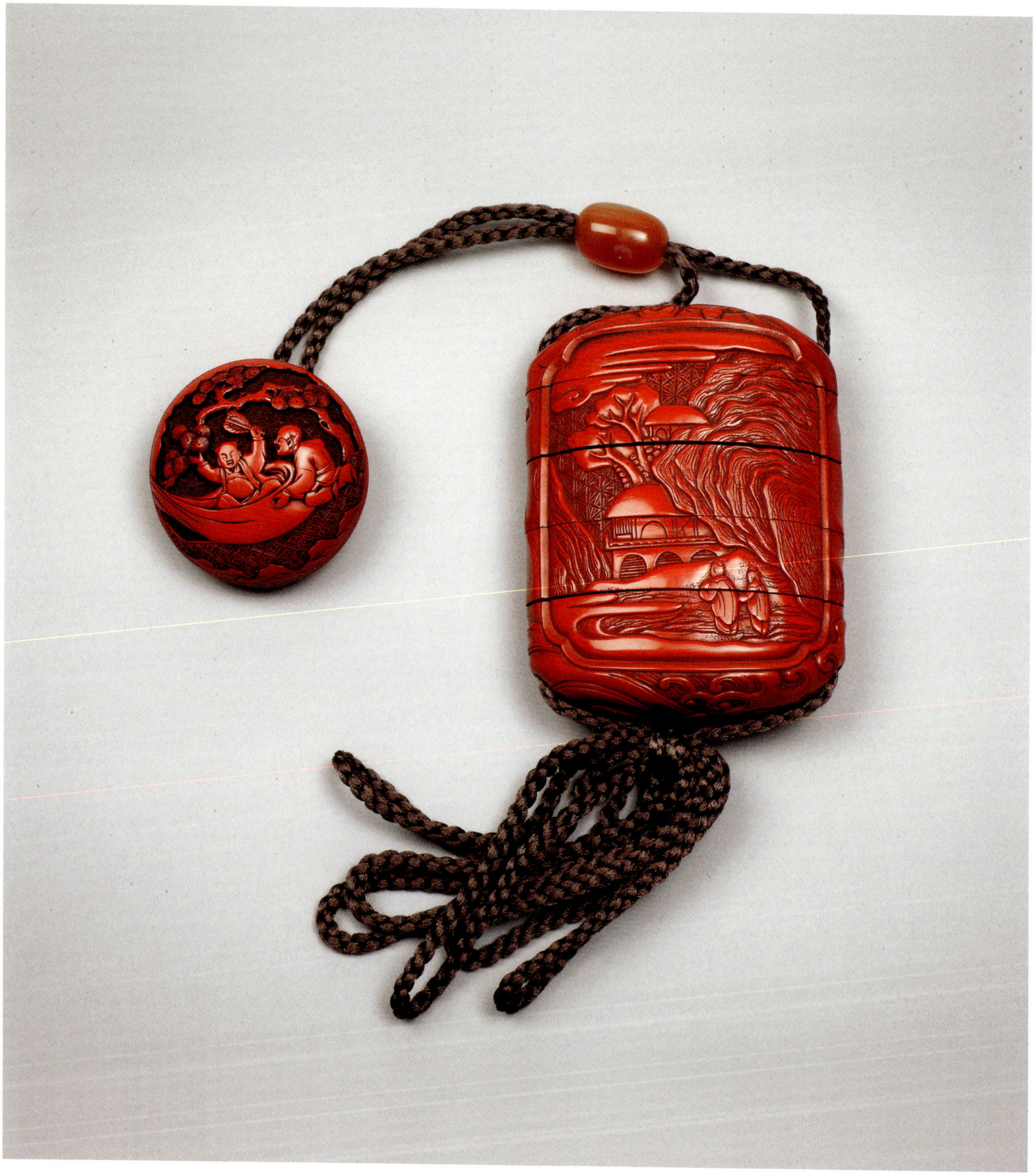

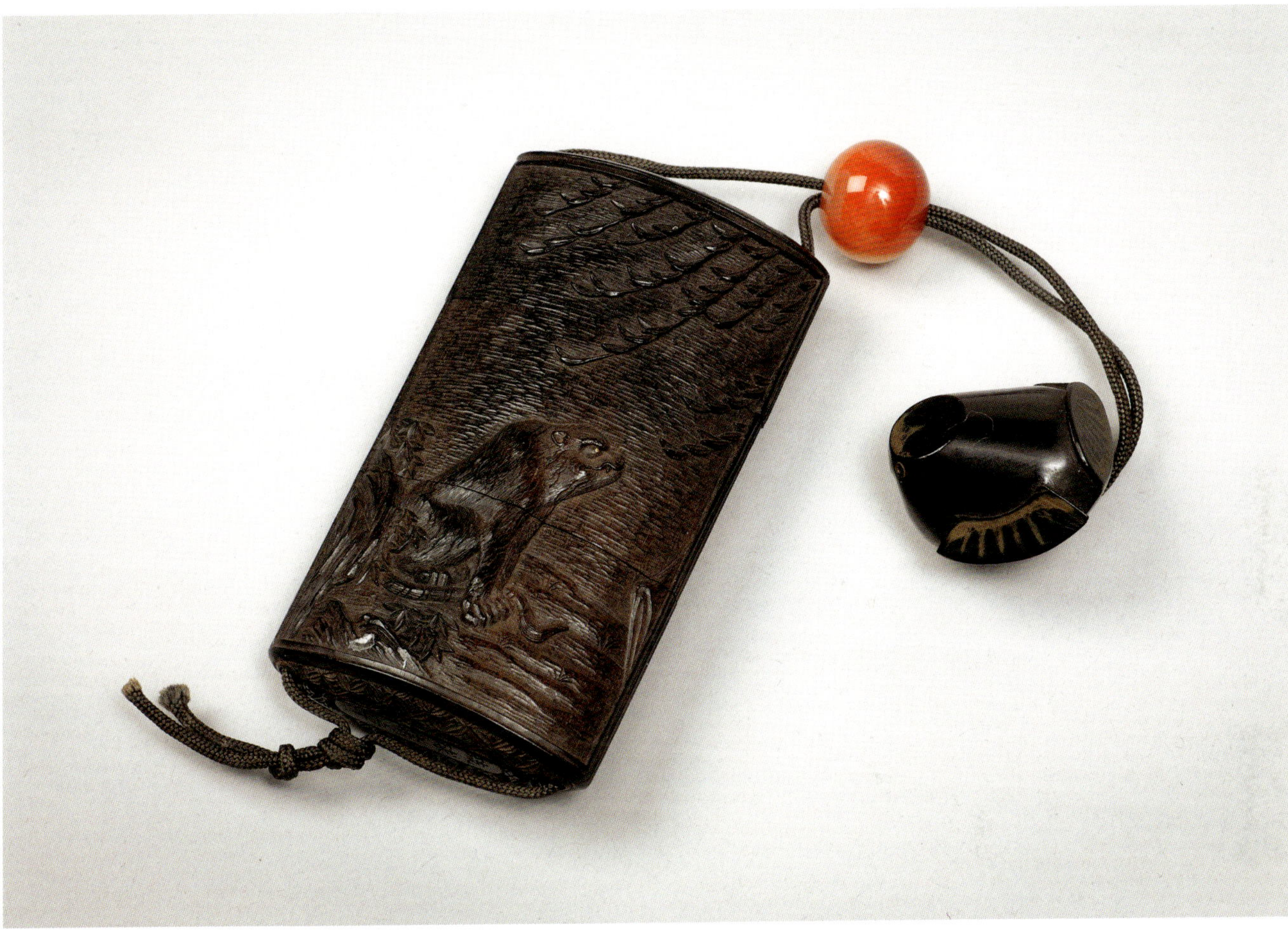

inro with design of a landscape • ***inro*** orné d'un paysage • wood, carved cinnabar lacquer • ***ojime***, carnelian • ***ojime***, cornaline • ***netsuke*** with design of man and boy in a sack under a pine tree wood, carved cinnabar lacquer, signed Shikoku late Edo period, mid 19th century • ***netsuke***, motif représentant un homme et un garçon dans un sac sous un pin, signé Shikoku, fin de la période Edo, milieu du 19e siècle • Fred and Isabel Pollard Collection, AGGV 1964.006.001

inro with design of a tiger with dragon in waves on verso ***inro*** orné d'un tigre avec dragon dans les vagues au verso • wood, carved lacquer • ***ojime***, carnelain • ***ojime***, cornaline • ***netsuke*** in the form of an owl • ***netsuke*** en forme de hibou • wood • late Edo period, mid 19th century • Fred and Isabel Pollard Collection, AGGV 1974.222.001

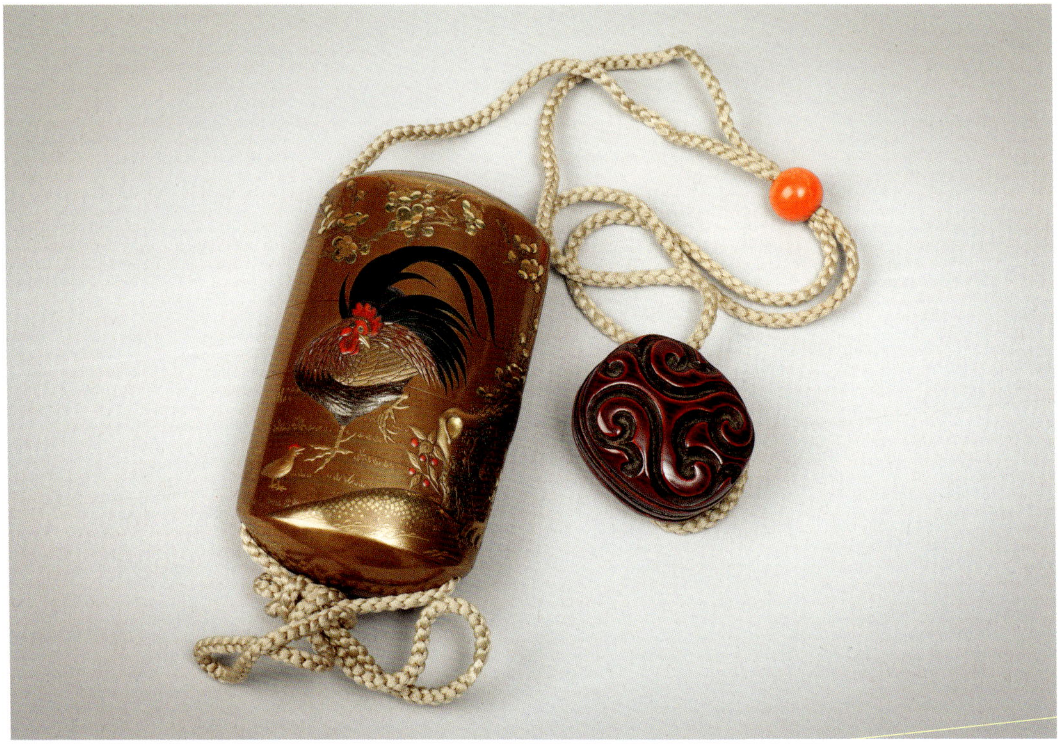

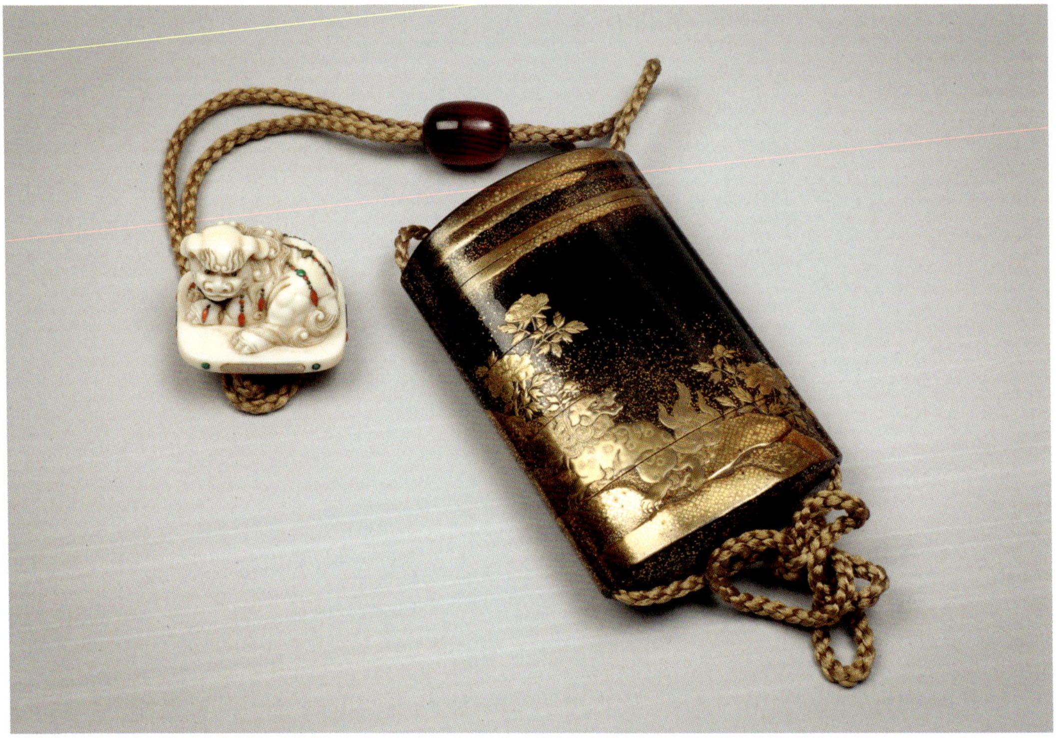

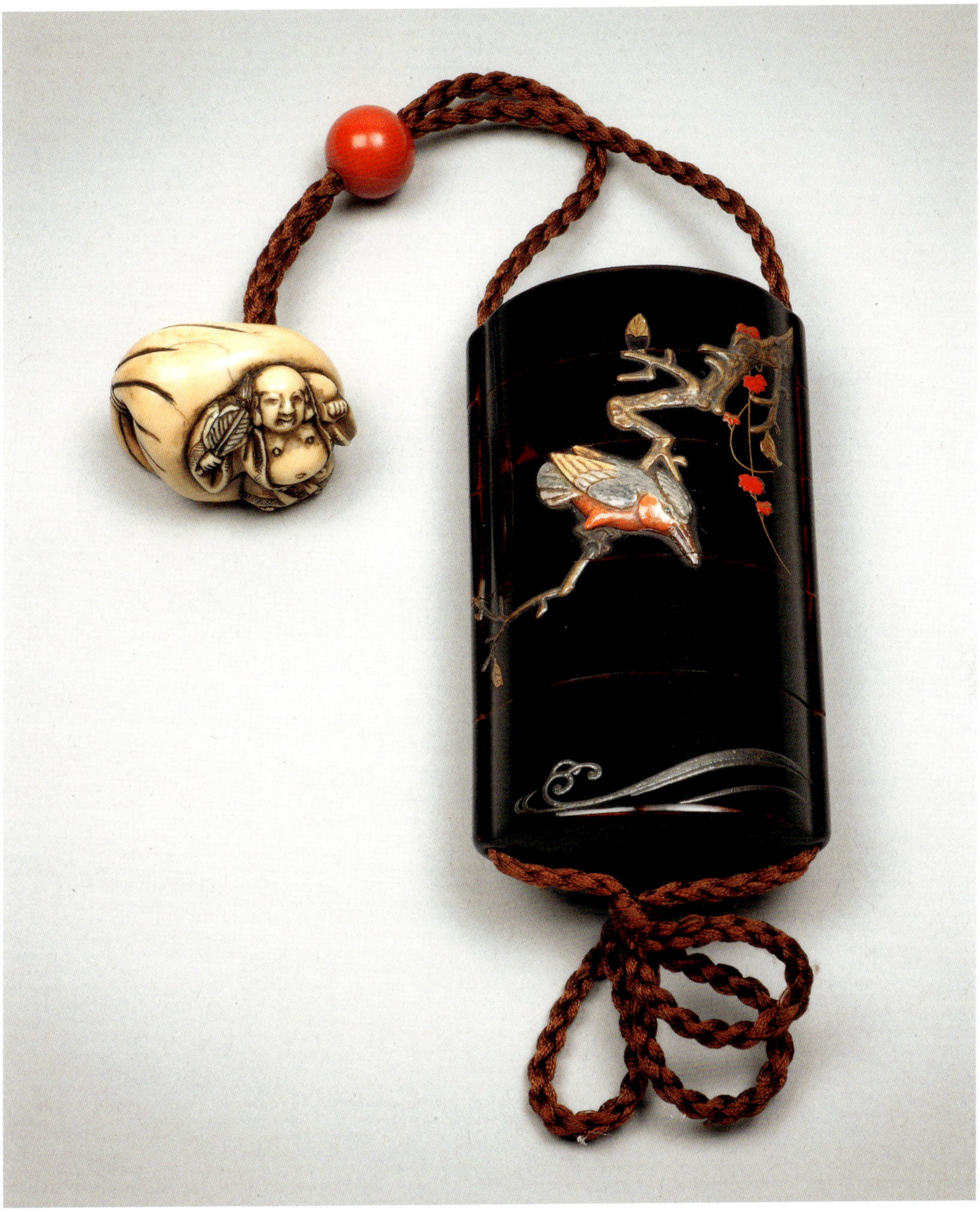

inro with design of red and black rooster with chick, hen and blossoms on verso, signed Kiyoharu • ***inro***, coq rouge et noir, avec poussin, poule et fleurs au verso, signé Kiyoharu • wood, lacquer • ***ojime***, orange bead • ***ojime***, perle orange • ***netsuke***, carved *guri* black and red lacquer • ***netsuke***, *guri* sculpté, laque rouge et noir • Edo period, early 19th century • Fred and Isabel Pollard Collection, AGGV 1977.121.001

inro with design of *shishi* lion dogs and peony • ***inro***, chiens lions *shishi* et pivoine • wood, lacquer • ***ojime***, agate • ***ojime***, agate • ***netsuke*** in the form of a *shishi* lion dog, signed Shibayama or Shinsai • ***netsuke*** en forme de chien lion *shishi*, signé Shibayama ou Shinsai • ivory, mother-of-pearl, coral, malachite • late Edo period, mid 19th century • Fred and Isabel Pollard Collection, AGGV 1964.008.001

inro with design of a kingfisher on a branch, grass spray on verso • ***inro***, martin-pêcheur sur une branche; bouquet d'herbe au verso • lacquer, mother-of-pearl • ***ojime***, coral • ***ojime***, corail • ***netsuke*** in the form of Hotei with a huge sack • ***netsuke*** en forme de Hotei avec un immense sac • ivory • late Edo period, mid 19th century • Fred and Isabel Pollard Collection, AGGV 1974.226.016

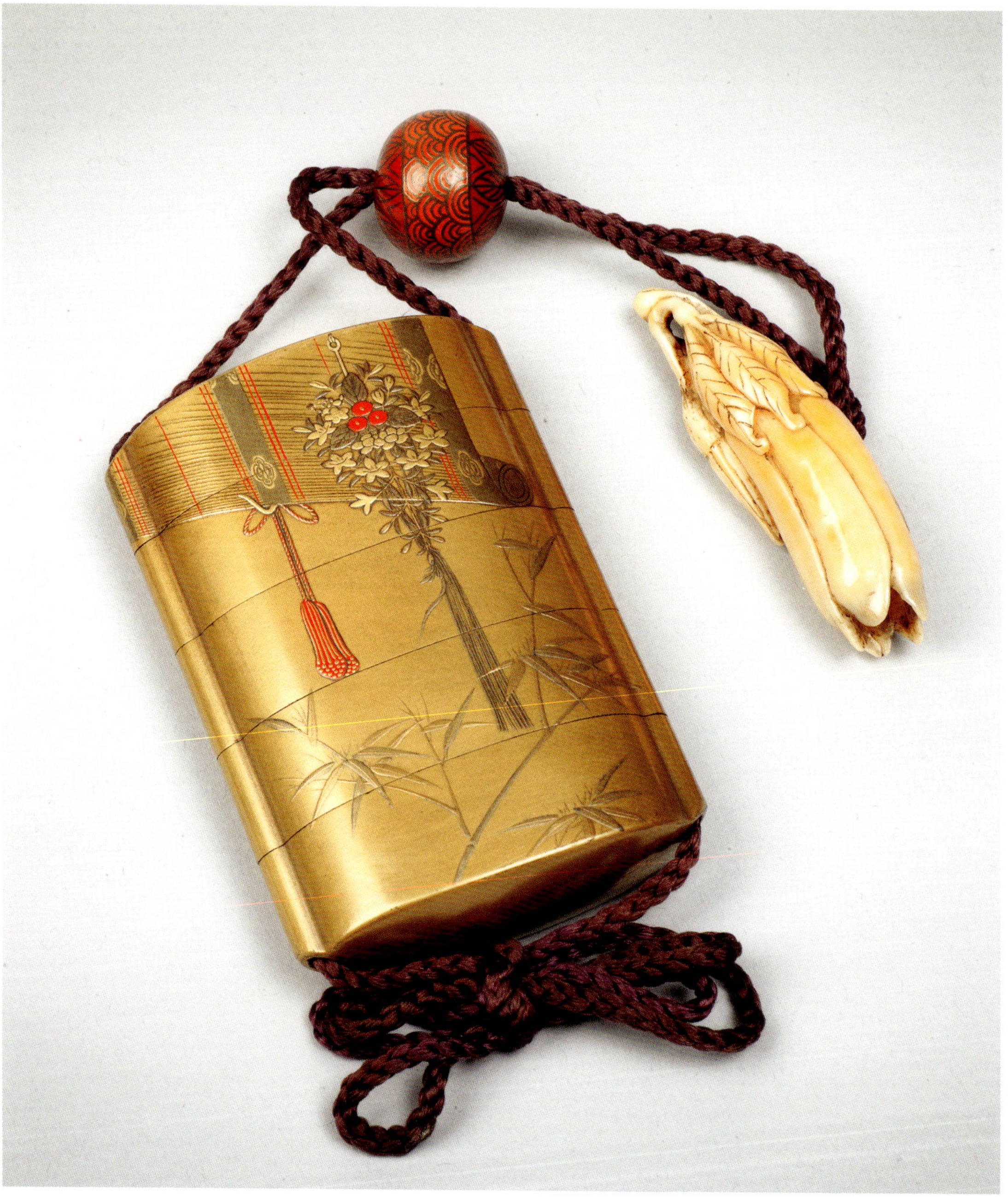

inro with design of bamboo blind and branch • ***inro***, store de bambou et branche • wood, lacquer • ***ojime*** with a wave design, wood, lacquer • ***ojime***, vague, bois, laque • ***netsuke*** in the form of a magnolia bud, signed Kajikawa Saku • ***netsuke*** en forme de bourgeon de magnolia, signé Kajikawa Saku • ivory • late Edo period, 19th century • Fred and Isabel Pollard Collection, AGGV 1964.009.001

inro with design of young pine trees and fans • ***inro***, motif de jeunes pins et éventails • ***ojime***, agate • ***ojime***, agate • ***netsuke*** in the form of a mask, signed Toshi Iizuka, circa 1800 • ***netsuke*** en forme de masque, signé Toshi Iizuka, vers 1800 • wood, lacquer • Gift of Peter de Trey, AGGV 1999.024.003

inro with tree, stream and rocks • ***inro***, arbre, ruisseau et rochers • wood, lacquer • ***ojime*** with design of foliage, ivory • ***ojime***, motif de feuillage, ivoire • ***netsuke*** in the form of reclining man holding a fan • ***netsuke*** en forme d'homme étendu tenant un éventail • ivory • late Edo/early Meiji period, mid 19th century • Gift of the Edith Low-Beer Estate, AGGV 1991.015.001

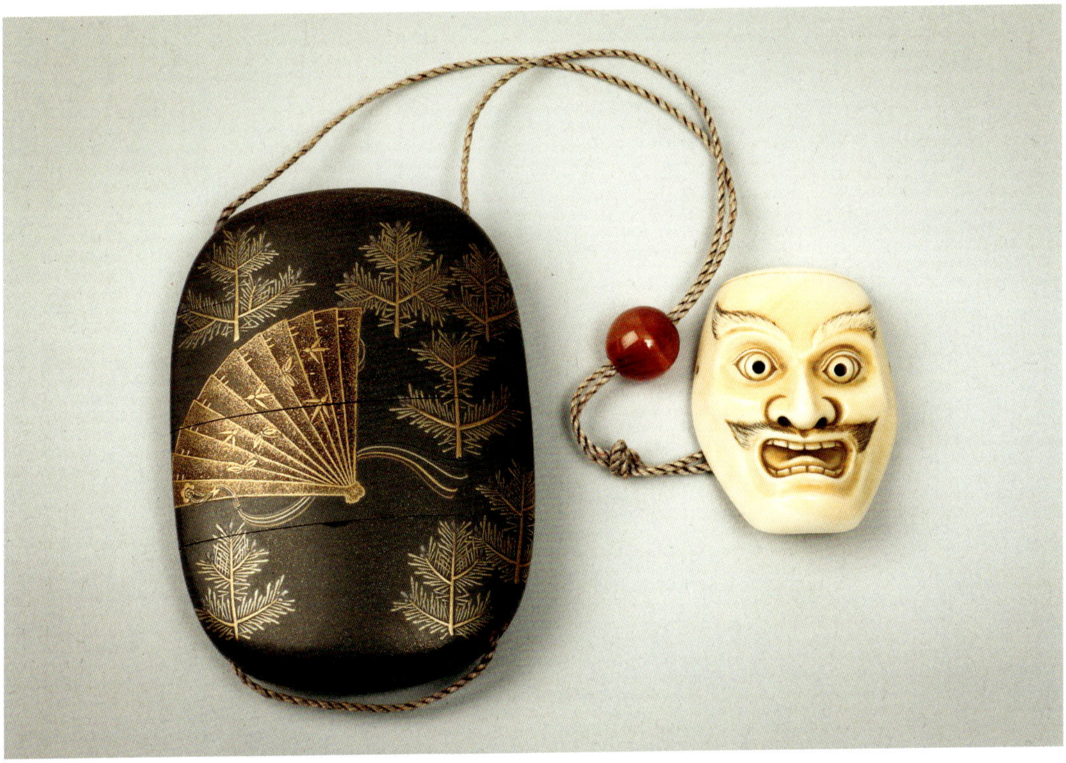

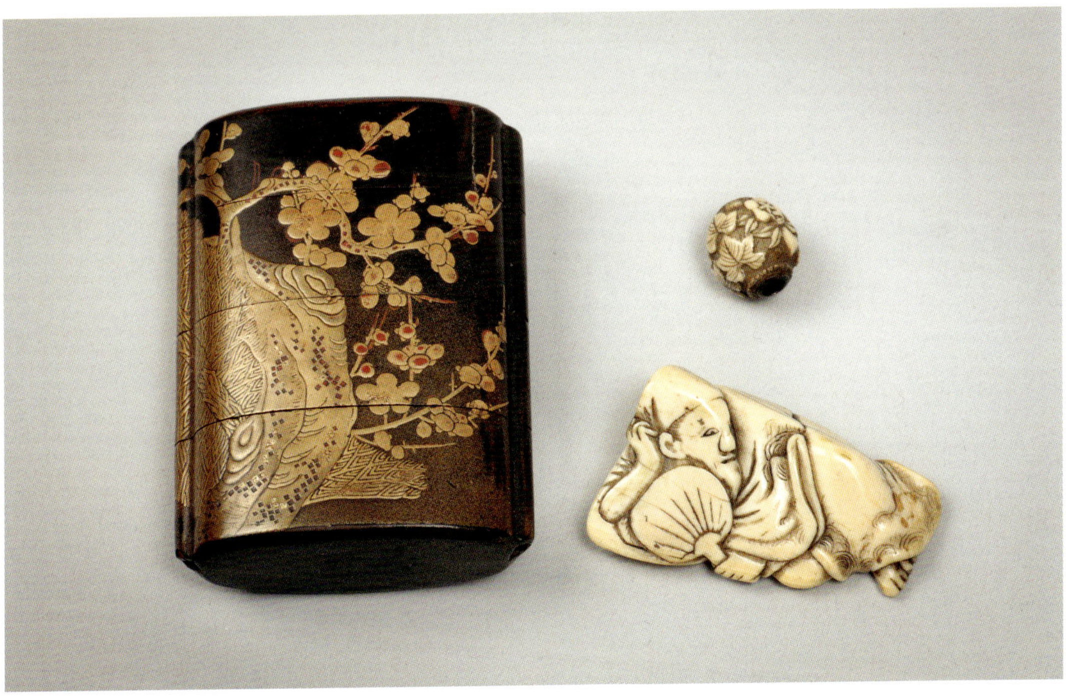

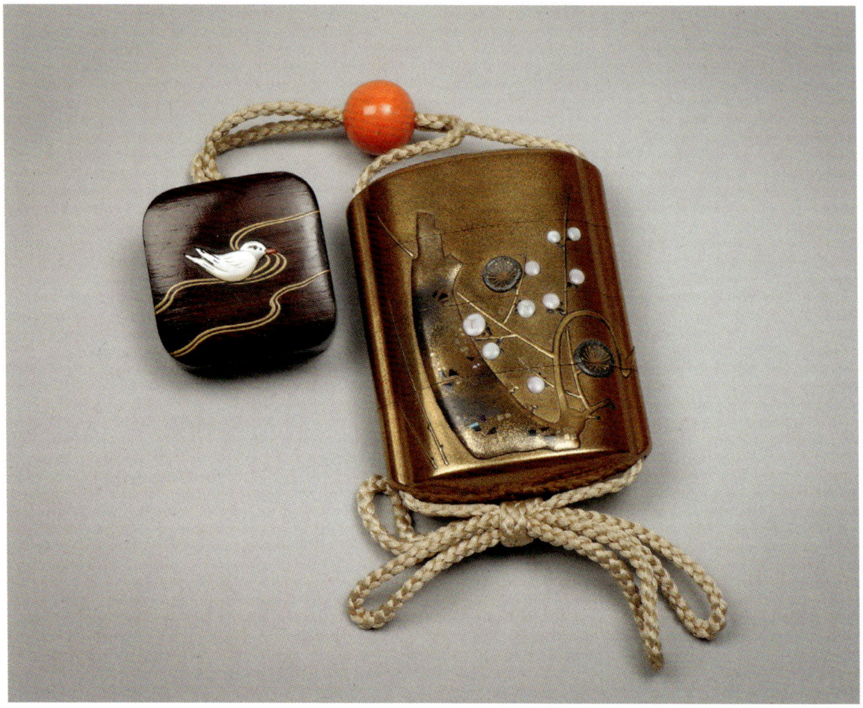

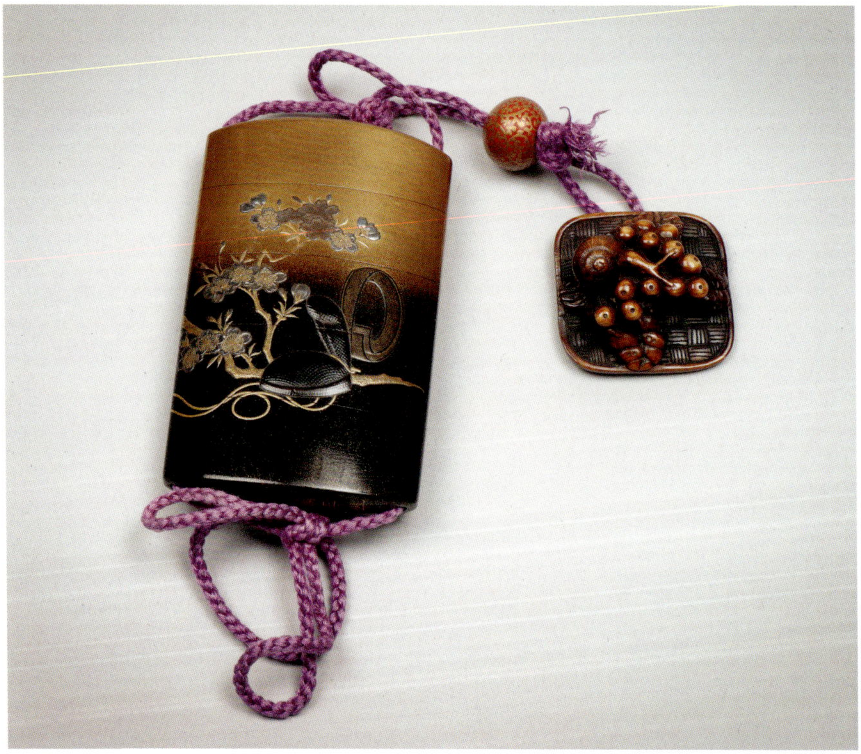

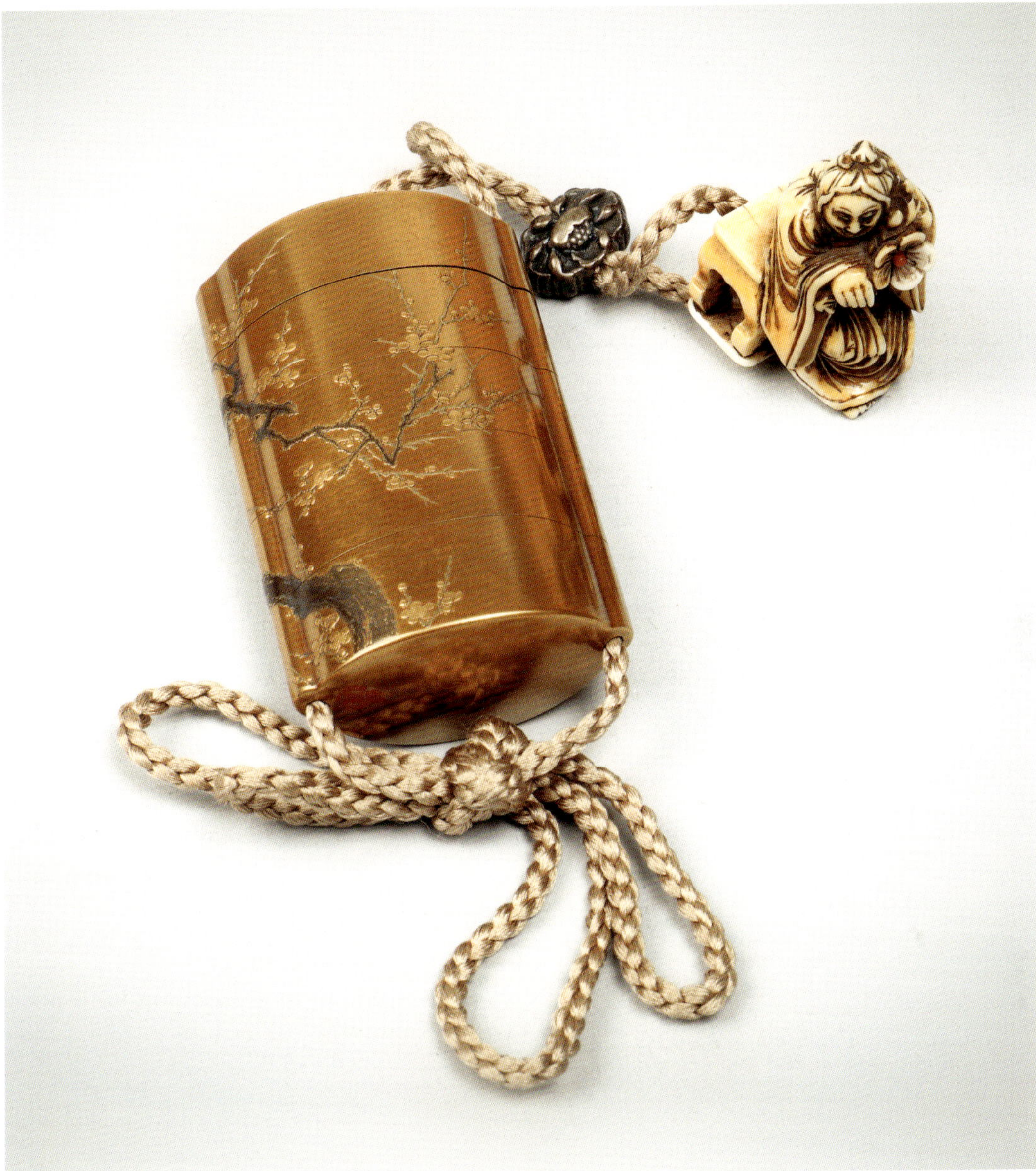

inro with design of plum blossoms, signed Shinsai (Urake Eishin) • ***inro***, motif de pruniers en fleurs, signé Shinsai (Urake Eishin) • wood, mother-of-pearl, lacquer • ***ojime***, coral • ***ojime***, corail • ***netsuke*** with design of bird on waves, signed Urake Eishin • ***netsuke***, motif d'oiseau sur des vagues, signé Urake Eishin • wood, lacquer, mother-of-pearl • late Edo period, mid 19th century • Fred and Isabel Pollard Collection, AGGV 1964.007.001

inro with design of fruit tree blossoms and hat, signed Tachibana Gyokuzan, Shinsai • ***inro***, motif d'arbre fruitier en fleurs at chapean, signé Tachibana Gyokuzan, Shinsai • lacquer • ***ojime***, red and gold lacquer • ***ojime***, laque rouge et or • ***netsuke*** with design of a snail on fruit on woven basket • ***netsuke***, motif de serpent sur un fruit sur un panier tressé • ivory • Edo period, early 19th century • Fred and Isabel Pollard Collection, AGGV 1964.005.001

inro with design of plum spray, signed Hasegawa Shigeyoshi • ***inro***, motif de bouquet de prunier, signé Hasegawa Shigeyoshi • wood, lacquer • ***ojime*** in form of flower, pewter, *shibuichi* alloy • ***ojime*** en forme de fleur, étain, alliage *shibuichi* • ***netsuke*** in the form of a flower seller sitting on a bench • ***netsuke*** en forme de marchande de fleurs assise sur un banc • ivory • late Edo period, late 18th/early 19th century • Fred and Isabel Pollard Collection, AGGV 1964.005.000

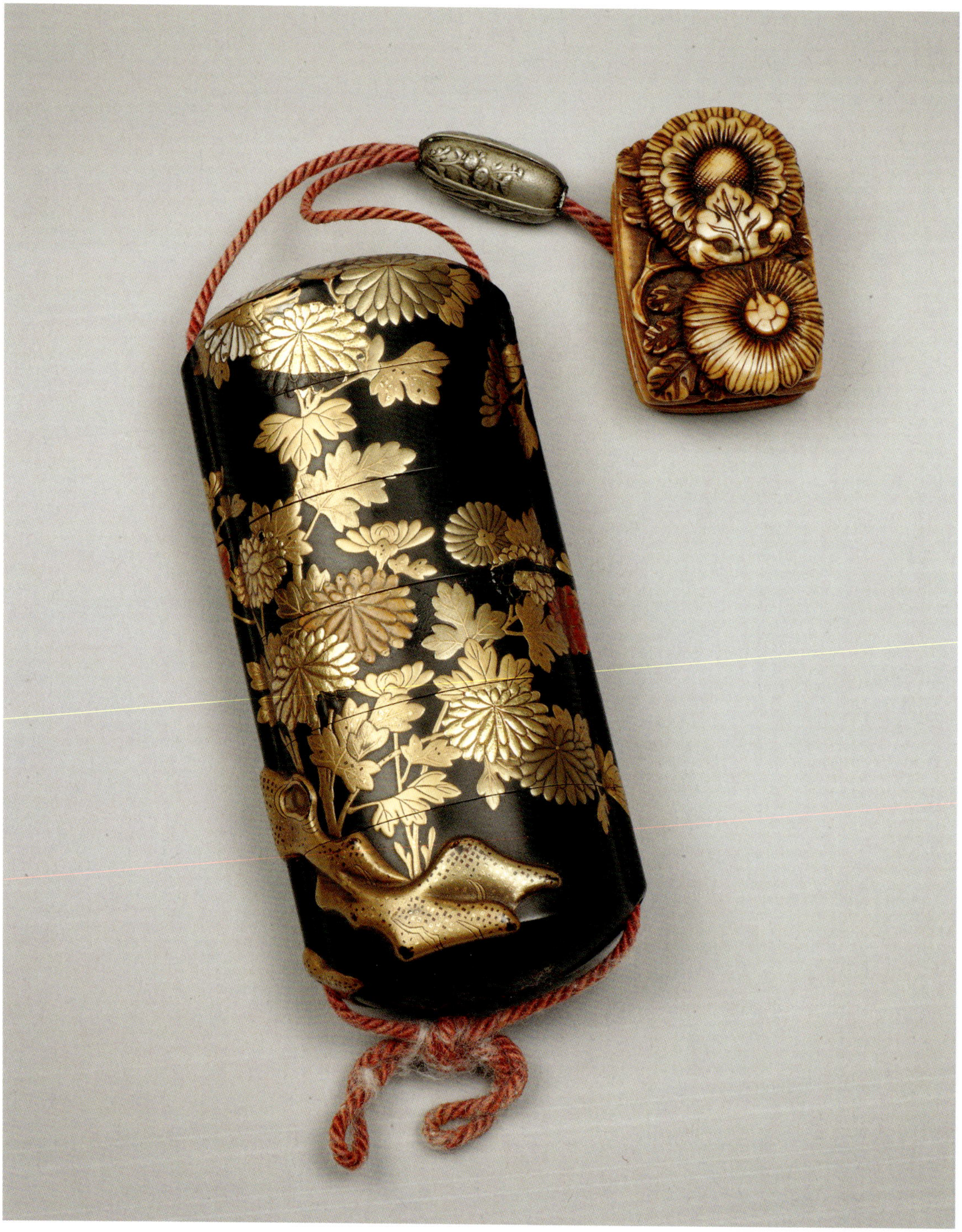

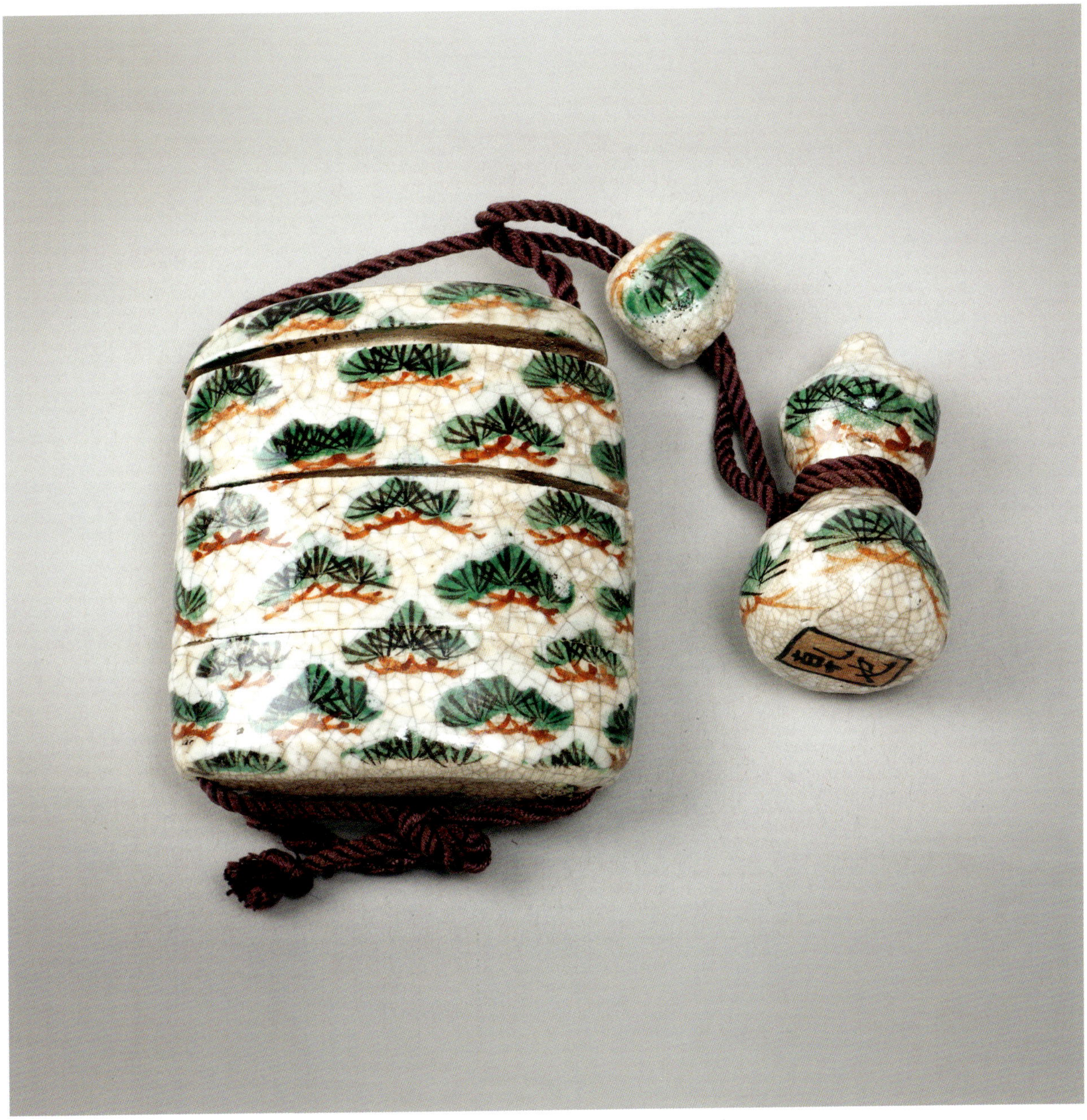

inro with design of chrysanthemums • ***inro***, motif de chrysanthèmes • wood, lacquer • ***ojime*** with iris design, metal • ***ojime***, motif d'iris, métal • ***netsuke*** in the form of two chrysanthemums on a stool • ***netsuke*** en forme de deux chrysanthèmes sur un tabouret • ivory • late Edo period, 19th century • Fred and Isabel Pollard Collection, AGGV 1974.224.001

inro, ***ojime*** and ***netsuke*** with design of pine trees, signed Kenya Miura (1821-1889) • ***inro***, ***ojime*** et ***netsuke*** avec motif de pins, signés Kenya Miura (1821 à 1889) • glazed stoneware, polychrome enamels • Gift of Bunzo Nakanishi, AGGV 1965.178.001

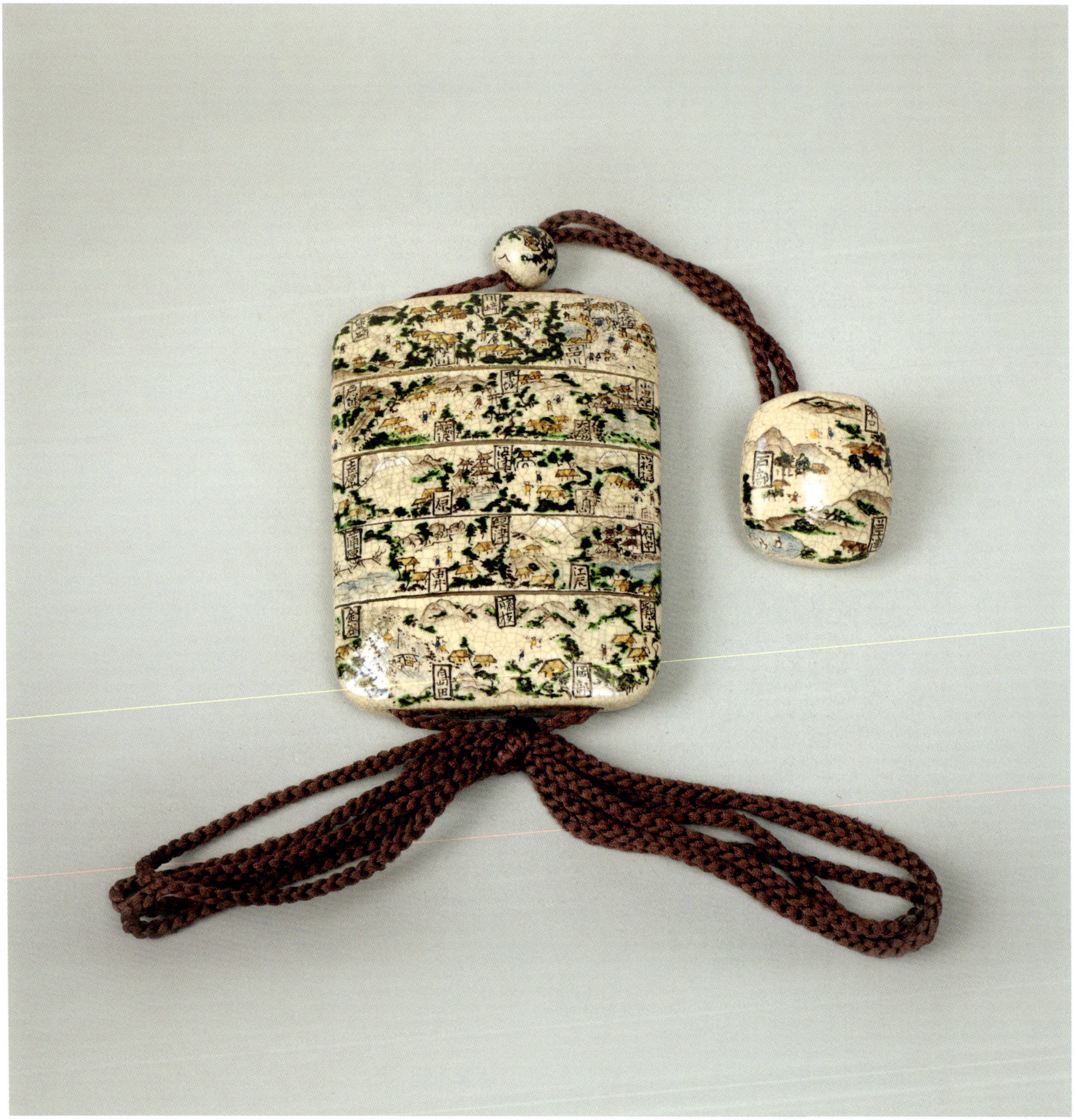

inro*, *ojime and ***netsuke*** with design of the stations of the Tokaido Road, signed Kenya Miura (1821-1889) • ***inro*, *ojime*** et ***netsuke*** ornés d'un motif représentant des postes sur la route Tokaido, signés Kenya Miura (1821 à 1889) • glazed stoneware, polychrome enamels • Gift of Bunzo Nakanishi, AGGV 1967.136.001

inro with design of snowflakes • ***inro***, motif de flocons de neige • porcelain, underglaze blue • ***ojime***, blue porcelain • ***ojime***, porcelaine bleue • late Edo period, 19th century • Fred and Isabel Pollard Collection, AGGV 1974.225.001

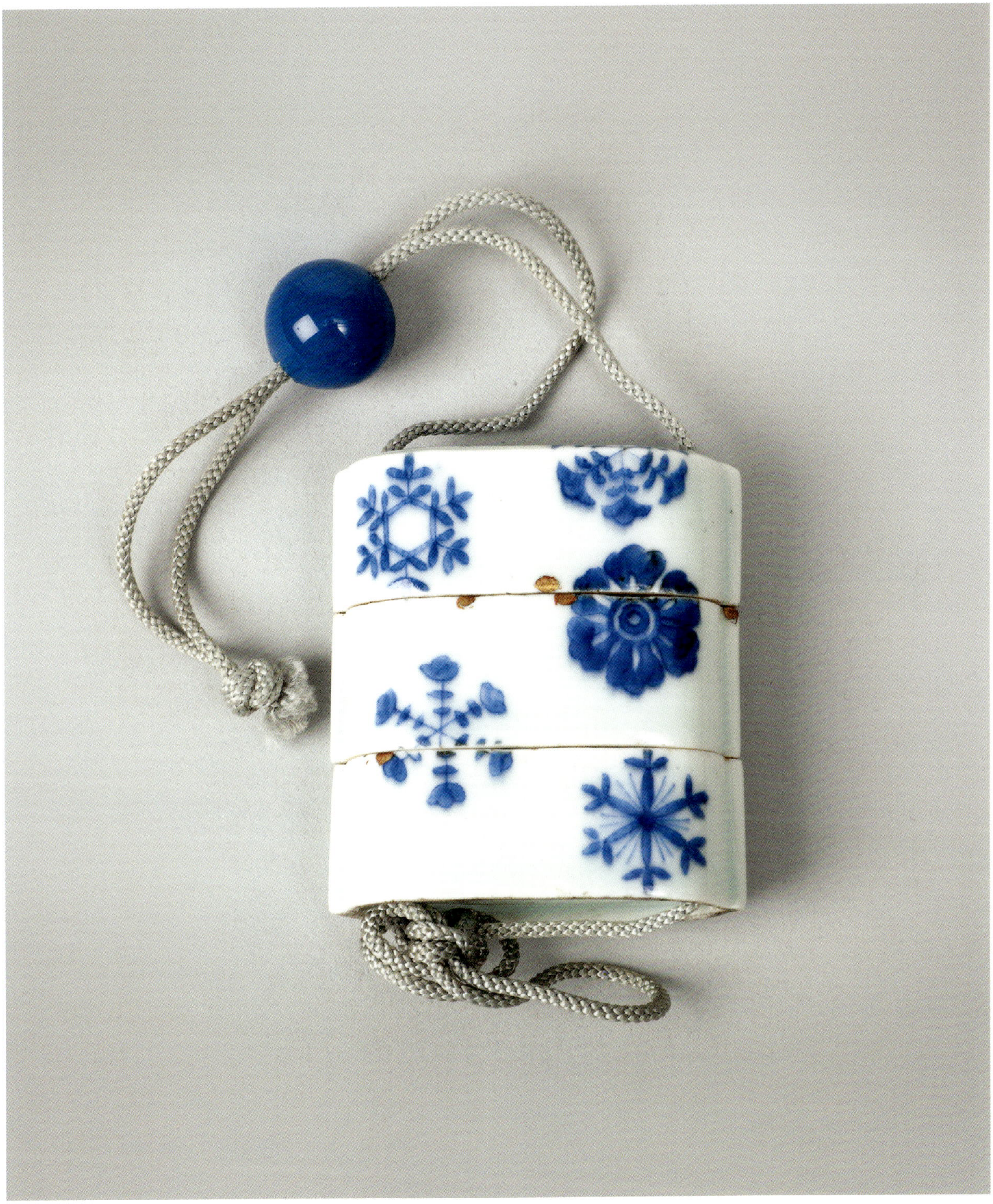

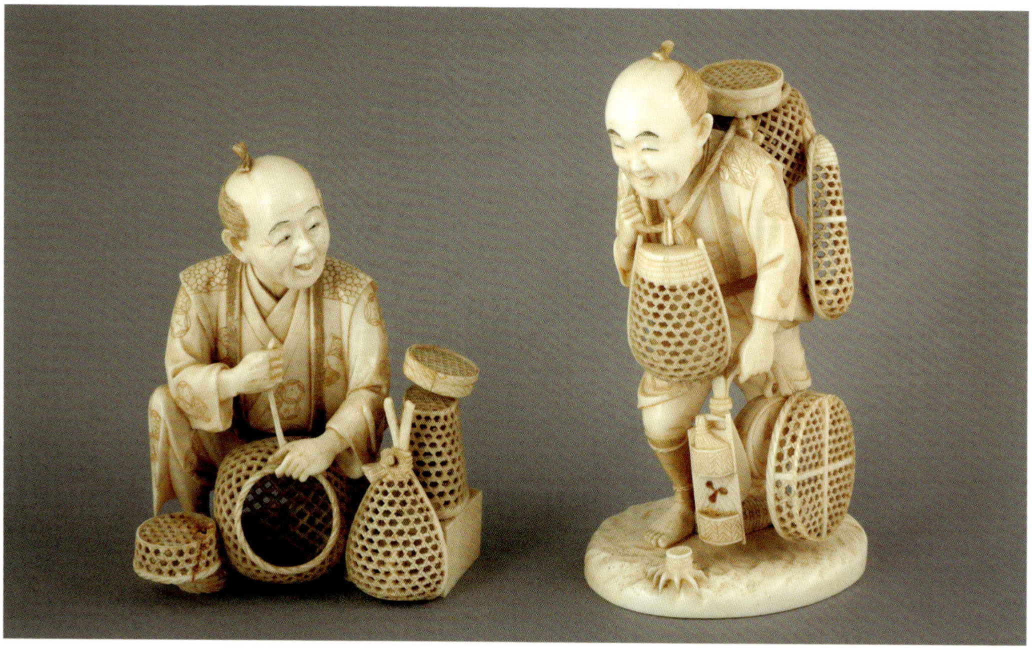

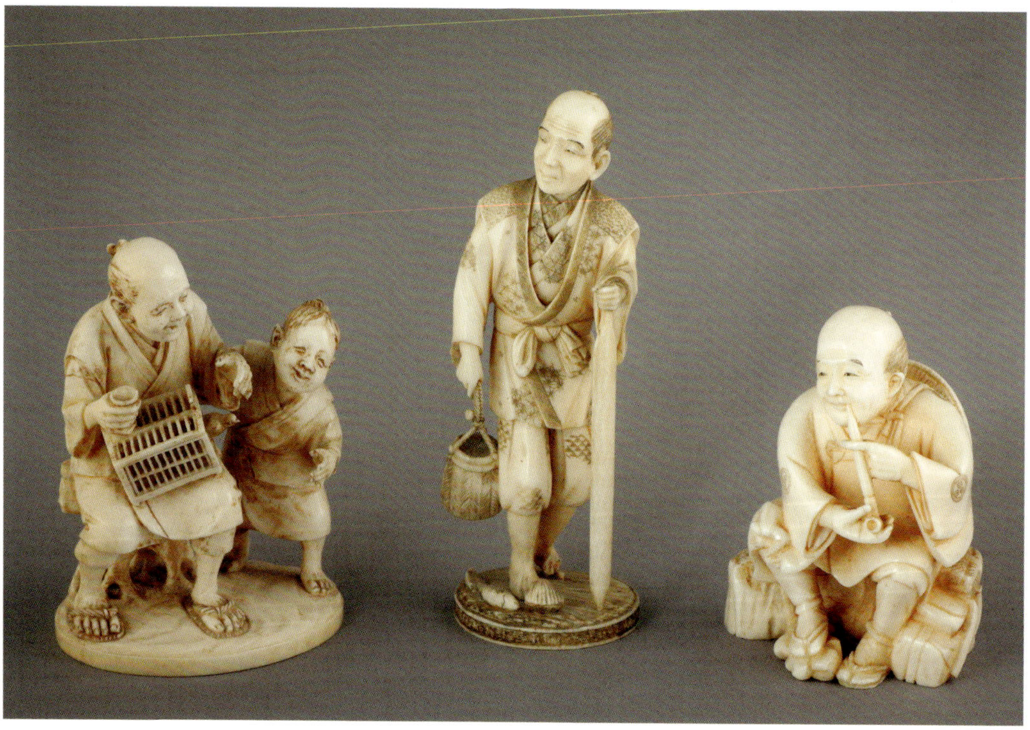

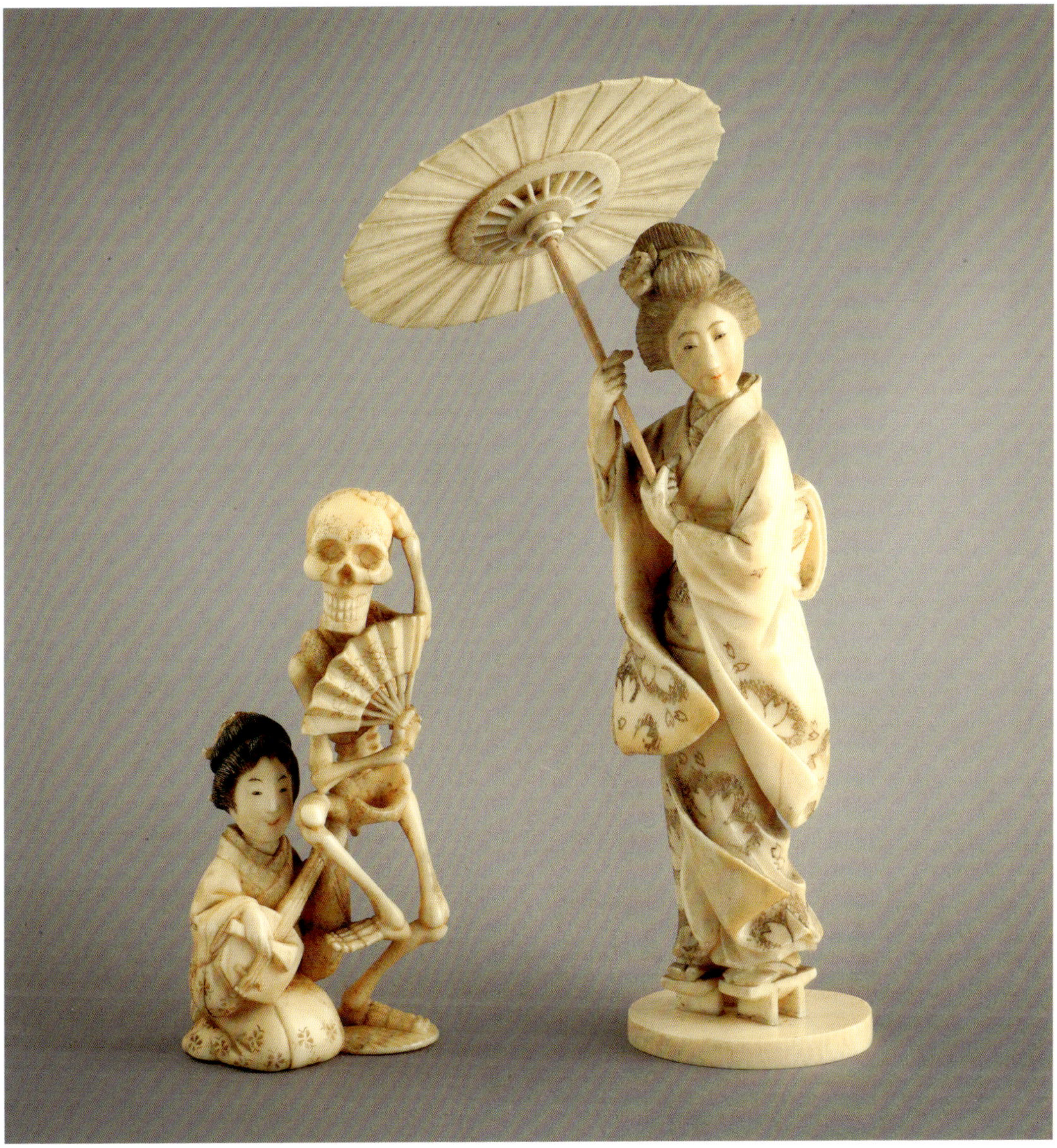

Two ***okimono*** of men with baskets, signed Toshimasa, Meiji period (1868-1912) • ***okimono*** d'un homme avec des paniers, signée Toshimasa, période Meiji (1868 à 1912) • ivory • Estate of Harold Rudolph Wright, AGGV SC446 and 447

(left) ***okimono*** of man with birdcage and child, signed Kyoko, Meiji period (1868-1912) • (à gauche) ***okimono*** d'un homme avec une cage d'oiseau et un enfant, signée Kyoko, période Meiji (1868 à 1912) • ivory • Estate of Harold Rudolph Wright, AGGV SC449 • (middle) ***okimono*** of man with a carrying pole, signed Shimura, Meiji period (1868-1912) • (au milieu) ***okimono*** d'un homme avec une perche de transport, signée Shimura, période Meiji (1868 à 1912) • ivory • Estate of Harold Rudolph Wright, AGGV SC448 • (right) ***okimono*** of man with a pipe, signed Suiten ? • (à droite) ***okimono*** d'un homme avec une pipe, signée Suiten? • Meiji period (1868-1912) • ivory • Gift of the Estate of Elizabeth Stewart, AGGV 2009.029.032

(left) ***okimono*** of *geisha* with a skeleton, signed Juei, Meiji period (1868-1912) • (à gauche) ***okimono*** d'une *geisha* avec un squelette, signée Juei • ivory • From the Collection of Bruce and Dorothy Brown, Given by their son Tony Brown, AGGV 2005.034.006 • (right) ***okimono*** of woman with umbrella, signed Tomotsugi or Tomochika, Meiji period (1868-1912) • (à droite) ***okimono*** d'une femme sous une ombrelle, signée Tomotsugi ou Tomotsugi ou Tomohide • ivory • Gift of the Estate of Nancy (Agnes) Simpson, (Collection of Harry Muncaster Hind), SC881.14

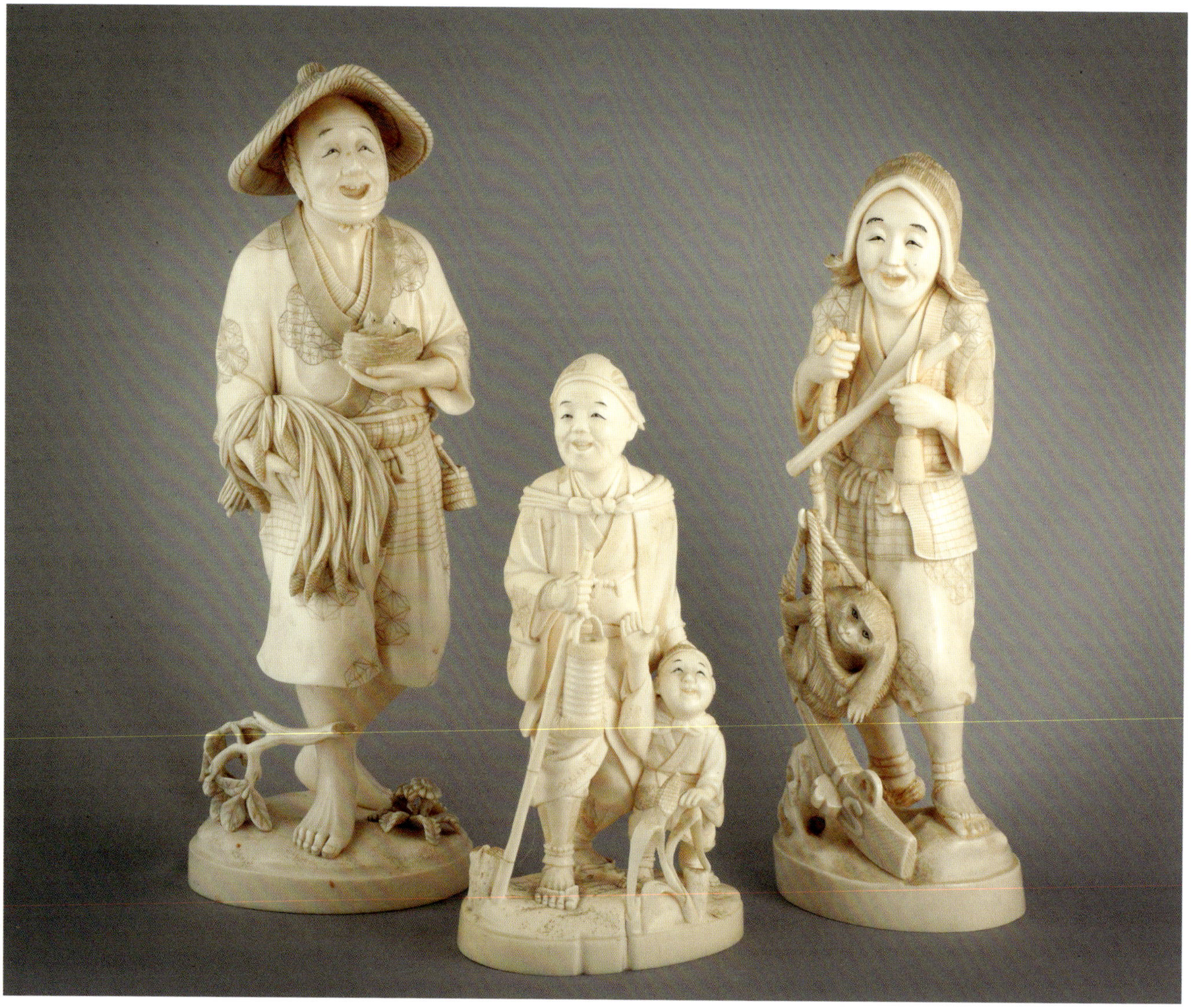

(left) ***okimono*** of man with two birds, signed Tenzan, Meiji period (1868-1912) • (à gauche) ***okimono*** d'un homme avec deux oiseaux, signée Tenzan • ivory • Gift of the Estate of Nancy (Agnes) Simpson, (Collection of Harry Muncaster Hind, AGGV 1998.036.037 • (middle) ***okimono*** of man and a boy, signed Seiso or Joso?, Meiji period (1868-1912) • (au milieu) ***okimono*** d'un homme et d'un garçon, signée Seiso ou Joso? • ivory • From the Collection of Bruce and Dorothy Brown, Given by their son Tony Brown, AGGV 2005.034.012 • (left) ***okimono*** of hunter with gun and monkey, signed Hozan, Meiji period (18686-1912) • (à gauche) ***okimono*** d'un chasseur avec un fusil et un singe, signée Hozan • ivory • Philip and Barbara Steel Bequest, AGGV SC1279

okimono of man with a cane wearing an *inro*, signed Tomoyuki, Meiji period (1868-1912) • ***okimono*** d'un homme avec une canne portant un *inro*, signée Tomoyuki • ivory • Philip and Barbara Steel Bequest, AGGV SC1272

okimono of long-legged Ashinaga with long-armed Tenaga reaching for an octopus, signed Minto, Meiji period (1868-1912) • ***okimono*** d'un Ashinaga aux longues jambes avec Tenaga allongeant son long bras vers une pieuvre, signée Minto • ivory • Gift of Hae Ran Dale, AGGV 2003.006.004 • The mythical personages of Ashinaga and Tenaga are said to have lived on a sea shore in northern China and lived upon fish which Tenaga catches with his long arms while being perched on the back of the long-legged Ashinaga

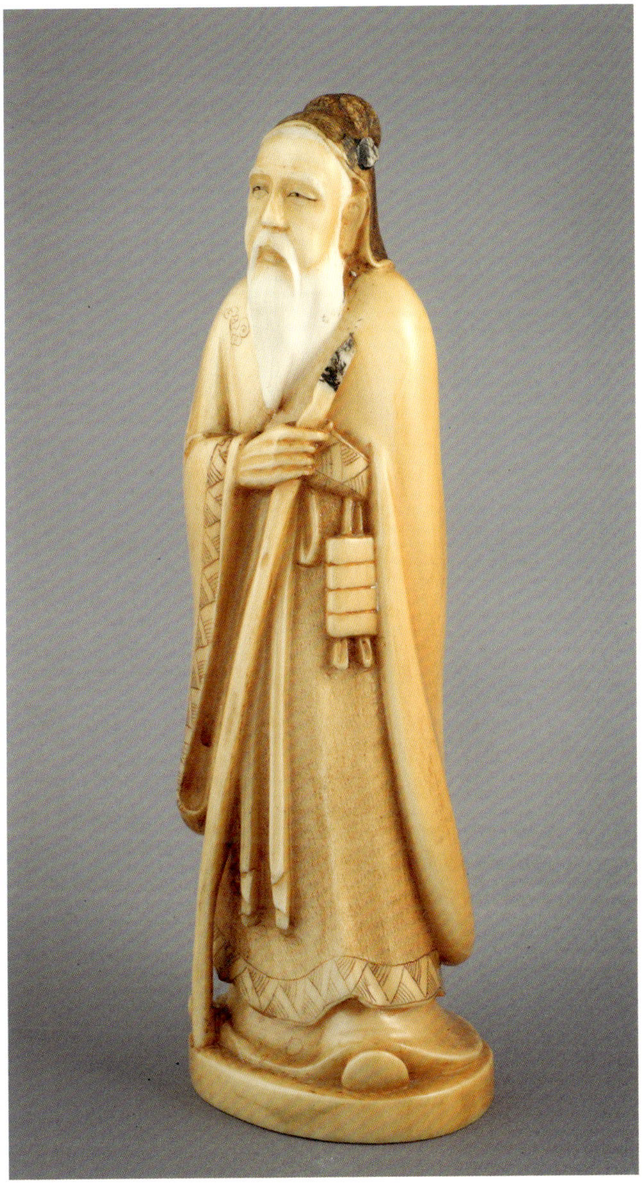

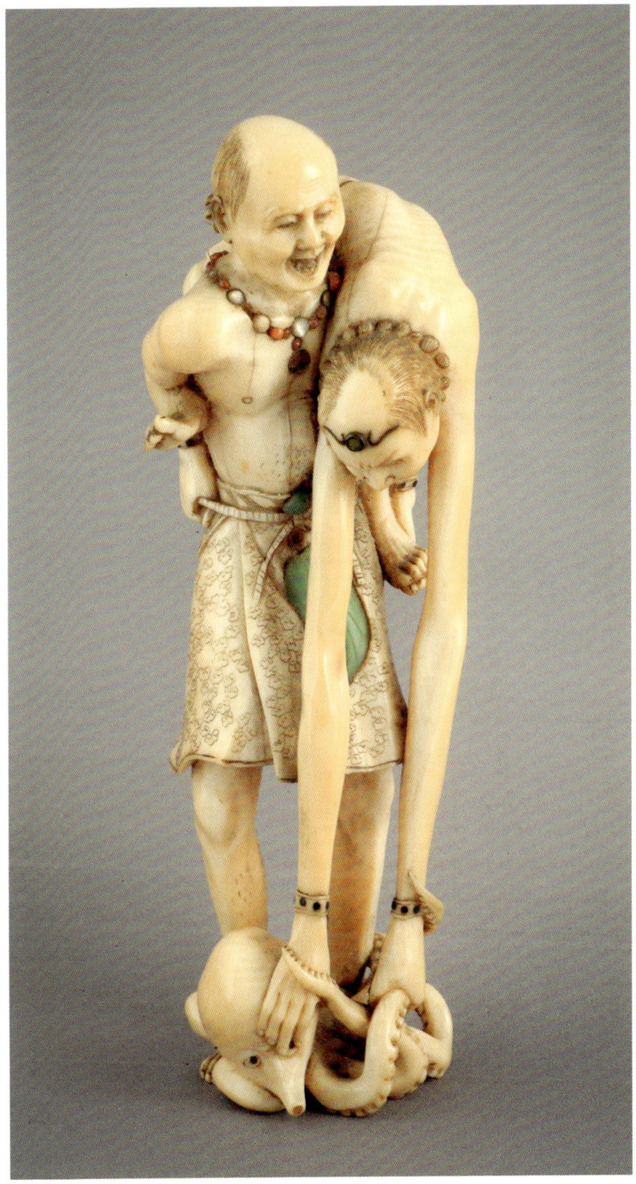

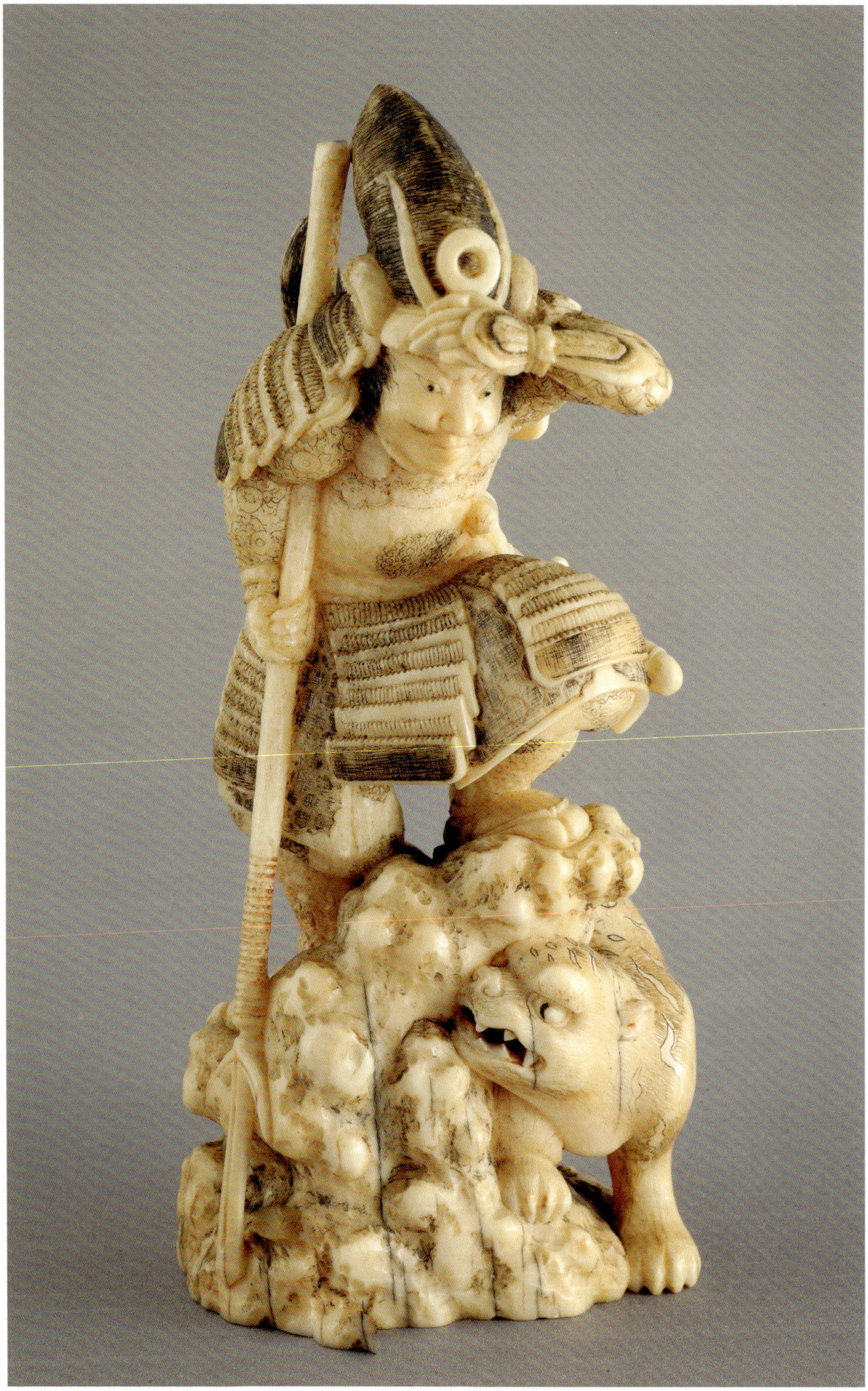

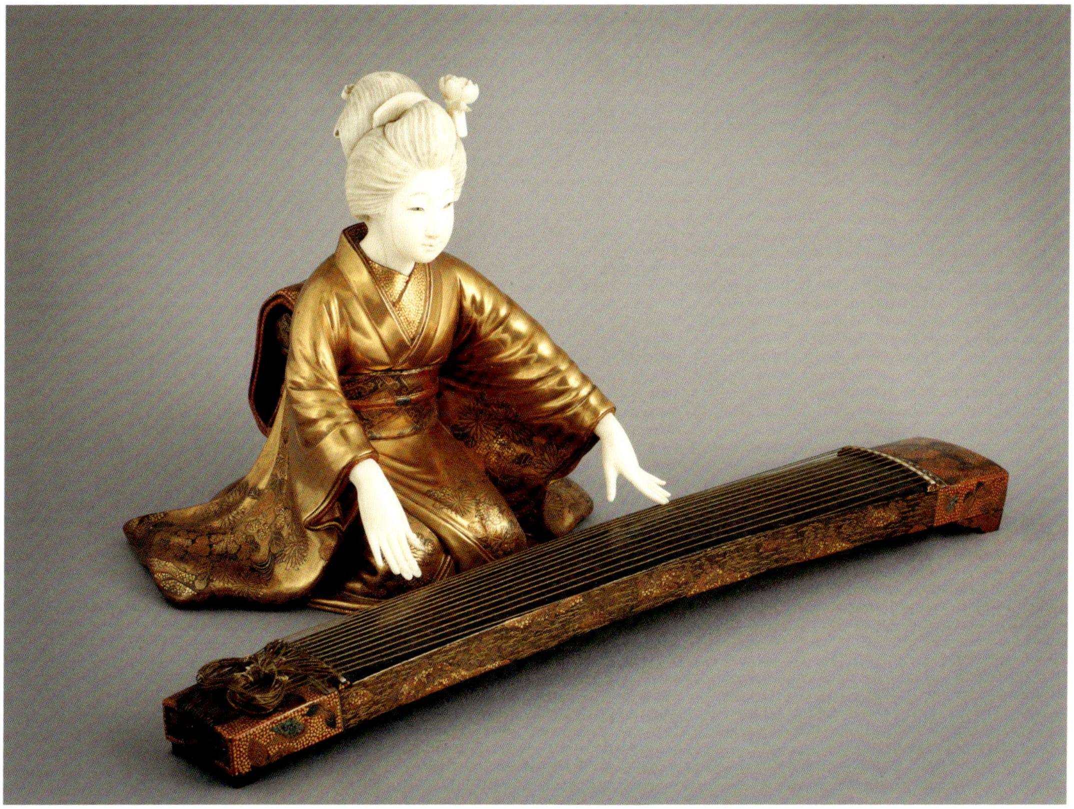

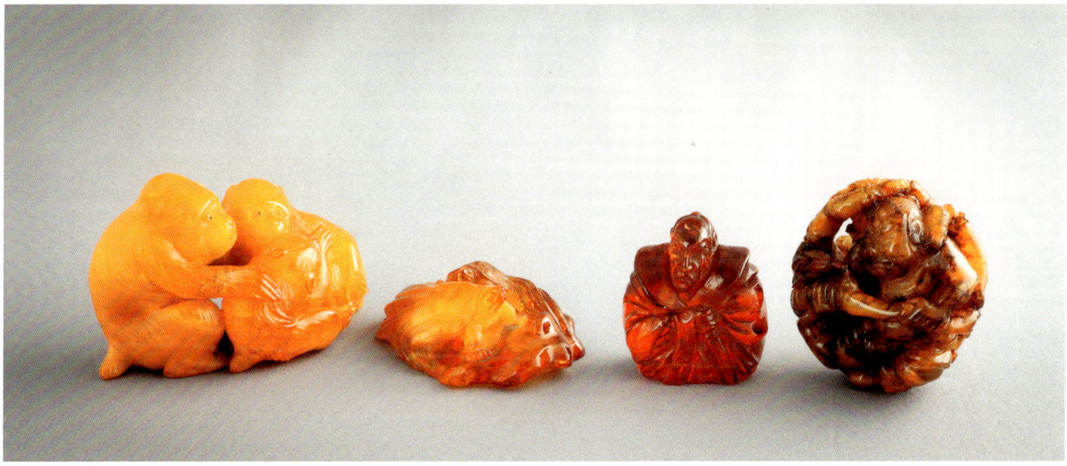

okimono of General Kato Kiyomasa hunting a tiger, signed Toshinaga or Juei, Meiji period (1868-1912) • ***okimono*** du général Kato Kiyomasa chassant un tigre, signée Toshinaga ou Juei, période Meiji (1868 à 1912) • ivory, black pigment • Irving Dwinnell Bequest Fund, AGGV 1967.086.001

okimono of *koto* player and *koto* • ***okimono*** d'un joueur de *koto* et *koto* • Meiji period (1868-1912) • wood, ivory, lacquer • Fred and Isabel Pollard Collection, AGGV 65.101

Miniature carvings (possibly ***netsuke***) of a group of monkeys/longevity turtles on a rock/of a kneeling samurai/a strongman in a bamboo groove • Sculptures miniatures (peut-être des ***netsuke***) d'un groupe de singes/tortues de longévité sur un rocher/un samouraï à genou/homme fort dans une rainure de bambou • 19th century • amber • (left, middle) Francis and Kay Reif Collection, AGGV 1998.042.125, 1999.023.044, 1999.023.043, (right) Gift of the Lewis and Ruth Sherman Foundation, AGGV 2007.016.039

Miniatures de Chine et du Japon

LA MINIATURE, CETTE FORME D'ART mise en vedette dans la présente publication, témoigne du grand plaisir que les petits objets procurent aux Chinois et aux Japonais, et de leur grande habileté à fabriquer ces articles minuscules. La Chine comme le Japon se glorifient d'avoir à leur actif un grand éventail de réalisations artistiques en miniature. Depuis les temps anciens, la miniature chinoise et japonaise se caractérise par sa délicatesse, sa précision et sa minutie d'exécution exceptionnelles.

Même si on qualifie souvent les formes d'art du présent catalogue d'arts mineurs, elles représentent tout de même l'excellence dans le milieu des arts de Chine et du Japon. Les miniatures conviennent mieux à un examen personnel, de près, qu'une grande œuvre d'art. Elles sont conçues pour tenir dans le creux de la main. Règle générale, elles ont une excellente qualité tactile et sont agréables à toucher. Les collectionneurs les aiment en raison de leur taille et parce qu'elles ont le pouvoir de faire grande impression sur les gens.

Malgré les limites de la matière employée, de la forme et de l'espace restreint qui s'offrent à l'artiste pour l'illustration, les fabricants de miniatures se sont révélés extrêmement patients, originaux et minutieux. Ils ont fait preuve d'élégance dans la forme et d'ingéniosité dans la variété des matières utilisées. Ils ont réussi à embellir des objets courants, fonctionnels ou utiles, jusqu'à créer des articles d'une grande beauté et complexité. Par leurs trésors miniatures, les Chinois et Japonais ont manifesté leur amour de la nature, du symbolisme et de la tradition. Dans l'ensemble, les œuvres d'art miniatures de Chine et du Japon passent haut la main le test de l'amplification.

Tous les types d'œuvres miniatures dont il est question dans cette publication, sans exception, ont été collectionnés par des étrangers qui ont contribué à les populariser, ainsi qu'à stimuler et prolonger les diverses formes d'art et d'artisanat de Chine et du Japon. La conséquence de leur reconnaissance de l'excellence de ces petits trésors et de leur intérêt à les collectionner est l'éventuelle promotion, conservation et appréciation de cette forme d'art en Chine et au Japon, qui l'avaient tous deux abandonnée pendant un certain temps, la jugeant non pertinente. De grandes collections de ces miniatures existent dans les musées et résidences privées du monde entier, et non seulement dans leur pays d'origine.

Tabatières chinoises

Ce sont les Européens à l'époque de la dynastie Ming (1368 à 1644), à la fin du16e siècle et au début du 17e siècle, qui ont fait connaître le tabac, puis la prise, en Chine. Au début de la dynastie Qing, on tente d'interdire l'usage du tabac, mais non la prise, en raison de ses propriétés thérapeutiques. La préparation du tabac à priser consiste à réduire les feuilles séchées de tabac en poudre fine que l'on mélange à des herbes, des épices et diverses substances aromatiques. Le tabac à priser chinois contient de la menthe, du camphre, du jasmin et de l'essence de rose. On le considère comme un médicament et on pense qu'il améliore la sensation de bien-être et guérit un grand éventail de maladies. On l'utilise pour traiter la congestion nasale et des sinus, les rhumes, les migraines, le mal de dents, la douleur dans les yeux et le mal de gorge. On s'en sert également pour faire transpirer, soulager de l'asthme, favoriser la digestion et apaiser des malaises intestinaux comme la constipation. Le tabac à priser finira par jouer un rôle social important dans la vie de la classe supérieure en Chine.

Pendant le règne de Kangxi (1662 à 1722), de Yongzheng (1723 à 1735) et de Qianlong (1736 à1795), les envoyés européens offrent du tabac à priser et des tabatières à la cour mandchoue en signe de leur volonté d'entretenir de bonnes relations avec la Chine. Toutefois, leurs tabatières ne sont guère pratiques en raison du climat humide de la Chine. C'est pourquoi les Chinois utilisent d'abord de petits flacons à médicament pour priser. Une toute petite cuiller, habituellement en ivoire ou en argent, ou parfois une carapace de tortue, est fixée à l'intérieur du bouchon et sert à prélever un peu de tabac du flacon. L'ouverture étroite du flacon empêche l'humidité d'entrer et préserve la fraîcheur du tabac à priser tout en empêchant le contenu de s'en échapper. Ces flacons deviendront des œuvres d'art miniature et des objets très intéressants à collectionner. Les empereurs mandchous offrent des tabatières en cadeau pour accorder la faveur impériale à des fonctionnaires ou des militaires très méritants, ou à des dignitaires ou envoyés étrangers. Ils fondent même des ateliers impériaux sur les terres du palais pour la production des tabatières. On en produit également ailleurs en Chine et elles servent parfois à soudoyer des gens afin d'obtenir des faveurs politiques. He Shen, un avide conseiller en chef corrompu de l'empereur Qianlong, possède une collection de 2 390 tabatières, qui serviront éventuellement de preuves de sa vénalité et de ses crimes.

Le tabac à priser est d'abord réservé aux riches de la classe supérieure, mais fera par la suite partie des articles de base de toutes les classes sociales. En vue de se distinguer, les classes supérieures commencent à privilégier une belle matière, élégante, originale et coûteuse pour la création de leurs tabatières. Par conséquent, les flacons de tabac à priser décoratifs de Chine en disent long sur la classe et le pouvoir social, et sur la situation économique de l'époque à laquelle ils ont été fabriqués. Les ateliers du palais se trouvent à Beijing, Jingdezhen, Suzhou et Yangzhou et ont pour mission de créer ces trésors miniatures pour la cour. D'autres tabatières sont fabriquées à Guangzhou, Boshan (province du Shandong) et dans la province du Liaoning. Les tabatières métalliques proviennent de Mongolie et du Tibet.

De nombreuses tabatières chinoises sont complètement dépourvues de décoration, laissant la matière parler d'elle-même, alors que d'autres portent des décorations ou dessins invraisemblables peints, sculptés, gravés, incrustés ou appliqués. On pourrait qualifier les tabatières chinoises de quintessence des arts chinois dans un microcosme, car elles combinent les techniques de la peinture, de la sculpture, de la calligraphie et de l'incrustation à l'habileté requise pour travailler diverses matières. Les paysages, la flore et la faune, ainsi que les scènes de genre représentées sur les tabatières de porcelaine bleu et blanc, en particulier, révèlent une grande habileté dans l'art de la peinture monochrome.

Les tabatières chinoises sont fabriquées dans un éventail apparemment inépuisable de matières qu'il est possible de répartir plus ou moins en cinq grands groupes : la pierre, le métal, les matières organiques, la céramique et le verre (y compris les flacons de verre peints de l'intérieur). Les bouchons de ces flacons sont également faits de diverses matières, qui contrastent avec l'esthétique du flacon, ou la complètent. Les divers types de pierre, et leurs sous-catégories, qui entrent dans la fabrication des tabatières sont très nombreux : jade (néphrite et jadéite), calcédonite, agate, quartz, améthyste, cristal, tourmaline, aigue-marine, béryl, lapis lazuli, turquoise, malachite, jaspe, topaze, saponite, mélantérite, poudingue, calcaire et jet. En sculptant, les habiles tailleurs de pierres précieuses utilisent souvent de façon ingénieuse la beauté naturelle inhérente à la matière et les diverses couleurs naturellement présentes dans la pierre ou sur sa surface, en vue de créer de beaux motifs en relief de couleurs contrastantes et d'exploiter les inclusions de couleur foncée distinctive dans la calcédonite, afin de créer un effet d'ombre. Les matières organiques utilisées pour les tabatières comprennent le corail, l'ambre, le bois, le bambou, la gourde, la coque de noix, la coque de noix de coco, l'ivoire, la corne, le calao, la carapace de tortue, la peau de poisson, la nacre et la laque, en particulier la laque de Pékin. Les métaux qui entrent dans la fabrication des tabatières sont l'argent, le cuivre et le *paktong/baitong* (alliage cuivre-zinc-nickel), et on se sert souvent d'une base métallique pour les surfaces émaillées et cloisonnées. Les tabatières de céramique sont composées de porcelaine de grand feu et de grès bruns des fours de Yixing, dans la province du Jiangsu.

À l'époque de la dynastie Qing, les potiers chinois produisent des chefs-d'œuvre de céramique parmi les plus impressionnants du monde, en particulier dans les fours impériaux de Jingdezhen, situé dans la province du Jiangxi. Ils créent de magnifiques récipients, y compris des tabatières, au moyen d'une grande variété de glaçures monochromatiques, peints en bleu de cobalt sous la glaçure avec motifs émaillés sur la glaçure. Ils peuvent même produire des glaçures qui imitent l'ivoire, la nacre, le métal, la laque, le bois, le bambou, le jade, l'agate, le marbre et le poudingue. La plasticité de la porcelaine permet également de la mouler et d'y sculpter des motifs. À l'exception des magnifiques tabatières de porcelaine destinées à la cour impériale et aux aristocrates, les tabatières sont relativement faciles à produire en grande quantité et, par conséquent, à prix abordable pour tout le monde. Les potiers, qui fabriquent les célèbres théières en grès brun de Yixing, fabriquent également des tabatières qui plaisent à la sensibilité des lettrés.

La matière la plus populaire, et la première à être utilisée pour les tabatières en Chine, est le verre. Les techniques européennes de fabrication du verre sont introduites au palais impérial de Beijing par les missionnaires jésuites durant le règne de Kangxi (1662 à 1722). Cette nouveauté mène à la création de nombreuses tabatières magnifiques en verre. On obtient de nombreuses couleurs par le mélange d'oxydes métalliques, certaines à pois, d'autres tachetées ou spiralées. On utilise également le verre aventurine durant cette période. Les artisans verriers chinois maîtrisent tous les aspects de la technique de fabrication du verre comme le soufflage, le pressage, le moulage, le laminage et le dressage. Tout comme les potiers, ils peuvent imiter d'autres matières que le verre, comme la porcelaine, le jade, l'agate, le réalgar (un sulfure rouge d'arsenic) et d'autres pierres. Les tabatières en verre avec un revêtement décoratif sont populaires. Cette technique, également appelée verre de Pékin, consiste à tremper un flacon de verre dans du verre liquide d'une seule couleur, ou de couleurs contrastantes, puis à sculpter cette couche externe jusqu'à dévoiler la couleur originale de base qui est habituellement claire ou blanc opaque, ou qui a l'aspect d'un « flocon de neige ». L'émail peint sur verre est également une forme populaire d'ornementation.

Le verre peut aussi servir à fabriquer des tabatières peintes de l'intérieur. L'artisan dépose d'abord du fer, du sable et de l'émeri dans un flacon de verre, le secoue, le frotte jusqu'à ce qu'il soit lisse, puis en peint l'intérieur avec un oxyde de fer mélangé à de l'eau, afin d'obtenir une surface d'un blanc laiteux qu'il peut peindre de motifs très élaborés. Il insère un pinceau courbé dans le goulot du flacon, de manière à peindre méticuleusement sous le verre de magnifiques paysages, portraits, caractères de calligraphie, fleurs ou animaux. Ces tableaux miniatures exécutés de main de maître à l'intérieur d'un flacon de verre sont extrêmement fascinants et populaires auprès des connaisseurs. Des artistes en produisent encore de nos jours et nombre d'entre eux se sont rendus célèbres à l'échelle internationale. Ma Shouxuan, Zhou Leyuan, Ding Erzhong, Ye Zhongsan, Yan Yutian, Guan Yutian et Tang Cichuan, sont quelques-uns seulement des artistes les plus connus pour leur peinture à l'intérieur de tabatières.

Les dessins, motifs et symboles qui ornent les tabatières sont vastes et diversifiés. Les symboles sont tirés de multiples sources telles que les récits légendaires, l'histoire, la religion, la philosophie et le folklore. Les symboles chinois de bon augure des tabatières prennent souvent la forme de jeux de mots visuels appelés rébus. Étant donné qu'un bon nombre de mots chinois ont la même prononciation, il existe bien des possibilités de rébus, mais seules les personnes qui maîtrisent vraiment bien la langue chinoise peuvent en comprendre les nuances. Au cours des siècles, certains rébus prendront une signification bien précise, parfois cachée. Les idées fréquemment exprimées sont des souhaits codés de bonne santé, prospérité, bonheur dans le couple, nombreux fils, bonne chance, joie, succès professionnel, longévité et même immortalité à l'intention du propriétaire ou du donateur de l'article.

De nombreux marchands étrangers qui fréquentent les marchés chinois des 18e et 19e siècles veulent rapporter chez eux un souvenir de cet étrange pays. Les petites tabatières, faciles à transporter, sont le bibelot idéal à cette fin. Au 20e siècle, les étrangers font l'acquisition d'un très grand nombre de tabatières chinoises qu'on peut maintenant admirer dans d'innombrables musées et collections privées d'Europe et d'Amérique.

Le Japon a produit un bon nombre de tabatières durant la période Meiji (1868 à 1912), en réaction à la demande des Occidentaux pour tout ce qui était oriental, de même que pour le marché chinois. Les tabatières produites au Japon à la fin du 19e siècle pouvaient être fabriquées par des sculpteurs de *netsuke* qui les ornaient de motifs originaux de style japonais, mais elles pouvaient aussi n'être que des copies pures et simples des tabatières chinoises. La base de nombreuses copies japonaises est gravée de la marque de l'empereur chinois Qianlong.

Bibliographie sélective

Hall, Robert and Ian Hardy. "chinois Snuff Bottles, the Japanese Connection." *Arts of Asia*, Vol. 35, No. 5, 2005.

Kleiner, Robert. *Chinese Snuff Bottles from the Collection of Mary and George Bloch.* Hong Kong, 1987.

____________. "The Tuyet Nguyet Collection of Snuff Bottles and Saucers." *Arts of Asia*, Volume 28, No. 6, 1998.

Moss, Hugh M. *Snuff Bottles of Chine.* London, 1971.

Moss, Hugh M., Victor E. Graham and Kabo Tsang. *The Art of the Chinese Snuff Bottle.* New York and Tokyo, 1993.

Scott, Rosemary. *The Miniature World, An Exhibition of Snuff Bottles from the J and J Collection.* Taipei, 2002.

Flacons à opium chinois

Les flacons miniatures à opium n'ont pas intéressé les collectionneurs au même titre que les tabatières. En fait, il n'existe qu'un petit nombre de collections privées, et publiques dans les musées. Néanmoins, ces flacons sont souvent délicats, très décorés et constituent des pièces extrêmement intéressantes à collectionner. Le flacon à opium est un petit contenant personnel à porter sur soi, utilisé pour ranger la provision d'opium de l'usager pour sa vie quotidienne ou des occasions spéciales.

L'opium, qu'on finira par appeler par euphémisme la « boue de longue vie », a probablement fait son apparition en Chine au 8e siècle comme médicament universel et aphrodisiaque. On le sert parfois avec du miel, des pruneaux ou des pelures d'orange. On croit qu'il soulage la diarrhée, l'asthme, les rhumatismes, la douleur au cœur et le mal de ventre. Les premiers marchands européens commencent à le fumer, ce qui permet à la substance d'entrer dans le sang plus rapidement qu'en la consommant par voie orale. À la fin du 18e siècle, l'habitude de fumer de l'opium se répand dans toute la Chine comme drogue récréative et, au 19e siècle, toutes les classes de la société chinoise s'y adonnent pour faire face aux difficultés de la vie. On croit que l'opium favorise la virilité et la vigueur sexuelle. On trouve occasionnellement cette idée dans les dessins érotiques cachés dans certaines parties du flacon. L'action de fumer de l'opium évoque les sombres fumeries peu recommandables, mais on fume également de l'opium à domicile chez l'élite de la société comme chez les pauvres. On sait que l'empereur Dowager Cixi (1835 à 1908) s'offrait une pipée ou deux en fin de journée.

L'opium s'est avéré un produit parfait pour des pays comme la Grande-Bretagne en vue d'équilibrer son commerce avec la Chine, inégal en raison de la grande demande de l'Europe pour le thé. Au 19e siècle, la Grande-Bretagne défie les lois chinoises sur la drogue, fait la promotion de l'exportation lucrative de l'opium indien, et gagne deux guerres (appelées les guerres de l'opium de 1839 à 1842 et de 1857 à 1860) afin de maintenir son marché de la drogue avec la Chine. C'est un héritage qui a laissé une multitude de récits de dépendances et de souffrances en Chine, et qui a persisté jusqu'au milieu du 20e siècle, alors que la toute nouvelle République populaire de Chine a éradiqué l'usage de l'opium.

L'opium s'accompagne de tout un attirail, comme une pipe à la forme distinctive, une petite lampe, une cuiller, une aiguille large et une balance portative pour mesurer la dose exacte, un oreiller d'une forme particulière sur lequel reposer la tête et des contenants ou coffrets miniatures. Les flacons d'opium qui sont suffisamment petits pour tenir dans la paume d'une main prennent diverses formes : cylindriques, oblongues, carrées. Ils sont fabriqués dans diverses matières, organiques et inorganiques : le laiton, l'argent, le *paktong* (alliage cuivre-zinc-nickel), le cloisonné, l'émail, le jade, les pelures de mandarines, la corne et l'ivoire. Certains sont même décorés de matières exotiques comme des piquants de porc-épic. La plupart sont en métal décoré par gravure, émaillage ou martelage de motifs en relief appelés « repoussé ». Certains flacons en argent sont décorés à l'aide d'une technique appelée *niello*, qui consiste à appliquer un motif fait d'un mélange d'argent, de cuivre, de plomb, de soufre et de borax sur la base de métal ou l'argent gravé, et à cuire.

Les thèmes décoratifs comprennent des fleurs et des animaux, des sujets tirés de la mythologie ou du folklore, des caractères calligraphiés, des symboles, des emblèmes religieux, les immortels de la légende taoïstes et des paysages. Certaines inscriptions du flacon font allusion au plaisir de fumer de l'opium. La décoration élaborée de certains flacons d'opium est souvent un signe de richesse. La plupart des flacons d'opium datent du 18ᵉ siècle jusqu'au début du 20ᵉ siècle. Ces contenants d'une substance très nocive, qui a causé des désordres politiques en Chine, sont néanmoins des exemples intéressants d'œuvres d'art miniatures. Ces flacons, qui ont souvent été offerts en cadeau, comprennent un couvercle et une grande ouverture qui permet d'en retirer une boule d'opium gélatineuse et collante, de la taille d'un petit pois. C'est peut-être pour cette connotation négative que les flacons d'opium n'ont jamais retenu l'attention des collectionneurs, car ils rappellent une époque où l'impérialisme étranger était endémique en Chine.

Bibliographie sélective

Armero, Carlos, and Ben Rapaport. *The Arts of an Addiction. Qing Dynasty Opium Pipes and Accessories.*(Édition privée) 2005.

Hodgson, Barbara. *Opium, A Portrait of the Heavenly Demon.* San Francisco, 1999.

Pagani, Catherine. *Chinese Opium Boxes, H. J. Eiley Collection.* Toronto, 1992.

___________. "Late Ch'ing Dynasty Opium Boxes", Arts of Asia, 1991, Vol. 21, No. 3

___________. "Opium, the Long Life Mud." *Rotunda, the Magazine of the Royal Ontario Museum.* Vol. 24, No. 2, 1991.

Peintures chinoises sur papier de moelle

Les peintures sur papier de moelle semblent remonter en Chine vers le début du 19ᵉ siècle et sont presque exclusivement destinées aux marchés de l'exportation, vendues comme souvenirs peu coûteux, un peu comme les cartes postales de nos jours, aux marchands étrangers, marins et missionnaires. On commence ensuite à les expédier en vrac aux Occidentaux pour satisfaire leur appétit d'images stéréotypées de la culture chinoise. Leurs années de gloire sont surtout les années 1830 et 1840. On en peint souvent en série pour les présenter dans de petits albums sous une fenêtre de papier ou dans des boîtes munies d'une vitre sur le devant. Leur qualité est très variable. La taille des peintures sur papier de moelle varie d'environ 10 cm par 8 cm jusqu'à une grandeur maximale de 30 cm par 20 cm. Des huit ateliers connus de peinture sur papier de moelle, six se trouvent à Canton et un à Beijing. On ne sait pas où se trouvait le dernier. Les seules peintures dont on puisse identifier la provenance sont celles qui se trouvent dans un album, sur lequel on a imprimé le nom de l'atelier. En règle générale, les peintres sur papier de moelle ne signent pas leurs œuvres, à l'exception de Sunqua. Carl Crossman, dans son livre intitulé *The Chine Trade*, énumère d'autres artistes connus comme Tingqua et Youqua de Canton, Chou Pai Chuen de Beijing et Chow Kwa de Shanghai. La production des deux derniers date de la fin du 19ᵉ siècle. On sait que Tingqua et Chow Kwa ont ouvert un atelier à Hong Kong après l'incendie des usines riveraines, ou *hongs* de Canton, durant la première guerre de l'opium (1839 à 1841) et en 1856.

Les peintures sur papier de moelle ne peuvent qu'être petites. Ce papier est de pauvre qualité et n'est pas traité. Il s'agit d'une matière spongieuse, semblable à du papier, extraite du cœur de la tige d'un arbuste appelé *tetrapanax papyrifera*, qui provient des zones marécageuses du sud de la Chine et de Taiwan.

Il faut d'abord faire tremper la tige avant de la couper. Au moyen d'une lame de rasoir tranchante, un artisan très habile découpe de minces feuilles tout en tournant la tige cylindrique. Après avoir séché au soleil plusieurs jours, ces feuilles sont taillées et ne subissent aucun autre traitement avant d'être utilisées. La surface obtenue est luisante, molle ou velouteuse et translucide. Du fait que la peinture appliquée ne coule pas, elle rend possible l'exécution d'illustrations très détaillées. Si on applique de la peinture à l'eau ou détrempe de couleur vive sur le papier de moelle, celui-ci se gonfle immédiatement sous l'action de l'humidité, ce qui donne une impression de profondeur ou de tridimensionnalité. L'éclat digne d'un bijou des couleurs vives fait penser à une broderie ou même à une mosaïque. Du fait que la peinture ne coule pas, on peut peindre la surface au moyen d'un pinceau aussi fin qu'un cheveu. Malheureusement, les peintures sur papier de moelle sont très fragiles, car ce papier devient très friable et se casse facilement. Il fait presque constamment l'objet de mesures de conservation.

On en sait bien peu sur les peintres sur papier de moelle, car seuls quelques-uns signent leurs œuvres. La plupart des peintures sont probablement produites par des équipes dans un atelier, peut-être même à la chaîne, chacun exécutant sans cesse un même aspect ou élément de la peinture : le visage, les vêtements ou l'arrière-plan. Il arrive que les visages d'une série se ressemblent trop et soient à peine esquissés. Un peintre expérimenté peut créer le dessin original, puis son armée d'apprentis reproduit d'innombrables copies au moyen de stencils ou en traçant les contours qu'ils colorient par la suite. Les thèmes des peintures, qui joueront un rôle très important pour faire connaître la culture chinoise à l'Occident, comprennent des paysages, des ports (en particulier les usines riveraines ou les *hongs* de Canton et les navires transportant leurs cargaisons), les coutumes, le jeu, les festivals, les mariages, les funérailles, les punitions ou les tortures, les métiers, le marché, des scènes de genre de jeux ou passe-temps traditionnels, ainsi que des séquences comme la culture du thé, la sculpture du jade, la production de céramiques et la fabrication de la soie. Parmi les autres thèmes populaires, on retrouve les portraits des habitants du lieu, allant des mendiants dans la rue aux riches aristocrates chinois et mandchous drapés dans leurs superbes habits. Les fleurs et les animaux sont souvent peints en détail, en particulier les plantes, les fleurs, les oiseaux, les insectes et les poissons locaux.

Bibliographie sélective

Clunas, Craig. *Chinese Export Watercolours.* 1984.

Crossman, Carl L. *The China Trade: Export Paintings, Furniture, Silver and Other Objects*, Princeton. 1972.

Williams, Ifan. "Beauty in Pursuit of Pleasure." *Apollo.* November, 2006.

____________. "Views from the West, Chinese Pith Paper Paintings." *Arts of Asia*, Volume 31, No. 5, 2001.

La garde du sabre japonais, la tsuba

Le sabre est l'objet le plus vénéré du samouraï. Il est considéré comme « l'âme » du samouraï, car il est l'incarnation de son code de conduite, appelé *bushido*, caractérisé par l'autodiscipline, un dévouement inconditionnel et la maîtrise suprême des arts martiaux. Seule la classe des samouraïs a le privilège de porter deux épées, un long sabre (*katana*) pour l'attaque et la défense, et une petite épée (*wakizashi*) pour se suicider au besoin. Les anciens sabres japonais, fabriqués depuis le 16e siècle jusqu'au milieu du 19e siècle, sont des exemples du savoir-faire artisanal le plus perfectionné du Japon. Ces sabres sont l'arme de combat la plus proche de la perfection de l'époque et la plus aiguisée jamais réalisée. Les accessoires de la lame sont considérés comme d'importantes œuvres d'art et, tout comme les lames, font l'envie de nombreux collectionneurs. La partie la plus décorée du sabre est la garde, appelée *tsuba*, un disque plat qui sépare la lame de la poignée. La *tsuba*, qui doit être à la fois solide et légère, contribue au contrôle et à l'équilibre général du sabre en procurant un centre de gravité précis. Elle a pour principale fonction d'empêcher la main du samouraï de glisser sur la lame et de se couper. Elle constitue également un important dispositif de défense en bloquant le sabre de l'opposant qui pourrait glisser contre la lame et trancher la main du samouraï.

La création de la garde du sabre est étroitement liée à l'évolution du sabre au Japon. Elle est probablement d'abord fabriquée par les forgerons pour leurs propres épées. Les premières *tsuba* de la période Muromachi (1333 à 1573) et de la période Momoyama (1573 à 1603) sont solides et fonctionnelles. Traditionnellement, elles sont souvent en fer peu ajourées et à peine ornées à la surface. Toutefois, durant la période Edo (1603 à 1868), une longue période de paix, la *tsuba* atteint son zénith en matière de qualité. Elle se démarque surtout par le travail artistique du métal mou et son aspect désormais extrêmement décoratif plutôt que pratique. Elle sert davantage à symboliser le statut. Elle n'a pas du tout été prévue pour la bataille. Les samouraïs, qui forment une grande classe influente, sont la clientèle des fabricants de *tsuba*, qui se multiplient en écoles ayant des styles distincts. Ces artisans se passent les secrets du métier de pères en fils. Les *tsuba* portent souvent le nom de leur fabricant gravé sur l'un des côtés du trou de lame. Durant la période Muromachi de la période Edo, des groupes de spécialistes de la fabrication des gardes de sabre finissent par constituer un grand répertoire d'ornementations variées. Les samouraïs propriétaires d'une *tsuba* les lèguent habituellement à des parents comme objet de famille, enveloppées dans un vieux brocart doux et rangées dans une boîte laquée d'une grande finesse. Cette boîte est parfois décorée des armoiries (*mon*), de l'insigne ou du seau de la famille. Même après avoir atteint un nouveau degré d'ornementation durant la période Edo, le décret interdisant de porter le sabre et l'épée suivra de peu la restauration du pouvoir de l'empereur durant la période Meiji (1868 à 1912), en 1876. Avec la disparition du sabre, les fabricants de *tsuba* perdent leurs clients samouraïs et doivent se recycler dans la fabrication de babioles en métal à l'intention des touristes. Au 20e siècle, les ateliers de fabrication ont envoyé un grand nombre de *tsuba* en cuivre aux usines de l'armée. Pendant la période Meiji, les étrangers se rendent compte de la beauté des *tsuba* et commencent à les collectionner à grande échelle.

Les *tsuba* avaient toutes sortes de formes pour les armes japonaises à lame, y compris les *tachi* ou *katana* (longs sabres) et les *wakizashi* (épées courtes) et parfois pour les *tanto* (poignards) et les *naginata* (hallebardes). Les principales formes de la *tsuba* se divisent en quatre catégories : *maru gata*, la plus courante, est une forme plutôt ronde, souvent elliptique ou ovale; *kaku gata*, est une forme plutôt carrée aux coins ronds, occasionnellement hexagonale ou octogonale, ou encore, rarement, trapézoïdale; *mokko gata*, est une forme à quatre lobes; *shitogi* a la forme d'un gâteau de riz, habituellement réservée aux sabres de cérémonie. À de rares occasions, la *tsuba* a la forme d'un insecte, d'un serpent, d'une grenouille ou d'un oiseau. La *tsuba* elle-même est habituellement percée de trois ouvertures : celle du centre est prévue pour le passage de la soie qui vient s'ajuster à la poignée de la lame; l'arc simple ou trou ovale, à gauche, sert au *kozuka*, soit la poignée d'un petit couteau appelé *kogatana* qui se glisse dans le fourreau du sabre; la troisième ouverture, à droite, comprend habituellement trois arcs et reçoit le *kogai*, une sorte de tige métallique. Le *kozuka* et le *kogai* ressortent tous deux du haut du fourreau, ce qui rend les ouvertures nécessaires dans la *tsuba*. Il arrive que le nom du fabricant de la *tsuba* apparaisse sur l'un des côtés ou sur les deux côtés de l'ouverture centrale de la soie.

Même si la taille de la *tsuba* est limitée, la multitude de thèmes qu'on y représente illustre tous les aspects de la culture japonaise, allant de la religion et de l'histoire à la mythologie, en passant par les paysages et la nature. Certaines *tsuba*, sont ornées de personnages dont des guerriers célèbres, des généraux et des figures légendaires chinoises comme le dieu de la guerre Guanyu ou Guandi (Kan'u en japonais), le démon queller Zhong Kui (Shoki en japonais), Bodhidarma (Daruma en japonais), les moines espiègles Hanshan et Shide (Kanzan et Jittoku en japonais), pour n'en nommer que quelques-uns. Les paysages représentés sur les *tsuba* sont souvent inspirés des peintures chinoises. Ces scènes se composent de hautes montagnes à l'arrière-plan sur lesquelles se dessinent des arbres, une rivière, un temple, une porte, des voyageurs ou des embarcations. Le tigre, le singe, le cheval, le serpent, le lièvre, la grue et la carpe sont les créatures animales les plus populaires. De nombreuses bêtes mythologiques illustrées s'inspirent du folklore chinois, comme le dragon, le phœnix et le *qilin (kirin* en japonais). Le dragon est associé à l'empereur et le phœnix (*ho*) à l'impératrice. Le *kirin* symbolise l'autorité impériale.

Les techniques et outils de décoration de la *tsuba* sont également assez variés. On travaille la surface en forgeant et martelant le métal et, dans le cas du fer, en le trempant. Traditionnellement, c'est le fer qui sert à la fabrication de la *tsuba,* lequel peut prendre un certain nombre de patines comme le rouge, le noir et le brun. On se sert également de métaux mous comme le cuivre et, plus tard, le laiton. Pendant la longue période de paix, Edo, qui a permis aux arts de s'épanouir, on utilise des alliages de cuivre comme le *shakudo* (qui contient de l'or), le *shibuichi* (qui contient de l'argent) et le *sentoku* (qui contient du laiton) pour fabriquer des *tsuba* d'une grande finesse. On complète l'ornementation avec de l'or ou une dorure. La *tsuba* est décorée des deux côtés. Le côté le plus visible, celui de la poignée, est le plus ouvragé. La *tsuba* est souvent décorée de dessins percés ou gravés et de perforations, ce qui permet d'appliquer les techniques de l'incrustation. Il n'est pas rare que les samouraïs possèdent plusieurs *tsuba* interchangeables pour leur unique épée, qu'ils chérissent. Le choix de la *tsuba* peut dépendre de la saison ou de l'occasion à laquelle le samouraï portait l'épée.

BIBLIOGRAPHIE SÉLECTIVE

Caldwell, R.B. "Tsuba, Handguards of the Japanese Sword." *Arts of Asia.* Vol. 23, No. 1, 1993.

Earle, Joe. "Japanese Sword-fittings in the Victoria and Albert Museum." *Orientations.* Vol. 17, No. 12, 1986.

Lorber, D. and H.B. Martin. "Japanese Sword Fittings." *Arts of Asia,* Vol. 7, No. 3, 1977.

Swart, Paula, Robert E. Haynes and John Berta. *The Soul of the Samurai, A Selection of Sword Guards from the Vancouver Museum.* Vancouver, 1993.

netsuke, billes ojime et boîtes à pharmacie du Japon

De tout petits boutons appelés *netsuke* (qui signifie littéralement « racine de fixation ») voient le jour au Japon au moins dès la fin du 16e siècle pour des raisons à la fois fonctionnelles et esthétiques. Les costumes traditionnels japonais, le *kimono* et le *kosode* ne comportent pas de poche pour transporter de petits articles. Les femmes peuvent glisser des articles personnels dans leur manche, mais les hommes suspendent leurs objets d'usage quotidien, appelés *sagemono* (objets suspendus) à des cordelettes. Ce peut être un sac à tabac, une pipe, un étui à pinceau, une bourse ou un coffret appelé *inro.* Ces objets sont suspendus à leur *obi* (ceinture de *kimono*). Pour retenir la cordelette à la ceinture, on utilise un petit bouton très chic, appelé *netsuke,* ou une sorte de contrepoids avec deux ouvertures dans lesquelles passe la cordelette et qui sert de point d'attache. On enfile une *ojime* (bille mobile) sur la cordelette, entre le *netsuke* et le *sagemono* pour resserrer ou relâcher l'ouverture du *sagemono.* Le propriétaire de ces trois éléments recherche la parfaite harmonie entre les couleurs, la matière et l'ornementation. La plupart du temps, ce n'est pas le même groupe d'artistes qui fabrique les trois éléments.

Pour remplir son rôle adéquatement, le *netsuke* doit respecter certains principes de base. Il doit être compact sans être trop lourd, mais assez massif pour empêcher la cordelette de glisser. Il doit être durable, car on veut le porter souvent et longtemps. Il doit être lisse et confortable, sans pièces coupantes ou qui ressortent et pourraient endommager le vêtement ou blesser la peau de son propriétaire. Enfin, il doit être chic, c'est-à-dire que son propriétaire peut le porter fièrement.

Pendant la période Edo, ou Tokugawa (1603 à 1868), les gens de toutes les classes, des fonctionnaires aux samouraïs, des riches marchands aux artisans, veulent se procurer de beaux *netsuke.* Même les paysans possèdent de simples *netsuke,* souvent faits de matières naturelles comme les gourdes, les coques ou les pierres. Le *netsuke* devient un moyen d'exhiber ses goûts personnels par des parures comme d'autres le font par des bijoux. La production de *netsuke* évoluera rapidement à partir de la fabrication d'un objet strictement utilitaire vers la création d'objets de collection convoités pour leurs grandes qualités artistiques et leur élégante complexité. Les *netsuke* deviendront également le symbole du statut social de leur propriétaire. Leurs propriétaires se comparent les uns aux autres et chacun tente de se procurer la collection la plus élégante. C'est leur individualité, leur originalité et leur caractère unique qui en feront rapidement des objets que les collectionneurs s'arrachent, de même qu'une forme d'art convoitée. Les *netsuke,* comme les bijoux, deviendront également un signe du statut social à mesure que l'habileté des artisans et la qualité des matières utilisées distingueront les classes.

au milieu du 18ᵉ siècle, les sculpteurs de *netsuke* ne considèrent plus leur métier comme un passe-temps ou un loisir insignifiant, mais comme une véritable forme d'art. Les artisans commencent à signer leurs œuvres et deviennent des sculpteurs professionnels et des maîtres. Ils en viennent à fonder diverses écoles régionales ayant leur propre style. Il leur faut les outils appropriés, un talent de sculpteur, une excellente vue et une grande imagination pour répondre à la grande demande car, à cette époque, presque tous les hommes du Japon doivent porter un *netsuke.* La complexité des motifs augmente progressivement à mesure que de nouvelles techniques de sculpture font leur apparition. Les artisans expérimentent toutes sortes de matières et tentent de concevoir le plus de sujets possible.

Un sculpteur établit sa réputation par le style, l'habileté et l'intelligence qui caractérisent ses œuvres. Celui-ci semble jouir d'une plus grande liberté en terme de parodie, satire et paraboles que les artistes de la période Edo qui exploitent d'autres techniques. Il ne semble pas tenu de respecter la tradition ou être entravé par la censure quant aux sujets de ses œuvres, comme c'était le cas des peintres et des graveurs. Un bon nombre de *netsuke* portent la signature du maître sculpteur, en particulier à la fin de la période Edo. Toutefois, étant donné que ses écoles (et ses élèves) utilisent souvent la signature du maître sans discrimination, le *netsuke* n'a pas nécessairement été fabriqué par le maître sculpteur lui-même. Même si le nom inscrit sur l'objet est véritable, on en sait très peu sur sa vie. La fabrication des anciens *netsuke* de luxe n'est considérée que comme une forme d'art miniature, mais leur création méticuleuse exige beaucoup de travail. La fabrication d'un seul *netsuke* prend beaucoup de temps, parfois jusqu'à un mois ou deux. Par conséquent, les sculpteurs de *netsuke* vivent très modestement. Puisque le *netsuke* est une sculpture en trois dimensions, il doit pouvoir être vu et apprécié sous tous ses angles, ce qui exige une finition presque parfaite à tous les points de vue. Le *netsuke* doit également être agréable à manipuler et avoir un certain attrait tactile, révélant ses profondeurs et ses textures. Avec le temps, de nombreux *netsuke* finissent par acquérir de belles patines, en vieillissant et à force d'être manipulés.

On fabrique les *netsuke* dans une grande gamme de matières, parfois en combinaison ou avec des incrustations, l'ivoire et le bois étant les plus populaires. Mis à part les défenses d'éléphant, on utilise aussi les dents (appelées simplement ivoire) d'autres créatures pour fabriquer des *netsuke,* y compris les défenses du mammouth de Sibérie, les dents du grand cachalot, la corne du narval, les défenses de morse, les défenses du sanglier ainsi que le casque du calao et, à l'occasion des dents d'hippopotame. Les *netsuke* de bois ne se limitent pas à un seul type d'essence. On utilise le cyprès, le buis, le camphre, le cerisier, le mûrier, le plaqueminier, le prunier, le camélia et le bambou, de même que l'ébène et le teck importés. On fait également des *netsuke* avec du métal, de la laque, des os, des coques de noix, des cornes (par ex., le bœuf, le rhinocéros, le cerf), des carapaces de tortue, de l'ambre, des coraux, du verre, de la saponite, des pierres semi-précieuses, de la céramique, des gourdes naturelles et sculptées, des coquillages et du rotin. Les sculpteurs de *netsuke* ne sont pas les seuls à en fabriquer, d'autres artisans comme les artistes de la laque, les fondeurs de métaux, les orfèvres, les fabricants de sabres et les potiers en fabriquent aussi en complément à leur principal métier.

Les *netsuke* se répartissent en quelques principales catégories : les *katabori*, les plus répandus, sont des sculptures compactes en trois dimensions qui représentent des êtres humains, des dieux, des animaux réels ou mythiques, des fruits ou des légumes; les *men*, les masques, qui sont souvent des imitations en miniature de vrais masques *noh* et *kyogen*, de masques de cérémonie bouddhistes *gigaku* et *bugaku* et de masques folkloriques utilisés dans les festivals; *les sashi*, longs et fins; les *kagamibuta*, sous forme de disque métallique qui servent de couvercle à un bol peu profond, habituellement en ivoire, en os ou en corne; et le *manju*, un *netsuke* habituellement rond, parfois carré ou ovale, qui fait penser à la forme d'un gâteau de riz appelé *manju* et souvent composé de deux moitiés en ivoire. D'autres types sont moins fréquents : le *ryusa*, une sorte de *manju*, qui représente souvent des fleurs et des oiseaux popularisés par l'artiste Ryusa; le *ichiraku*, un *netsuke* souvent en forme de gourde fabriqué à partir d'une matière tressée ou tissée comme les cannes ou baguettes de bambou; et le *kurawa*, appelé *netsuke* cendrier, car il est utilisé par les fumeurs.

Compte tenu de la très petite taille du *netsuke*, le sculpteur ne peut guère réaliser une œuvre très élaborée. Le *netsuke* mesure habituellement quatre centimètres, mais cette dimension peut varier de deux à neuf centimètres, et parfois plus. Pour ce qui est des sujets du *netsuke*, on retrouve les activités quotidiennes des diverses classes sociales du Japon de la période Edo, souvent représentées de façon fantaisiste : des scènes de moines en méditation, la pipe aux lèvres, buvant du thé, jouant des jeux ou accomplissant leurs tâches quotidiennes, ou encore des marchands étrangers dans leur costume occidental. C'est avec ingéniosité qu'on représente tous les types de personnages, réels ou imaginaires, célèbres ou ordinaires, vieux ou jeunes, dieux ou démons, historiques ou contemporains, étrangers ou natifs du pays. Il arrive qu'on exploite le thème de la sexualité. De nombreux personnages humains sont inspirés du folklore chinois ou japonais, de légendes ou de religions, dont le *sennin*, ermite légendaire, Zhong Kui (Shoki), le démon queller, Bodhidarma (Daruma), le saint bouddhiste indien qui a fondé le Chan (Zen), et les sept dieux de la chance. Parmi les sujets animaliers les plus populaires se trouvent les douze animaux du zodiaque, les créatures de la mer, les oiseaux, des animaux magiques comme le loup et le blaireau, des bêtes mythiques comme le dragon, *kirin* (un animal de bon augure habituellement muni d'une corne, parfois appelé licorne), *baku* (l'avaleur de cauchemars), *oni* (démons), *kappa* (créatures malicieuses avec les mains et les pieds palmés), *tengu* (farfadets de la forêt) et *shishi* (lion-chien), de même que des reptiles et des bestioles. Les végétaux les plus courants sont les châtaignes, les champignons, les fleurs et divers fruits et légumes. Les objets inanimés comprennent les pièces de monnaie, les outils, les jouets, les articles ménagers, les instruments de musique, les tuiles de couverture. On a également une préférence pour tout ce qui est pittoresque, bizarre, grotesque ou macabre, comme les crânes humains.

À la fin de la période féodale Edo et au début de la période Meiji (1868 à 1912), les Japonais commencent à adopter les vêtements occidentaux munis de nombreuses poches, contrairement à leurs *kimono* traditionnels. Les *netsuke* perdent donc leur raison d'être et finissent par disparaître comme accessoire de mode dans la vie de tous les jours. Les familles japonaises mettent de côté tout un héritage sous forme de coffres aux trésors remplis de *netsuke*, reliques d'un temps révolu. Les marchands européens et américains s'intéressent immédiatement aux *netsuke* en tant que magnifiques exemples d'une forme d'art miniature et commencent à les collectionner à pleines boîtes. Même si on porte moins le *kimono* et le *netsuke*, la demande des étrangers pour les *netsuke* de haute qualité alimente l'industrie. L'exportation florissante permettra aux artistes du *netsuke* de prospérer et de survivre pendant encore plusieurs autres décennies. C'est ainsi que se bâtiront d'immenses collections privées et muséales en Hollande, en Angleterre, en France et aux États-Unis. En fait, en raison de l'indifférence des Japonais envers le *netsuke*, un grand nombre des plus magnifiques collections de *netsuke* anciens se retrouveront à l'extérieur du Japon. La plupart des *netsuke* fabriqués à partir du début de la période Meiji n'ont jamais été portés. Ils étaient uniquement destinés à l'exportation. D'habiles artisans les sculptaient et ils étaient de haute qualité, mais la grande demande des Occidentaux mènera également à la production de nombreux *netsuke* de moindre qualité.

Par conséquent, les étrangers, (*gaijin*) ont joué un rôle de premier plan dans la préservation et la prolongation de l'art du *netsuke*, amenant les sculpteurs à s'adapter et à satisfaire une nouvelle clientèle avec de nouvelles idées et de nouvelles matières. Les thèmes érotiques sont même devenus un genre assez courant pour les *netsuke* destinés aux marchés étrangers.

De nos jours, la valeur d'un *netsuke* peut varier, allant d'une centaine de dollars à une centaine de milliers de dollars, selon la qualité de l'exécution et la célébrité de l'artisan.

L'acheteur doit être vigilant, car il s'en fabrique maintenant en quantité partout dans le monde, en particulier en Chine. La tradition artistique de la sculpture du *netsuke* a survécu jusqu'à ce jour avec environ une centaine d'artistes professionnels répartis dans le monde entier (japonais et non japonais) qui continuent de produire de magnifiques *netsuke*. En fait, un *netsuke* novateur créé par un artiste contemporain du *netsuke* peut se vendre dans les quatre chiffres.

Les sculpteurs contemporains de *netsuke* qui font revivre l'art font souvent preuve du même talent, de la même créativité et de la même originalité que les grands maîtres d'autrefois. Les artistes japonais contemporains du *netsuke* sont Kangyoku, Bishu, Hideyuki, Akihide et Keiun. Les sculpteurs étrangers de *netsuke* qui se sont consacrés à cet incroyable art de la minutie sont les Britanniques Guy Shaw, Nick Lamb et Michael Webb; l'Américain David Carlin; et le sculpteur juif George Weil, pour n'en nommer que quelques-uns. Un grand nombre d'artisans chinois sculptent également depuis des décennies.

Tel que mentionné plus tôt, le bouton *netsuke*, la bille *ojime* et le coffret *inro* font partie d'une panoplie d'articles à porter sur soi. La bille *ojime* est une perle ou une barrette qui se glisse sur deux cordelettes jusqu'au haut de l'*inro* pour le refermer ou l'ouvrir. Elle doit généralement s'harmoniser au *netsuke* et à l'*inro*. Comme le *netsuke*, on le fabrique à partir de nombreuses matières : divers métaux, or, pierre, ivoire et bois, parmi les plus populaires. Elles représentent également la mythologie, la tradition et la nature mais, en raison de sa taille et de sa forme limitées, l'illustration est beaucoup moins détaillée et attrayante.

L'*inro* (qui signifie étui de sceau personnel) est un petit coffret dont les compartiments s'emboîtent parfaitement. On dit que les samouraïs furent les premiers à porter l'*inro*, et que cet article était très populaire parmi les membres de cette classe. Par contre, les membres prospères des autres classes commencèrent aussi à en porter. Les compartiments (habituellement de deux à cinq qui s'emboîtent avec précision les uns dans les autres) servent à transporter de petits sceaux, des poudres et des comprimés de médicaments, et des herbes aromatiques. L'*inro* est plat, rectangulaire ou rond et comprend quatre ou cinq compartiments horizontaux retenus par des cordelettes qui passent par les bouts de chaque compartiment. Comme le *netsuke* et d'*ojime*, on fabrique l'*inro*, ce coffret compartimenté, à partir de diverses matières dont la plus populaire, et de loin, est le cyprès laqué. La laque est la sève de l'arbre à laque appliquée par couches successives (jusqu'à soixante couches selon certains) sur le bois de cyprès. Une fois sèche, on la polit jusqu'à ce qu'elle devienne luisante. Pour créer différentes couleurs et textures sur les pièces de haute qualité, les artistes de la laque utilisent une technique de décoration appelée *maki-e*, qui consiste à pulvériser sur la surface laquée, avant qu'elle soit sèche, diverses poudres métalliques, dont l'or, l'argent, le cuivre, le laiton, le plomb l'aluminium, le platine, l'étain ainsi que leurs alliages. Un décorateur peut appliquer une décoration externe somptueuse avec différentes laques de couleur, ou ajouter un appliqué de différentes matières, comme la nacre, l'ivoire, la carapace de tortue ou le corail. Certaines *inro* sont des chefs d'œuvre d'application de l'art de la laque, que seuls les samouraïs, puis les marchands les plus riches, peuvent s'offrir. Alors que les *netsuke* sont généralement des sculptures en trois dimensions, les *inro* se rapprochent davantage d'œuvres en deux dimensions, parfois inspirées de la littérature, des peintures ou des gravures sur bois classiques. Certains ornements raffinés d'*inro* sont d'extraordinaires exemples du savoir-faire japonais dans l'art de la laque. Comme dans le cas du *netsuke*, les collectionneurs en raffolent.

Bibliographie sélective

Barker, Richard and Lawrence Smith. *netsuke, The Miniature Sculptures of Japan*. London, 1976.

Bushell, Raymond. *Collectors' netsuke*. Tokyo, 1971.

Davey, Neil K. *netsuke*. London, 1973.

Kotler, Philip. "Judging Quality in netsuke." *Arts of Asia*. Vol. 6, No. 2, 1976.

Okada, Barbra Teri. *netsuke, Masterpieces from the Metropolitan Museum of Art*. New York, 1982.

O'Brien, Mary Louise. *netsuke, Guide for Collectors*. Ruthland and Tokyo, 1973.

Olson, Eleanor. "A Panorama in Miniature: Japanese netsuke". *The Museum*. Vol. 9, No. 4, 1957.

Roth, Stig. *netsuke in the Collections of the Röhss Museum of Arts and Crafts*. Göteborg, 1970.

Ryerson, Egerton. *The netsuke of Japan, Legends, History, Folklore and Customs*. London, 1958.

Stern, Harold P. *The Magnificent Three: Lacquer, netsuke, and Tsuba, Selections from the Collection of Charles A. Greenfield*. London, 1972.

Ueda, Reikichi. *The netsuke Handbook of Ueda Reikichi*, adapted from Japanese by Raymond Bushell. Tokyo, 1961.

Webb, Glenn T. *Masterworks in Miniature: Japanese netsuke*. Vancouver, 1967.

Yoshiko, Kakudo. *netsuke: Myth & Nature in Miniature*. San Francisco, 1981.

Les Okimono, sculptures japonaises

En lien avec le *netsuke* miniature, on retrouve des sculptures plus grandes, non fonctionnelles et purement décoratives, appelées *okimono* (qui se traduit littéralement par « objet à exposer ») habituellement installées dans le *tokomono* ou alcôve. Quand les Japonais commencent à se vêtir à l'occidentale, à la période Meiji (1868 à 1912), ils ont des poches et n'ont plus besoin de boutons *netsuke* ni de contenants *sagemono*. Par conséquent, de nombreux sculpteurs *netsuke* commencent à sculpter aussi des pièces plus grandes pour capter l'intérêt des marchands prospères qui sont en train de former la nouvelle classe de connaisseurs et de clients des œuvres d'art, et pour répondre à l'avidité des Occidentaux pour des bibelots ou souvenirs japonais, en particulier à la fin du 19e siècle. Les Occidentaux sont friands des articles originaux et si bien exécutés du Japon. Le gouvernement japonais de l'époque contribue également au commerce des *okimono* par sa participation aux expositions internationales, à commencer par l'Exposition universelle de Paris en 1867, où les étrangers ont l'occasion de voir des produits exotiques du Japon.

Les sculptures *okimono* sont exposées à côté de céramiques, de cloisonnés, d'articles de ferronnerie, de laques et de textiles spectaculaires à la fin du 19e siècle, durant la période Meiji, dans le cadre d'expositions industrielles au pays de même qu'à des expositions internationales, où le Japon se démarque par la grâce et l'élégance de ses illustrations et par la parfaite exécution des œuvres.

Toutefois, les sculpteurs d'*okimono*, sans modifier leurs caractéristiques qui les distinguent en tant que Japonais, tentent de plaire au goût des étrangers en chargeant certaines de leurs sculptures d'un excès de détails finement sculptés et en s'orientant davantage du côté du naturalisme occidental. Les sculptures de personnages et de groupes, représentant des aspects des métiers traditionnels japonais, sont particulièrement populaires, les êtres et animaux mythiques et surnaturels étant moins attrayants pour leur clientèle. Les *okimono* pouvaient varier, allant de belles pièces uniques à d'innombrables objets produits en masse et de piètre qualité. Les sujets représentés par les *okimono* sont extrêmement variés et s'inspirent de nombreux thèmes exploités dans les *netsuke*. La plupart des *okimono* sont faits en bois ou en ivoire, mais on en trouve aussi en laque, céramique, ambre, cloisonné et métal.

Bibliographie sélective

Bordignon, Laura. *The Golden Age of Japanese Okimono, Dr. A. M. Kanter's Collection*. London, 2010.

Earle, James. *Splendors of Imperial Japan: Arts of the Meiji Period from the Khalili Collection*. London, 2002.

Lester, Gerd. "Okimono: Decorative Wood and Ivory Carvings for the Tokonoma." *Arts of Asia*, Vol. 19, No. 6, 1989.

Credits

Curator: Barry Till

Publication Project Manager: Barry Till

Editor: Joan Padgett

Translator: Marie-Hèléne Duval

Publication Design: Frank Reimer

Photography: Bob Matheson

Printed in Canada by Friesens Corp.

Gallery Associates
ART GALLERY OF GREATER VICTORIA

British Columbia Arts Council
Supported by the Province of British Columbia

Canadian Heritage Patrimoine canadien

CRD
Making a difference...together

Art Gallery of Greater Victoria
1040 Moss Street
Victoria, British Columbia
Canada V8V 4P1
250-384-4101 aggv.bc.ca